Thomas D. Cook (Ph.D., Psychology, Stanford University) is Associate Professor of Psychology, Northwestern University. He was Director of the Social Psychology Training Program at Northwestern (1969-1972). He is Consulting Editor to *Evaluation* magazine and the co-author of two books, *The Design and Conduct of Quasi-Experiments in Field Settings* (with D. T. Campbell, 1976) and *The Design and Conduct of Randomized Experiments in Field Settings* (with S. S. Diamond, 1976).

Hilary Appleton (Ph.D., Psychology, Northwestern University) is Assistant Professor of Psychology, University of Winnipeg.

Ross F. Conner (Ph.D., Psychology, Northwestern University) is Assistant Professor of Social Ecology, University of California, Irvine.

Ann Shaffer (M.B.A., University of Cincinnati) is an executive with Procter & Gamble.

Gary Tamkin (Ph.D., Psychology, Northwestern University) is Director of Community Services, Division of Drug Rehabilitation, Massachusetts Department of Mental Health.

Stephen J. Weber (Ph.D., Psychology, Northwestern University) is Assistant Professor of Psychology and Sociology, University of New Hampshire.

"Sesame Street" Revisited

Thomas D. Cook, Hilary Appleton, Ross F. Conner, Ann Shaffer, Gary Tamkin, and Stephen J. Weber

Continuities in Evaluation Research

Russell Sage Foundation   New York

PUBLICATIONS OF RUSSELL SAGE FOUNDATION

Russell Sage Foundation was established in 1907 by Mrs. Russell Sage
for the improvement of social and living conditions in the
United States. In carrying out its purpose the Foundation conducts
research under the direction of members of the staff or in close
collaboration with other institutions, and supports programs
designed to develop and demonstrate productive working relations
between social scientists and other professional groups. As an inte-
gral part of its operation, the Foundation from time to time publishes books or pamphlets resulting from these activities. Publication
under the imprint of the Foundation does not necessarily imply
agreement by the Foundation, its Trustees, or its staff with the
interpretations or conclusions of the authors.

Russell Sage Foundation
230 Park Avenue, New York, N.Y. 10017

To the children—past, present, and future—
of Rock Ferry Primary School

Contents

Foreword

I took the draft of this book by Thomas Cook and his associates with me to Mexico City, where I was on leave from Brandeis University and Russell Sage Foundation. The initial preparation of this Foreword took place during my first months there. In thinking about what to write, I found myself coming back to two experiences I had during this brief period: One was my own, trying to learn a new language; the second was as an involved observer, watching a young girl from the Mexican countryside, who had never worked outside her own home, become a maid.

It may be my limited facility to learn new languages, but it is nevertheless quite crippling for someone with a self-image of being highly verbal to find himself inadequate at communicating. I think I appreciate now, much more than I ever did before, what it means in terms of emotional and interpersonal impact to suffer from a deficiency in communication and other educationally related skills.

That was only a part of the experience of not knowing Spanish. The other was the method by which I was taught the language, which was essentially the way a child learns his native tongue—little emphasis on the rules of grammar, on the subtlety of Spanish syntax, or on perfect pronunciation. Rather, I learned on a one-to-one basis from two exceedingly intelligent tutors with unbelievable patience who treated me as a child and educated me in the same way most of us taught our children in their preschool years. Repetition, rewards for saying the right thing, and an introduction to many aspects of Mexican life were unavoidable parts of my carefully planned, albeit individualized, course of programmed learning.

It is no wonder I feel compelled to begin this Foreword to *"Sesame Street" Revisited* in a personal way. Indeed I came to identify with the children who watch "Sesame Street" and even watched the Spanish version of "Sesame Street" and programs like it a few times.

Watching Angelica, our maid, learn was a less stressing and unusually interesting experience. Of Indian background, she was recruited by a colleague's maid. I was not only surprised when I found out that she could not read or write but also was shocked that she did not know how to lock a door with a key, dial a telephone, or tell time. Then, after she was with us about three days, one of my tutors told me her Spanish was not much better than mine—she, too, was learning it as a second language. Other than the skills of bargaining in the food market and handling money, she was no more equipped for Mexico City than I was.

When I realized that Angelica would not stop working in the evening until I had, I discovered she could not tell time. Both one of my tutors and I tried to explain to her about telling time with our wrist watches, without much success. However, once she was introduced to a digital clock, all her acumen with counting money came to the fore, and the transfer learning from a digital clock to an ordinary one was virtually astounding.

The second illustration has to do with her vocabulary. In order to improve mine, every time I saw an article lying about I would ask her what it was. I received an answer every time, only to find to my chagrin from my tutors that a good part of my vocabulary was not Spanish at all but her first language, Indian. In time, similar requests almost invariably brought the appropriate Spanish word or a "no se." Where did she learn? Undoubtedly from her new Spanish-speaking friends, but I also suspect that she learned from the television she watched in our living room, from the radio we constantly played, and from "listening in" on my Spanish lessons. A digital clock as a teaching aid and opportunities for day in and day out exposure to primary and secondary communication brought astonishing results.

I think both Angelica and I learned to be more competent in Mexico City and in our work. I also believe television represents an effective means of education or at least of learning a language. Also, I think somehow that training aids, like digital clocks, and the environment in which Angelica found herself had an impact. And so do the designers and sponsors of "Sesame Street" believe in their approach. Presumably, also, do millions of parents and perhaps their children-viewers as well. But, of course, the stakes are much higher in the case of "Sesame Street."

First, there is the dollar investment involved. While "Sesame Street" is inexpensive on a "per-child" basis, the total costs are extensive. We therefore have to ask: "What are the returns?" Moreover, any massive effort, such as "Sesame Street," must compete for dollars with other educational efforts, and thus the benefits need to be either impressive or in some way demonstrable as more efficient in—to use that offensive concept—their "costs to benefits."

Second, and more important, there is the polarization effect. Not only do "Sesame Street" and similar programs compete for dollars; they also have an impact on the ideological and philosophical frameworks that guide efforts at educational, cultural, and social development. Why pay teachers more money, run programs such as Headstart, build new schools, and experiment with complex teaching machines when there already is a relatively inexpensive, easily expandable approach? Here, "Sesame Street" has a decided advantage. Millions of adults, including public officials, academicians, foundation executives, and just parents, are intimately acquainted with the program and "understand" how it works. The mothers, fathers, aunts, uncles, and grandparents of its millions of child-viewers have literally shared in the excitement of watching children learning to count, read, and conceptualize. Clearly, unless the "Sesame Street" approach really is efficacious, there is the concern that the swell of enthusiasm for it could drown out other educational efforts to improve human resources. Certainly, while it is unimportant to challenge my impressions of how Angelica and I profited from educational programs, policymakers, behavioral scientists, educators, parents—and yes, even children—have a right to expect that so sweeping an innovative development as "Sesame Street" be subjected to careful study and evaluation.

But there is still another issue—perhaps *the* issue of the 1970s—that needs to be raised. This is the distributive effects of any social action program. When programs are freely available to all persons, who in fact makes the most use of them? If they are freely available and equally consumed by various social groups, who benefits the most? Given the great sensitivity to reducing inequality, is there any defense for allocating public funds, foundation resources, and creative talents to any human service activity that widens the gap between the "haves" and the "have-nots"? The commitment of the times, politically and morally, is to reduce inequality. Where it cannot be reduced, the commitment is to introduce new programs from which all social groups benefit equally. To put it in the extreme, who derives the most benefit from "Sesame Street," the white middle class child or the poor black child barely surviving on public welfare? Which of these children is more likely to view the show? If they both watch it for the same amount of time, which one is more likely to learn from it? Which one is more likely to view the show in quiet surroundings and to have adults around with the time and inclination to rehearse what was seen and heard? Which one is more likely to have commercially franchised "Sesame Street" books, toys, and records bought for him, items that permit practice-learning and that stimulate further interest in the program?

What happens to one sociologist in a foreign country or even one Mexican country girl is not important, but the consequences of "Sesame Street" are. "Sesame Street" is viewed by millions of children in the United States and in more than sixty other countries. The educational procedures in the United States and many other countries are being shaped by it, and the distance between socioeconomic groups may be affected as well.

The commitment to evaluate "Sesame Street" in a rigorous manner was wise and most rational. So, too, was the selection of the well-respected Educational Testing Service (ETS) to undertake the job. Certainly, their evaluation could not be perfect: There were strong pressures to get "Sesame Street" underway rapidly and to a national audience; there were the inevitable blinders that accompany the enthusiasm of the developers and sponsors of action programs and which interfere with any objective effort that requires their cooperation and collaboration; and there were the frailties of both the state of the evaluation-research art and of the humans doing the work. As an outsider who peeked in from time to time, admittedly usually secondhand at that, I would say, however, that all the parties concerned—and they had many important stakes in the outcome—were honestly interested in finding out just what was the effect of their social invention.

But this book is only secondarily a report on the evaluation of "Sesame Street." When Russell Sage Foundation sought out Cook and his associates to undertake the work reported here, we had a catchy phrase, "The evaluation of an evaluation." It sort of backfired because we did not mean that we were out to hang anyone, to undertake a Nader's Raiders-type project, or to destroy any social action effort. Rather, as a foundation whose purpose is to put social science to work in supporting the welfare of the country, we were striving to improve the state of social research and its utility in relation to the development of social policies.

The Foundation has been active similarly in the past: Eleanor Bernert Sheldon, president of the Social Science Research Council, played a strong role in the social indicator movement when she was a Russell Sage Foundation staff member; Orville Brim, Jr., former president of the Foundation, chaired the National Science Foundation–National Academy of Sciences' committee on the utilization of social science; and the Foundation initiated social science teaching and research programs in medical, public health, and law schools. Involving the Foundation in the evaluation research arena has been a somewhat different venture. Assessments of social action programs are not new: Social scientists in the 1930s conducted such studies, World War II saw a great number of persons examine various military and civilian crash programs, and the Great Society days brought assessments of many of the programs of the President's Committee on Youth Crime and Delinquency and later of the activities supported by the Office of Economic Opportunity. But the popularity of evaluation research is a phenomenon of this decade. The recent growth of interest and activity in evaluation research is evidenced by the large number of profit-making companies, and non-profit groups, as well as academic research centers now engaged in such endeavors.

But cynics can still say, "Show us many studies that really have counted in influencing social policy." Optimists might rephrase the matter and ask, "Are we not ready to learn, from work completed and going on, how to do evaluation research that really counts?" Both camps would agree that the time is ripe for "doing something" about the evaluation-research field. It is large in dollars expended, growing as a methodological specialty in universities, and supported by more and more public policymakers and human service practitioners. But the existing situation, even when looked at by those who believe in the utility of the approach, is that many promises about usefulness have been made but few definitive, hard-nosed evaluations have been delivered that have changed national policies.

This book is the first to be published in the Foundation's "Continuities in Evaluation Research" series. It is one of several studies commissioned by the Foundation to get inside the activities that constitute evaluation research. Others are being done by Peter H. Rossi of the University of Massachusetts, on the New Jersey guaranteed annual wage experiment, and by Henry Levin and Richard Snow of Stanford University, on the Office of Economic Opportunity's evaluation of contract incentive education. Each shares the same objective: to describe what went on during an evaluation effort and to examine further the methods, findings, and conclusions of important investigations.

Each differs, however. They differ in part because of the different points in time in which the studies started, in part because the designs vary in complexity and in scope, and in part because of the nature of the interpersonal relationships between the original research teams, their sponsors, and the groups the Foundation is supporting. Also, the teams have had to make their own decisions on what they would look at and the style of—if I can use the term—their evaluations of evaluations.

Early in this volume, Cook and his associates conceptualize their task and consider the alternative ways of conducting such reviews. Trying to summarize these views, like abstracting the findings, would be unfair to the author as well as to the readers and I am sure that this part of the book, as well as the data chapters, will be of value. Cook and his co-authors describe fully and with great gratitude the openness of ETS toward the endeavor and the complete access he and his colleagues had to the data tapes and other materials at hand. Although this is their book, I want to add Russell Sage Foundation's appreciation to the ETS evaluation staff for their collaboration, which continued after they knew that Cook and his associates would provide a different picture of "Sesame Street's" efforts than the one they published.

The Foundation's support of this and other evaluation studies was not intended to create adversary relationships between the original evaluation groups and the investigators. In this book there are critical assessments of some of the ETS work, even though they are muted because Cook and associates chose to evaluate "Sesame Street" as an educational phenomenon rather than simply to redo the ETS procedures step by step. Nevertheless, Cook and his associates challenge any feelings of complacency that may exist that "Sesame Street" is the answer, either for maximizing educational development during the pre- and early school years, for remedying educational deficits, or for modifying the distributive character of learned competences in language, conceptualization, and social development. It is important, in pointing to the critical character of some parts of this volume, to underscore the different positions of the original evaluation team and the evaluation-research team. The latter group approached the data as academicians who, in formulating their analysis plans and in looking at their data, developed a commitment to a wider perspective on "Sesame Street" than that of ETS. That this results in different interpretations and conclusions is not totally unexpected; that Cook and his colleagues make a clear effort to explicate the framework they use in their analysis allows the reader, and the ETS research group, to judge the reanalysis of the data not just in terms of technical expertise but within the context of their own perspectives on social policy and the advisability of this particular social action program.

Essential to any re-evaluation effort is feedback from the original investigators. Therefore, when Russell Sage Foundation approached ETS about its participation and cooperation in this project, it was agreed at that time by all parties involved that ETS would review any resulting manuscript and prepare a chapter to be published as part of the volume.

This monograph was first submitted for publication in August 1972. The delay in publication was the result of a dialogue that ensued between Cook and his associates and the Educational Testing Service–Children's Television Workshop groups after the manuscript was completed. Naturally, Samuel Ball and his associates at ETS, as well as the Children's Television Workshop (CTW), were concerned about the reanalysis, since it questioned the highly positive statements of impact contained in the original publications. Because of the reactions of ETS and CTW to the manuscript, the Foundation convened an expert review committee. Wilfred Dixon of the University of California, Los Angeles, read the manuscript with particular emphasis on questions of scaling and data analysis. Peter Rossi read it with special reference to the survey data and relationship between viewing and socioeconomic status. Donald Campbell of Northwestern University and James Coleman of the University of Chicago reviewed the manuscript in its entirety. The committee met with Cook, with representatives from ETS, and with representatives and advisors of CTW. The reviewers recommended additional ways that Cook and his group could look at the data, and some of their suggestions were acted upon. The rejoinder of Ball and Gerry Bogatz of ETS appears as the last chapter of this book. It expresses well the sentiments of the original investigators about the "re-evaluation." They take issue with some specific points but also with the scope of the "re-evaluation."

As I have already noted, Cook and his colleagues did more than either check the accuracy of the statistical procedures or use different modes of analysis. Their perspective was to look at "Sesame Street" from the standpoint of its being a "public good," rather than as an innovative program of uncertain worth. The ETS position that they were evaluating an experimental program and not an established "public good" is understandable, since they planned their first-year's work before the program was broadcast. Few persons anticipated the large audience and the national attention "Sesame Street" would attract.

When the Foundation made the original agreement with ETS, it did not realize the reanalysis would be placed in a social policy framework. It is clear now that I and others at Russell Sage Foundation should have been much more definitive in our negotiations and on the scope of the re-evaluation. As a matter of record, when we at the Foundation started the series of evaluations of evaluations, we were not certain in our own minds about the end results. We know now that evaluations of evaluations must follow one of two models. The first requires explicit contractual arrangement between the parties involved. Otherwise the original researchers, in the face of strong criticisms, may feel unfairly treated. The second model is more compatible with the notion of free inquiry that surrounds the scientific enterprise. It requires guidelines specifying the time after completion of a study that data and questionnaire materials must be placed in a national data bank and made freely available.

Ideally, all parties—regardless of their political ideologies or research orientations—should have an opportunity to examine for themselves the data which influence public decisions. This should be true in the case of drugs available to the public and the television shows we watch. Since funds and technical acumen limit the number of persons who can in reality assess and interpret relevant data, the task remains for a few foundations to provide funding and a small cadre of researchers, without vested interests in the products or programs being evaluated, to undertake the work. However fallible the existing surrogates, their watchdog function is critical.

I believe efforts to review evaluation studies are essential. It is consistent with the traditions of the research community to critically review completed work and, if there is a reason, to reexamine the original data. Such reviews are critical especially for studies which have important national implications. It is only through the free and open exchange of information and through thorough reviews such as the one provided in this volume that the technical quality of evaluation studies and the emerging art that now guides their implementation will be improved.

Howard E. Freeman

Acknowledgments

This book would not have been possible without the aid of many people. A special debt is owed to Diana Williams for typing three drafts of the work and for her general encouragement and help in a myriad of other tasks. She was helped in her work, most competently and cheerfully, by Jo Ann Gengler, whose contributions to this and other projects have been invaluable over the years.

A preliminary draft of the manuscript was discussed at a meeting at Russell Sage Foundation where valuable advice was offered us by Donald T. Campbell, James S. Coleman, Wilfred J. Dixon, Peter H. Rossi, and Eleanor Bernert Sheldon. Others in attendance were Gerald S. Lesser and Lloyd N. Morrisett from Children's Television Workshop and Samuel Ball and Gerry A. Bogatz from the Educational Testing Service. The latter four helped considerably in clarifying their points of view about our work; and Ball and Bogatz provided us with extensive written comments as well. In addition, Dixon was especially helpful in pointing to the need for scaling the learning data, and we hope that Chapter 8 has benefited from this. Rossi skillfully analyzed for us some of the methodological inadequacies in existing surveys of the audience of "Sesame Street," and we hope that Chapters 8 and 9 have benefited from his comments.

An earlier draft of the manuscript was usefully commented upon by persons who are conducting other secondary analyses under the auspices of Russell Sage Foundation and by persons at the Foundation who are responsible for coordinating these efforts. We would like to thank Hugh F. Cline, Howard E. Freeman, Henry M. Levin, Peter H. Rossi, and Richard E. Snow for their advice. In particular, Freeman has been a great support and a wise counsel, and without him this project would not have been possible; while at all the meetings we have attended, Rossi has continued to enlighten us about survey research.

Since we did not act upon all of the advice given us, we want to make it especially clear that the persons we have thanked deserve credit for what is useful in this book, but they are not responsible for any of its failings.

A word of appreciation has to be extended to officials at the Children's Television Workshop, in particular Edward L. Palmer, who sent us most of the material about "Sesame Street" we requested. Their willing cooperation was a great help.

We want to extend a very special final word of appreciation and thanks to Samuel Ball and Gerry A. Bogatz of the Educational Testing Service. This book involves the reanalysis of data they collected in two evaluations of "Sesame Street." We suspect that if the roles had been reversed and they had wanted to use any primary data of ours for secondary analysis purposes, we would have been more suspicious, defensive, and reluctant than they, both to let the data be used and to cooperate with secondary analysts. Ball and Bogatz were not: They were at all times eminently professional, fine examples of the position that a scientist is accountable to others when he publishes a report and that his raw data should be made available to all who want to use them. Releasing data is not easy for it necessarily entails the risk that one's professional performance might be found wanting. As it turns out, our analyses corroborated those parts of the Ball and Bogatz work that were most central to their purposes. We, therefore, would not like the very real differences between some of our conclusions and theirs to obscure the similarities which emerged when we examined the topics that most concerned them.

Thomas Cook

Chapter 1
Objectives and a Summary of the Major Findings

PURPOSE OF THE STUDY

Introduction

The major purpose of this report is to present a case study of evaluation research that might be useful in the training of future evaluation researchers. Every society needs systematic feedback about the effects of its institutions or social programs, be they old or new. Most feedback today is in the form of personal testimony, which often comes from an unsystematic sample of persons who have an interest in the institution or program being evaluated. When this type of feedback occurs, it is often difficult to disentangle the effects of a program from the idiosyncracies of the parties giving the feedback.

Evaluation research has recently become popular as a purportedly scientific means of gaining valid feedback about the intended and unintended outcomes of programs. The hope is that such feedback will permit society to retain and improve successful programs and to modify or abolish unsuccessful ones. Unfortunately, there are not yet as many trained evaluation researchers as are needed, and the quality of data-based evaluations occasionally leaves something to be desired. We hope our evaluation will be useful in training the next generation of researchers so that the quality of evaluations can be enhanced by building upon what we have done well and by improving on what we have not done so well.

"Sesame Street" is a good choice for an instructional evaluation for several reasons. First, it is a television program for preschool children that enters into millions of homes and may be affecting millions of children. Secondly, the program has been twice evaluated by Samuel Ball and Gerry Ann Bogatz of the Educational Testing Service (ETS),[1] and the conclusions of their analyses, together with the testimony of many parents and children, have helped establish "Sesame Street's" reputation as an effective teaching instrument in the eyes of educational policymakers and many members of the general public. Third, the popularity and presumed teaching ability of "Sesame Street" have led to the development of similar television programs that are aimed at other social problems. Hence, the national importance of "Sesame Street" goes beyond the program itself to encompass the potential of television for solving educational problems. Finally, the United States is currently undergoing a flurry of deliberate social experimentation, much of it in education.[2] Exposure to the problems of evaluating "Sesame Street" may have some utility for persons who will have to evaluate these future educational programs.

We have not conducted an evaluation of "Sesame Street" from scratch. We did not select samples of respondents, or make sure that some preschool children saw the show more than others, or develop measures of the possible intended and unintended effects of the show. Rather, we took data about "Sesame Street" from several sources, especially the evaluations by Ball and Bogatz, and reanalyzed them. Thus, we were secondary analysts, and a minor objective of our work was to present a case study of one particular way that secondary analyses might be carried out. However, there is nothing to prevent many of our techniques from being used in primary evaluations, too.

The national need for the secondary analysis of evaluations is closely related to the need for "objective" conclusions about programs.[3] However, it is becoming increasingly obvious that there are many barriers to "objec-

---

[1] S. Ball and G. A. Bogatz, *The First Year of Sesame Street: An Evaluation* (Princeton, N.J.: Educational Testing Service, Oct. 1970); G. A. Bogatz and S. Ball, *The Second Year of Sesame Street: A Continuing Evaluation,* vols. 1 and 2 (Princeton, N.J.: Educational Testing Service, Nov. 1971).

[2] Perhaps the best general introduction to this recent social experimentation for the purposes of evaluating the effects of policy-relevant treatments is found in H. W. Riecken, R. F. Boruch, D. T. Campbell, N. Caplan, T. K. Glennan, J. Pratt, A. Rees, and W. Williams, *Social Experimentation: a Method for Planning and Evaluating Social Intervention* (New York: Academic Press, 1974).

[3] A summary of other reasons for conducting secondary evaluations is contained in T. D. Cook, "The Potential and Limitations of Secondary Evaluations," which appears in M. Apple, H. S. Lufler, and M. Subkoviak, eds., *Educational Evaluation: Analysis and Responsibility* (Berkeley, Calif.: McCutchan, 1974).

tive" evaluations. For example, many evaluation researchers are commissioned to perform their work by the administrators of the program being evaluated, and the researchers may hope for future work from these administrators. Thus, there will often be subtle pressures on the evaluator to provide outcomes that flatter the program. (This pressure is rarely overt, and we found no evidence that it applied to the ETS evaluations. Rather, the pressure is exerted at critical decision points when evaluators may unwittingly opt for solutions that are in a program's favor rather than against it.) In addition, most primary evaluations are conducted in haste because speedy feedback is demanded about a program. Clearly, such speed can be a barrier to asking and answering a wide range of sophisticated questions and might even lead to simple errors being made that reduce the usefulness of an evaluation. Finally, the science of evaluation research is not very well developed yet, and honest men can have sincere differences about such matters as the appropriate questions for an evaluation, the analyses that are appropriate for a particular body of data, the way to handle missing data, or the ways to aggregate data. Thus, no evaluation will (or should) produce outcomes that are beyond dispute, and secondary analyses should be welcomed as opportunities for a second group of persons to examine a body of previously analyzed data in their own way.

The Advantages and Limitations of Secondary Analysis

We might presume that secondary analysts should be competent in evaluation research if they are to do a good job. They will often have the advantage over the original evaluators in that they are removed from contact with the administrators of the program being evaluated, and so they will not have to deal with them or anticipate their desires or reactions to particular ideas, They will probably also have the advantage of less stringent deadlines to be met, and, as most of us know, deadlines help to focus energy but they also facilitate carelessness and the failure to examine important questions that had a lower priority rating than other questions. Also, secondary analysts typically have the reports of the original analysts to work with, and this should sensitize the secondary analysts both to the limitations in the original data and analyses as well as to any new techniques that the original evaluators may have developed. Certainly, we were helped considerably in our evaluation of "Sesame Street" by knowing what Ball and Bogatz had done in their two studies. Once the data have been secured (the difficult task), most secondary analysts will probably enjoy the same benefits that we did.

University researchers who conduct secondary analyses without time pressure, without contact with program administrators, and with the original evaluation reports in front of them enjoy advantages that a primary evaluation researcher does not have. If the latter are like the brave men in front-line trenches who are pushing us towards a self-monitoring society in the face of numerous difficulties, then university secondary analysts might be likened to "Monday-morning generals" who occasionally deign to applaud the heroic efforts and mud-splattered dignity of the men in the trenches but who, much more often, offer their lofty counsel as to why the front-line fighting did not go as well as it should have.

Such counsel is invariably ill-placed. Although the secondary analyst does enjoy a more comfortable distance, it would be naive to think that he avoids all of the problems of the original evaluator. The secondary analyst has deadlines, too, for if he is an academic it is not in his best self-interest to spend too many years analyzing other people's data unless his aim is to develop new methods of data analysis. Moreover, the secondary analyst will require funds and any agency that sponsors him will demand deadlines and may insist that they be kept. Also, it is easy for the investigator to be unaware of particular new methodological techniques, and it is natural for him to have preferences for certain modes of data analysis over others. In addition, the secondary analyst has his own values relevant to the program being evaluated, and although he will hopefully strive to minimize the role these play in his work, his own values will indubitably have some effect on the formulation of problems, the choice of analysis, and the interpretation of data. Finally, while the secondary analyst will probably not have the administrators of a program symbolically looking over his shoulder as he proceeds, other persons will be there, and they may unwittingly constrain the secondary analyst's freedom. For example, in our case we felt grateful to Ball and Bogatz for the promptness and willingness with which they supplied information when needed, for their candidness, for their nondefensive interest in what we did, and for their professional manner at all times.

The relative advantages of secondary analysis obviously do not guarantee any more valid conclusions about a program than can be obtained from primary analyses. Secondary analyses only permit the potential for better work. Secondary analyses are bound to be flawed, and the most one should hope from them is that the values of the analysts are not too obtrusive, that the analysts are methodologically competent, that their assumptions about evaluation research are spelled out, that the limitations of their perspective and analyses are detailed, and that their inadequacies are different from those of the original evaluators. Because secondary analyses are not definitive, Ball and Bogatz were invited, before we began our work, to comment on it when it was finished.

The Model of Secondary Analysis that We Shall Follow

There are many ways[4] of conducting secondary analyses. Perhaps the most common is to obtain a research report and to read it critically, perhaps even with some reanalysis of data from the tables in the report. The most obvious limitation of this *evaluation of the evaluation report* is that the raw data are not on hand to check that important analyses have been properly executed and to explore additional questions.

A second model involves obtaining the raw data and then *evaluating the evaluation* by recomputing some analyses, by conducting different analyses to answer some of the original research questions, and by exploring new questions. This method permits one to assess how well the original evaluation answered the questions it set out to answer and how adequately it formulated these questions in the first place. One would then be in a position to infer the effectiveness of the program from the robustness of the original findings and from any other findings.

This second model of secondary analysis has many advantages, for it both checks and expands upon previous work. Its major limitation is that it takes the original evaluation as its starting point, and the secondary analyst may be inadvertently trapped into the same general framework of questions and analyses as the original investigator. It is this general framework, of course, that the secondary analyst must question in great detail, for many of the lower-order decisions flow from it. There is a second drawback to the model we have just described. It places the secondary and primary analysts in what can easily become an adversary relationship, for the former's aim is a critical analysis of the latter's work rather than a critical analysis of the program being evaluated. It is for this reason that many primary analysts will be reluctant to let secondary analysts have access to their data.

If secondary analyses are to become as widespread as we think they should be, this goal is less likely to be achieved by evaluations of evaluations than by *alternative evaluations of a program*. In the case of "Sesame Street," this latter perspective places the emphasis on using the data of Ball and Bogatz (and of others) to evaluate "Sesame Street" rather than to evaluate Ball and Bogatz' two reports. We follow this model in our study, and the reader will look in vain for a systematic exposition and critique of the ETS reports. Rather, we asked what "Sesame Street" was intended to achieve, what accomplishments were claimed for it, and to which national problems it might be relevant. Then, we set about exploring the ETS data, and other

---

[4] A more comprehensive list of possible models is given and discussed in the previously mentioned chapter by T. D. Cook.

data, to see what "Sesame Street" is actually achieving, what it might be achieving, and what still needs to be examined about the program.[5]

Although our strategy was to evaluate "Sesame Street" and not Ball and Bogatz' work, there were occasions when we were forced to do the latter. This happened in particular when one of our conclusions differed from one of theirs. We checked their work when this happened, because such obvious discrepancies implied that a mistake had been made somewhere by someone. Sometimes, we found that the mistake was ours and corrected it; at other times the discrepancy was resolved in a way that indicated to us that Ball and Bogatz may not have been correct. We shall point out instances of this last occurrence so that readers are not left bewildered by contradictory findings. Another context where we were critical of Ball and Bogatz' work is when we could not conduct a particular analysis, used estimates from the ETS report on "Sesame Street," and would have computed the estimates differently. This was a very infrequent occurrence, however. Nonetheless, it serves to point out that we sometimes had to evaluate the work of Ball and Bogatz, and so our model of secondary analysis was not followed in the finest detail.

The major limitations of our model were those of all secondary analyses. It is rare that two evaluators would choose to answer the same research question with identical samples, identical measures of outcomes, or identical procedures for collecting data in the field. Moreover, the secondary analyst may not have a good firsthand understanding of testing procedures or the exact nature of a complex experimental treatment, and he may have to rely for an understanding of these on written reports or the testimony of a small sample of persons. Certainly, Ball and Bogatz were always willing to provide us with information about their experiences and instructions to field staff, and this reduced our ignorance. However, it did not make us fully informed (this may have been our fault, but we suspect that it is inevitable).

Finally, and perhaps most importantly, in evaluating a program rather than an evaluation the secondary analyst will pose questions that were peripheral to the primary evaluators or were irrelevant to them. Therefore, the secondary analyst may have to analyze data for a purpose other than

---

[5] It would be naive to think that evaluating programs instead of evaluations will necessarily induce primary evaluators to allow their data to be reanalyzed by others. A better method of gaining access to data would probably be for the sponsors of research to require that all evaluation data be placed in an easily available archive. It would also be naive to think that evaluating programs rather than evaluations removes all the adversary relationship. It will probably only reduce it. Nonetheless, we still believe that secondary analysis is most useful if it involves the evaluation of a program rather than the evaluation of an evaluation.

the one for which they were originally collected, and the data might not be entirely appropriate for the new purpose. Moreover, there may not even be any data of relevance to some of the secondary analyst's new questions. In this case he has to look elsewhere for data (which may not necessarily be of high quality), or he has to do without the data and fall back on suggesting that they be collected if the program is ever to be comprehensively evaluated.

As we shall see in later chapters, some data that we considered crucial for the evaluation of "Sesame Street" were not collected by Ball and Bogatz because they were not commissioned to do so by the Children's Television Workshop (CTW). However, once it was clear that we wanted to evaluate the national impact of "Sesame Street" rather than the work of Ball and Bogatz, we needed these additional data. Fortunately, some of them had been collected for CTW by other research agencies, and CTW did not hesitate to supply us with the reports containing the data. Had it not been for the prompt help of both CTW and ETS, we would not have been able to follow the secondary analysis model we did, for it absolutely required access to *all* of the data collected by the ETS team and to many research reports commissioned by CTW.

OUR PRE-DATA ANALYSES

The Questions Guiding Our Evaluation

We began by asking what "Sesame Street" was meant to accomplish. In her proposal for the funding of "Sesame Street," Joan Cooney, president of CTW, stated that "the general aim" of the program was "to promote the intellectual and cultural growth of preschoolers, particularly disadvantaged preschoolers."[6] In a related section of the proposal she referred to the need to teach children how to think as well as what to think. Cooney's statement is quite clear in indicating that one objective of "Sesame Street" is to cause intellectual and cultural growth in *all* groups of children. However, the reference to stimulating "the growth of preschoolers, *particularly disadvantaged preschoolers*" is ambiguous as a second objective of the show. It does not make clear whether the special focus of "Sesame Street" on the economically disadvantaged is: (1) to make these children a special target group for receiving "Sesame Street"; (2) to make sure that one major outcome of the program is that the disadvantaged learn from it; or (3) to make sure that the economically disadvantaged benefit more from the program than their economically advantaged counterparts.

---

[6] J. G. Cooney, "Television for Preschool Children: A Proposal" (New York: Children's Television Workshop, Feb. 19, 1968).

We chose to test whether "Sesame Street" successfully teaches a wide variety of children of different backgrounds. We also chose to ask the preceding three questions about the show's effects on the economically disadvantaged. The first required us to ascertain what efforts were made to stimulate the economically disadvantaged to view the program and how effective it was in reaching the national audience of disadvantaged children. The second question required us to ascertain whether the economically disadvantaged children who viewed the series made *absolute* learning gains from it. The third question required us to ask whether the average achievement of economically disadvantaged children across the nation increased more than the average achievement of advantaged children.

One reason why we asked this last question was that this is what Cooney's ambiguous statement may have meant since there is no reason to single out the economically disadvantaged once it has been stated that "Sesame Street" is meant to teach all children. After all, the economically disadvantaged are merely a subgroup of all children. A second reason was that the ETS evaluations of "Sesame Street" contained statements in their summary sections which indicate that "Sesame Street" may have been helping disadvantaged children more than others and thereby narrowing the gap in academic achievement between advantaged and disadvantaged preschoolers. We thought that it was especially important to evaluate the significant claims that were made for the series by responsible persons like the ETS team. Third, we agreed with Cooney's own statements in her paper on the goals of "Sesame Street" when she said that narrowing the academic achievement gap is an important national problem. Because of "Sesame Street's" undisputed special emphasis on the economically disadvantaged and its widespread popularity, we considered it worthwhile to ascertain how this particular educational resource affected a national problem that it might plausibly influence.

In our opinion, social programs should be evaluated in terms of their effects rather than in terms of the extent to which they meet those of their goals that are unambiguously stated. Such a preference is implicit in the widely held belief that evaluations should attempt to measure a program's *unintended* side effects, for these are effects that were not goals. Of course, program objectives serve as an important clue to some possible effects, but they obviously do not exhaust all the effects that a program has or can have.

A Possible Conflict between the Goals that We Explicated

It appears at first glance that there is a conflict between stimulating the growth of all children, and either causing absolute growth in the economically disadvantaged or causing relatively more growth in the disadvantaged as a group than the advantaged. Stimulating all children would seem to be best served by a *universalist strategy* that made "Sesame Street" equally available to all children, made it so universally attractive that the opportunity to view the program was equally used by all groups, and made the program's content so geared to the general intellectual and cultural needs of all preschoolers that, on the average, all groups learned from viewing.

Teaching the disadvantaged or narrowing the academic achievement gap would seem to be best served by a *selective strategy* based on some combination of three sub-strategies: "Sesame Street" could be made particularly available to the economically disadvantaged; it could be made particularly attractive to these children, so that they would want to view the show; or it could be particularly geared to their intellectual and cultural needs. In all three cases, though, the series would have to be especially tailored to the economically disadvantaged.

However, it is possible simultaneously to teach all preschoolers, including the economically disadvantaged, and to narrow the achievement gap. This would happen:

1. if an equal percentage of children in all social groups watched the series, and if economically disadvantaged children who watched for a certain time learned more than economically advantaged children who watched the show for the same amount of time;

2. if a higher percentage of economically disadvantaged children viewed "Sesame Street" regularly and if, among children who viewed for an equal amount of time, economically disadvantaged children learned at least as much as advantaged children.

The preceding summarizes our pre-data analyses which indicated to us that the focus of our evaluation would have to be on the size and social composition of "Sesame Street's" viewing audience, on whether the children from all social groups who viewed the show learned from it, and on whether children of different socioeconomic status levels learned equally if they viewed the show equally.

THE EDUCATIONAL TESTING SERVICE'S EVALUATION DESIGNS

Encouragement-to-View Treatment

It was originally feared before "Sesame Street" went on the air that the show would not be popular. Hence, the major treatment in the ETS evaluations of "Sesame Street" was "encouragement-to-view 'Sesame Street'." Encouragement-to-view involved a visit to the home before the

1970 or 1971 viewing season began in order to impress on the parents and child the importance of viewing "Sesame Street" and in order to leave promotional materials in the home—buttons, balloons, magazines, etc. During the 1970 season, the child was also visited weekly when the same encouragement was given him.[7] In 1971, visits and telephone calls were made to the home on a monthly basis. All of the visitors lived in the neighborhood, and some of them were responsible for collecting continuous measures of the frequency of viewing "Sesame Street" during the week or month as well as the testing to see how much the child knew at the pretest and posttest. This encouragement-to-view treatment was provided on a random basis to two-thirds of the children in the 1970 evaluation, and to one-half in the second-year evaluation.

The economically disadvantaged children in the first-year study came from poorer neighborhoods in Boston, Durham, and Phoenix; others came from a rural northern California area. Economically advantaged children came from the Philadelphia suburbs. Both the research sites for the second year (in Los Angeles and Winston-Salem) were chosen because their inhabitants were economically disadvantaged. In all cases, the labeling of sites as advantaged and disadvantaged was done by the ETS team on the basis of their acquaintance with the neighborhoods from which the research samples came.

---

[7] The first-year ETS report describes the encouragement treatment as follows:

The encouraged group was told about *Sesame Street,* was given publicity material, and was paid a weekly half-hour visit by ETS-trained staff during the *Sesame Street* morning telecasting time. The control (not-encouraged children) did not receive these treatments (p. 21).

The second-year report describes the second-year encouragement treatment as follows:

All children who were encouraged to view the show were visited once a month by testers who told the parents and children about the show and its importance for all preschool-aged children. The testers distributed CTW publicity materials to all encouraged parents and gave *Sesame Street* buttons and other souvenirs to the children. In Los Angeles and Winston-Salem, the homes of encouraged children were given the capability of receiving the show, if the capability was not already there, by installing UHF adapters or by arranging for a cable to be brought into the home. As will be shown in Chapter III, encouragement had the desired major influence, almost all encouraged children becoming viewers of *Sesame Street.*

The not-encouraged parents in all sites were told that ETS was conducting a survey of children's television viewing habits. Testers visited the not-encouraged homes once a month to collect viewing data, but *Sesame Street* was not mentioned to these parents. The not-encouragement came in the form of not mentioning the show, rather than in any active effort to discourage viewing (p. 34).

Major Outcome Measures

The outcome measures in the first year were predominantly measures of cognitive learning that were closely and skillfully tailored to the explicit behavioral objectives of "Sesame Street" that had been established by CTW's Research Advisory Board and Research Division. The measures were mostly of symbolic representation (knowledge of Forms, Body Parts, Letters, Numbers) and simple cognitive processes (Classification, Relations). These represented the focus on intellectual growth. There were few outcomes of relevance to cultural growth, which we understand to be knowledge of society and of nature.

The second-year evaluation was more congruent with the objectives of "Sesame Street" that we cited earlier. Items measuring symbolic and cognitive processes were still by far the most numerous, but there were four questions about the roles of mailmen and firemen and a test of attitudes towards race and school. These represent aspects of what we considered cultural growth. Also, the Peabody Picture Vocabulary Test (an IQ test) was administered at the second-year pretest and posttest, and although this is a vocabulary test, we assume that changes in Peabody IQ provided an indicator of growth in knowing how to think.

The ETS tests revealed a distinct preference for tests of cognitive skills, and there were noticeably fewer measures of social and personal development or of tests that measured the higher-order skills we associate with knowing how to think. This preference faithfully reflected the goal priorities that were established by CTW's Research Advisory Council and Research Division, although it did not as faithfully reflect the total range of goals that was established.

Some Consequences of Using the ETS Evaluations as Our Major Source of Data

The ETS evaluations were primarily designed to test whether disadvantaged children who were encouraged to watch "Sesame Street" learned cognitive skills. This objective created difficulties for us in our attempt to answer the questions we posed. First, while it was important to establish the effects of encouragement on both viewing and learning, we considered it more important to establish how viewing affects learning independently of encouragement. To answer this last question, we had to conduct analyses of viewers and nonviewers within the experimental groups of encouraged and nonencouraged children, thereby losing the advantages of randomization that apply when comparing the encouraged and the nonencouraged.

Second, two evaluations with six disadvantaged sites and only one advantaged site made it difficult to assess whether "Sesame Street" stimulated the growth of children who were not disadvantaged and whether it affected the achievement gap. These problems were exacerbated since the emphasis on the disadvantaged led to the creation of learning tests whose psychometric properties were excellent with respect to the economically disadvantaged but deficient with respect to the one advantaged site, in which the children scored so high at the pretest that there was restricted room for them to grow by the posttest.

Third, we wanted to assess "Sesame Street's" effects over a wide range of intended and unintended effects. However, we were limited by the tests for which data were collected, most of which were explicitly tailored to what was taught on the program. While such measures were imperative if the program was to·be evaluated sensitively, they were not sufficient if it were to be evaluated comprehensively. Hence, we had better data for assessing the cognitive growth of children in areas taught by "Sesame Street" than we had for ascertaining more general "intellectual skills" or social and personal development.

It is quite understandable that the ETS data should be better for the purposes for which they were collected than for some of the purposes to which we wanted to apply them. This does not mean, however, that the data were totally inappropriate for our questions. It merely means that we had to identify carefully the particular problems that arose because we wanted to ask some questions that were not directly addressed in the ETS evaluations; that we had to be careful in how we used the ETS data to answer these questions; and that we had to look beyond the ETS data for other studies that might have corroborated or disconfirmed any tentative conclusions about "Sesame Street" that emerged from our analyses of the ETS data.

THE EFFECTS OF ENCOURAGEMENT-TO-VIEW
"SESAME STREET"

We have added conclusion sections to the end of our major data analysis chapters, and these specify the conclusions in detail. Our present purpose is to give a broad overview of findings rather than the detailed web. To gain the latter perspective, the reader should read the appropriate chapters or—at the very least—their conclusion sections.[8]

In Durham, Phoenix, and northern California in the first year and in both Los Angeles and Winston-Salem in the second year, encouraged children viewed more of "Sesame Street" than nonencouraged children. For

---

[8] References to particular empirical studies to which we refer other than the ETS reports are cited in the appropriate chapters.

each of the first- and second-year sites where encouragement led to increased viewing, we first made sure that the various encouraged and nonencouraged learning means did not differ at the pretest and then we analyzed the posttest learning scores using each test's pretest learning scores as covariates. We found on a wide variety of tests that the adjusted posttest means were higher among encouraged children than nonencouraged ones.

We then used two different methods for predicting what the posttest learning means of encouraged children would have been at each site if there had been no "Sesame Street." We used the pretest learning scores for this purpose, and each of the prediction methods resulted in a comparable estimate of posttest knowledge at each site. The observed posttest mean for the Grand Total (a sum of all the test items that was weighted to reflect the behavioral objectives of "Sesame Street") was significantly different from the predicted mean at all the sites, including Boston and Philadelphia where the encouraged and nonencouraged children had not differed in viewing. Thus, it seems that encouragement to view "Sesame Street" was effective in modifying learning at all seven sites.

Encouragement affected means on a wide range of the ETS tests, including the attitude items and knowledge about two social roles. It could also be demonstrated that encouragement prevented Peabody IQ from decreasing (which was what tended to happen in the nonencouraged group). Moreover, the size of the learning differences was such that they met several different criteria of social significance, and there were no observed differences between the program's effects on viewers who were boys or girls, blacks or whites, or on viewers who were at different levels of IQ, age, or socioeconomic status (SES). It seems, therefore, to be a powerful treatment that promoted the growth of all children. (For more details, see Chapters 5 and 6.)

But three points must be made about the effects of encouragement. First, it decreased the amount of reading time that parents reported spending with their children. Second, encouragement is not a construct that can be adequately described *solely* in terms of television and viewing. Since some data indicated that encouragement affected learning independently of viewing, it is possible that the complex encouragement treatment had *some* of its effects for reasons that had nothing to do with viewing the show (see Chapter 7). Third, the only children in the nation who have ever received this particular encouragement treatment are in the ETS research samples. We can, therefore, be certain that encouragement is not promoting the growth of many children in the United States today, although a better understanding of the process whereby encouragement affects learning may have important consequences for obtaining significant amounts of learning in the future.

THE EFFECTS OF VIEWING "SESAME STREET"
WITHOUT ENCOURAGEMENT-TO-VIEW

It was not possible for us to form viewing and nonviewing groups at random in order to test whether viewing caused learning among nonencouraged children. Hence, we had to conduct a number of quasi-experimental analyses to examine the issue. None of them was perfect when taken singly. However, some of them were presumed to underestimate the effects of viewing on learning while others were presumed to overestimate them. Thus, the quasi-experimental strategy was to conduct multiple tests and create a sort of confidence interval in which the true effects of viewing on learning should lie. As it turned out, each mode of quasi-experimental analysis produced essentially comparable results, although slightly larger effects did tend to be found from the modes of data analysis that should have overestimated effects.

Our analyses of the first-year data indicated that the amount of viewing was related to learning at conventional levels of statistical significance (p. < .05) for two of the eight ETS learning tests (Letters and Numbers). Analyses of the nine second-year tests indicated one effect (Relations). However, Relations was almost marginally related to viewing in the first year (p. < .20), and the Grand Total, a composite that is disproportionately weighted in favor of the Letters and Numbers tests, was marginally significant in the second year (p. < .10). We concluded, therefore, that watching "Sesame Street" teaches some letter, number, and relations skills.

The direction of most of the statistically nonsignificant effects suggested that viewing might have caused learning. As with all nonsignificant effects it was not clear whether "Sesame Street" did not teach the skills tapped by these tests or whether more statistically significant effects would have emerged if additional sources of extraneous variance had been controlled, if tests of greater statistical power had been conducted, or if sample size had been increased. However, even if additional sources of extraneous variance had been controlled, it was unlikely that the results for nonsignificant effects would have reached conventional statistical criteria of educational significance. As a matter of record, of the seventeen first- and second-year tests, the only one to account for more than 5 percent of the learning gain variance in our analyses was the Letters Test in the first year.

Judith Minton evaluated "Sesame Street" at the end of its first season and asked whether the show taught the skills tapped by the Metropolitan Readiness Test (MRT), an instrument that is often used to assess a child's readiness to enter school. Three of the MRT subtests are directly relevant to "Sesame Street's" goals (letter recognition, number skills, and matching visual forms); the other three tap what could be positive side effects of the show (vocabulary gain, phrase recognition, and copying). Minton's basic design involved comparing the subtest means for 524 children who attended a kindergarten in "Sesame Street's" first year with the respective subtest means of children who had attended the same kindergarten the two years before the show went on the air. Of the children who had the chance to watch "Sesame Street," 54 percent reported being daily viewers and 97 percent reported viewing at least once during the season. The mean letter recognition of this group was significantly higher than that of the groups from the pre-"Sesame Street" years, but no other interpretable effects of the show were obtained. In a very important subsidiary analysis, Minton was able to rule out the possibility that the kind of child who had attended the kindergarten in "Sesame Street's" first year differed from the kind of child who had attended it in previous years. Her design to accomplish this is outlined in Chapter 7, and it indicated once again that "Sesame Street" raised the group mean on the Alphabet Test but on no others. Minton's data provided an independent corroboration of the Letters effect from our first-year analyses and they also suggested that the Letters effect was stronger than other effects. Indeed, no other effects emerged from her work.

The learning gains from viewing without encouragement did not seem to be as large or as generalized as the gains from encouragement-and-viewing.[9] It must be remembered, however, that despite our strategy of replication across years and bodies of data, (1) we only tested the results of six-months' viewing in 1970 and 1971 and many children view the program for a longer period; (2) our own analyses of the ETS data were restricted to economically disadvantaged children; (3) we used several different measures of viewing in our work and none of them was perfect; (4) there were only 108 at-home children in one-year's tests and 117 in the other year's. This last point must be balanced, however, against the larger Minton samples and our corroborating analyses (reported in Chapter 7) where the effects of viewing were examined both within the larger sample of first-year encouraged children and with the encouraged and nonencouraged pooled.

THE VIEWING AUDIENCE OF "SESAME STREET"

Since we demonstrated that heavy viewing was required for gains to appear, we were primarily interested in determining the size of "Sesame Street's" audience of regular viewers (four times a week or more) who were

---

[9] We deliberately use the expression "encouragement-and-viewing" rather than "encouragement-to-view" in this context to reflect the fact that encouragement enhanced viewing and that viewing was independently related to learning.

between two and five years of age. To make estimates of the size of this viewing audience we used Harris audience surveys commissioned by the Public Broadcasting Service in 1969, 1970, and 1971; Nielsen ratings; two audience surveys conducted by Daniel Yankelovich, Inc. in urban ghetto neighborhoods in 1970 and 1971; and the two ETS reports. None of these, taken singly, was an adequate survey of the nationwide audience, although the Harris surveys were the best.

After making many assumptions that are spelled out in Chapter 9, we were able to place the audience of regular viewers somewhere between 28 percent and 36 percent of all the nation's children between two and five years of age in the 1969–1970 season and between 33 percent and 42 percent in the 1970–1971 season. These are impressive figures. Since only 63 percent of the households in the nation can receive public television, the figures would be even more impressive if they were computed against a baseline of children living in areas where the show is available. We calculated that the average cost of reaching regular viewers was between $1 and $2 per season and was probably at the upper end of this range in the first season and at the lower end in the second season. Most other preschool programs have wider curricula than "Sesame Steet" but involve face-to-face interaction between teachers and children which means that the programs reach many fewer children and at costs that often exceed $1,000 per child per annum! A large measure of "Sesame Street's" national importance lies in its ability to attract and hold such a large audience of viewers that the per capita costs are so strikingly low.

The per capita costs of reaching the economically disadvantaged were higher than those of reaching the advantaged. This was because CTW used utilization centers in inner-city areas in attempts to stimulate viewing and because much of CTW's research budget was spent on the disadvantaged. If we consider only utilization centers, they consumed 8.6 percent of CTW's budget in 1969 and 15 percent in 1970. These costs made "Sesame Street" a program which was universally available to children in areas where public television was available but which was also compensatory because more resources were spent on disadvantaged than advantaged children during the years in question.

THE EFFECTS OF "SESAME STREET" ON THE ACADEMIC ACHIEVEMENT GAP

Children from advantaged homes outscore children from disadvantaged homes on tests of academic achievement even before the children enter school. There are many kinds of academic tests on which this difference can be observed, and in this sense there are many different gaps. Also, there are many ways of conceptualizing disadvantagement (in terms of parental income, education, race, place of residence, or the like). With the data that were available to us we checked (1) how viewing "Sesame Street" was related to income, education, and race in the nation at large; (2) how gains from "Sesame Street" were related to the SES level of sites as chosen by the ETS team; and (3) how learning was related to indicators of SES in Minton's work.

Viewing and Indices of Advantagement

Ball and Bogatz concluded that their Philadelphia advantaged sample viewed more heavily than their disadvantaged samples, and we replicated this. We also demonstrated that viewing "Sesame Street" was correlated with the educational climate of the home and the child's pretest learning scores within each first-year site. In addition, the Nielsen data indicated that families with large incomes are more likely to tune in to "Sesame Street." Finally, the Harris surveys—the best available data—documented that in 1970 and 1971 viewers of the program came disproportionately from homes where the adults were better educated. All this evidence suggests that "Sesame Street" was watched more in homes of higher socioeconomic status.

There were some difficulties, however, about accepting this conclusion. The Harris surveys reported that whites tended to view more than blacks in 1970 (by eight percentage points) but not in 1971. However, the Harris estimate of viewing by black children may not have been stable since the Harris sample of black households with a child under six years of age in public television areas was about sixty in 1971. In addition, for the Harris estimate of viewing by blacks to have been correct it would have had to follow both from the preponderance of blacks among the economically disadvantaged in the nation and from the positive overall relationship of viewing and other indices of advantage that disadvantaged black children would have viewed "Sesame Street" more than disadvantaged white children. No such trend was noticeable in the ETS viewing data.

A second difficulty arose because the rating services have, in Joan Cooney's words, "middle class biases." These presumably result because the ratings are not sensitive to multiple viewing at home or in day-care centers. Moreover, in the case of the Nielsen samples, there is an unknown bias associated both with that organization's greater need for accurate data on the more affluent sections of society and with the kinds of families which do and do not agree to have a mechanical device attached to their television set. Unfortunately, we could not estimate by how much the bias from such sources accounted for the positive relationship of viewing and indicators of socioeconomic status.

Finally, it must be noted that the national viewing surveys we consulted did not report the data in terms of cross-tabulations by indicators of socioeconomic status (including race) and the region of the country in which a child lived. There was, for example, considerable evidence suggesting that in 1971 children in the northern part of the United States viewed more educational television than children in the South and that children in urban areas viewed more than children in rural areas. Moreover, northerners and city-dwellers tended to have higher incomes and more years of education than southerners and country- or town-dwellers. Hence, it would seem that viewing may have been related to income and education only because the series was more popular in some parts of the country than others. This possibility was examined with the ETS data which, it will be remembered, produced a positive relationship between viewing and indicators of socioeconomic status *within the ETS research sites.* Thus, it was possible to obtain the positive relationship of viewing and status independently of region. (For further details, see Chapter 8.)

Effects of Viewing on the Learning Gains of Children from Different Social Backgrounds

The children in the ETS studies about whom we most wanted to generalize were the children who watched "Sesame Street" without any encouragement from members of the ETS research team.

There are several problems that had to be faced before using the data from these children to investigate the effects of "Sesame Street" on the average knowledge level of nonencouraged children of different socioeconomic backgrounds. First, the second-year ETS evaluation contained no economically advantaged children. Hence, we had to restrict ourselves to the first-year samples. Second, there was only one first-year site that the ETS team labeled as advantaged. However, we were able to demonstrate that the Boston and California samples were relatively more advantaged than the Durham and Phoenix samples on a variety of tests, and this helped us generate three levels of advantagement—Philadelphia, the highest; Boston and California, the next; and Durham and Phoenix, the lowest. However, the absence of valid SES measures meant that no meaningful absolute differences could be attributed to the sets of sites. Indeed, it is worth remembering that the Boston children came from a site that was deliberately chosen because poorer persons lived there. Hence, in comparing a set of sites including Boston with a set including Durham and Phoenix, we were comparing two sets of deliberately chosen poor communities! Third, the samples of nonencouraged children who viewed the show at home were smaller than we would have liked—twenty-seven in Philadelphia, sixty-two in Boston and California, and forty-six in Durham and Phoenix. Fourth, the learning mean and standard deviation were correlated, thereby violating an assumption of the statistical tests we wanted to use. Hence, we rescaled the data and demonstrated that the means and standard deviations of the transformed scores were not correlated. Finally, the ceiling effect that operated on the highest-scoring Philadelphia sample artificially restricted their growth and deflated the estimate of their learning gain from pretest to posttest. This meant that, if "Sesame Street" were increasing the gap—at least on the tests administered by the ETS team—then we would presumably have underestimated such effects.

Our analyses of the rescaled gains scores revealed that the mean gains were systematically related to the status level of sites across the first-year tests but that the effects were weak statistically. That is, in a comparison of the highest and lowest SES groups (Philadelphia *versus* Durham and Phoenix), acceptable levels of statistical significance were only obtained for a test of alphabet skills, and marginally significant effects were obtained for the Grand Total. Such results may have reflected the fact that viewing had weak effects on learning, or the bias in the analysis which was against finding a widened gap, or both of these factors.

Minton's Dissertation

In a dissertation which we mentioned earlier and which would not be definitive by itself for examining the gap issue, Minton demonstrated that economically disadvantaged children who had previously been in a Headstart program did not differ in knowledge on any of the MRT subtests from Headstart graduates who had entered the same kindergarten in the two years before "Sesame Street" was broadcast. However, greater gains than their respective controls were obtained on the alphabet subtest (a) by advantaged children who came from a suburban community in New York state and (b) by a group of children who were ambiguously described as being "white," "lower class," "middle-income," "representing all socioeconomic levels," and bound for parochial schools once they left kindergarten. (Of course, all the children in Minton's research attended the same kindergarten.) These results suggested the same conclusion as our analyses of the ETS data: A gap in letter-related skills may have been widening because of "Sesame Street." (For further details, see Chapter 8.)

We could draw four general conclusions about the gap issue. First, there was no evidence that any gaps were being narrowed because of "Sesame Street." This contradicted the conclusions drawn by the ETS re-searchers. Second, there was little indication that "Sesame Street" was hav-ing pedagogically significant effects in a single season except for some letter-related skills. Hence, the program was not likely to be having socially significant effects on most gaps despite the SES-related pattern of viewing the show. Third, if the series was having any effects on the academic achievement gap, then the data from viewing surveys, from our analyses of the ETS data, and from Minton's dissertation indicated that the direction of such effects was toward widening rather than narrowing the gap. Fourth, the Letter Test findings from our analysis of the gap issue, and the letter recognition findings from Minton's analysis, suggested that gaps were most likely to be widened in those cognitive domains where "Sesame Street" was most successful in teaching.

PLACING A VALUE ON "SESAME STREET"

The Value of Six-Months' Viewing

Assigning value to "Sesame Street" has to start from what we know about the show. The major positive findings were: (1) encouragement-and-viewing caused statistically reliable learning gains on most of the tests that were developed to fit the show's curriculum and on a test of knowledge of so-cial roles. Moreover, it prevented IQ, as indexed by a vocabulary-based test, from declining; (2) encouragement-and-viewing cost between $100 and $200 per child per year over and above the costs of producing "Sesame Street"; (3) viewing "Sesame Street" for six months without encouragement caused learning gains in some letter, number, and relationship skills; (4) the 1971 audience of regular viewers (at least four times per week) was between 33 percent and 42 percent of all the nation's children between the ages of two and five; (5) the cost per regular viewer per year was about $1.

The less positive findings were: (1) encouragement-and-viewing de-creased the amount that disadvantaged parents reported reading to their chil-dren; (2) in most analyses, the effects of viewing without encouragement were less generalized and of lesser magnitude than the effects of encourage-ment-and-viewing; (3) effects of viewing could only be demonstrated on a minority of the ETS tests, albeit the more reliable ones, and only one test (Letters) reached conventional statistical criteria of educational significance; (4) viewing the show seems to be positively correlated with indices of pa-rental income and education, though less strongly with indices of race (how-ever, the size of black samples was small for making confident estimates of viewing by black children); (5) "Sesame Street" is probably increasing achievement gaps in those domains where it effectively teaches.

Information that is still not known, and that is vital for a comprehensive understanding of the show's effects, includes: (1) what are the effects of viewing "Sesame Street" for more than six months? (2) how do schools capitalize upon any gains that "Sesame Street" may be causing during a child's total viewing career? (3) how is race related to viewing? and (4) how is the program affecting non-cognitive growth among children of different backgrounds?

How does one weight the positive and the negative findings that we detailed above in order to come to an estimate of how valuable "Sesame Street" is? How can one make any judgment at all about the show's value, when so much that is important is still unknown? Should the evaluator make any judgments at all about a program's value? These are issues we deal with in Chapter 3, and especially in Chapter 10. Suffice it to say here that we are prepared to make judgments, that we are not impressed with the educational consequences of viewing without encouragement that have been demonstrated to date, but that we freely acknowledge that a convincing, comprehensive analysis of "Sesame Street's" national impact is still lacking.

A Note to Parents

In discussing the results of our work we have been struck by the frequency with which parents were skeptical about our finding that six-months' viewing of "Sesame Street" led to little cognitive gain. This finding seemed to contradict the parents' own experience from observing their children. One possible reason for this may be that our analyses of this issue, together with Minton's analysis and the ETS analyses of the effects of viewing independently of encouragement, all underestimated the effects of viewing. This is possible, but we think that any underestimation by a large magnitude is unlikely. Another possibility is that most children view "Sesame Street" for more than one season. Hence, the opinion of parents might be based on the effects of several seasons' viewing while our judgment is based on the effects of one season's viewing. A third possibility is that most of the analyses we reviewed were conducted on samples of disadvantaged children while most of the parents we talked to were relatively more advantaged. A final possibility is that some parents may have overestimated the extent of learning gains by their children in any of the following ways.

First, they may have been thrilled that their child learned something from the program and might have generalized from the learning of some items to the learning of a more significant number of items. Second, it is easy to confuse learning from the program with gains from it. That is, viewers might have learned some items from the program which, at their stage of development, they would have learned from their environment anyway. It is possible, therefore, that "Sesame Street" *taught* more than our analyses of *gain* indicated. Since the outcome variable of policy relevance is learning gains rather than learning from a new source what one would have learned elsewhere, it is important for parents not to confuse learning from "Sesame Street" with gaining from it. A third possibility is that parents generalized from the relatively narrow and—to them—salient gains in preschool skills (principally letter skills other than reading or alphabet recitation) to gains in more general cognitive domains or in the domains of social and emotional development. These broader areas are included among the program's goals and formed part of its televised content, but it has not yet been demonstrated that viewing caused significant gains in these areas. Finally, it is also possible that parents estimated their child's learning on the basis of testimony from friends about the program's ability to teach. "Sesame Street" has received a favorable press and is popular with both children and parents because it entertains and is believed to teach. If the attitudes and beliefs of parents have indeed been influenced by this publicity, it too may have contributed towards overestimating the program's effects.

SOME IMPLICATIONS OF OUR FINDINGS

The Selective Use of Universally Available Social Goods

We have considered "Sesame Street" as a national resource. As such, it is universally available over the airwaves, which means that nearly all children have potential access to it in areas where public television is available. The program has been selectively promoted in the past so that economically disadvantaged children were more likely to have been the targets of CTW personnel in utilization centers. Despite being universally available and selectively promoted in a way that should have especially benefited the disadvantaged, the program is in fact selectively used by children in a way that especially benefited advantaged children who were heavier viewers of it. This gives rise to the need to understand why universally available social goods, like "Sesame Street," are selectively used so that the groups in society which least need them may benefit most from them.

It also gives rise to the need to make explicit the difficulty of pursuing compensatory goals by means of a universalist strategy. Compensatory goals are based on the notion of giving poor children extra learning opportunities so as to compensate for any differences in environmental learning opportunities that might favor the advantaged. Such compensatory programs are less politically and ethically attractive to some persons than are universal programs because compensatory programs favor some children over others and because the persons who receive them may be stigmatized as deficient in some way. It would be naive to expect that universal programs will be equally used by all segments of society. Since benefits come from using opportunities rather than from merely having them, it is difficult to pursue compensatory aims by means of a universalistic strategy. It is especially difficult to pursue both universal and selective aims with a single program. In our opinion, this is a major lesson to be learned from "Sesame Street," and it leads directly to the crucial question: What should the program's priority be, if it cannot be both universal and selective simultaneously?

Defining Priorities for Preschool Education

A universal strategy is crucial if the highest priority for preschool education is defined as reaching and teaching the maximum number of children. This will enable many children to know more so that they, and society at large, might enjoy the particular benefits that follow from many persons being more knowledgeable. (These benefits are described in Chapter 10.) A selective strategy is called for if the highest priority for preschool education is defined as reaching and teaching the maximum number of economically disadvantaged children so that they as individuals and society at large might enjoy the benefits that accrue from the least fortunate in society knowing more. (These benefits are also described in Chapter 10.)

There can be little doubt that teaching all children and focussing special teaching resources on the economically disadvantaged are each important national objectives. But since the two priorities are in large part countervailing, the crucial issue is which of them has a higher priority than the other. This issue is complicated and difficult, and many persons will (and should) have different ideas on the topic. Our own thoughts appear in Chapter 10 and are intended as inputs into an important area of public debate. They are obviously not the data-bound results of an evaluation research project.

Is the Achievement Problem of the Economically Disadvantaged of an Absolute or Relative Nature?

If "Sesame Street" had had larger effects in a single season or if viewing for several seasons has larger effects than viewing for a single season, then one would be faced with the problem of deciding between an absolute and a relative conception of the educational problem of economically disadvantaged children. The problem would arise because, under the conditions already outlined, the disadvantaged might absolutely gain from the show but might relatively lose by falling even further behind the advantaged. How can absolute gains be justified if there are relative losses? Which is more important to the disadvantaged or to the nation at large: that disadvantaged children know more than at present or that gaps between specific social groups be narrowed? Is the problem of the disadvantaged one of what they do not know or of what the advantaged know more than they? This general issue is discussed in Chapter 10 and is intended as an input into the public debate about whether the relative or absolute problem should receive higher priority in future policy decisions in the preschool area.

The Implications of Encouragement-to-View

Encouragement-to-view "Sesame Street" had more desirable consequences than viewing "Sesame Street." One reason for this is probably that encouragement increased viewing among disadvantaged children almost to the level of the advantaged children at Philadelphia. But since encouragement probably had effects over and above those directly attributable to viewing, it is also possible that the encouraged children were especially conscious of being in a research study, or that the testers behaved differently with encouraged children, or that the parents of encouraged children interacted more with the child in ways relevant to "Sesame Street." Some of these last possibilities do not involve acquiring new information due to viewing the program, but establishing social relationships which may permit the child to demonstrate his previous knowledge or which may have caused new learning for nonviewing reasons. It should not be forgotten that these last possibilities involve face-to-face rather than television-mediated processes and, as such, they take "Sesame Street" out of the technological arena of mediated, focussed, and entertaining instruction and put it back into the traditional arena of learning caused by face-to-face interaction with other persons.

The major advantage of television is its low per capita cost once a large audience has been reached, and one of the major disadvantages of programs that deal with each child or group of children separately is their higher per capita cost. If part of the causal learning variance associated with the global encouragement treatment was indeed related to special relationships between the encouraged children and the ETS research personnel or the children's parents, it would imply that the maximal effectiveness of "Sesame Street" involved greater per capita costs than those associated with merely reaching into homes with a television program. However, our *gross* estimate (indeed, *very* gross estimate) of the annual per capita cost of encouragement ($100 to $200 above the cost of producing "Sesame Street") was lower than the cost of many other preschool programs of a face-to-face nature, and this fact alone should warrant further research on understanding why encouragement-to-view had the effects it did.

OUR RECOMMENDATION

We believe that the evidence we have examined casts reasonable doubt about whether "Sesame Street" was causing as large and as generalized learning gains in 1970 and 1971 as were attributed to the program on the basis of past evaluations. We believe that the evidence also casts reasonable doubt about whether "Sesame Street" had a totally beneficial effect on children from economically disadvantaged social groups during these years in that the program may have been widening achievement gaps in those curriculum areas where it taught with success. However, most of the evidence we have examined came from research that was not specifically designed to test whether viewing "Sesame Street" caused learning gains or whether the show affected national achievement gaps. Hence, the data base and our analyses do not carry the more definitive stamp of research which was deliberately designed to test a small number of specific issues of maximal policy relevance. Furthermore, we could find no data of any reasonable quality to assess the crucial question of the long-term effects of viewing "Sesame Street" on both learning and social development. There is, we feel, a real sense in which "Sesame Street's" national impact has not yet been adequately or definitively evaluated.

These considerations lead us to recommend that a committee be appointed by the commissioner for education and/or the president of the Ford Foundation and/or the president of the Carnegie Corporation (the major financial sponsors of CTW) to commission research in order to ascertain whether larger and more widespread learning gains are caused by viewing "Sesame Street" than have been demonstrated to date, and also to ascertain how the series may be affecting the more important achievement gaps between children of different socioeconomic and racial groups. We also recommend that CTW be free to take whichever steps it wants in the interim to change the program's content or its distribution so as to increase the level of gains or to decrease the chances of the program widening achievement gaps. These recommendations are discussed in Chapter 11.

Chapter 2
The General Objectives of "Sesame Street" and of Our Evaluation

A BRIEF INTRODUCTION TO "SESAME STREET"[1]

The Program

"Sesame Street" is a television series aimed at entertaining and teaching children aged three to five, with special emphasis on four-year-olds. The program is produced by the Children's Television Workshop (CTW), a nonprofit organization that was created in March 1968. The prime mover of the workshop and its current president is Joan Ganz Cooney, whose media experience was gained as a public affairs producer on Channel 13 in New York. She is largely responsible for the original idea of "Sesame Street" and for the specification of its objectives.

Each "Sesame Street" program is fast-moving and action-packed, and it portrays humans and puppets interacting in a way designed to teach letters, numbers, principles of classification, body parts, and elementary problem-solving. The televised lessons are independent of each other in the sense that mastery of one day's program is not a precondition for mastery of the next day's. Indeed, since children will inevitably miss some programs and since the show's implicit philosophy of education stresses the role of repeti-

---

[1] An account of the origins and activities of the Children's Television Workshop can be found in Phyllis Feinstein, *All About Sesame Street* (New York: Tower Publications, 1971).

27

tion in inducing learning and retention, the same learning sequences are sometimes broadcast several times during each viewing season.

Much of the action in "Sesame Street" takes place in a setting reminiscent of an inner-city ghetto, and the principal adult actors are black. Many of the children who appear on the show are also black, and the remainder appear to be carefully chosen to represent most of the social groups in the United States today. Because "Sesame Street" is not merely a program for learning letters and numbers, the social interaction that is portrayed is exemplary in its harmony, and the whole tone of the series is one of friendly interracial and intergroup acceptance and cooperation. Thus, the series is designed to appeal to a wide range of children, although to inner-city black children in particular, and is intended to promote a certain basic social philosophy of social and racial integration.

"Sesame Street" is distributed and partly funded by the Corporation for Public Broadcasting (CPB) and is designed to be viewed at home or at nursery school. In most parts of the country it is only available on educational television channels; about 75 percent of U.S. children live in areas reached by public television, although the extent of coverage is increasing annually. Moreover, there are some areas of the country where public television is only available on ultra-high frequency channels, and not all sets in these areas can pick up UHF signals. For these two reasons, the program is not available in all homes that have television sets.

The series was originally broadcast for one hour a day during the school week. Later during its highly successful first year, the five weekday shows were run consecutively on Saturday mornings, permitting Saturday viewers to see any shows they had missed or to see other shows for a second time. In the next season, "Sesame Street" went on the air twice a day in many areas—once in the morning and once in the afternoon. And in later years, it was screened even more frequently. For example, in the Chicago area, during 1972, "Sesame Street" could be seen four times a day Mondays through Saturdays and twice on Sunday. If we assume that most children of four do not view after 9 P.M., "Sesame Street" was broadcast in Chicago for twenty-six of the ninety-one hours when preschool children could view television.

The Sources of Funds

The following table[2] indicates the sources of funds for the development and first two broadcast years of "Sesame Street," and it can be seen that

---

[2] Office of Economic Opportunity, "Hearings Before the Subcommittee of the Committee on Appropriations," House of Representatives, 92nd Cong., 1st Sess., 1970, p. 63.

Funding of Children's Television Workshop
(Fiscal years 1968–1971)

Source	Amount
Federal	
Office of Education	$ 6,225,000
Office of Economic Opportunity	350,000
Office of Child Development	300,000
National Institute of Child Health and Human Development	15,000
National Foundation on the Arts and Humanities	10,000
Total Federal Support	$ 6,900,000
Private	
Carnegie Corporation	$ 2,100,000
Ford Foundation	2,025,000
Corporation for Public Broadcasting	1,650,000
Public Broadcasting Service	600,000
Markle Foundation	237,800
Learning Resources Institute	150,000
3M Company	37,200
Total Private Support	$ 6,800,000
Total Support from Above Sources	$13,700,000

about one-half of the total funding came from public or government sources and that most of this came from the Office of Education.

The income from foundations and federal sources does not represent CTW's sole source of income. Private interests other than those listed contribute money, and the recent expansion of CTW has been partly financed by the overseas sale of "Sesame Street" and by the sale within the United States of records, film strips, books, films, and toys that deal with "Sesame Street" and for which CTW holds the copyright.

The Historical Context in Which "Sesame Street" was Developed

Joan Cooney planned much of the guiding philosophy for "Sesame Street" during a year in which, with the aid of Carnegie Corporation funds, she examined the feasibility of using television to provide entertaining instruction for preschool children. She submitted a final report to the Carnegie Corporation[3] that was paraphrased in later grant proposals.[4]

---

[3] Joan G. Cooney, *The Potential Uses of Television in Education: A Report to the Carnegie Corporation* (undated).

[4] Joan G. Cooney, *Television for Preschool Children: A Proposal* (Feb. 19, 1968); Joan G. Cooney, *Children's Television Workshop in 1970–71: A Proposal* (Apr. 1970).

The first grant proposal, dated February 19, 1968, began by describing what Cooney believed to be the "Educational Wasteland" of preschool education, a wasteland where preschoolers were encouraged to spend their day in play rather than in more structured formal instruction. She objected to what she called the play-oriented "Sandbox" approach, because she did not consider it adequate for solving two pressing national problems that we briefly describe below.

Narrowing the Academic Achievement Gap. The first problem is that, on entering school, children from economically disadvantaged homes score lower on academic achievement tests than do their cohorts from more economically advantaged homes,[5] and Cooney pointed out that these performance differences increase with each year that the child is in formal schooling. The challenge to preschool education, as she viewed it, was to reach children at a young age when the gap between the economically advantaged and disadvantaged is at its narrowest. She wrote in the 1968 proposal with reference to narrowing the gap that:

> The earlier the gap . . . can be narrowed, the easier the task will be and the better (the lower class child's) educational chances. To many, the neglected years before school have seemed the best place to begin (pp. 1, 2).

Joan Cooney's statement must be seen in its historical context. The War on Poverty in the 1960s was largely responsible for the reemergence of the academic achievement gap as a national problem of high priority. At that time, formal education was considered to be one of the more potent means of breaking out of the poverty cycle. This cycle was believed to operate by providing poorer children with few educational opportunities, thereby preventing them from securing good jobs, keeping them poor, and subsequently not allowing them to provide the educational opportunities that would help their children get good jobs. It was believed by the advocates of the War on Poverty that poverty was transmitted in this fashion from generation to generation and that enough new educational opportunities had to be provided so that a whole generation of poor children could break out of the cycle.

The Economic Opportunities Act of 1964 clearly indicated that poverty was considered a national problem of high priority and that education was viewed as one means of alleviating the problem:

> . . . [P]overty continues to be the lot of a substantial number of our people. The United States can achieve its full economic and social potential as a nation

---

[5] Edmund W. Gordon and Doxey Wilkerson, Compensatory Education for the Disadvantaged, 1966, College Entrance Examination Board, p. 14.

only if every individual has the opportunity to contribute to the full extent of his capabilities and to participate in the workings of our society. It is therefore the policy of the United States to eliminate the paradox of poverty in the midst of plenty in this nation by opening to everyone the opportunity for education and training, the opportunity to work, and the opportunity to live in decency and dignity . . . (Sect. 2).

It was assumed that several factors operated together, even before the child entered school, and decreased the effectiveness of formal school education as a means of breaking the poverty cycle. President Nixon made this very clear in his message to Congress of February 19, 1969, when he said:

The immense contribution the Headstart program has made simply by having raised to prominence on the national agenda the fact—known for some time, but never widely recognized—that the children of the poor mostly arrive at school age seriously deficient in the ability to profit from formal education, and already significantly behind their contemporaries. It also has been made abundantly clear that our schools as they now exist are unable to overcome this deficiency.

Since it was believed that the schools alone could not reduce the academic achievement gap, the need arose for an alternative method of instruction, and one was preschool education. The following section from the Elementary and Secondary Education Act of 1965 (known as Title 1) makes this clear. The act states:

In recognition of the special educational needs of children of low income families and the impact that concentrations of low income families have on the ability of local educational agencies to support adequate educational programs, the Congress hereby declares it to be the policy of the United States to provide financial assistance (as set forth in this title) to local educational agencies serving areas with concentrations of children from low income families to expand and improve their educational programs by various means (including preschool programs) which contribute particularly to meeting the special educational needs of educationally deprived children (Sect. 201).

Stimulating All Children to Grow Intellectually and Culturally. According to Joan Cooney, the second national problem is that, for all the nation's children, life is becoming increasingly complex. As a result, it is frequently assumed that more and more stringent demands are being made on our intellectual capacities. The challenge that this problem poses is to develop ways of teaching children how to learn. Once they have mastered this skill, it is assumed that they will be better able to handle the complexities of our fast-changing technological society. Such thinking is also reflected in the same Economic Opportunities Act that outlined the War on Poverty, for it also manifested an awareness that "the United States can achieve its full economic and social potential as a nation only if *every* individual has the opportunity to contribute to the full extent of his capabilities" (italics ours). In 1966, the National Education Association gave its support to a proposal to begin public education at age four. Much mention was made during that meeting of the special problems of the economically disadvantaged, but the speeches also reflected the second problem. W. G. Carr stated in one of the opening addresses:

> . . . People are (our) most valuable resource. . . . Are twelve years of universal education enough? The question arises in part because of new events such as a sudden rise in the percentage of jobs which require extensive education. . . . I believe that twelve years are no longer enough to satisfy American ideals or to conform to society's needs for human development. This nation would take better account of its ideals and potentials if it offered universal education opportunity from the age of four. . . .[6]

In a similar vein, John W. Gardner, then secretary of the Department of Health, Education and Welfare (HEW), addressed the assembly of educators:

> . . . Our future is full of problems that are being created by our advancing technology . . . if we create new problems while we're solving the old, then this has implications for the kind of society we need and the kind of education we need. . . . It should be a self-renewing society, ready to improvise solutions to problems it won't recognize until tomorrow. And we want an educational system that can create that kind of society.[7]

The same social scientists who, as we shall see, expressed concern about the problem of narrowing the educational opportunity gap between economically disadvantaged and advantaged children were also quick to point out the necessity for an increase in mental ability in the whole society. Hunt, for example, stated:

> Ours is a technological culture of increasing complexity. Its development continually demands an ever larger proportion of the population with intellectual capacity at the higher levels. It calls also for intellectual giants to solve the problems that become increasingly complex. The fact that it is reasonable to hope to find ways of raising the level of intellectual capacity in a majority of the population makes it a challenge to do the necessary research.[8]

---

[6] W. G. Carr, "Unity, Growth and Responsibility," in *Addresses and Proceedings* (National Educational Association of the United States, 1966), p. 19.

[7] John W. Gardner, "Education for the Great Society," in *Addresses and Proceedings* (National Educational Association of the United States, 1966), p. 34.

[8] J. McV. Hunt, *Intelligence and Experience* (New York: Ronald Press, 1961), p. 363.

Bloom expressed a similar interest:

A society which places great emphasis on verbal learning and rational problem solving and which greatly needs highly skilled and well-trained individuals to carry on political-social-economic functions in an increasingly complex world cannot ignore the enormous consequences of deprivation as it affects the development of general intelligence.[9]

Preschool Education as a Solution to Both National Problems. Preschool education was suggested as a single solution to the dual problems of narrowing the achievement gap and developing the full potential of all children in the United States. The assumptions behind this choice of strategy were outlined in two historically important books, *Intelligence and Experience* by J. McV. Hunt and *Stability and Change in Human Characteristics* by Benjamin Bloom. Each argued that intelligence develops and changes *at its fastest rate* during the first few years of the child's life. Also, it is during this early period that environment has the strongest impact on development. It is therefore imperative that any attempt to increase a child's mental ability should occur when he or she is very young—preferably during the first five years of life. Bloom explained:

Variations in the environment have [the] greatest quantitative effect on a characteristic at its most rapid period of change and [the] least effect on the characteristic during the least rapid period of change.[10]

Bloom went on to say that intelligence seems to be one of the human characteristics that appears to be modifiable through the environment:

There is little doubt that intelligence development is in part a function of the environment in which the individual lives. The evidence from studies of identical twins reared separately and reared together, as well as from longitudinal studies in which the characteristics of the environment are studied in relation to changes in intelligence test scores indicate that the level of measured general intelligence is partially determined by the nature of the environment. The evidence so far available suggests that extreme environments may be described as *abundant* or *deprived* for the development of intelligence in terms of the opportunities for learning verbal and language behavior, opportunities for direct as well as vicarious experience with a complex world, encouragement of problem solving and independent thinking and the type of expectations and motivations for intellectual growth. The effects of the environments, especially of the extreme environments, appear to be greatest in the early (and

---

[9] Benjamin Bloom, *Stability and Change in Human Characteristics* (New York: John Wiley & Sons, 1964), p. 89.

[10] Ibid., p. vii.

more rapid) periods of intelligence development and least in the later (and less rapid) periods of development.[11]

Both authors assumed that deprivation during the preschool years can cause developmental deficiencies which cannot be made up at a later stage. But it is also during these early years that an optimal environment can most stimulate a child's development. Hunt was optimistic about the possibilities of early intervention:

> . . . [I]t is no longer unreasonable to consider that it might be feasible to discover ways to govern the encounters that children have with their environment, especially during the early years of their development, to achieve a substantially faster rate of intellectual development and a substantially higher adult level of intellectual capacity.[12]

Although Hunt and Bloom saw great possibilities for preschool intervention, both clearly pointed out that it is extremely difficult to say precisely what constitutes abundant and deprived environments for the development of intelligence. Furthermore, these conditions may vary for different individuals. Innovators in preschool education, therefore, have worked on the assumption that early stimulation is imperative but that optimal environments for child development have not yet been established. However, they believe the problem is technical, and consequently they continue to experiment with new methods and techniques, all of which are based on increasing environmental stimulation to the child. It is within this climate of innovation that many preschool programs, including "Sesame Street," were created.

The Objectives of "Sesame Street"

After mentioning the national problems of narrowing the achievement gap and increasing the intellectual skills of all children, Cooney went on in her 1968 proposal to outline the objectives of "Sesame Street." She wrote: "The general aim . . . is to promote the intellectual and cultural growth of preschoolers, particularly disadvantaged preschoolers" (p. 10).

Let us examine this statement and a few remarks following it more closely. In keeping with the need for developing citizens who can deal with the complex new world, Joan Cooney specified that the program was to be aimed at *all* kinds of preschoolers—rich and poor, black and white, urban and rural, bright and less bright. She also specified that the program would not only teach a certain amount of specific information (letters, numbers, language tools, etc.) but that it would also, citing Jerome Kagan, "teach

---

[11] Ibid., p. 80.
[12] J. McV. Hunt, p. 363.

the children *how* to think, not *what* to think" (p. 12). Thus, in Cooney's opinion, our complex world requires persons who are knowledgeable "culturally" and "intellectually" and who know how to think for themselves. There is, in these statements, ample evidence of ambitious learning goals for an undifferentiated viewing audience, and it is clear that these goals refer to the national problem of increasing all children's intellectual capacities.

Cooney's statement of "Sesame Street's" objectives also includes a reference to the series causing growth "particularly (for) disadvantaged preschoolers." The word "particularly" is of special importance, for it makes clear that the intellectual and cultural growth of economically disadvantaged children is a major objective. But the word "particularly" is ambiguous. It can also be construed as implying that the economically disadvantaged should be "particularly stimulated" and should show "particular growth" relative to other children. This would entail not merely that these children learn from the show but also that, as a group, they learn more than others. What is important here is to note that the achievement gap between the economically advantaged and disadvantaged would not be narrowed if each group learned from the show and the advantaged learned more than, or as much as, the disadvantaged. The first of these outcomes would widen the gap and the second would not affect it. The gap would only be narrowed if the economically disadvantaged learned more as a group than the advantaged. Only this outcome would be relevant to solving the first national problem in education that Cooney mentioned in her grant proposal.

There is evidence that "Sesame Street" received its funds because of its focus on economically disadvantaged children. For instance, the Office of Economic Opportunity and the Office of Child Development were noted for their emphasis on programs with this focus during the 1960s when "Sesame Street" was first funded, and there is also evidence that the Office of Education funds were initially allotted because of the emphasis. Lawrence P. Grayson, acting director of the Office of Technology Development in the federal Office of Education, wrote:

> Preschool education for culturally disadvantaged children . . . has been deemed important. With the decision made to provide the needed education, alternatives could be explored. One resultant approach to reaching the children was the development of the television series Sesame Street.[13]

What is not clear, of course, is whether the sponsors' focus on economically disadvantaged preschoolers was to see if "Sesame Street" taught these

---

[13] Lawrence P. Grayson, "Costs, Benefits, Effectiveness: Challenge to Educational Technology" 175 *Science* (1972): 1216–1222.

children anything at all or to see if it narrowed the academic achievement gap between them and their more affluent counterparts. This is a fundamental ambiguity about the higher order objectives of the series, and we return to it later.

The ETS Reports and their Conclusions about "Sesame Street"

Each of the ETS evaluations of "Sesame Street" contained conclusions that were pertinent both to stimulating the growth of all preschoolers and to stimulating the particular growth of economically disadvantaged children. Our aim at this point is not to evaluate whether the data supported the conclusions. Rather, we want to document what is currently believed with regard to the effectiveness of "Sesame Street," and we want to see how these claims are related to the two national problems to which Joan Cooney referred.

The summary of the first-year report by ETS suggested that heavy viewers of "Sesame Street" learned more from the program than light viewers. It also suggested that this relationship held for boys and girls; for children aged three, four, and five; for economically advantaged and disadvantaged children; for children who viewed at home or in school; for children who were English- or Spanish-speaking; and for children who lived in urban and rural settings. The results of further analyses of the first-year data were reported in the second-year summary where it was suggested that heavy viewers had learned more than light viewers among both black and white children. Thus, a positive relationship between viewing and learning was reported for all of the groups examined.

It was further reported that the heavier viewers in all groups gained approximately equal amounts, indicating that "Sesame Street" was not only effective with all groups but that it was also equally effective with all groups. The only exception to this last conclusion was that three-year-old viewers seemed to gain more than four- and five-year-olds.

The summary of the second-year evaluation also mentioned that heavy viewers gained more than light viewers in all the groups examined (except for a small sample of Spanish-speaking children), and that all heavy viewers gained in approximately equal amounts. (However, there were no children in the second-year study who were advantaged or attending school or living in a rural setting.)

The summary to the first-year report also contained statements that are relevant to narrowing the academic performance gap. Ball and Bogatz wrote:

> Although the disadvantaged children started out with considerably lower achievement scores on the skills being taught, those who watched a great deal

surpassed the middle-class children who only watched a little. It thus appears that such television programs can reduce the distinct educational gap that usually separates advantaged and disadvantaged children by the time they enter first grade.[14]

The summary of the second-year report contained a statement with a similar implication. However, the evidence in the second year was not based on the heavy viewers among the economically disadvantaged overtaking the light viewers among the advantaged. Instead, it was based on the disadvantaged learning more than the advantaged at all levels of viewing.

The relationship between socioeconomic status and (learning) gains is partly indicated by the fact that the correlation between SES and total gain score was low and negative but significant (—.24). Note that the children studied were relatively homogeneous with respect to SES, thereby lowering the possibility of finding a significant relationship. Thus, the fact that there was a negative relationship between SES and gain scores suggests that the show may be having its greatest impact among those with the lowest socioeconomic status.[15]

The ETS findings from the first-year evaluation were reported in the national press in uniformly glowing terms. For example, *Time* magazine in its November 16, 1970, issue reported the results under the heading of "Sesame Street Report Card" and stated that "Sesame Street has earned straight A's." In *Newsweek*'s issue of the same date, it was reported that all groups benefited from the show and that ghetto children who watched five days a week learned more than middle-class children who saw the show less frequently. A *Time* article of November 23, 1970, commented that the ETS report demonstrated that " 'Sesame Street' has been sharpening the cognitive skills of poor kids by as much as 62%," and it goes on to add, "Theoretically, their ideal viewer is poor and culturally deprived. Actually, the show catches the preschooler almost before his society does. Thus 'Sesame Street' is as popular with the well-to-do as it is with the slum dweller." The only remotely negative comment that we found in the most popular press was the statement in *Newsweek* of November 16 that "The ETS study . . . prepared in cooperation with 'Sesame's' producers, was designed to measure the program's self-selected goals, thus avoiding the issue of whether those goals were exactly on target."

These brief statements from the ETS reports and the press suggest that

[14] Samuel Ball and Gerry Ann Bogatz, *The First Year of Sesame Street: An Evaluation* (Princeton, N.J.: Educational Testing Service, Oct. 1970).

[15] Gerry Ann Bogatz and Samuel Ball, *The Second Year of Sesame Street: A Continuing Evaluation,* vols. 1 and 2 (Princeton, N.J.: Educational Testing Service, Nov. 1971).

it may be widely believed that "Sesame Street" is succeeding in stimulating the cognitive growth of all children, including the economically disadvantaged, and that it is also narrowing the academic achievement gap. The important point to be noted at this juncture is that claims were made to the effect that "Sesame Street" taught all the groups it reached and that it was narrowing the gap.

FROM NATIONAL PROBLEMS, "SESAME STREET'S" OBJECTIVES, AND CLAIMS MADE FOR THE SERIES TO OUR EVALUATION OBJECTIVES

There is an obvious case to be made for evaluating programs in terms of their stated intermediate objectives[16] if realizing these objectives would ameliorate problems that are considered urgent in the society. The two national problems that Joan Cooney outlined are probably urgent ones, and many other persons in the 1960s agreed.

A good case can also be made that evaluations should be concerned with the significant claims that are made for a program by a wide range of persons, including persons other than the administrators of a program. This perspective emphasizes that evaluations should check what is claimed for a program against what is attained by it, and from this perspective the major importance of stated objectives is that they provide a clue to some major claims. But stated objectives typically do not provide the universe of significant claims. Nor, indeed, do they provide the universe of recognized social problems to which a program is relevant. The alert evaluator has to understand and explicate (a) the stated objectives of a program, (b) the claims made on its behalf by a wide range of other persons; and (c) the problems of society to which a program may be relevant.

In considering "Sesame Street" from the standpoints of stated objectives, significant claims, and recognized social problems, we had no difficulty in establishing that the series had to be tested for its success in reaching and teaching a wide range of children so that their "intellectual and cultural" growth would be enhanced. There was no difficulty in this because this objective was unambiguously expressed by Cooney; because relevant

---

[16] E. A. Suchman, *Evaluative Research* (New York: Russell Sage Foundation, 1967). Suchman distinguishes between ultimate, intermediate, and immediate objectives. In "Sesame Street's" case, one ultimate objective would be to help children handle the complex world better as they pass through life; an intermediate objective would be to foster intellectual and cultural growth in many preschoolers; and the immediate objectives would be to teach preschoolers specific skills (e.g., recognition of the letter "J"). We have been concerned in this chapter with ultimate and intermediate objectives, especially the latter.

results were claimed as outcomes of the series in the press and in the ETS evaluations; and because the need to increase the intellectual skills of children is generally recognized as an important national problem.

We had no difficulty in establishing that "Sesame Street" should also be evaluated in terms of its ability to reach and teach economically disadvantaged children so that their "intellectual and cultural" growth would be enhanced. Once again, Joan Cooney stressed such an aim in her grant proposals; ETS and the press claimed that the series reached and taught these children; and how to stimulate the potential of these children is widely acknowledged as a national problem.

We had more difficulty in establishing whether to evaluate "Sesame Street" for its success in narrowing the academic achievement gap. The difficulty arose because Cooney never explicitly referred to this as an objective of the program. Rather, she presented "Sesame Street" in the context of the national problem of narrowing the gap and then went on to mention only that the "general aim . . . is to promote the intellectual and cultural growth of preschoolers, particularly disadvantaged preschoolers." She never defined the phrase, "particularly disadvantaged preschoolers." However, the ETS research reports did make the claim that "Sesame Street" was narrowing the gap; and the gap is widely acknowledged to be an important national problem in the area of preschool education. We, therefore, attempt to evaluate what effects, if any, the show had on the achievement gap.

Some Relationships between Stimulating the Growth of All Children and Narrowing the Gap

There are many gaps between the economically advantaged and disadvantaged (nutritional, health, knowledge, availability of models of social success, etc.), and there are many ways of conceptualizing advantaged and disadvantaged (along ethnic, racial, income, education, urban-suburban-rural lines, etc.). We discuss these distinctions in Chapter 8.

Right now, we want to point out that most federally funded preschool programs in the 1960s were aimed at narrowing some of the gaps that existed between economically advantaged and disadvantaged groups. Some programs were made available only to economically disadvantaged children on the grounds that, if successful, they would raise the mean performance level of these children without affecting the performance of advantaged children. Other programs were made available to a wider range of children but were tailored to remedy the particular performance deficits that were attributed to the economically disadvantaged. In this way, it was hoped to raise the mean level of the disadvantaged by a greater amount than that of the advantaged. If we translate this into the context of "Sesame Street," it implies that one way to narrow the performance gap would be to have economically disadvantaged children view "Sesame Street" as much as other children but to have them gain more from viewing. Another way would be to have proportionately more of the economically disadvantaged view the series. A third way would be to have economically disadvantaged children both view more and learn more from equivalent amounts of viewing. In each case, the target group of economically disadvantaged children would have to be treated specially.

There are different requirements for stimulating the growth of all preschoolers, including the disadvantaged. For this to happen, all children would have to be given the opportunity to view the series and would have to be so entertained by it that they would actually use the opportunity. There need not therefore be a special target audience. Moreover, for all groups of preschoolers to learn from the series, its content would have to have a general appeal and capacity to teach all the groups. There would be no question of tailoring the series to the learning needs of one particular group.

There is an inevitable negative relationship between the most potent means for stimulating the growth of all children and narrowing the academic achievement gap. Stimulating the growth of all preschoolers would be best realized by a *universalist strategy* based on making "Sesame Street" universally available, making it equally used by all groups of children, and making it equally beneficial to all the groups. Stimulating the growth of economically disadvantaged children in particular would be best realized by a *selective strategy* based on making "Sesame Street" selectively available to the disadvantaged, making it more attractive to these children so that they would want to view it more than others, and making it relevant to the learning needs that are unique to this one group of children.

Fortunately, it is possible to achieve both objectives simultaneously. Each would be achieved if:

—*the economically advantaged and disadvantaged viewed "Sesame Street" in equal amounts;*
—*each group learned from viewing;*
—*the disadvantaged learned more than the advantaged.*

Both objectives would also be reached:

—*if the economically disadvantaged viewed "Sesame Street" more heavily than the advantaged;*
—*and if, as a consequence of viewing, the two groups learned the same amount or the disadvantaged learned more than the advantaged.*

This analysis indicates the major outline of what we had to look for in answering the questions we posed about whether all groups of children, including the economically disadvantaged, gained from the show and about whether the achievement gap was narrowed, widened, or not affected thereby. Put quite simply, our major task was to ascertain whether the data fitted either of the patterns that were detailed in the immediately preceding paragraphs.

A second noteworthy relationship between the questions we have asked is that "stimulating the intellectual and cultural growth of preschoolers" subsumes stimulating the particular growth of economically disadvantaged preschoolers. Hence, there is no logical need to mention "Sesame Street's" objective of reaching and teaching disadvantaged children independently of the objective of reaching and teaching all children. If we appear to stress the questions of teaching all groups of children and narrowing the gap over the question of teaching the economically disadvantaged irrespective of whatever the advantaged learn, it should not be taken to reflect our emphasis of the low importance of the last question. Rather, the low salience of the question in some of the following chapters should be construed in the light of the fact that teaching all kinds of preschoolers includes teaching economically disadvantaged preschoolers.

"SESAME STREET" AS THE FORERUNNER OF OTHER EDUCATIONAL TV PROGRAMS

We decided to ask a fourth question in our evaluation. An unstated objective of "Sesame Street" was to establish the effectiveness of television as a means of public instruction over the regular airwaves. For some persons, this objective was salient from the very inception of the program. For others, "Sesame Street" started out as a modest experiment and went on to achieve great success in terms of audience appeal and a favorable press. It was then that, for these other persons inside and outside of CTW, "Sesame Street" became an example of television's realized potential in education. It was then that the objective crystallized of considering "Sesame Street," not as a program aimed at two national problems, but as a symbol of an effective mass instructional technology to solve part of the problem of improving the quality of education.

Once "Sesame Street" was conceptualized as a successful demonstration of television's instructional potential, it was no surprise that other programs were developed that resembled it in many ways. CTW itself produced "The Electric Company," a show aimed at seven-year-old children with reading problems, and "Feeling Good," a show aimed at the health needs of adults. And in testimony before a subcommittee of the Committee on Appropriations of the House of Representatives in 1970, Dr. Sidney Marland, then commissioner of education, stated:

I would like to have a Sesame-type creativity going on on drug abuse, or a Sesame-type creativity going on in vocational education for maybe as many as twenty or thirty of the crafts and technologies to draw young people in at fourteen, sixteen, and eighteen, the way they draw in the three-, four-, and five-year-olds into "Sesame Street." We need persons with the same kind of exquisite talent and creative leadership as Joan Ganz Cooney who is the creative force behind "Sesame Street." We need more Joan Ganz Cooneys.

Moreover, John Macy, then president of the Corporation for Public Broadcasting, said in testimony before a subcommittee of the Senate Committee on Appropriations:

The Corporation has received a grant of $600,000 from the Office of Education for the purpose of undertaking a major activity dealing with the environment and the quality of life in the environment. We have organized the Public Broadcasting Environment Center for the purpose of undertaking the initial development work and for the eventual management of the program production process. In so doing, we borrowed liberally from the precedent provided by the Children's Television Workshop. Research and evaluation of the activity will be an important concern of PBEC just as it is to CTW.

We should also take note of the following press release, dated April 3, 1972, from the Office of the Secretary of Health, Education, and Welfare:

The first of a series of fifty 3½ minute films, made for the Office of Child Development, Department of Health, Education, and Welfare, will be shown on CBS' "Captain Kangaroo" show, Monday, April 3.

Dr. Edward Zigler, (former) Director of OCD, will appear on this first broadcast with host Bob Keeshan.

The films, which are part animation, part live action, deal with subjects ranging from good nutrition and care of the body, to learning to cope with emotions such as fear, anger, loneliness, disappointment, to understanding the senses, and the rights of each individual child and of other people.

Made by Sutherland Learning Associates, of Los Angeles, California, under a $500,000 contract from OCD, the films are aimed at the more than three million three- to six-year-olds who watch the "Captain Kangaroo" show. The fifty films will be rebroadcast in the fall season.

This undertaking represents the first time that a Federal agency has funded a project to be broadcast over a commercial network.

Plans and accomplishments like these indicate how important it is to arrive both at a realistic estimate of "Sesame Street's" impact and at an estimate that is nonetheless based on high standards. More is at stake than "Sesame Street" alone. The series' importance from a historical perspective *may* well be as a catalyst for other television programs aimed at large national audiences or for programs that aim to teach by capturing a child's attention with a medium he uses and then repeating a focussed message that is some part of a general learning curriculum. "Sesame Street" probably gains additional importance in this regard from analyses which claim to indicate how ineffective the formal educational system is, for in this context television may appear to be a "better" or "alternative" or "adjunct" teaching resource in which large financial investment would be worthwhile.[17]

We are not able to use empirical means to establish the desirability of further televised programs based on the kind of model that underlies "Sesame Street." This is because no such programs had been evaluated at the time of this writing (1973) and because it is logically impossible to extrapolate from one program like "Sesame Street" to future programs which are like it in many ways but which are different from it in others. Instead, we will restrict ourselves to a later conceptual analysis of the usefulness of the "Sesame Street" example as a model for generating other television programs that are aimed at solving significant national problems in education and other areas.

---

[17] Charles E. Silberman, *Crisis in the Classroom* (New York: Random House, 1970); see also Christopher Jencks et al., *Inequality* (New York: Basic Books, Inc., 1972).

Chapter 3
Formative and Summative Evaluation Research in the Context of "Sesame Street"

AN INTRODUCTION TO FORMATIVE AND SUMMATIVE RESEARCH

The Children's Television Workshop makes use of two kinds of research: formative and summative. Bloom, Hastings, and Madaus have characterized the difference between these kinds of research in terms of their *purpose, timing,* and level of *generalizability.*

Formative research is used in education to determine whether a particular skill has been acquired and, if it has not, to examine the sub-processes necessary for learning the skill. Once these sub-processes are known, it is possible to modify teaching so that the skills can be learned and a curriculum developed. Summative research, on the other hand, "is directed towards a much more general assessment of the degree to which the larger outcomes have been attained over the entire course or some substantial part of it."[1] The major question for summative research is what the children have gained and lost from a program of instruction.

Formative research is particularly beneficial when the theory behind a reform is nonexistent or vague. It is one thing to argue that preschool environmental stimulation will enhance cognitive development and quite an-

---

[1] B. J. Bloom, J. H. Hastings, and G. F. Madaus, *Handbook on Formative and Summative Evaluation of Student Learning* (New York: McGraw-Hill, 1971), p. 61.

other thing to specify the precise kinds of stimulation that will enhance specific kinds of cognitive development in a specific target audience of four-year-old, inner-city children. It is a sad fact that most social science theories are so deficient as to be of little help to social reform agents. The theories are simply too global and too lacking in rigorous empirical corroboration. Even if our theories were better, their successful application to specific problems would not be guaranteed. Just as an engineer cannot take some well-tested theory in physics and apply it to bridge-building, so an educational innovator cannot take some psychological theory of development and apply it in schools. There are just too many gaps between the abstract elegance of our few well-tested formal theories and the concrete problem-ridden reality of implementing changes in complex settings.

The planners of "Sesame Street" had the great foresight to allow themselves eighteen months of formative research before they went on the air. This time was invaluable and was used to make filmed segments and to test them on economically disadvantaged children to ascertain whether the films held the children's attention and caused short-term learning.[2] Segments that succeeded in these tasks were retained while others were modified or rejected. This procedure provided some minimal assurance that the program might have some impact and might avoid the classic problem that Weiss[3] and Rossi[4] have detailed for so many other reforms—that despite great hopes and conviction on the part of planners, the programs are puny when compared to the magnitude of the longstanding problems to which they are addressed.

Since formative research is aimed at feedback and program modification rather than at comprehensive evaluation, it is not surprising that formative and summative evaluations are conducted at different times. Formative research is typically carried out before instruction begins or at frequent intervals during a course of instruction. In this way, the flow of information for detecting and correcting mistakes can start before a program is implemented or shortly after its implementation. Summative research, on the other hand, usually takes place after a course of instruction has ended, although it may also take place once or twice during the course.

---

[2] Much of the following discussion is taken from the second volume of CTW's report to its sponsors by B. F. Reeves, *The First Year of Sesame Street: The Formative Research* (Children's Television Workshop, Dec. 1970). Unless otherwise stated, quotations are from this source.

[3] C. H. Weiss, "The Politicization of Evaluative Research," *Journal of Social Issues* 26 (1970): 57–68.

[4] P. H. Rossi, "Practice, Method and Theory in Evaluating Social Action Programs," in James L. Sundquist, ed., *On Fighting Poverty: Perspectives from Experience* (New York: Basic Books, Inc., 1969).

Finally, formative research is typically concerned with a lower level of generalizability than is summative research. For example, if the aim of a program is knowledge of the alphabet, formative research might be directed toward discovering which letters or series of letters children have difficulty in learning. Summative research would only be concerned with knowledge of the alphabet and with any unintended positive or negative side effects. Furthermore, formative research is typically conducted on small and non-random samples of the subject population, rather than on a sample believed to be representative of the target population. Generalizability is not as important in formative research as is speed of feedback—although to choose research subjects who are markedly different from target subjects would increase the risk of obtaining formative data that are of little value. In summative research, generalizability to a particular target population is usually more important.

FORMATIVE RESEARCH BY THE CTW STAFF

Almost from its inception in 1968, CTW employed a research division. One of its most vital first tasks was the operational specification of the goals of "Sesame Street." These were worked out at five seminars held in the summer of 1968 and attended by members of the CTW staff and Research Advisory Board as well as by well-known consultants in the fields of psychology, education, sociology, filmmaking, and television production.

The goals were divided into four major categories:

1. *Symbolic Representation* dealt with knowledge of letters, numbers, and geometric forms.

2. *Cognitive Processes* was concerned with perceptual discrimination, relational concepts, classification, ordering, and reasoning.

3. *The Child and the Physical World around Him* dealt with knowledge of the natural and man-made environments.

4. *The Social Environment* was related to social interaction.

These categories were then subdivided, sometimes more than once, so that highly specific objectives finally emerged. For example, a Letters Test goal read: "Given a verbal label for certain letters the child can pick the appropriate letter from a set of letters," and one of the goals for the Physical World section required that "The child should realize that the earth is made of land and water, and that the earth's surface differs in various places."

These last goals were highly specific and, if well chosen, should have had a high correspondence with "Sesame Street's" more general aim of stimulating "the intellectual and cultural growth of preschoolers, particularly disadvantaged preschoolers." We shall later examine the degree of correspondence between the general aims of the program and its specific goals. For the time being, however, it should be noted that the specificity of the goals helped the summative research team from ETS develop its test items and helped production teams plan the content of the particular films they were to make. To this latter end, the formative research staff developed *The Writer's Workbook,* a book in which each objective was listed and various technical strategies for achieving the objective were highlighted. The book was modified and supplemented as experience and data were accumulated. The fact that the production and evaluation teams were working from the same list of specific goals increased the likelihood that the test items in the summative evaluation would reflect in direct fashion what was actually produced on the show.

Data were initially collected to describe the level of competence of the proposed audience of disadvantaged children. This resulted in the identification of general problem areas and of areas in which the economically disadvantaged children lacked cognitive skills. For example, the proportion of children (from admittedly biased samples) who knew each letter of the alphabet was computed, as were the series of letters with which children had least or most difficulty. Such information enabled the producers to concentrate on some things more than others.

An important phase of the research involved measuring the audience appeal of possible programs before they went on the air, since appeal was a vital ingredient, if "Sesame Street" was to reach and keep its audience. Most of the CTW in-house research on audience appeal used the distractor method, whereby a child or group of children viewed a program while slides were projected onto the wall at an angle to the child. Observers rated the proportion of each 7.5 second schedule that the child viewed the program rather than the projected slide. Producers could then relate the content of the program at any one time to the degree of attention that it claimed, and from this generalizations were developed about program features that do and do not hold the attention of economically disadvantaged children. The formative research team played a crucial role here in reducing (but not eliminating) the risk that "Sesame Street" would not hold its target audience once it reached them.

To justify its funding, "Sesame Street" had to gain and hold attention, and it had to be effective in its teaching. Efforts were made during the prebroadcast formative research phase to test the learning from particular films and to test how films could be improved as teaching instruments. Simple before-and-after designs and crude measures were used for this part of the formative research. Some of the problems investigated were: the effect of being exposed to a letter once, four, or even ten times; the way learning letters is affected by massed and distributed practice; and the way interference operates in learning sequences of letters. Readers acquainted with the literature on human learning will recognize classical research problems in such formative experiments. The policy researcher will hopefully recognize a strategy of low-cost pilot-testing that reduces the chances of implementing social reforms that have little impact.

Collaboration of the Formative and Summative Research Teams

The members of the CTW formative research team were in contact with the ETS summative research team almost from the first days of CTW. Samuel Ball was one of the consultants at the original five CTW goal-planning seminars and was later given an office in the Workshop's New York headquarters. Thus, the person who was eventually to be responsible for the summative evaluations of "Sesame Street" (the same evaluations we reanalyzed) was invoked in establishing the series' behavioral objectives and came to know the major planners of "Sesame Street."

Later, when Ball knew he was to be responsible for the evaluation, but before the series went on the air, he and the CTW formative research staff collaborated in a joint project to evaluate five hour-long programs. From a formative research perspective, the purpose of the project was to evaluate a complete program for the first time, to observe children in their own home settings, and to evaluate some of the recommendations that had been made earlier to producers. CTW's report of its formative research findings stated that the most important results of the project were determinations that simple pretest–posttest gain scores "were related to 1) the amount of emphasis on the specific goal in the programming, 2) the manner in which the goal-related subject matter was presented, and 3) the extent to which the children exhibited relevant overt responses to the given program segment."

The purpose of the project from a summative perspective was to pilot-test instruments to determine length and ease of administration, how well children performed, and how ambiguous or reliable obtained responses were. The information gathered from the pilot-tests was then used to refine the measures that were developed for the summative evaluation.

SUMMATIVE RESEARCH

The Criteria Used in Summative Research

The value and comprehensiveness of summative research depends on the criteria used for evaluation. This section is an attempt to review the ETS evaluation of "Sesame Street" in the light of a rigorous set of six criteria, five of which are taken from Suchman's book entitled *Evaluative Research*.[5]

---

[5] E. A. Suchman, *Evaluative Research* (New York: Russell Sage Foundation, 1967).

Suchman's criteria for a comprehensive evaluation are:

1. A demonstration that the promised effort has been expended and the treatment has been received by those who were meant to get it.
2. A demonstration of performance. This means that statistically significant and desired effects have been obtained and can be unambiguously attributed to the treatment.
3. A demonstration of the adequacy of performance. This means that any effects that are caused by the treatment are of social significance.
4. A demonstration of the efficiency of performance. This means that the benefits of the program outweigh its costs.
5. A demonstration of the process that caused the effects.

Scriven[6] has added a sixth criterion to the list:

6. An examination of the value of the program and of the social values that it promotes or puts in jeopardy.

Each of these criteria can be related to the two major questions we were asking about "Sesame Street." If the *promised effort* is expended, we should expect to see this reflected in data on the size and social composition of the show's audience. "Sesame Street" could only plausibly stimulate the growth of all categories of preschool children if a "high" proportion of the preschool population watched the series. For purposes of narrowing the gap, the right audience would be reached if it were also demonstrated that the special target group of four- and five-year-old economically disadvantaged children viewed more, or at the very least, if it could be demonstrated that they did not view less than their economically advantaged counterparts.

The specification of a *program's performance* or effectiveness, the second criterion, is the major thrust of most summative research. With respect to stimulating the growth of all children, the objective would be achieved if the program caused measurable gains in development on the part of children from all social groups. The achievement gap might be narrowed, however, if the gains by economically disadvantaged children were greater than those for advantaged children.

It is no problem to test the *adequacy of a program* if a specific criterion for success is given. Thus, in a performance-contracting situation it might be specified that a class of children should gain more than one year's achievement growth in one academic year. It can then be measured whether they do or do not meet this criterion.

Unfortunately, the criteria for most programs are rarely so specific, and the problem is to decide what makes a statistically significant difference socially significant. In the case of "Sesame Street," we need to ask how much

---

[6] M. Scriven, *Value Claims in the Social Sciences,* Publication No. 123 (Lafayette, Ind.: Social Sciences Education Consortium, 1966).

of which kind of knowledge a child needs for effective functioning in our complex society. Frankly, we do not know and cannot find out. However, it is clear from the statement of "Sesame Street's" general objective that Joan Cooney thought that "intellectual and cultural growth" is a central part of such a knowledge store and that children will be able to handle our complex world more easily if they know "how to think." We also need to ask how much of a decrease in the performance gap between economically advantaged and disadvantaged children is a socially significant decrease. Again, we do not know. All we do know is that statistical significance is not enough to justify claiming that a social innovation is adequate. There are purely statistical conventions for establishing social significance and we shall deal with these in what follows. But these conventions are arbitrary and not accepted by all. Despite these problems, we should not be deterred from asking how adequate any social reform is. But we should also be mindful of the problem of determining adequacy when no specific performance criterion is set.

The *efficiency* of a program refers to the ratio of its benefits to its costs. It is difficult to conceptualize and measure each of these, partly because each is so multidimensional. At the simplest level, we can compute the dollar cost per child of viewing "Sesame Street." We cannot, however, assess the cost of not watching some other program, not interacting with other persons, not reading, eye strain, or of many other things. All we can say is that for meeting both of its goals "Sesame Street" should be inexpensive.

It is especially useful if we can specify that one program has a more favorable ratio of benefits to costs than some other program with the same objectives. Unfortunately, rigorous determination of such relative efficiency is even more difficult than the determination of absolute efficiency. There are two major reasons for this. First, most programs in a given problem area do not have totally overlapping goals and the successfully attained effects might be different for each program. To take a hypothetical example, program X might modify the learning of simple rote items, while program Y might fail in this (or not be relevant to it) but might affect the child's motivation to learn, while program Z might not affect either of these two goals (or may be irrelevant to them) but might improve the child's nutritional health. This makes it extremely difficult to identify the programs that should be compared with each other to establish relative efficiency. A second reason is that programs differ in the adequacy with which they are evaluated. If two programs had equal effects, for example, and one was better evaluated than the other, then it is likely that the poorly tested program may appear to have fewer benefits than the better tested program. But this would be a result of the evaluation and not of the program. What we need are designs where *a priori* designated alternative programs are pitted against each other and are evaluated by a set of criteria that are common to each program. This does not preclude the use of criteria that are unique to one program. It merely means that some common measures should be used as well as some unique ones.

It is important to specify the *social and psychological processes* that lead to any innovation or reform being effective. This knowledge can often be used to refine a program by placing greater stress on those aspects that cause change and a diminished stress on those that do not. For example, if "Sesame Street" were effective because children paid particular attention to puppets and little attention to humans, then the programming might be modified accordingly.

In the context of narrowing the academic achievement gap, there might be some processes correlated with social class that increase the effectiveness of "Sesame Street." For example, viewing or discussing the program with adults might facilitate learning and this social process might be more frequent in one social class than another. In the context of stimulating the growth of all children, television at an early age might facilitate the passive acquisition of knowledge and might make the child less able to ask questions and discover answers for himself. Such an active questioning frame of mind might be particularly useful as our world becomes increasingly more complex.

The final criterion for a good evaluation has been especially stressed by Scriven. He believes that an evaluation should also be concerned with *the value of the program's objectives and effects.* He is not content to see evaluation researchers as the technicians who manipulate data to determine the effects of a program. He enlarges the evaluator's role so that it encompasses value judgments about the relevance to national needs of the program's objectives and effects. Glass[7] echoed this when he wrote: "The current meaning of the term 'evaluation' in several recent writings and in federal legislation is that it is the gathering of empirical evidence for decision making and the justification of the decision-making policies and the values upon which they are based." In the case of "Sesame Street," an evaluation should consider the importance of narrowing the performance gap between economically advantaged and disadvantaged children, the importance of reaching and stimulating the growth of all children, and the relative priority of each of these objectives if realizing one objective conflicts with realizing the other. Also, we have to inquire whether there are any other values of greater importance that could be realized by "Sesame Street."

---

[7] G. V. Glass, "Comments on Professor Bloom's Paper," in M. C. Wittrock and D. Wiley, eds., *The Evaluation of Instruction* (New York: Holt, Rinehart and Winston, 1970).

The six criteria for comprehensive evaluation are related in Table 3.1 to the outcomes that would be expected if "Sesame Street" were successful in solving the problems we have explicated. The table makes three things clear. First, the criteria for solving the problems differ with respect to performance and effectiveness. Second, the most stringent criteria for adequacy are either very vague or unrealistically high and, as will be apparent later, we shall have to modify them and substitute less strict criteria. Third, if "Sesame Street" is effective, it is particularly important to check whether home factors are necessary conditions for effectiveness. If they are, then

Table 3.1. Outcomes Indicating that "Sesame Street" is Solving the Problems of Relevance

	Relevant Problems	
Evaluation Task	Stimulating the intellectual and cultural growth of all kinds of preschoolers*	Narrowing the academic achievement gap
Performance	Number of children who view nationally should be high	Disadvantaged should view more than advantaged
Effectiveness	All children should learn something	Disadvantaged should learn more than advantaged
Adequacy	Enough is learned for children to function in a technological society	Academic achievement gap is narrowed or closed
Efficiency	Inexpensive	Inexpensive
Process	Process should facilitate learning to learn	Process should not be dependent upon cultural advantages
Value Relevance	Increasing the potential of all children is of greater social value than other goals that Sesame Street could attain or that could be attained for the same expenditure as on Sesame Street	Narrowing the achievement gap is of greater social value than other goals that Sesame Street could attain or that could be attained for the same expenditure as on Sesame Street

* This column includes stimulating economically disadvantaged children, for their growth was one of "Sesame Street's" unambiguous objectives. The criteria for meeting this objective can be ascertained by substituting "disadvantaged" for "all children" wherever the latter appears in the column.

"Sesame Street's" effectiveness may be limited to some kinds of homes, e.g., those where there is rehearsing of the program content with one's parents or where there is viewing with minimal distraction in the room.

THE MEDICAL AND TAILORED MODELS OF EVALUATION RESEARCH

It is not sufficient to show that a reform or innovation has reached its target audience and that its major immediate goals have been realized. The purpose of education is to change people. But after any desired changes have taken place, it is important "to try and define what kinds of unanticipated outcomes have been achieved."[8] Unanticipated outcomes can typically be expected. At the most simple level, watching television takes time away from other activities, which was not a goal of "Sesame Street" but which is a result. Or, more importantly, "Sesame Street" might have made viewers more "passive," or the program might have been so exciting that school seemed dull by comparison. Or, parents might have become more or less interested in the academic achievement of their offspring. Medical research has frequently shown the importance of assessing the unanticipated effects of drugs as well as the anticipated ones. Evaluation researchers who look for unanticipated changes for some period after a treatment has been implemented are said to follow the *medical model* of evaluation research.[9]

Bloom, Hastings, and Madaus also pointed out the importance of assessing the long-term consequences of educational experiences, and this point was stressed by Postman.[10] Obviously, programs which have only a temporary effect are less beneficial than programs which have more permanent effects.

Postman went beyond the importance of assessing temporal effects and also stressed the importance of measuring the transfer of learning from one context to another, from one kind of test to another.

I want to underscore especially (the) call for the use of measures of retention and of transfer in the assessment of learning outcomes. Since the objective of instruction is preparation for future activities, long-term retention and the potentialities for transfer to the mastery of new tasks must be the primary criteria of the success of our methods of teaching.

---

[8] Bloom, Hastings, and Madaus, p. 19.

[9] For a fuller explanation of medical and tailored models of evaluation research, see T. D. Cook, " 'Sesame Street' and the Medical and Tailored Models of Summative Evaluation Research," in J. Albert and M. Kamrass, eds., *Social Experiments and Social Program Evaluation* (Cambridge, Mass.: Ballinger Publishing Co., 1974).

[10] Bloom, Hastings, and Madaus, p. 22; L. Postman, "Comments on Professor Gagne's Paper," in Wittrock and Wiley, eds., *The Evaluation of Instruction.*

To pursue the medical analogy further, long-term effects correspond to the time period during which a drug continues to affect bodily processes, while transfer corresponds to finding a drug that cures one intended ailment and helps control other illnesses as well.

There are many problems associated with following the medical model. For instance, a time delay of several years is typically required for estimating long-term impact. Yet policymakers frequently need immediate feedback. Also, it is very difficult to measure unanticipated side effects since these, by definition, cannot be anticipated in advance! Finally, measuring the transfer of learning requires resources that could alternatively have been used for measuring a program's direct impact on the variables it was designed to affect. This last problem is particularly acute when conducting research on preschool children, for their attention span is relatively limited and they cannot be given test after test in order to measure both intended and transfer effects.

Other problems are perhaps less obvious. The more one follows the medical model, the greater is the risk that a program will have few demonstrable effects. Delayed measures of impact do not measure a program's impact alone. They measure *both* the residue of a program's initial impact *and* the effects of any post-program experiences that have influenced outcome measures. Typically, graduates of a program return to the same environment that they left for the program, and this is the very environment that caused them to need the program in the first place. It is small wonder, then, that long-term impact is difficult to obtain. Consider the case of "Sesame Street." The program may have given children a better start in school. But if schools and homes could not capitalize upon any advantages that "Sesame Street" might have bestowed, then the long-term impact of the program would be slight. In what sense, though, would the failure to obtain long-term impact be due to "Sesame Street"? (Of course, if the schools and homes were successful in capitalizing upon any advantages conferred by the program, then "Sesame Street's" effectiveness would "snowball," and the series would be all the more socially important because it would be feeding its graduates into institutions which, without major and difficult reform, were capable of building upon what "Sesame Street" had taught.)

The risk of no-difference findings is also present when an evaluation places heavy emphasis on the transfer of learning. If we assume that a program is more likely to succeed with what it teaches directly than with what it teaches indirectly, then it will be more successful in achieving its intended goals than in achieving indirect goals through transfer. Thus there will be more no-difference "findings" in an evaluation which stresses transfer than in one which does not. The matter of transfer effects is particularly troublesome in education where the principal transfer measures are tests of academic achievement, aptitude, or intelligence. For good or ill, these measures form a kind of social currency in the sense that, together with grade point averages, they are used by parents, teachers, counselors, some employers, and college admissions officers for allowing children access to social opportunities. And they are also used to test whether children learn something of greater general utility than mastery of a specific curriculum. But it is not easy to modify scores on the commonly available standardized tests of aptitude or intelligence. Hence, if such transfer measures are used in an evaluation and are not affected by a program, then it naively appears as though the treatment has failed to influence a very important aspect of current social life.

Let us give an example of a high-risk evaluation based on the medical model. An attempt was made to evaluate the Headstart program,[11] and the major criterion variables in the study were academic achievement and self-concept. The achievement tests had not been developed either for testing what Headstart centers taught (which varied considerably) or for testing economically disadvantaged children in particular. Moreover, the global self-concept measures did not tap into the particular areas of self-concept that Headstart programs were most likely to have tried to modify, e.g., academic self-concept—"Myself as a student" or racial self-concept—"Myself as a black" or even sex-role self-concept—"Myself as a boy." Instead the test measured "myself," a much more global and fluid concept. Such tests, since they have no close correspondence to what was taught in Headstart centers, are primarily measures of the transfer of learning rather than of the acquisition of what was taught. Moreover, since the tests were administered from one to three years after the children had graduated from Headstart, any program effects may well have dissipated by then. It would have been much easier to detect effects of the program if testing had taken place immediately after graduation.

What was missing from the Headstart evaluation was all sense of the uniqueness of the different Headstart centers. The evaluation was not at all tailored to the specific goals of each center, and so we do not know if the centers were successful in what they wanted to accomplish. The purpose of evaluations following a tailored model is to measure the impact of a program at its strongest point, to measure the program's intended effect and not the effect that others might want it to achieve. Instead of using nationally available normed tests that are only tangentially related to a program's goals, evaluations following the tailored model use tests that have been derived from a list of highly specific behavioral objectives that have been set for a

---

[11] Westinghouse Learning Corporation–Ohio University, *The Impact of Head Start* (Springfield, Va.: U.S. Clearinghouse for Federal Scientific and Technical Information, 1969).

program and that have been incorporated into the program. The tests are therefore unique to the program. Moreover, there is little emphasis on the possible long-term effects since these are not effects of the program; they are effects of the program that have been influenced by maturation or by the post-program environment. Finally, there is little stress on unintended side effects or on positive transfer since these are not part of the goals of the program. Thus, evaluations following the tailored model fit the measures to the program's finely specified behavioral objectives and they do not aim to do more.

In a sense, the tailored model is biased toward illustrating whether a program achieves the operational goals it has set for itself and biased against illustrating whether a program achieves the long-term and generalized effects that most members of society value highly. Conversely, the medical model is biased against illustrating whether a program achieves the objectives it has set for itself and biased toward achieving the kind of effects that society values most. Thus, evaluations like the Headstart study, while they run a high risk of obtaining no effects at all, also hold out promise of a dramatic impact of great social importance if effects are obtained. It should be obvious by now that the criteria set by the medical model are more stringent than those set by the tailored model. It might also be obvious that an evaluation can and should incorporate elements of both models, for the models define imprecise endpoints on a single continuum.

Our own values should manifest themselves at this point. We think it most important that a program be evaluated at its strongest points, for what it is rather than for what some persons would like it to be. Thus, the first priority is tailoring an evaluation to a program's behavioral objectives if any exist. However, tailoring is not sufficient for a comprehensive understanding of how a program fits into the lives of its recipients and of how these lives are modified by the program. Social changes are more important if they are long-lasting, if they have no deleterious side effects, and if, in education at least, the intended effects generalize to measures that indicate an intellectual growth which is not tied to a specific curriculum. Since the medical and tailored models are by no means mutually exclusive, a comprehensive evaluation should place first stress on tailoring but should not ignore the major aspects of the medical model.

THE SCOPE OF THE ETS EVALUATION OF "SESAME STREET" AND OF OUR EVALUATION

The foregoing explication of evaluation research was intended to present one framework of questions that the researcher might ask before undertaking his work. In our estimation, one needs to ask the five questions posed by Suchman and the value question posed by Scriven. In addition, the evaluator has to decide the extent to which the evaluation will follow the tailored or the medical model. We now enquire about the extent to which, *in our estimation,* the ETS evaluations met these criteria. We also propose how we intend to extend the scope of the evaluation beyond that of the ETS team.

According to Suchman, the first fact that an evaluation should demonstrate is that the promised *effort* has been expended (i.e., the program has reached its target audience). The ETS team was less interested in this question than we were, although they carefully pointed out how many of their sample viewed "Sesame Street," and they related this to socioeconomic status. However, the ETS team conceived of the target audience as the children in their research sample, while we conceived of "Sesame Street's" target audience as being all children in the nation, particularly those who lived in areas where public television could be watched. Information about "Sesame Street's" national audience was crucial if we were to discover whether the program was having any significant effects on national problems. We could not answer any of these questions with confidence on the basis of the ETS sample, which was unrepresentative of the nation (it was not meant to be, of course, in any strict sampling sense) and which contained children and parents who were conscious of being in a research study. Hence, we turned to surveys to discover how frequently "Sesame Street" was watched in the United States. The first row of Table 3.2 illustrates how, in our opinion, we differed from the ETS team with respect to the kinds of viewing data that should be evaluated to determine the national impact of "Sesame Street."

Suchman also maintained that an evaluation has to assess the *effectiveness* of an innovation. The major thrust of the ETS evaluations was directed towards this goal, and our evaluation reflected the same priority. However, in some cases we conducted different analyses from those of Ball and Bogatz.

Adequacy refers to whether a program is having a socially significant impact, and Suchman conceived of it in terms of the magnitude of effects relative to the magnitude of the need that gave rise to the problem in the first place. There was no systematic attempt in the ETS reports to determine this particular aspect of adequacy. The long-term and transfer criteria of the medical model can also be considered in the context of adequacy, since any program whose effects persist is better than one whose effects dissipate, since any program with prosocial generalized effects is better than one without such effects, and since any program without unintended negative consequences is better than a program with these consequences. The ETS reports did consider some transfer items, and its second report examined

Table 3.2. The Scope of the ETS Evaluation and of Our Evaluation

Evaluation Task	ETS Evaluation		Our Evaluation	
	Extent of Treatment	Method of Treatment	Extent of Treatment	Method of Treatment
Assess Effort	Partial	Assessment of characteristics of heavy and light viewers in the ETS sample	More detailed	National survey data on the number and characteristics of regular viewers
Assess Effectiveness	Substantial	Analysis of learning scores	Substantial	Different analyses of learning scores
Assess Adequacy	Partial	Examination of some transfer and long-term effects	More detailed	More criteria of adequacy
Assess Efficiency	None		Partial	Evaluation of others' estimates of costs
Assess Process	Substantial	Assessment of characteristics of high learners and of effects of viewing on different kinds of children	Substantial	More comprehensive analyses of characteristics of viewers and nature of treatment
Evaluate Value of Program Objectives and Values Promoted by the Program	None		Substantial	Logical analysis and review of value statements by other social scientists and social theorists

effects one year after children had first seen "Sesame Street." Nonetheless, the evaluations were more tailored than they were medical, *although neither was exclusively tailored and the second was markedly less tailored than the first.* In later chapters, we examine whether the learning gains from "Sesame Street" were large enough to be considered "socially significant," and we also examine issues of transfer and unintended effects that were not elaborated upon by the ETS team.

Efficiency refers to the ratio of benefits to costs, particularly in the context of different programs with similar objectives. The ETS researchers did not consider this issue, and we considered only part of it. Because of the difficulty of comparing programs that overlap only partially and that have been evaluated with different degrees of skill, we contented ourselves with reporting others' estimates of the cost per child per year of producing "Sesame Street," and we related this to cost differences in reaching different kinds of children.

The *process* whereby a program causes learning is worth study, and we concentrated upon the aspects of the complex viewing treatment that lead to learning, upon the conditions of viewing that most promote learning, and upon the kinds of children who learn most. A great deal of the ETS reports were concerned with these three problem areas, particularly the last two.

Finally, most of one of our chapters is concerned with a value analysis of the relative importance of stimulating the growth of all social groups of preschool children and of narrowing the academic achievement gap. It also deals with other value issues raised by "Sesame Street." There were no such analyses in the ETS reports.

It is instructive to examine why there were differences between the ETS evaluation and our own. Why did Ball and Bogatz cite only their own viewing data and not those that were available from national surveys about the size and social composition of "Sesame Street's" audience? One reason is that they were not commissioned to cite national figures. Another is that they were most interested in the question, "Did 'Sesame Street' cause learning if children of various kinds viewed the show?" This question could be competently answered with the kind of design they used, for all that was required was to stratify the sample into various social groups and various levels of viewing "Sesame Street." Ball and Bogatz did not ignore the issue of "who views?"—but they did not assign it either a national perspective or a crucial role in making decisions about whether "Sesame Street" was achieving what it set out to achieve or was solving significant national problems.

There are also fairly compelling reasons why Ball and Bogatz did not cite data about "Sesame Street's" efficiency. On the one hand, they were not commissioned to do so by CTW, and on the other, they are not the experts in this area that they are in the area of measurement and evaluation. Moreover, it is a thankless task to try and scale the social, psychological, and economic costs and benefits of any program. Nonetheless, we thought it important at least to evaluate estimates of dollar costs, for such costs are obviously an important element in reaching any decisions about the program's future disposition.

We also have great sympathy for the arguments against examining the values implicated by a program. Quite apart from the extra time this involves and the subjectivity of judgment, there is the additional problem that there is no unanimity among evaluation researchers that their role includes even interpretation of data, let alone evaluation of the values of a program. The following quotation from Lumsdaine expressed a cautious perspective on the evaluator's role that stresses the primacy of the data rather than their interpretation. Lumsdaine's position serves as an indispensable end-anchor for comparison with Scriven's position.

> We should consider quite seriously whether the evaluator's role of reducing something to numbers—measuring the effects of an educational program— ought to be kept quite separate from the function of choosing among alternatives, given the facts about the effects of the program. I fear that if these functions are not kept separate, the inevitable uncertainties and shifting winds that will surround the question of which values ought to be achieved will tend to discredit the factual basis of evaluation, that is, the data.
>
> The factual basis—and I don't think this is a narrow technicality—must be kept unchallenged, at least unchallenged for improper reasons. The administrator must see that *only by keeping facts separate from interpretations can he defend the integrity of the facts.*[12]

Nonetheless, policy decisions typically entail making choices that have long-range implications for realizing some social values and for lessening the chance of realizing others. Policymakers may appreciate any help in pointing out the larger societal implications of possible decisions. At the same time they should—as Lumsdaine correctly pointed out—be confident that they are getting the facts before they get the interpretations.

---

[12] A. A. Lumsdaine, "Comments on Lortie's Paper," in Wittrock and Wiley, eds., *The Evaluation of Instruction.*

Chapter 4
Preliminary Descriptive Analyses of the First-Year ETS Data

INTRODUCTION

The purpose of this chapter is to illustrate how descriptive analyses of the first-year ETS evaluation can be used (1) for establishing a list of independent, moderator, and dependent variables that will help answer the questions we have raised; and (2) for describing these variables so that we can assess whether there are pitfalls in the data because of confounded relationships among independent variables, non-normal distributions of moderator or dependent variables, or inadequate fits between operationalizations and their referent constructs.

Some terms have to be defined before we can proceed to this task. We use the term *true experiment* to refer to designs in which experimental units are assigned to experimental conditions on a random basis. This assures the probabilistic comparability of the various conditions at the pretest, so that any observable posttest differences must be due to the experimental treatments. (Actually, this last statement is true only so long as the randomization procedure has been successfully carried out, the number of experimental units is "sizable," and the statistical analysis has not capitalized upon chance.)

Following Campbell and Stanley,[1] we use the term *quasi-experiment*

---

[1] The terminology about experiments and validity is from D. T. Campbell and J. C. Stanley, *Experimental and Quasi-Experimental Designs for Research* (Chicago:

to refer to designs in which the experimental units are assigned to experimental conditions on a systematic basis which makes the various experimental groups non-comparable at the pretest. Such designs are typically more difficult to interpret than true experiments for a number of reasons.

The major difficulty with quasi-experiments concerns *internal validity*. Internal validity is threatened whenever an observable relationship between *A* and *B* can be alternatively interpreted in terms of some third variable affecting *B*. Threats to internal validity do not involve the denial of an *A–B* relationship; they merely question whether *B* can be interpreted as a consequence of *A* or of some third variable. Campbell and Stanley have provided a list of such third variables, and Cook and Campbell have recently added others.

Doubts about whether an *A–B* relationship has ever been established are doubts about *statistical conclusion validity*. Statistics are used to demonstrate that *A* and *B* covary, and such covariation is a necessary condition for concluding that *A* might have caused *B*. But conclusions about covariance can be wrong—in some cases an *A–B* relationship might be expected by chance; in other cases it might emerge because statistics have been incorrectly used; and in yet other cases, a true *A–B* relationship might be obscured because of the high error variance associated with the particular measures, procedures, or participants in a study. Some quasi-experimental designs that we shall later use cannot be sensitively analyzed,[2] and it is a second advantage of true experiments that well-known and accepted statistical tests are available for determining whether *A* and *B* covary.

Even when the covariation of two variables has been established and can be interpreted causally, it is still not clear how the cause and effect should be labeled. *Construct validity* concerns the correspondence between operationalizations of a treatment or dependent variable and the construct to which the operationalization is meant to refer. Construct validity is threatened whenever this correspondence is low. For example, if one introduced a new curriculum with a blaze of publicity, the curriculum might be related to learning and this relationship might be causal. But we would not know whether the effect was due to the curriculum, the publicity, or both of them combined, and we would be wrong in attributing the learning to the curriculum alone.

Rand-McNally, 1966); and from T. D. Cook and D. T. Campbell, "The Design and Conduct of Quasi-Experiments and Randomized Experiments in Field Settings," in M. D. Dunnette, ed., *Handbook of Industrial and Organizational Research* (Chicago: Rand-McNally, 1975).

[2] Cronbach and Furby have gone so far as to state that experiments with nonequivalent treatment groups cannot be analyzed in a way that permits valid inference about a treatment's effects. See L. J. Cronbach and L. Furby, "How We Should Measure 'Change'—or Should We?" *Psychological Bulletin* 74 (1970): 68–80.

Even if we could demonstrate covariation, could establish cause, and could label our treatment and effects in some satisfactory manner, we would still not know the range of persons, settings, and times across which a particular relationship could be generalized. *External validity* refers to such a range of generalization, and high external validity implies greater generalizability.

THE ORIGINAL DESIGN

Ball and Bogatz planned the first-year evaluation as a true experiment and ETS field personnel randomly assigned the children in the research sample to one of two major experimental groups. Children in the first group were encouraged to watch "Sesame Street" in the hope that the encouragement would increase viewing. This treatment is described on page 21 of the first-year report, and it makes clear that encouragement-to-view involved more than mere viewing:

> The encouraged group was told about "Sesame Street," was given publicity material, and was paid a weekly half-hour visit by ETS-trained staff during the "Sesame Street" morning television time.

The second group consisted of children who did not receive the encouragement treatment and were left to view the show as they chose. Their function was to be the base line against which the performance of the encouraged children could be compared if the encouraged children did in fact view more than the nonencouraged children.

Children in the encouraged group were further divided into experimental conditions of being "observed" or "not observed." The former children were observed by ETS personnel for one-half hour per week as they watched "Sesame Street," and observation records were kept of the children's reactions to various segments of the show. No such records were kept for nonobserved children.

Five research sites were chosen for the first-year study in order to test *and replicate* the effectiveness of "Sesame Street" in regions that differed in several important ways. The Durham children ($N = 218$) came from a southern city, were 85 percent black, and were all economically disadvantaged; the Boston children ($N = 402$) came from a large northern inner-city and were about two-thirds black and one-third white; the Phoenix children ($N = 262$), all of whom were economically disadvantaged, came from a southwestern city and were about 55 percent black, 27 percent Spanish-speaking, and 18 percent English-speaking whites; the Philadelphia children ($N = 177$) were middle-class white children living in the suburbs of that city; and the northern California children ($N = 65$) came from a rural environment and were more than 90 percent white. (The California sample was not part of the original ETS design but, since the data were voluntarily collected for ETS by cooperating authorities, they were included in the first-year analyses.)

The sample of sites was purposive rather than random, and its purpose was to ensure heterogeneity and quasi-representativeness rather than formal, national representativeness. For practical reasons of finance and organizational control, it would have been difficult to collect data from a randomly selected set of national sites or from many other sites however chosen. Despite the obvious unrepresentativeness of the sites in any strict sampling sense, there is at least some heterogeneity of sites so that, if "Sesame Street" were effective in all of them, it would give us a considerable degree of confidence in the program's general ability to teach. This does not mean we would have as much confidence in conclusions about the program's ability to teach particular kinds of children as about children in general. After all, there is only one site (Boston) with considerable numbers of poor white children and only one site (Philadelphia) with clearly advantaged children.

Ball and Bogatz also wanted to test the effect on children of viewing "Sesame Street" at home or at school, and so at all the sites except in California, they selected groups of children who watched the program in either setting. All the at-home children in a particular neighborhood block were assigned to the same encouraged or nonencouraged treatment, and the treatments were randomly assigned to blocks. All the children in a particular classroom received the same treatment, and the treatments were assigned to classes at random. Each classroom in the at-school encouraged condition received two television sets, and the teachers were allowed to integrate "Sesame Street" into the school day in whatever way seemed best to them.

All children in the experiment were given a battery of pretests which had been developed by ETS to measure knowledge in areas to be covered by "Sesame Street." These tests covered knowledge of Body Parts, Letters, Forms, Numbers, Object Sorting, Object Relations, Object Classification, and Problem-solving. The tests were sensitively designed in such a way that they required a minimum of verbal response from the child. The battery was expanded somewhat during the production of "Sesame Street" to accommodate new operationalizations of CTW goals and the expanded version was administered to all children when the "Sesame Street" season was over, about six months after the pretest.

Thus, the planned design of the first-year evaluation involved a true experiment, and children were randomly assigned to an encouraged-to-view experimental group or to a not-encouraged-to-view control group. Then, each child received a pretest, and six months later, a posttest. Samples of children were chosen from school and home viewing situations and from five sites in the continental United States which differed in SES level or in the racial composition of the sample. (Moreover, there was variability due to sex, age, and intelligence within each of the sites, making it also possible to examine the effects of these variables on learning.)

INDEPENDENT VARIABLE CONFOUNDS

Table 4.1 gives a detailed breakdown of the 943 children from the first-year study for whom there were both pretest and posttest data. The children have been categorized according to research site, sex, pretest age, the at-home or at-school setting, and the experimental manipulation (encouraged-to-view and observed while watching, encouraged-to-view but not observed, or not-encouraged-to-view and not observed).

Before discussing the table, it should be noted that thirty children could not be listed, because twelve were at least six years old at the pretest and eighteen had uninterpretable classifications for the encouragement factor. Moreover, there were five children in Boston and one in Phoenix who were listed as being at-school and encouraged but not observed. This combination was not possible. Finally, one California child was listed as being at-school, whereas all the California children were reportedly in the at-home condition. These misclassifications were omitted from the analyses to be reported.

The table reveals that not all of these factors were crossed with each other. For example, site was not crossed with the at-school/at-home factor since there were no at-school children from California but there were from the other four sites. Also, the at-school/at-home factor was not crossed with age since—understandably enough—there could be no three-year-olds among at-school viewers.

There are also instances of large disparities in cell frequencies. For example, the group of five-year-old children from Boston is larger than the group of five year olds from any other site; the at-school groups from Phoenix or Boston are large in comparison to the other at-school groups; and the at-home groups from Durham and Philadelphia are larger than similar groups in the other sites.

The major problem of such a design is that potential causes are confounded. For example, if we were naively to compare the at-home and at-school children, the Phoenix and Boston children would contribute most to the at-school scores while the Durham and Philadelphia children would contribute most to the at-home scores. Hence, it would not be clear whether we were comparing viewing at-school with viewing at-home or whether we were comparing viewing at two sites with viewing at two other sites.

The major confoundings revealed in Table 4.1 are:

1. *Age and Site:* The three- and five-year-olds came predominantly from Boston.

Table 4.1. Number of Children in the Different Cells of the Design

MALE

	Encouraged-Observed						Encouraged-Not Observed						Not Encouraged-Not Observed					
	Home			School			Home			School			Home			School		
	Age 3	Age 4	Age 5	Age 3	Age 4	Age 5	Age 3	Age 4	Age 5	Age 3	Age 4	Age 5	Age 3	Age 4	Age 5	Age 3	Age 4	Age 5
Boston	11	14	5	7	24	19	2	3	0	1	1	0	1	10	8	6	12	22
Philadelphia	1	23	2	0	19	4	1	9	0	0	0	0	0	9	3	0	12	5
Durham	7	22	8	0	13	1	3	8	12	0	0	0	3	7	5	1	3	5
Phoenix	3	19	11	0	23	4	0	10	4	0	0	0	2	10	2	0	20	4
California	0	0	0	0	0	0	2	12	3	0	0	0	0	10	1	0	0	0
Total	126			114			69			2			71			90		

Table 4.1 (*cont.*)

FEMALE

	Encouraged-Observed						Encouraged-Not Observed						Not Encouraged-Not Observed					
	Home			School			Home			School			Home			School		
	Age 3	Age 4	Age 5	Age 3	Age 4	Age 5	Age 3	Age 4	Age 5	Age 3	Age 4	Age 5	Age 3	Age 4	Age 5	Age 3	Age 4	Age 5
Boston	11	12	4	13	11	16	1	6	2	0	1	2	11	7	7	7	18	17
Philadelphia	1	22	2	1	15	1	0	15	0	0	0	0	1	14	0	0	6	3
Durham	5	17	12	0	10	4	3	10	4	0	0	0	0	8	3	2	6	2
Phoenix	1	11	3	0	20	5	1	6	3	0	1	0	0	5	0	0	31	7
California	0	0	0	0	0	0	0	18	7	0	0	0	1	4	3	0	1	0
Total	101			96			76			4			64			100		

2. *Setting and Site:* At-school children predominated in Boston and Phoenix, while at-home children predominated at the three other sites.

3. *Encouragement and Site:* The encouraged-to-view and not observed children predominated over the encouraged-to-view and observed children in California.

4. *Encouragement and Setting:* The encouraged-to-view and not observed children were overrepresented among children in the at-home setting relative to the at-school setting.

These four confounds are not exhaustive, though they are the major ones and have important implications. One implication is that the data should be analyzed within each site before they are analyzed across sites. To sum across sites without first inspecting the within-site data would mean that many effects of great importance (e.g., age, encouragement, and setting) would be confounded and we would not know what we were dealing with.

There is an obvious danger to disaggregating data by sites, for we risk basing estimates of particular cell means on small samples. While the validity of causal constructs is enhanced by even finer breakdowns of the data, these same finer breakdowns can have the side effects of introducing large sampling biases as cell sizes diminish and of reducing statistical conclusion validity as degrees of freedom decrease.

The need to analyze data within sites would be all the more crucial if heavy viewers were more likely in one site than another. Imagine that viewing was heavier in Boston than in Durham and that Boston children gained more than Durham children between the pretest and posttest for reasons that had nothing to do with "Sesame Street" (e.g., their rate of cognitive maturation was higher). Then, any learning gain associated with viewing "Sesame Street" might be interpreted, not as consequences of viewing, but as a possible consequence of a higher rate of cognitive growth in urban Boston than in the more rural Durham. This hypothetical example illustrates the special importance of checking the data carefully for evidence of confounds involving the amount of viewing "Sesame Street."

A preliminary estimate of this possibility can be gained by classifying the children from each site according to the viewing measure that Ball and Bogatz used to divide the total sample of children into equal-sized viewing quartiles which represent four different levels of viewing. Since the ETS viewing measure was a composite of four items (see p. 88), some of which did not directly ask how frequently the child viewed, it is difficult to interpret the quartiles in absolute terms that state "Children in Quartile 4 viewed n times per week." Instead, the best interpretation of the quartiles is a relative one: "Children in Quartile 4 (Q_4) viewed more than children in Quartile 1 (Q_1)."

Table 4.2.   Number of Children from Each Site in
Each Original ETS Viewing Quartile*

Site	Lightest Viewers (Q_1)	Next Lightest Viewers (Q_2)	Next Heaviest Viewers (Q_3)	Heaviest Viewers (Q_4)
Boston	51	99	78	87
Philadelphia	16	31	57	65
Durham	51	43	53	39
Phoenix	76	42	32	19
California	23	16	8	14

* Spanish-speaking children not included.

Table 4.2 illustrates how many children at each site were in each view-ing quartile. It can be seen that children from the advantaged Philadelphia suburbs were overrepresented among the heaviest viewers, while the disad-vantaged children from Phoenix and California were overrepresented among the lightest viewers. It would seem, then, that advantaged children tended to be heavier viewers. However, it is dangerous to state categorically at this stage that the relationship between viewing and site was a real one. The danger arises because of the multiple confoundings involving site and because we have yet to examine the validity of the viewing measure that Ball and Bogatz used.

Another implication of the design concerns the at-school/at-home var-iable which is confounded with the encouragement and observation manip-ulations. We must be careful to differentiate the at-school and at-home samples, for without separate analysis of the two settings, we could not dis-tinguish effects of encouragement-to-view from effects of encouragement-to-view plus observation.[3]

MODERATOR VARIABLES

A moderator variable is one which affects the magnitude or direction of a presumed cause-effect relationship. Such variables typically take two forms. Either they are variables that cannot be manipulated, like sex or social class or age or setting, and which may codetermine the strength and direction of a relationship, or they are processes that directly mediate an effect by taking place immediately after the cause has varied and before the effect has been obtained. In the case of "Sesame Street," sex and age

---

[3] We later note that there is an even more compelling reason for analyzing the at-home and at-school samples separately.

were obvious moderator variables of the first kind, while aspects of the mother's interaction with the child after viewing "Sesame Street" were measured as potential mediators of the second kind. We shall now discuss each moderator variable that will be used later.

Peabody Picture Vocabulary Scores

The Peabody Picture Vocabulary Test is intended as a vocabulary-based measure of IQ and is frequently used to measure vocabulary alone. It also has a distinct cultural bias in favor of middle-class children and should inflate their IQ scores over the scores of other children. Moreover, preschool IQ scores correlate less than .5 with IQ scores from the same child at a later age, a fact which should make us question the validity of the test as a measure of intelligence. Therefore, little weight should be placed on the Peabody as a stable measure of culture-free intelligence, in the sense in which intelligence is popularly understood. However, it is all that we have to use.

The raw data from the Peabody can be converted into three scores: one for mental age, one for IQ, and a third for the child's percentile rank. We plan to use IQ scores in our analyses rather than mental age or percentile rank. This is because IQ is not confounded with chronological age, and because chronological age is confounded with other variables in the basic design. The major confound is with site, and if we were to classify children by mental age most of the youngest and oldest would come from a single site—Boston.

The test was normed on a sample of 4,012 white children in and around Nashville, Tennessee, and the IQ scores derived from the test have a mean of 100 and a standard deviation of 15. We should expect the mean IQ of the 731 disadvantaged children in the ETS sample to be less than 100 and we should also expect a positively skewed distribution. The frequency distribution of scores for the combined sample of economically disadvantaged children is shown in Figure 4.1; the modal IQ falls within the 63–70 category (the mean is 85.05), and there is an obvious positive skew to the data. We can confidently conclude that the disadvantaged group scores lower than national norms on this particular IQ test.

We used these IQ scores in two ways: first, to check that there were no differences in IQ between groups that were randomly constituted and should be comparable at the pretest; and second, to see if children with different IQ scores learned differently from "Sesame Street." Since the Peabody data were collected only at the pretest in the first-year evaluation, it is not possible to study the effects of viewing on this one particular measure of IQ. Post-test data are an absolute necessity if we are to examine IQ as an outcome variable as well as a moderator variable.

Figure 4.1. Distribution of Peabody IQ for Disadvantaged Children
from First-Year Report

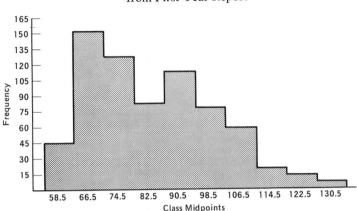

Class Midpoints

Pretest Indicators of Socioeconomic Status

There are advantages to testing whether any effects of "Sesame Street" are found among children of different social status. Hence, a reliable and valid index of socioeconomic status needs to be developed. There were twelve items relevant to socioeconomic standing in the Pretest Parent Questionnaire that parents filled out. A description of these items follows, and we shall retain the same system of numbering items that ETS used.

Pretest Item 10—Interaction with Child—asked, "What do *you* usually do when you are with your child?" Only three of the six answers listed actually dealt with interaction. These were 1) play with him; 2) read to him; and 5) watch television with him. A code of 1 was given for every item indicated, allowing a range from 0 to 3.

Pretest Item 12—Reading Exposure—was phrased: "How often is your child read to?" Its answer alternatives were coded from 1 to 5: 1) never; 2) less than once a week; 3) about once a week; 4) several times a week; 5) at least once a day.

Pretest Item 13—Art Activity—asked, "How often does he use such things as paper, crayons, or paints at home?" and again the response items were coded 1 through 5: 1) never; 2) less than once a week; 3) about once a week; 4) several times a week; 5) at least once a day.

Pretest Item 24—Preferred Education—asked, "If you could have your wish, what grade in school would you like him to complete?" Responses were: 1) 8th grade or less; 2) some high school; 3) all of high school; 4) some college; 5) college or beyond. Responses were coded from 1 to 5.

Pretest Item 25—Expected Education—asked, "Since things don't always turn out the way we want them to, how far do you think he will actually go in school?" The answers, coded 1 to 5, were: 1) 8th grade or less; 2) some high school; 3) high school; 4) some college; 5) college or beyond.

Pretest Item 29—Child's Possessions—asked "Does your child have his own: (a) room; (b) art things like crayons, paints, blackboard; (c) toys like puzzles, blocks, games; (d) books; (e) toy box or other place to keep his own things; (f) television?" A score of 1 was coded for every item indicated and the scores were summed.

Pretest Item 30—Event Attendance—asked, "How often does your child go to each of these things?" The list included seven events, but only six were used in this analysis. "Summer day camp," event (a), did not have an adequate list of response alternatives for the children tested. The remaining events included were: (b) public library; (c) playground; (d) museum; (e) live theater (for plays or puppet shows); (f) zoo; (g) movie theater. The child received a code of 1 for every event attended. The scores were then summed.

Pretest Item 36—Family Possessions—asked, "Which of the following things do you have?" The fourteen objects which followed all received a 1 code if parents indicated possession, and 0 if they did not. The objects were: (a) automobile; (b) black and white television set; (c) color television set; (d) hi-fi or phonograph; (e) telephone; (f) encyclopedia; (g) dictionary; (h) still or movie camera; (i) refrigerator; (j) oven; (k) stove; (l) dishwasher; (m) clothes washer; (n) clothes dryer. The responses were summed.

Pretest Item 37—Education of Parent—Almost Invariably Mother—asked, "What was the last grade in school that you completed?" The answers, coded 1 to 5, were: 1) 8th grade or less; 2) some high school; 3) all of high school; 4) some college; 5) college graduate or beyond.

Pretest Item 40—Education of Male Head—asked, "What was the last grade in school the male head of the household completed?" and again had five response alternatives, coded 1 to 5: 1) 8th grade or less; 2) some high school; 3) all of high school; 4) some college; 5) college graduate or beyond.

Pretest Items 44–47—Occupant/Room Ratio involved a ratio of the answer to Item 44, "What is the total number of people living in your home at the present time?" to the answer to Item 47, "How many rooms are there in this apartment or house?," the response alternatives to which were: 1) one or two; 2) three or four; 3) five or six; 4) seven or eight; 5) More than eight.

Pretest Item 50—Books Read—asked, "About how many books do you read each year?" The responses, coded 1 to 5, were 1) none or one; 2) two to four; 3) five to ten; 4) ten to twenty; 5) More than twenty.

The distributions of these items were examined and, although the range of scores was limited in some cases, none of the distributions appeared grossly non-normal. Hence, the pretest data for all the disadvantaged children were intercorrelated,[4] and two clusters of high intercorrelations emerged (see Table 4.3).

The first cluster involved the ETS items numbered 24, 25, 37, and 40 which have just been described. A glance at them shows that they referred to the parents' own years of education or to their educational aspirations and expectations for the child.

Simple visual inspection of the correlations revealed a second cluster consisting of the ETS items numbered 10, 29, 30, and 36. Inspection of these items indicates that they referred to the amount of environmental stimulation available to the child with his mother, with art objects, with his own home possessions, and with family possessions in general.

The data were examined more closely by factor analysis. A principal components analysis was used and the data were rotated to give orthogonal factors. Inspection of the eigenvalues revealed two sharp discontinuities, and Table 4.4 shows that the two factors which emerged from the factor analysis completely overlapped with the two factors that emerged from the simpler correlational analysis.

One index was formed by summing responses to items 24, 25, 37, and 40, each of which had a similar number of response alternatives, was answered by all the parents, had a factor loading of .50 or above, and had face validity because it dealt with education in the home. The composite was therefore labeled the Home Education Index. (Naming factors is, of course, a somewhat arbitrary process, and the most one can hope is to give a sense of the underlying construct.)

A second factor was formed from responses to items 10, 29, 30, and 36. Each of these items was composed of multiple subquestions that could be answered with a "Yes" or "No." The number of subquestions differed across the items, and no responses were available at all for some of the subquestions. Thus, an item score was derived for each mother by dividing the number of her "Yes" responses by the total number of "Yes" and "No" responses recorded for her. The resulting percentage of "Yes" responses was then simply summed across the four items. This method prevented items with more response alternatives (especially item 36) from predominating in the index, and it also meant that scores were not biased by the

---

[4] These correlations will presumably be inflated because they were obtained by summing across all the economically disadvantaged sites. A major determinant of site differences is that the samples from each site differed on measures of socioeconomic status.

Table 4.3. Intercorrelations from Pretest Parent Questionnaire:
Economically Disadvantaged Only*

Item Number	Variable	PE-PRE	EXE	EOP	EOM	IC-PRE	CP-PRE	FPO	EA-PRE	RE-PRE	AA-PRE	ORR	BRD
24	Preferred Education-Pre (PE-PRE)												
25	Expected Education (EXE)	.474											
37	Education of Parent (EOP)	.276	.407										
40	Education of Male Head (EOM)	.256	.381	.463									
10	Interaction with Child-Pre (IC-PRE)	.067	.140	.112	.075								
29	Child's Possessions-Pre (CP-PRE)	.120	.233	.310	.226	.541							
36	Family Possessions (FPO)	.187	.309	.319	.264	.604	.644						
30	Event Attendance-Pre (EA-PRE)	.165	.261	.335	.332	.438	.490	.564					
12	Reading Exposure-Pre (RE-PRE)	.140	.144	.188	.130	.258	.231	.175	.243				
13	Art Activity-Pre (AA-PRE)	.114	.113	.161	.175	.129	.175	.179	.211	.286			
44/47	Occupant/Room Ratio (ORR)	−.081	−.163	−.163	−.006	−.053	−.315	−.152	−.125	−.036	−.018		
50	Books Read (BRD)	.095	.150	.149	.118	.093	.175	.046	.177	.241	.146	−.109	

* PRE refers to variable scores at the pretest.

Table 4.4.   Factor Loadings from the Varimax Rotation:
Pretest Parent Questionnaire

Factor	1	2
Variance Accounted For	59.739	44.918
Variable Name:		
Preferred Education	—.053	.520
Expected Education	—.156	—.635
Education of Parent	—.222	—.592
Education of Male Head	—.152	—.570
Interaction with Child	—.718	.001
Child's Possessions	—.741	—.202
Family Possessions	—.765	—.235
Event Attendance	—.596	—.318
Reading Exposure	—.283	—.226
Art Activity	—.206	.224
Occupant/Room	—.193	.142
Books Read	—.140	—.225

absence of data from mothers who did not respond to some of the subquestions.

It was more difficult to label this index than the Home Education Index since it dealt with the number of home possessions, the number of the child's possessions, the frequency of attending events outside the home, and the amount of interaction between child and mother. Clearly, the items referred to numerosity, or to environmental richness, or affluence. Finally, and of course somewhat arbitrarily, the factor was labelled the Home Stimulation-Affluence Index.

The distribution of these indexes was plotted, and each was normal. Then, the indexes were correlated for the total disadvantaged sample. The correlation was .397 ($p < .01$). Thus, we had two indexes of the child's home environment, and they were not totally independent of each other.

The Posttest Parent Questionnaire included only six items of a socioeconomic nature, and they were all repetitions of items on the pretest. These dealt with the child's art activities, his interaction with parents, his exposure to reading materials, his own possessions, his attendance at events outside the home, and the educational goals that his parents had for him. Unfortunately, it was impossible to construct the same posttest as pretest indexes with the smaller pool of posttest items. As a consequence, the posttest items are not used for classifying the SES level of a child's home. Rather, they are mostly used singly to see how they were correlated with encouragement to view "Sesame Street."

Because the necessary items were not available on the posttest, it proved impossible to compute the test–retest correlation for the two indexes we constructed. However, inspection of the test–retest correlations of the six socioeconomic status items that were common to pretest and posttest (see Table 4.5) showed that these correlations ranged from only .56 (the educational level preferred for the child) to .29 (the frequency of the mother's interaction with the child).

These reliability estimates may be so low because of the relatively few response alternatives for each question or because a different parent answered at the posttest than at the pretest. Alternatively, however, it may have been that the responses of parents were not stable over six months, and because of this we have to question the reliability of our indexes of socioeconomic status. The indexes are suspect from another viewpoint. They were derived from analyses in which all the economically disadvantaged were treated as a single population. A different pattern of inter-item correlations appeared when the socioeconomic status data were analyzed within sites (where variability is more restricted), and the difference between sites obviously contributed to finding the particular indexes of socioeconomic status that we obtained. While socioeconomic status may be one major determinant of site differences, it would be naive to think it was the only determinant.

We have to resort to three strategies for assessing socioeconomic status in our attempts to understand the relationship between socioeconomic status, viewing, and learning.

1. The strongest tests involve direct comparisons between the Philadelphia children and those from the four economically disadvantaged sites since the sites were chosen with this difference in mind. (We see later that SES distinctions can also be made between the four disadvantaged sites in a way that reduces our dependence on the single comparison between the Philadelphia and other children.)

2. The second strategy, albeit a weaker one, is to assign each child socioeconomic status scores based on the indexes derived from the preceding correlational analyses. The problem with this strategy is that the scores are of dubious reliability and, for comparisons within the economically disadvantaged, they are restricted in their variability. Nonetheless, where it is absolutely necessary we assign children their scores on the two indexes.

3. Occasionally, we also replicate analyses using the number of years of mother's education as a single proxy for SES. This variable has proven in previous research to be a high correlate of learning among preschoolers

Table 4.5.   Test-Retest Correlations Parent Questionnaires:
Disadvantaged Only*

Variable		PE-PO	IC-PO	CP-PO	EA-PO	RE-PO	AA-PO
Preferred Education-Pre	(PE-PRE)	.555					
Interaction with Child-Pre	(IC-PRE)		.288				
Child's Possessions-Pre	(CP-PRE)			.369			
Event Attendance-Pre	(EA-PRE)				.430		
Reading Exposure-Pre	(RE-PRE)					.399	
Art Activity-Pre	(AA-PRE)						.414

* **PRE** refers to variable scores at the pretest.
   PO refers to scores on the same variables at posttest.

and, as we see later, its use is particularly appropriate with children from the evaluation of "Sesame Street's" second year.

It is unfortunate that no SES indexes could be computed from the ETS Parent Questionnaire data that would meet the stringent requirements of a hardheaded sociologist. To do this, information about occupation or income would have been required in addition to education, but it is often very difficult to collect information on these sensitive topics. Nonetheless, the evaluation is weakened without such measures and an even greater reliance has to be placed on the difference between the children from Philadelphia and those from the less advantaged sites.

THE LEARNING TESTS

The test battery was composed of 203 items that were common to the pretest and posttest. The items were grouped into eight major tests, each of which was divided into different numbers of subtests, and each of these subtests was composed of different numbers of single items. Most of the analyses that follow are based on the eight tests that covered knowledge of Body Parts, Letters, Numbers, Forms, Object Sorting, Object Relations, Object Classification, and Problem-solving. (The last was called the Puzzles Test, and—following the ETS team—we shall omit "Object" when referring to the Sorting, Relations and Classification tests.)

The Eight Tests

The distribution of pretest scores was plotted for each test, and inspection revealed that all the distributions were approximately normal. The posttest scores were then separately plotted for the encouraged and nonencouraged conditions. Once again, most of the distributions were approximately normal. The major exception was the Body Parts Test which, in both the encouraged-to-view and control conditions, was negatively skewed because most of the children obtained high scores. Thus, the Body Parts Test was the only test where transformation of the data might have been appropriate.[5] However, since it was the only non-normal distribution, and since the analysis of variance is rather robust to violations of the normality assumption, the data for this one test were not transformed.

The eight learning tests were not completely independent of each other. As Table 4.6 shows, 14 percent of the individual items were counted into

---

[5] The robustness of analysis of variance to violations of normality has been commented upon in E. F. Lindquist, "The Norton Study of the Effects of Non-normality and Heterogeneity of Variance," in B. Lieberman, ed., *Contemporary Problems in Statistics* (New York: Oxford University Press, 1971).

Table 4.6.   Overlapping Items in Tests of Dependent Variables

Test	N Items	N Items Belonging to this Test Which Appear in Another Test
Body Parts	32	0
Letters	65	11
Forms	8	0
Numbers	54	0
Sorting	12	5
Relations	8	0
Classification	18	10
Puzzles	5	2
Total N	202*	28

* One item seems to have been in none of the tests.

the total of more than one test. For example, a correct answer on the item which required the child to sort objects according to their form (an item which is officially classed under Sorting) would result in the child's being given a point in both the Forms and the Sorting tests. The distribution of such overlapping items across tests is indicated in Table 4.6.

When we originally obtained the data from ETS, we had no information about individual items and so were unable to classify the items into mutually exclusive tests.[6] Thus, all the data on single tests that will be presented involve nonindependent tests, as described, and effects of viewing on some tests (e.g., Forms and Sorting) might be due to items the tests share rather than to the unique demands associated with, say, learning Forms and Sorting.

The original absence of information about item responses made it impossible to compute a sensitive estimate of internal consistency—the extent to which items in a test are measuring some unique construct. Had we had item information we would have computed a reliability for each test at the pretest and posttest using the Kuder-Richardson Formula 20. We would only have used the economically disadvantaged sample for this since the magnitude of reliability estimates increases with the heterogeneity of the

[6] When we asked for item data at a later date for another purpose, Ball and Bogatz did not hesitate to provide us with them. However, we did not recompute the many analyses with independent tests since the overlap was only 14 percent.

sample of subjects. Hence, putting economically advantaged and disadvantaged children into the analysis inflates reliabilities. Table 4.7 gives the

Table 4.7. Internal Reliability of Learning Tests:
First-Year Report—All Children*

Body Parts	.98
Letters	.96
Forms	.82
Numbers	.95
Relations	.69
Sorting	.53
Classification	.87
Puzzles	.50
Grand Total	.98

* These are overestimates of internal reliability.

estimates computed by Ball and Bogatz on the basis of all 943 children. The estimates for Body Parts, Letters, Forms, Numbers, and Classification were all above .80 while the estimates for Relations, Sorting, and Puzzles were below .70. Interestingly enough, reliabilities tended to be higher for tests measuring symbolic representation (Letters, Numbers, and Body Parts) rather than for tests measuring more intellectual cognitive skills (Sorting, Classification, Puzzles). Since low reliability makes it more difficult to reject the null hypothesis, any effects indicating that "Sesame Street" affected some learning tests but not others have to be carefully scrutinized, for differences in the learning of tests may have reflected differences in the reliability of measures rather than differences in the goal areas actually influenced by "Sesame Street."

Test–retest correlations are estimates of the temporal stability of a measure, while internal consistency estimates measure the commonality between items at any one point in time. Estimates of internal consistency are inflated when respondents complete the different parts of a test at a single sitting, because any chance or situational factor leading to high performance on one part of a test should lead to enhanced performance on the rest of the test or on related tests. Test–retest correlations also normally result in high estimates of reliability because the same test is administered at two different times, (say, two weeks apart), and the respondent might remember his previous responses at the second test session.

In the present instance, however, we might expect test–retest correlations to produce low estimates of reliability for two reasons. First, when many tests are administered at any one time, recall should be depressed because of interference at the time of testing. Second, when a six-month interval intervenes between testing and retesting, interference from the environment should be high and should depress recall of previous responses. As a consequence, we assume that the test–retest correlations for the first-year "Sesame Street" evaluation will be lower—to an unknown degree—than is normally obtained with this particular estimate of reliability.

It is incorrect to compute test–retest correlations across the total sample if an experimental treatment has intervened between the first and second testings. In such a case, effects of the treatment could affect the magnitude of the correlations. It is more appropriate to estimate test–retest reliabilities within experimental conditions. The problem with this general strategy in the particular context of "Sesame Street" was that it was not clear what the treatments were. In one sense, the experimenter-controlled treatment was being encouraged to view "Sesame Street." In another sense, the subject-controlled treatment was the amount of reported viewing of "Sesame Street." Since the need for estimating reliability is more acute in quasi-experiments than in true experiments, and since we use the subject-controlled treatment based on reported viewing in the quasi-experiments, we report here test–retest correlations using three levels of treatment.

Heavy viewers of "Sesame Street" were classified as children whose parents scored 5 or 6 on the Posttest Parent Questionnaire viewing measure (see p. 91); moderate viewers scored from 1 to 4; and nonviewers scored 0. The number of economically disadvantaged children in each category is in Table 4.8 together with the appropriate correlations. The test–retest correlations for Body Parts, Letters, Numbers, and for the Grand Total are consistently above .50, while for Relations, Sorting, and Puzzles they are consistently below .40.

These last three measures did not have entirely desirable psychometric properties when we considered either test–retest reliability or estimates of internal consistency. The other measures seemed entirely satisfactory.

Composite Learning Measures

Ball and Bogatz summed all of the items into a Grand Total index that they used freqently when they were investigating the global question of whether "Sesame Street" caused learning. In this case, they added the single items so that, unlike the test totals, no item appeared twice. Forming a composite in this way has the potential problem that it will weight the tests with higher variance more than those with lower variance. Thus, the Letters Test (with a total possible score of 58) and the Numbers Test (with a possible maximum of 54) accounted for about one-half of the Grand Total items and had more variability associated with them than other measures. It

Table 4.8.   Test-Retest Correlation within Posttest Parent Questionnaire
Viewing Groups for All Learning Tests*

	Test-Retest Correlations		
Test	Viewing Group 0 N = 78	Viewing Group 1–4 N = 219	Viewing Group 5–6 N = 510
Body Parts	.538	.601	.641
Letters	.627	.578	.526
Forms	.469	.525	.429
Numbers	.702	.703	.707
Sorting	.055	.246	.235
Relations	.399	.377	.380
Classification	.277	.495	.476
Puzzles	.190	.288	.291
Grand Total	.718	.731	.716

* This excludes all Spanish-speaking children and all children for whom pretest
or posttest parent questionnaire data were not available.

is often advisable to weight tests equally in forming a composite total. We
did not do so in the present instance because content analysis of "Sesame
Street" (see Ball and Bogatz, p. 256) showed that numbers and letters were
taught somewhat more than other concepts. Thus, the bias in the composite
roughly corresponded to the biases in the program which makes the Grand
Total particularly suitable for testing the program at its strongest points. It
was a measure of good psychometric properties (normal distributions at
pretest and posttest; internal consistency above .90; and test–retest reliabilities about .72), although it was presumably biased in favor of the simple
kind of associative learning tapped by the majority of items in the Numbers
and Letters tests.

The Fit between Intermediate Objectives, Behavioral
Objectives, and the Learning Tests Used

The first report by Ball and Bogatz contained a document by CTW entitled "The Instructional Goals of Children's Television Workshop." The
document had a section called "Interpretative Guidelines" that is divided
into four parts. The first part stressed the "experimental nature of the
('Sesame Street') project" and stated "we have not attempted to restrict our

goals to those which may be achieved with certainty." The second part commented on the "overlapping of goal priorities" and noted that certain instructional goals could be placed under any one of several more general categories. The third part dealt with goal priorities, and the fourth part dealt with "measurement plans" for the formative and summative research. The summative research was described as "probably emphasizing typical conditions of broadcast viewing, the evaluation of long-term gains, and the use of standardized instruments." (As it turned out, hardly any of these features were incorporated into the ETS designs—the major treatment was encouragement-to-view, not a typical condition of viewing; no standardized tests were used as dependent variables in the first year; and there were inevitably no measures of long-term gains at the end of the first viewing season.)

It was the third part of the document concerning goal priorities that is of special interest here. The following statement was made:

> The goals fall into two major sets in terms of priorities. The first set consists of those objectives currently seen as the primary instructional goals of CTW. Each of these is marked with an asterisk. Those goals not preceded by an asterisk may be dealt with somewhere in the program, but it is not anticipated that they will necessarily be the subjects of concentrated production efforts. The follow-up, or summative research, will focus predominantly upon the higher-priority goals, and will include the measurement of the remaining goals only to the extent that the programs as produced appear to be capable of achieving them.

This statement was followed by a list of program goals which were specified at three levels of generality. We call these: goal areas, goals, and subgoals. One general goal area was *Symbolic Representation*. It was divided into lower-order goals which included knowledge of Letters, Numbers, and Forms. These goal areas were themselves divided into a total of nineteen specific subgoals that included learning to recognize uppercase letters, learning to recognize lowercase letters, learning the alphabet, etc. These subgoals should be thought of as behavioral objectives of "Sesame Street," and of the nineteen listed under Symbolic Representation, twelve have asterisks by them to signify their high priority.

A second general goal area is *Cognitive Processes*. This was divided into six goals: Relational Concepts, Perceptual Discrimination, Classification, Ordering, Reasoning, and Problem-solving. These goals were further divided into a total of seventeen specific subgoals, nine of which were marked by asterisks.

A third general goal area related to knowledge of the *Physical and Man-made Environment*. None of the specific subgoals had an asterisk next to it, and so we can infer that CTW did not ascribe as high a priority to this general goal area as it did to Symbolic Representation and Cognitive Processes.

The fourth and last general goal area involved teaching children about the *Social Environment*. Two goals were mentioned: Social Units and Social Interactions. A total of six subgoals were listed, three of which were accompanied by asterisks. These were:

1. Differences in Perspective—a single event may be interpreted differently by different individuals.
2. Cooperation—"in certain situations it is beneficial for two or more individuals to work together toward a common goal."
3. Rules Which Insure Justice and Fair Play—this involves behaving by rules, recognizing fairness, evaluating rules, and generating rules.

These goals are important for our purposes since they served as the operational specification of the intermediate level objectives of "Sesame Street." The goal priorities and their behavioral referents tell us what CTW understood by intellectual and cultural growth in the description of the program's aim of "stimulating the intellectual and cultural growth of preschoolers, particularly disadvantaged preschoolers." But the step from broad intermediate level objectives to specific behavioral objectives of highest priority is crucial in a different way, for if there is a low correspondence between the specific goal priorities and a program's general objectives, then the evaluation runs the risk of being irrelevant to the objectives. In fact, of a total of twenty-four asterisked goals, the twenty-one for Symbolic Representation and Cognitive Processes implied that major stress was placed by CTW on the child's cognitive growth, which includes symbolic representation. There were fewer priority goals relating to the child's growth in most moral and social domains as the three asterisks for knowledge of social interaction and of social units indicated. Yet these are presumably important areas if the child is to grow, in Cooney's words, "intellectually and culturally," and if we are not to restrict the definition of cultural to knowing how to classify forms or to label body parts.

There is also some discrepancy between the tests that were asterisked and the tests that were administered to children. In the first year, the ETS team did not administer any tests of knowledge of social units or of social interaction. Nor, if we examine the individual tests, were there well-constructed tests of cognitive processes that would be adequate operationalizations of what Jerome Kagan called "knowing how to think" as opposed to knowing "what to think." It is difficult to know just what Kagan and Cooney meant when they stressed the importance of knowing how to think, but it is clear from the ETS tests that 46 percent of the items dealt with the simple association of a verbal label with a shape (including numbers, letters, forms, and body parts).[7] The other items included questions dealing with the ability to sort, relate and classify by size, shape, number, or function, and there was a Puzzles Test of five items that required children to point out what was wrong in a picture. Unfortunately, to judge by the reliabilities, these tests were not as well constructed as the associative tests, and it is not obvious to us that they measure knowing "how to think."

Of course, we must realize the difficulty of expanding the pool of items to cover more goals or to cover more adequately those goals to which fewer items were relevant. It would have been almost impossible to give more tests to the experimental children, and it would have been expensive to increase the sample size and give each child in the expanded sample part of the total universe of test items. Moreover, there is more knowledge available at present about tests of simple cognitive skills for preschoolers than there is about tests of aspects of their self-concepts, or their knowledge of the social world, or of the higher-order cognitive skills that are relevant to children of four. Thus, it is probably easier to develop new tests based on old wisdom, experience, and research than it is to create new tests or to trust existing tests that may not be of the same standard as the tests that Ball and Bogatz created for themselves.

Nonetheless, the fact remains that there was some discrepancy in the first year between "Sesame Street's" intermediate and behavioral objectives, and between each of these and the tests that were actually administered to the children in the research sample. In particular, strong tests of attitudes, knowledge of the social world, of moral concepts, such as justice, cooperation, and fairness, and of problem-solving, were missing, while tests of

---

[7] The 46 percent figure was reached by summing the number of items involving the recognition or naming of, or the pointing to, a number, letter, form, or body part. The total, eighty-four, was then divided by the total number of items that were included in both the pretest and posttest battery and that were included by the ETS term in their subgoal analyses. There were 184 such items. If we use the same procedure for individual tests, 72 percent of the Letters Test items were associative in the sense described (recognizing letters, naming capitals or lowercase letters, recognizing letters in words), while 28 percent were not (matching letters in words, initial sounds, and reading words). For the Numbers Test, 49 percent of the items were associative (recognizing and naming numbers), while 51 percent were not (numerosity, counting to twenty, adding and subtracting). Interestingly, the trend was reversed in the second year where twelve of fifty-seven Letters Test items were associative (recognizing and naming letters), while the remainder (83 percent) were not (letters, sounds, initial sounds, decoding, reading, left-right orientation, and alphabet recitation). For the Numbers Test in the second year, 10 percent of seventy-eight items were associative (recognizing and naming numbers), while the remainder (87 percent) were not (enumeration, conservation, counting strategies, number/numeral agreement, adding and subtracting, counting to thirty).

associative learning in the cognitive domain provided about 46 percent of the items and made the ETS evaluation primarily an evaluation of "Sesame Street's" effectiveness in teaching the association between verbal labels and numerical, alphabetic, or physical shapes.

VIEWING MEASURES

Although Ball and Bogatz had the commendable foresight to collect multiple measures of the amount of viewing "Sesame Street," there were some cells in the design where no data were collected for a particular viewing measure. Table 4.9 shows that Viewing Logs data were not collected

Table 4.9.   Viewing Measures Obtained in Four Cells of the Basic Design

Treatment Condition	Viewing Measures			
	S.S. Test	Parent's Questionnaire	Viewing Logs	Viewing Records
Home-Encouraged	√*	√	√	√
Home-Not Encouraged	√*	√	√	
School-Encouraged	√*	√		√
School-Not Encouraged	√*	√		

√ Measure available.
* Validity dubious.

from at-school children and that Viewing Records data were not collected from nonencouraged children. This placed special emphasis on the Sesame Street Test of viewing and on the Posttest Parent Questionnaire measure of viewing since these provided the only relevant viewing data from the total sample. We now deal with the four viewing measures separately, paying special attention to the two measures for which all the children had scores.

Sesame Street Test

The distribution of Sesame Street Test scores was negatively skewed among the economically disadvantaged and showed definite ceiling effects (see Figure 4.2). The modal frequency was 10 on a test where the maximum was 10, indicating that most children recognized all of the "Sesame Street" characters they were called upon to identify at the posttest.

The assumption behind the test was that higher recognition reflects higher viewing. This may have been so. However, the test may also have reflected other factors, some of which could be co-symptoms of both learning

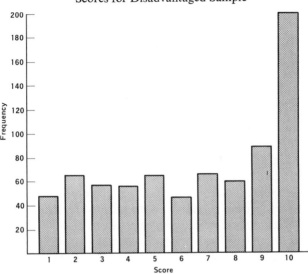

Figure 4.2. Distribution of Sesame Street Test
Scores for Disadvantaged Sample

gains and high scores on the Sesame Street Test (e.g., intelligence). If viewing and learning were common co-symptoms of intelligence, it would not be clear if the relationship of the Sesame Street Test to learning gains was due to viewing causing learning or to the more intelligent children being more able, thereby both recognizing more "Sesame Street" characters and maturing at a faster rate than other children. This last interpretation would be a threat to the internal validity of any relationship between viewing and learning gains and would explain the relationship without any reference to "Sesame Street" *causing* learning. All the interpretation requires is that there be nonequivalent groups that are maturing over time at different rates. It would not seem advisable, therefore, to classify children into viewing groups by using one learning test (the Sesame Street Test) in order to study the effects of this learning test on other learning tests (the eight principal outcome measures).

Another reason for not using the Sesame Street Test is that it was probably more highly correlated with posttest learning than with pretest learning for reasons that were irrelevant to the efficacy of "Sesame Street." For example, the Sesame Street Test was administered to each child at the same time posttest learning was assessed. Hence, each of these measures reflects the communalities of the testing session, and these communalities presumably inflate the correlation of the measures. It is also possible that the tester knew at the posttest how much the children had viewed either because she was responsible for implementing the encouragement manipulation or for keeping the continuous viewing records (see p. 93), or because the Sesame Street Test or the Posttest Parent Questionnaire was administered before the learning tests. If the tester did know this, it might have affected the tester–child relationship at the posttest, thereby inflating the correlation of posttest learning and posttest viewing measures.. (This inflation was much less likely at the pretest since the tester could not have known how much the children had viewed.)

"Treatments" (like viewing) that are more highly correlated with posttest outcome measures than pretest ones will give rise to a problem of differential statistical regression[8] that can cause spurious treatment effects. Let us illustrate the problem in two different ways. In a randomized experiment there should be no correlation between the treatment and pretest because the experimental groups have been randomly formed. However, if the treatment is effective, there should be a correlation between the treatment and posttest. In a quasi-experiment, on the other hand, there will often be an initial pretest-treatment correlation, since treatments are assigned to nonequivalent groups that differ in pretest learning, and a treatment effect would only be suggested if the posttest-treatment correlation were higher than the pretest-treatment correlation. However, testing communalities alone could lead to such a pattern of differential correlation in any quasi-experiment where the treatment levels were determined at the posttest—especially if recognition tests were used both for assessing experimental outcomes and for assessing the treatment, as was the case with the learning tests and the Sesame Street Test measure of viewing. (No differential correlation would be expected because of testing communalities in a true experiment, because viewing groups are determined by the experimenter's assignment rather than by posttest questionnaire responses to a viewing test.)

Let us now state the problem a second way that more explicitly refers to regression. The Sesame Street Test defined the level of viewing in a way which was probably more highly correlated with posttest than pretest learning scores. Thus, high scorers on the Sesame Street Test should have known more at the posttest than low scorers, and we should have nonequivalent groups of children selected on the basis of a correlate of the posttest outcome measures. These high scorers at the posttest presumably regressed downwards on the pretest to their population mean (thereby inflating their raw learning gains), while the low posttest scorers presumably regressed up-

---

[8] Statistical regression in this situation is discussed in D. T. Campbell and K. N. Clayton, *Avoiding Regression Artifacts in Panel Studies of Communication Impact* (University of Chicago, Department of Sociology, Studies in Public Communication, No. 3, 1961), pp. 99–118. A briefer version is in D. T. Campbell and J. C. Stanley, *Experimental and Quasi-Experimental Designs for Research.*

wards on the pretest (thereby deflating their raw gains). Thus, high scorers on the Sesame Street Test probably had higher raw gain scores than low scorers for reasons of statistical regression.

The co-symptom and statistical regression problems made it dangerous to classify children into viewing groups for quasi-experimental purposes when the Sesame Street Test was the sole or major factor in the classification index. However, the test can be used as an index of viewing in a true experiment where we want to discover whether the encouraged-to-view and the not-encouraged-to-view groups differed in viewing. The test is permissible in this instance because random assignment to experimental groups ensures that selection factors (e.g., intelligence) will not be confounded with viewing as they are in quasi-experiments.

The Posttest Parent Questionnaire

The second index of viewing was derived from the Posttest Parent Questionnaire. Four items were involved. First, the parents responded to an open-ended question about the educational television programs their child watched, and a score of 1 was assigned by ETS if "Sesame Street" was spontaneously mentioned. Next, the parent was asked directly if the child viewed "Sesame Street." A "Yes" response was scored as 2 and a "No" as 0. Third, the parent was asked how often the child viewed per week. Four alternatives were available and scores ranged from 0 to 4. Finally, the parent was asked how much of each program the child usually watched. There were four alternatives (nearly all; about one-half; less than one-half; none). Each child received a score between 0 and 3. The responses to these four questions were then summed by ETS to give a weighted index with a 0 to 10 range.

We were not able to interpret the ETS coding for the first item that went into the index, but we were able to re-create the index based on the other three items. It had a total of nine possible points and should be very similar to the ten-point ETS original. A frequency distribution of scores was plotted within the encouraged and nonencouraged groups and examination showed that there were no children scoring 1, 2, or 3. This reflects the way the index was constructed. A mother who claimed that her child viewed the minimum possible (from zero to one program per week and for only about one-quarter of that program) received four points, and so there was an inevitable gap of three points between no viewing and absolutely minimal viewing. So, we subtracted three points for each child who scored four or more, resulting in a viewing index with a range from 0 to 6. The distribution of scores was heavily skewed with most children falling in categories 5 and 6.

The skewed distributions meant that it would be difficult to use the Posttest Parent Questionnaire to divide children into multiple viewing categories to test the relationship of viewing and learning. Moreover, one logical division would have been to classify children as viewers and nonviewers. However, a problem arose in doing this because there were only seventy-eight nonviewers in all of the disadvantaged sites combined.[9]

There were also two minor validity problems with the Posttest Parent Questionnaire measure of viewing. Parents were called upon to estimate their children's viewing, and the parents of at-home children probably made reasonable estimates. However, the parents of at-school children, when they answered the question, could have been responding to the frequency of viewing at-school, at-home (weekends or vacations), or in both settings, and it would have been difficult for them to estimate sensitively the amount of viewing in preschool classrooms. It is important, therefore, to analyze the at-home and at-school children separately whenever the Posttest Parent Questionnaire is used for classifying children by the amount of time they viewed "Sesame Street."

The second validity problem occurred because the parents of encouraged children knew that the purpose of the encouragement was to get them to watch the show. Any desire that such parents might have had to please the interviewer or to present a favorable picture of their child could have led to an overestimation of the amount of time the child had watched.

It would seem that one indirect way of examining whether social desirability inflated the viewing estimates of the parents of encouraged children would be to compare how encouraged and nonencouraged children scored on the Sesame Street Test—a presumed measure of viewing—and how their parents scored on the Posttest Parent Questionnaire measure—a presumed measure of viewing plus social desirability. However, this comparison would not be definitive, for the Sesame Street Test scores of encouraged children may have been inflated by the nonbroadcast material that was left in the

---

[9] We tried to construct a different index by multiplying the frequency of reported viewing per week by the average length of time spent viewing each program. The last measure was obtained by treating the entire program as sixty minutes of viewing, most of the program as forty-five minutes of viewing, one-half of the program as thirty minutes of viewing, and less than one-half as fifteen minutes of viewing. Such a multiplicative index should reflect the total numbers of minutes the child spent viewing "Sesame Street." Unfortunately, this index was very heavily skewed, and scores piled up at the heavy viewing end of the scale. In addition, the single item measuring the weekly frequency of viewing predicted nearly all the variance in the index. This one question discriminated best perhaps because of the nature of the question or because of the relatively high number of response alternatives.

home as part of the encouragement treatment, and some parents may have looked at this information with their children. Hence, the Sesame Street Test scores may measure viewing, parent–child interaction style, or the child's use of CTW's nonbroadcast information.

Nonetheless, it is instructive to describe the relationship between encouragement and different viewing estimates at each site. We would have to doubt whether the encouragement manipulation had had its desired effect if there were no statistically significant differences between encouragement conditions for either the Sesame Street Test or the Posttest Parent Questionnaire. And we would have to doubt the validity of the viewing measures if they were not related to encouragement in the same way at each site.

Because of the validity problem with the Posttest Parent Questionnaire for the at-school sample and because of evidence (see p. 109) that randomization was not successfully accomplished or maintained over time with the at-school sample, Tables 4.10 and 4.11 report only the data for the at-home children.

There was an impressive correspondence between the measures at the different sites when one-way analyses of variance were conducted to test whether the encouraged conditions differed in viewing. When one viewing measure failed to discriminate between encouragement conditions, the other did too (Boston and Philadelphia), while when one measure discriminated between encouragement conditions, the other did also (California, Durham, and Phoenix). This overlap between the viewing measures may have reflected the fact that each of the tests measured viewing in addition to any unique features that it did not share with the other test.

Viewing Records

The third measure of viewing in the ETS report was derived from records which the parents of encouraged children kept. Beginning with the third month of the "Sesame Street" season, parents were asked to record the days on which the child had viewed "Sesame Street"; the data were collected monthly. The maximum number of months for which data could be collected was four. The collected number of records per child is reported in Table 4.12. It is noteworthy that about 16 percent of the children have no viewing records and that 38 percent have data for two or fewer months. The average frequency of viewing per month was not correlated with the number of records available for each child ($r = -.02$), indicating that there was probably no relationship between the number of records and the reported frequency of viewing.

The most serious problem with the Viewing Records from our perspective is that the data were not collected from the nonencouraged children.

Table 4.10. Description of Viewing Measures for All Sites

Site	Factor		Variable	
			Posttest Parent Questionnaire	Sesame Street Test
Boston	Encouraged 69	N	60	69
		X̄	5.30	6.93
		SD	.74	2.88
	Nonencouraged 44	N	42	44
		X̄	5.10	6.84
		SD	1.10	3.21
Durham	Encouraged 111	N	109	111
		X̄	4.52	6.48
		SD	1.69	3.18
	Nonencouraged 28	N	26	28
		X̄	2.77	2.82
		SD	2.36	2.72
Phoenix	Encouraged 52	N	49	52
		X̄	4.45	6.08
		SD	1.42	3.53
	Nonencouraged 18	N	17	18
		X̄	3.29	3.61
		SD	2.23	3.03
California	Encouraged 41	N	36	41
		X̄	4.56	6.93
		SD	1.98	3.37
	Nonencouraged 19	N	18	19
		X̄	1.56	2.63
		SD	2.09	2.57
Philadelphia	Encouraged 76	N	76	76
		X̄	5.00	8.93
		SD	1.34	1.75
	Nonencouraged 27	N	27	27
		X̄	4.78	8.44
		SD	1.37	2.33

Table 4.11.   Analyses of Variance of Viewing Measures at Each Site

		Variable			
		Posttest Parent Questionnaire		Sesame Street Test	
Site	Factor	MS	F	MS	F
Boston	Encouragement	1.04	1.26	.20	.02
	Error	.82		9.07	
Durham	Encouragement	64.56	19.26†	298.88	31.21†
	Error	3.35		9.58	
Phoenix	Encouragement	16.83	6.13*	81.30	6.10*
	Error	2.75		11.62	
California	Encouragement	108.00	26.57†	239.53	24.24†
	Error	4.06		9.88	
Philadelphia	Encouragement	.98	.54	4.78	1.30
	Error	1.81		3.68	

* $p < .05$
† $p < .01$

Table 4.12.   Number of Encouraged Children Having Viewing Record Scores

Number of Children	Number of Viewing Records Turned in per Child
66	1
71	2
100	3
269	4 or more
506	

Since we used the data from nonencouraged children in all the major analyses to be reported, we had no further use of the Viewing Records.

Viewing Logs

The parents of at-home children were asked once every month to note whether their child had viewed "Sesame Street" the previous day. If the child had not viewed, he was assigned a 1; if he had viewed once, he was assigned a 2; and if he had viewed twice, he was assigned a 3. There were many children without logs. As Table 4.13 shows, less than 50 percent of

Table 4.13.   Number of Children by Site and Encouragement Condition
for Whom Viewing Logs Were and Were Not Available

	Viewing Logs Available			Viewing Logs Not Available		
Site	En-couraged	Non-En-couraged	Total	En-couraged	Non-En-couraged	Total
Boston	70	46	116	5	1	6
Philadelphia	74	26	100	3	1	4
Durham	89	23	112	10	4	14
Phoenix	60	19	79	14	1	15
California	24	6	30	19	14	33

the California children had logs, and of these only six were not-encouraged-to-view. In addition, there were numerous children with only one or two logs. However, we computed a score for each child who had logs by adding up his total raw score, dividing this by the number of logs for that child, and then—for the sake of convenience alone—multiplying this average log viewing score by 10.

The resulting Viewing Logs score had problems of both reliability and validity. Reliability was a problem because of the fact that most children had only a single log recording based on a single viewing item. Validity was a problem because we were forced to assume that the child's level of viewing at the time of measurement was maintained over time. Moreover, the parents in the encouraged condition might have said that their child did view because, as encouraged parents, they were expected to get their child to view. As a single measure of viewing, the Viewing Logs would not be impressive.

Combining Viewing Measures

Ball and Bogatz followed the strategy of combining all four viewing measures into a composite index that was presumably more reliable than any single item. Given their design, the problems with this strategy were that many scores had to be estimated and that the composite may have been determined more by some measures than others. Ball and Bogatz estimated a great deal of missing data because neither the Viewing Logs nor Viewing Records were completed by all the parents. These scores had to be estimated on the basis of scores from the Sesame Street Test and the Posttest Parent Questionnaire. To judge by Table 7 in Chapter 2 of Ball and Bogatz, the Sesame Street Test predominated in the composite. The correlation of the two measures was .85, whereas the composite correlated .66 with the Posttest Parent Questionnaire measure, .38 with Viewing Logs, and .42 with Viewing Records. Thus, the composite must have taken on, in attenuated form, the deficits of the Sesame Street Test. Since these were severe deficits, an unbiased composite cannot include the Sesame Street Test unless it is first demonstrated that the sources of bias we outlined did not in fact operate. Nor can an unbiased composite include data from the Viewing Logs or Viewing Records which were not collected from all the children in the sample. As a consequence, no composite was possible in analyses of the total sample.

In their second report, Bogatz and Ball sensibly shifted strategy and analyzed the data for the first year of "Sesame Street" by using each viewing measure separately. This turned the focus from an attempt to gain a single reliable measure of viewing to an attempt to replicate relationships using multiple imperfect indicators of viewing. And there was no problem of estimating missing data since each viewing measure was used only in analyses of children from whom a particular measure was collected.

We applaud this last strategy, and we used it wherever possible in this report. But in conducting analyses that minimize bias it is important to plan the analysis first and to use whichever measures of viewing are appropriate to that analysis. The more numerous the imperfect measures are the better, providing that the imperfections of each measure are unique. It is much more dangerous to determine a viewing measure first and then to plan analyses around it. The latter strategy means that any systematic biases associated with that measure appear and re-appear in all analyses.

Bias Associated with the Sesame Street Test

Bias in an evaluation has two principal dimensions of interest: direction and magnitude. *Positive bias* can be said to occur when biasing factors increase the chances of showing that a program is effective. Sometimes, positive bias will inflate the magnitude of true effects, but at other times it will produce "findings" that are totally spurious and have no relationship to the program being investigated. *Conservative bias* operates in the opposite direction and can be said to occur when bias or error decreases the chances of obtaining a true difference. Conservative bias, as we understand it, can result because certain forces affect mean values; because statistical tests have low power when they are based on small samples, or when sources of extraneous variance cannot be removed from the error term for testing effects, or when it is necessary to partition respondents into categories that do not differ greatly. To illustrate this last problem, sample size and the realities of viewing might force us to create a group of light viewers to contrast with a group of combined moderate and heavy viewers. Tests of the effects of viewing that rely on such a simple dichotomy would be less powerful than tests in which nonviewers are contrasted with heavy viewers.

It is typically impossible to eliminate all sources of bias, especially in quasi-experiments, and it is the evaluator's job to decide how he is going to live with this. Our general position is simple. *If there has to be bias, then we want to conduct analyses that minimize the magnitude of bias and make it conservative in direction.* The reason for preferring conservative bias to positive bias is based upon two considerations. First, we avoid the real danger of using tests of statistical significance to endorse social programs that are noneffective and that only appear to be effective because positive bias inflates trivial relationships or causes spurious ones. Second, although conservative bias will sometimes result in concluding that a program is ineffective when an unbiased test might have demonstrated that the program made some difference, the undetected difference will have limited social consequences because it is small enough that a "limited" amount of conservative bias makes it disappear.

There is an obvious cost to preferring conservative over positive bias. We could never be fully confident that a failure to find treatment effects is due to the absence of treatment effects or is due to the countervailing force of conservative bias. Thus, in a strict sense, only one-sided inference is permitted by conservative analyses. For this reason, we will occasionally adopt a second strategy if an important effect is not obtained after conservative tests. We shall conduct a second analysis in which the bias is minimal in magnitude and positive in direction. This means that the positive and conservative analyses, when taken together, should bracket the true effect. Thus if no effects emerge with an analysis of this last kind, we can conclude that a program is ineffective. If effects do emerge when bias is positive but not when it is conservative, we can conclude that no conclusion about the effectiveness of a program can be drawn, but that the program may well be inadequate in that it fails to produce large effects. Let us now look at the Sesame Street Test to see if there is empirical evidence for our contention that it is associated with positive bias.

In response to comments by us and others about the nature of the Sesame Street Test, Bogatz and Ball reanalyzed the first-year data using each viewing measure as the sole indicator of viewing. Their analyses are used here to demonstrate that the Sesame Street Test may well have inflated estimates of the effectiveness of "Sesame Street."

In one set of analyses, Bogatz and Ball divided the total sample of economically disadvantaged children into the best-balanced quartiles that could be computed for each viewing measure, thereby creating groups that differed in the amount "Sesame Street" had been watched. Then, they analyzed the raw gain scores from the Grand Total in univariate analyses of variance with viewing group as the major factor. (The other factors were sex and, where appropriate, the at-school or at-home setting.)

The results of the analyses are in Table 4.14. They indicate that the pretest Grand Total means varied with the particular measure of viewing. When the Posttest Parent Questionnaire was used to classify children into viewing groups only 5 points separated the lowest viewing quartile (Q_1) and the highest (Q_4); but 9.2 points separated Q_1 and Q_4 when the composite of all measures except the Sesame Street Test was used to classify viewers; and adding the Sesame Street Test to the composite made the difference between Q_1 and Q_4 as large as 21.6 points. Note that this differentiation took place merely by adding the Sesame Street Test. If Bogatz and Ball had reported the results for the Sesame Street Test by itself, we can confidently predict that the pretest difference between Q_1 and Q_4 would have been much larger.

The means for the pretest–posttest raw gains are the most interesting, for the difference between the lowest and highest Grand Total gains (always Q_1 and Q_4 respectively) was about 20 points when the Posttest Parent Questionnaire was used, was 17.7 when the composite minus the Sesame Street Test was used, and was 28.8 points when the Sesame Street Test was added to the composite.[10] We can only conclude from this that the difference in gains between high and low viewers must have been well in excess of 28.8 points if the Sesame Street Test had been used alone.

The second set of analyses involved correlating each measure of viewing with the pretest and posttest Grand Total. These correlations from Bogatz and Ball are reproduced in Table 4.15. Three features of that table are worth commenting upon. First, the Sesame Street Test had the strongest relationship with the pretest Grand Total even though "Sesame Street" had not yet been broadcast ($r = .36$; other individual viewing measures vary from .12 to .07). Second, the correlation of posttest and viewing was greater than the correlation of pretest and viewing for each of the four viewing measures. And third, the raw difference between pretest-viewing and posttest-viewing correlations was greater for the Sesame Street Test (.27)

---

[10] We do not want to imply that this design, which Ball and Bogatz called their "Inferential" design, is by itself adequate for demonstrating that "Sesame Street" caused learning. The viewing groups were not equivalent at the pretest and might have been maturing at different rates, with the more knowledgeable heavier viewers maturing most quickly of all. If they were, a difference in growth rates would have appeared as larger raw gains by heavy viewers than by light viewers, and this pattern of data would have been indistinguishable from the pattern predicted if "Sesame Street" caused learning. In addition, since the encouraged children viewed more heavily than the nonencouraged children at some sites, the effects of viewing are confounded with those of encouragement when we use the ETS composite to classify viewers across the encouragement conditions. Since few children in the nation are encouraged as the ETS sample was, we are more interested in coming to conclusions about viewing than encouragement.

Table 4.14.   The Magnitude of Grand Total Gains in the First Year
with Viewing Computed in Three Different Ways

Measure		Q_1*	Q_2	Q_3	Q_4
	Pretest	83.9	81.6	85.0	88.9
Posttest Parent Questionnaire	Gains	22.2	30.4	32.2	44.2
	N	172	136	204	171
Posttest Parent Questionnaire plus Viewing Logs and Viewing Records	Pretest	80.4	84.6	85.3	89.6
	Gains	22.8	29.0	37.1	40.5
	N	172	172	159	180
All First-Year Measures Including Sesame Street Test	Pretest	75.6	84.4	87.7	97.5
	Gains	18.6	29.1	37.9	47.4
	N	198	197	172	164

* Higher quartiles mean heavier viewing.
SOURCE: G. A. Bogatz and S. Ball, *The Second Year of Sesame Street: A Continuing Evaluation,* vol. 2 (Princeton, N.J.: Educational Testing Service, Nov. 1971).

Table 4.15.   Correlation of Grand Total Scores with Various Viewing
Measures: Disadvantaged Children Only

	1 Sesame Street	2 Posttest Parent Questionnaire	3 Viewing Records	4 Viewing Logs	5 Viewing Composite Score
Pretest Grand Total	.36	.07	.12	.10	.26
Posttest Grand Total	.63	.23	.29	.28	.50
N	731	683	354	307	731

than for the other measures (range .18 to .16). It certainly seems from these analyses by Bogatz and Ball that the apparent effectiveness of "Sesame Street" was greater by about 33 percent when the Sesame Street Test was used for classifying viewers.

It must be stressed that the Sesame Street Test may not have inflated the viewing–learning relationship. It may be that the other measures, whose weakness we have explained, deflated the relationship, or it may even be that both inflation and deflation occurred. Since the possibility of an inflated relationship follows from two well-tested principles (differential statistical regression and group differences in maturational rate), we cannot afford the risk of analyzing quasi-experimental data when a source of plausible positive bias is present which could cause us to conclude that a program is effective when it is not. For this reason we do not use the Sesame Street Test when relating viewing and learning in quasi-experiments. We are better served by multiple viewing measures that have convergent validity (as these do) and no known sources of bias of any magnitude than by a single composite measure that might inflate any viewing-learning relationship.

It must be stressed, however, that inflated effects are not the same as spurious ones. The ETS team conducted multiple analyses of their data with and without the presumed bias from the Sesame Street Test, and they always found effects that they attributed to viewing "Sesame Street."

Correlates of Viewing among the Nonencouraged At-Home Children

The correlations of viewing and pretest Grand Total scores that Bogatz and Ball computed and that we reported in Table 4.15 show that viewing was not strongly related to learning among the total disadvantaged sample except for the flawed Sesame Street Test. These correlations of pretest knowledge and viewing level could have been attenuated by the pooling of at-school and at-home children, for the at-school children may have learned from school in a way that the at-home children could not. Also, viewing measures other than the Sesame Street Test were based on mothers estimating how much their child viewed at school, and for this reason the measure may not have been as valid for at-school children as for at-home ones.

For these reasons, we wanted to examine the correlation of viewing with pretest learning and moderator variables in a way that would allow us to understand the relationship among the at-home children in whom we were primarily interested. The viewing behavior of nonencouraged children is also of special interest, since most American children view "Sesame Street" without encouragement from a research team. Hence, we took the nonencouraged, at-home children from each site and correlated the two available and least-biased measures of viewing with learning and moderator variables. The ETS sampling plan called for two encouraged children for every one nonencouraged child and so the number of target children was small within sites. We averaged the within-site correlations using the weighting procedure outlined in McNemar.[11] The results of the analysis are presented in Table 4.16.

---

[11] Quinn McNemar, *Psychological Statistics,* 4th ed. (New York: John Wiley and Sons, 1971). The procedure weights each correlation in proportion to the size of the sample on which it is based.

Table 4.16.   Correlates of Viewing at Four First-Year Sites

Site	Viewing Measure	Grand Total Pre-test	Pea-body IQ	Home Educ. Index	Home Stim.-Affl. Index	Age
		Correlates				
Boston (N = 37)*	Posttest Parent Questionnaire	.12	.10	.22	.20	−.02
	Viewing Logs	.06	.02	.06	.03	−.19
Durham (N = 24)	Posttest Parent Questionnaire	.22	.17	.44†	.34	.11
	Viewing Logs	.06	−.44†	.11	.23	.19
Phoenix (N = 17)	Posttest Parent Questionnaire	.22	.53†	−.06	−.09	−.29
	Viewing Logs	.35	.29	.24	−.44	−.50†
Philadelphia (N = 26)	Posttest Parent Questionnaire	.46†	.06	.41†	.30	.09
	Viewing Logs	.23	.02	.34	.23	−.36
Average Correlation	Posttest Parent Questionnaire	.24†	.17	.28†	.21†	−.01
	Viewing Logs	.14	−.05	.18	.04	−.20

* N = number of children with all of the data; no missing data were estimated.
† p < .05.

The level of viewing reported in the Posttest Parent Questionnaire was significantly correlated with the pretest Grand Total, the Home Education Index, and the Home Stimulation-Affluence Index. The correlation with Peabody IQ $(r = .17)$ fell short of conventional levels of statistical significance. None of the correlations involving the Viewing Logs measures was statistically different from zero, and only those involving the pretest Grand Total $(r = .14)$ and the Home-Education factor $(r = .18)$ even approached the same relationship that was obtained with the Posttest Parent Questionnaire. For reasons given earlier, we believed that the latter measure had greater face validity, and we assumed, henceforth, that the heavier viewers were more knowledgeable than lighter viewers at the time of the pretest and came from homes where the level of education and interest in education were also higher. Thus, by classifying children into different viewing groups, one would be classifying them into nonequivalent groups that may be maturing at different rates. This would present a threat to internal validity, for the highest viewers may well have been the children who gained most in knowledge between the pretest and posttest for reasons that had nothing to do with "Sesame Street."

SOME SITE DIFFERENCES

We have previously characterized some of the differences between sites in terms of geographical region, racial composition of the sample, and an urban-suburban-rural dimension. Other site differences can be ascertained from the data, and Table 4.17 reports data from the at-home sample on the two SES indices, Peabody IQ, and pretest Grand Total.[12]

One striking feature of Table 4.17 is the superiority of the Philadelphia children on all four measures, indicating that these suburban children came from more advantaged homes, had higher IQ's, and knew more at the pretest. (The pretest Grand Totals have not been adjusted for the slight differences in mean age between sites. Correction would have made no difference to the superior standing of the Philadelphia sample.)

A second striking feature of the table is the similarity of the Phoenix and Durham samples and the fact that they scored lowest of all on the four measures. These were the most obviously disadvantaged sites.

Another noteworthy feature is the relative comparability on these measures of the racially mixed, northeastern, urban Boston sample and the white, western, and rural California sample, with the latter having a slight edge on both SES indicators and IQ but not on pretest knowledge scores. (In fact, the superiority of the Boston sample increases when the scores are corrected for age in order to account for the fact that the Boston sample is more than four months younger than the California sample.)

These analyses suggested that we could consider the sites as representing three distinct levels of economic advantagement and its correlates —Philadelphia being the highest, Boston and California the next highest, and Durham and Phoenix the lowest.

Tables 4.10 and 4.11, which were presented earlier, revealed that the encouraged and nonencouraged children did not differ in viewing at Boston and Philadelphia but did differ at California, Durham, and Phoenix. Moreover, the absolute level of viewing was high among nonencouraged children at the first two sites and was far from zero at the last three sites. These data on absolute viewing level corroborated the widely held belief that "Sesame Street" was successful in its first year in attracting a large audience.

---

[12] The data in Table 4.17 are also broken down by encouragement condition, and this breakdown is used in Chapter 5 as part of our check on the pretest comparability of the encouraged and nonencouraged children. Such comparability is crucial for true experiments.

Table 4.17. Summary of Pretest Data from At-Home Children

Site	Factor	N	Grand Total	Home Education Index	Home Stimula-tion-Afflu-ence Index	Peabody IQ	Mean Age in Months
Boston	Encouraged	69	85.145	244.593	10.678	89.836	47.52
	Nonencouraged	44	90.386	260.211	11.553	89.256	50.23
California	Encouraged	41	88.047	263.195	13.439	97.146	53.73
	Nonencouraged	19	80.850	261.000	12.526	96.450	53.55
Durham	Encouraged	111	72.432	219.266	9.890	74.990	52.29
	Nonencouraged	28	73.714	201.321	9.893	76.000	54.07
Phoenix	Encouraged	52	75.096	209.458	10.542	74.808	51.77
	Nonencouraged	18	77.222	205.235	9.882	93.889	50.78
Philadelphia	Encouraged	76	104.908	268.868	15.105	104.671	50.43
	Nonencouraged	27	109.296	283.148	15.630	108.111	52.96

The unexpectedly high level of viewing by nonencouraged children led Ball and Bogatz to abandon the true experiment they had planned on the grounds that the encouraged and nonencouraged children did not differ enough in viewing to make the comparison meaningful. Thus, they analyzed the data as coming from a quasi-experiment with four levels of viewing derived from the ETS composite, and this strategy led to the problems of differential growth rate and statistical regression that we mentioned earlier. Moreover, to conduct these analyses they summed across the encouraged and nonencouraged children, thereby confounding encouragement-to-view with viewing. This confounding arose because encouraged children viewed more than nonencouraged children at some sites and were therefore disproportionately represented in the heavy viewing quartiles of the ETS analysis. This meant that the causal construct in the ETS report was neither encouragement-to-view, a complex treatment composed of multiple factors including viewing "Sesame Street," nor viewing alone. The latter was of greater interest for evaluation research purposes than was encouragement-to-view, because few children in the nation have been encouraged to view by ETS field staffs while many have viewed the program without encouragement from researchers.

In the next chapter we attempt to analyze the ETS data as coming from a true experiment in which the manipulated treatment can perhaps best be described as encouragement-to-view "Sesame Street" rather than level of viewing "Sesame Street." Later, we analyze the effects of viewing independently of encouragement-to-view.

Chapter 5
The Effects of Encouragement-and-Viewing in the First-Year Evaluation

THE ADVANTAGES OF ANALYZING THE FIRST-YEAR DATA AS COMING FROM A RANDOMIZED EXPERIMENT

We have previously commented upon three advantages of treating the ETS data as coming from a randomized experiment with encouragement-to-view as the experimental treatment. The first advantage is that random assignment to conditions should make the encouraged and nonencouraged groups equivalent on the average at the pretest, thereby avoiding the threats to internal validity which arise when analyzing the performance of nonequivalent groups which receive different treatments. The second advantage is that powerful and accepted statistical tests exist for the analysis of randomized experiments whereas this is not always the case with quasi-experiments, especially when comparing the differences in pretest–posttest performance of nonequivalent groups. And thirdly, use of the Sesame Street Test or the ETS composite may cause positive bias in quasi-experiments where they are used to classify children into different levels of viewing. But the measures are not biased in this way when they are used as dependent variables in a randomized experiment to test whether equivalent groups that do or do not receive the encouragement treatment differ in viewing as a result of the treatment.

Analyzing "Sesame Street" as a randomized experiment has disadvantages. A comparison of the encouraged and nonencouraged children involves comparing a treatment group with a control group that really received some version of the treatment because many of the nonencouraged children did in fact view the program. Thus, it is more exact to state that two different amounts of the same treatment are to be compared than it is to state that the comparisons involve a treatment and a no-treatment control group.

Conservative bias is introduced when two groups that inadvertently received similar treatments are compared. In the limiting case where the treatments, however planned, are identical in the way respondents received them, the conservative bias should obscure all true effects of the treatment. In cases where the treatments actually turn out to reduce the planned experimental contrast without eliminating it, the resulting bias makes it difficult both to detect true differences and, if any are detected, to estimate their true magnitude. Thus, the failure to find effects in a randomized experiment is uninterpretable when there is "large" conservative bias, and additional data analyses are required that might be less powerful for making inferences about cause but which would permit a stronger differentiation of the dimension being evaluated—viewers and nonviewers in the "Sesame Street" case.

Strategy of Analysis

The process of analyzing the data from a randomized experiment involves several crucial steps. First of all, the experimental (encouraged) and control (nonencouraged) groups must be checked to see if they are comparable at the pretest. Because of sampling error, randomization sometimes results in nonequivalent pretest groups even if the randomization process has been correctly carried out. Another reason for checking the pretest equivalent of experimental groups is that randomization may not be maintained throughout an experiment and attrition from the experiment may be related to the experimental conditions. If it is, we can confidently conclude that the treatments caused differences in dropping out of the experiment. But for all other dependent variables the experimental groups will not be comparable at the posttest and the randomized experiment can be considered to have broken down. The threat of selective attrition is very real in those policy experiments where treatments differ in desirability or in the closeness of supervising respondents' behavior. The latter obviously applies to the encouraged children in the "Sesame Street" evaluation.

Once it is decided that the treatment groups are comparable and that certain other assumptions have been met, posttest scores can be analyzed using an analysis of covariance. This analysis adjusts group posttest scores for any chance differences between group pretest scores. But this is not its major function, since randomization ensures that any group pretest differences will be slight. The major function of covariance analysis is that it adjusts the error term for the correlation between pretest and posttest scores within conditions, and the magnitude of the adjustment is determined by the correlation between these scores. In order to take advantage of the statistical power of covariance analysis it is important, therefore, to check that the assumptions for its use have been met.

It is also important in true experiments to check that the independent variable has been successfully manipulated. We need to make sure that the experimental and control groups actually viewed "Sesame Street" for different amounts of time. If they did not, the treatment groups would be indistinguishable with respect to the amount of viewing. However, if they did differ in viewing, this would be no guarantee that they differed *only* in viewing. A later step in the analysis has to be the explication of other correlates of encouragement in addition to the amount of time that "Sesame Street" is watched.

THE TRUE EXPERIMENT

At-School Sample

Ball and Bogatz attempted to assign all the children on a random basis to conditions where they were or were not encouraged to view "Sesame Street." Unfortunately, the randomization procedure was not entirely successful, especially among the at-school children. For example, two teachers insisted that their classes should view "Sesame Street," and one insisted that the class should not view the program. These wishes were accommodated. In a strict sense, then, randomization was not accomplished, because some teachers selected the condition they were in. However, these teachers were all from the Boston sample (according to statements to us by Ball and Bogatz), and so this particular form of bias is restricted to the one site.

One tester from Durham was found to be fabricating data, and the data she collected were omitted from all analyses by ETS. She worked only with the at-school encouraged children which explains why only nine Durham children provided usable data in this particular condition. The small sample size precluded further use of these Durham children.

Neither of these particular threats to randomization occurred for the children in the Phoenix at-school sample. However, only two classes were randomly assigned to the control group and only three to the experimental group. Even if randomization procedures are perfectly unbiased it is unlikely, because of sampling error, that they will result in pretest equivalence if the units differ from each other and if a total of only five units is assigned to the two experimental conditions.

Because of these considerations, we analyzed the pretest data from the school children in Boston and Phoenix without much hope that randomization had resulted in the pretest equivalence of experimental groups. We had no information from the Boston sample about the particular classrooms that children attended, and so we used the child rather than the class as the unit of analysis. This procedure meant that the unit of analysis (the child) was not the same as the unit of assignment (the class). However, we would have had to use this procedure in any case because of the small number of classes.

Table 5.1 presents the pretest means and standard deviations for all economically disadvantaged, English-speaking, at-school children who were four years old in Boston and Phoenix. As we would expect, there are pretest differences between experimental and control groups for some learning measures among the Boston children. The encouraged children scored significantly higher than the nonencouraged on the Forms and Letters tests ($p < .05$) and marginally higher ($p < .10$) on the Sorting, Classification, and Puzzles tests as well as on the Grand Total.

There were no such learning differences among the Phoenix sample. However, as Table 5.2 shows, there were differences for the moderator variables at Phoenix. The encouraged children scored higher on the Home Education and Home Stimulation-Affluence indices and marginally higher in IQ.

In conclusion, the at-school sample of children cannot be analyzed as coming from a randomized experiment because pretest learning scores differed between treatment groups in Boston and moderator variables differed in Phoenix. Moreover, all the pretest bias was positive. This means that the more advantaged among the economically disadvantaged probably had the opportunity to see "Sesame Street." As a consequence, any effects of "Sesame Street" would be confounded with differences in maturational rate between noncomparable groups. Moreover, since all the children were at-school and so few classes were assigned to treatments, it is possible that the classroom or quality of the teacher were confounded with encouragement.

Encouraged and Nonencouraged At-Home Children

Did the Encouragement Group Differ at the Pretest? We analyzed the pretest learning and moderator variables within sites to determine whether the encouraged and nonencouraged at-home groups were comparable at the pretest. The important summary of Grand Total means at each site has already been presented in Table 4.17.

Table 5.1. Description of Pretest Learning Measures for Disadvantaged Four-Year-Old At-School Children at Boston and Phoenix

Site	Factor		Body Parts	Letters	Forms	Numbers	Sorting	Relations	Classification	Puzzles	Grand Total
						Dependent Variables					
Boston	Encouraged	$\bar{X}$	21.865	17.459	12.297	22.459	2.838	10.676	13.946	2.405	97.892
	N = 37	SD	6.079	10.381	3.886	9.700	1.424	2.539	4.796	1.518	30.457
	Nonencouraged	$\bar{X}$	21.250	14.725	10.600	18.200	2.300	10.025	12.350	1.800	87.275
	N = 40	SD	5.795	7.355	2.610	7.907	1.324	2.750	3.416	1.344	22.250
Phoenix	Encouraged	$\bar{X}$	21.081	14.054	10.000	18.973	2.216	9.459	12.027	1.919	85.243
	N = 37	SD	5.866	4.515	3.543	7.679	1.250	2.364	3.848	1.299	22.553
	Nonencouraged	$\bar{X}$	20.364	13.614	9.364	17.886	1.977	9.432	11.341	1.841	81.386
	N = 44	SD	5.843	6.066	3.458	7.192	1.338	2.905	3.941	1.293	23.853

Table 5.2. Description of Moderator Variables for Disadvantaged
Four-Year-Old At-School Children at Boston and Phoenix

Site	Factor		Home Education Index	Home Stimulation-Affluence Index	Peabody IQ
				Variables	
Boston	Encouraged	N	25	25	37
		X̄	261.200	11.800	81.243
		SD	61.821	3.937	14.677
	Nonencouraged	N	36	36	40
		X̄	256.806	11.361	83.800
		SD	47.958	2.810	16.185
Phoenix	Encouraged	N	35	35	37
		X̄	270.457	12.771	85.676
		SD	53.010	3.300	14.428
	Nonencouraged	N	43	43	44
		X̄	216.302	10.860	79.795
		SD	63.269	3.777	12.429

The means for the eight individual learning tests at Boston are in Table 5.3, and analysis of the pretest learning and moderator variables resulted in only one statistically significant difference (at the .05 level) due to the encouraged children outscoring the nonencouraged on the Letters Test. This one effect may well have been due to chance since we did not control for error rate.[1]

The pretest learning means for the at-home Durham children are in Table 5.4. Analyses of variance of these tests, the Grand Total, and

---

[1] Our general strategy of analysis was to look for patterns of replication across tests within sites and, particularly, across tests *and* across sites. The stress on patterns of replication reduced our dependence on single tests of a particular effect. It was for this reason that we did not take the error rate into account that would be expected after making as many comparisons as we did. As a matter of record, if we had used Scheffé's Test or had we adjusted the expected p value for the error rate per experiment in the manner outlined by Ryan, this effect of Letters would not have been statistically significant. The classic paper on error rate is by T. A. Ryan, "Multiple Comparisons in Psychological Research," *Psychological Bulletin* 56 (1959): 26–47.

Table 5.3. Description of Pretest–Posttest Learning Measures for Disadvantaged Children at Boston

		Variable									
		Body Parts		Letters		Forms		Numbers		Sorting	
Factor		Pretest	Posttest	Pretest	Posttest	Pretest	Posttest	Pretest	Posttest	Pretest	Posttest
Encouraged	$\bar{X}$	20.797	24.493	13.348	23.420	10.145	13.406	18.696	26.029	2.797	3.768
N = 69	SD	6.889	6.009	8.758	12.398	4.268	4.092	11.328	13.087	1.389	1.457
Nonencouraged	$\bar{X}$	19.636	23.364	17.341	26.295	10.500	12.864	22.659	30.068	2.477	3.545
N = 44	SD	6.506	6.481	10.214	15.664	3.739	4.598	13.987	15.511	1.285	1.784

Table 5.3 (cont.)

		Variable							
		Relations		Classification		Puzzles		Grand Total	
Factor		Pretest	Posttest	Pretest	Posttest	Pretest	Posttest	Pretest	Posttest
Encouraged	$\bar{X}$	10.232	11.435	12.174	15.754	2.290	2.826	85.145	114.478
N = 69	SD	3.092	3.041	4.991	4.812	1.436	1.372	32.682	37.740
Nonencouraged	$\bar{X}$	9.500	11.409	11.773	15.432	2.023	2.705	90.386	119.386
N = 44	SD	3.467	3.208	5.425	5.916	1.470	1.503	36.398	44.935

Table 5.4. Description of Pretest–Posttest Learning Measures for Disadvantaged Children at Durham

		Variable									
		Body Parts		Letters		Forms		Numbers		Sorting	
Factor		Pretest	Posttest	Pretest	Posttest	Pretest	Posttest	Pretest	Posttest	Pretest	Posttest
Encouraged	$\bar{X}$	18.072	23.351	12.622	20.847	7.523	12.054	15.820	24.955	2.072	3.225
N = 111	SD	6.287	6.205	4.332	9.974	2.873	4.072	7.561	10.640	1.340	1.582
Nonencouraged	$\bar{X}$	18.107	21.679	13.071	16.214	7.750	9.857	15.679	21.071	2.643	2.929
N = 28	SD	6.408	6.230	5.868	6.844	3.181	4.214	8.305	10.180	1.311	1.538

Table 5.4 (cont.)

		Variable							
		Relations		Classification		Puzzles		Grand Total	
Factor		Pretest	Posttest	Pretest	Posttest	Pretest	Posttest	Pretest	Posttest
Encouraged	$\bar{X}$	8.505	11.036	9.775	14.081	1.775	2.622	72.432	106.514
N = 111	SD	2.760	2.733	4.029	4.549	1.050	1.294	21.287	31.472
Nonencouraged	$\bar{X}$	8.321	10.536	10.321	12.321	1.786	2.286	73.714	92.179
N = 28	SD	2.829	3.049	3.044	4.722	1.258	1.272	24.329	27.097

the moderator variables resulted in only one effect of encouragement. This was on the Sorting Test.

The Phoenix pretest learning means are in Table 5.5, and analyses of variance of these tests and of the Grand Total showed no statistically significant differences. However, analyses of the moderator variables resulted in a significant difference in Peabody IQ scores between the encouraged ($\bar{X} = 74.81$) and nonencouraged children ($\bar{X} = 93.89$). This difference must decrease our confidence in the comparability of the two groups, although it is in some ways fortunate that the nonencouraged children had higher scores. It implies that they may have been brighter and so would presumably be maturing faster, thereby leading to conservative rather than positive bias at this one site.

The means for the pretest learning measures in California are presented in Table 5.6. The encouraged children performed significantly better on the Sorting Test, but not on any other individual learning tests, the Grand Total, or the moderator variables.

If we turn now to the advantaged children in Philadelphia, it is noteworthy that the encouraged and nonencouraged children did not differ on any learning tests (see Table 5.7) or on any moderator variables. The groups can be considered equivalent.

We also analyzed the pretest and moderator variables in two-way analyses of variance with disadvantaged site as one factor and degree of encouragement as the other. The results involving encouragement were similar to those in the analyses within sites. There was, first, an interaction of encouragement and sites on the pretest measure of Sorting; second, there was an interaction of encouragement and sites for Peabody IQ; and third, there were no effects for any of the other learning tests or moderator variables.

The foregoing analyses indicated a heartening degree of comparability between the encouraged and nonencouraged at-home children. We conducted sixty tests without correcting for the inevitable error rate problem, and four effects were statistically significant at the .05 level. They may well have been due to chance since about three false differences would be expected from sixty tests. Even if the effects were real, they should introduce a small degree of conservative bias both at Boston, where the encouraged children scored lowest on the Letters Test, at Phoenix where the encouraged children had lower Peabody IQ scores, and at Durham where the encouraged children scored lowest on the Sorting Test. Only in California was there any possibility of positive bias. But the single effect obtained there was so small that, even if it were real, it did not indicate anything but a small degree of noncomparability. Even more important than such considerations, however, is the fact that we shall place

Table 5.5. Description of Pretest–Posttest Learning Measures for
Disadvantaged Children at Phoenix

		Variable									
		Body Parts		Letters		Forms		Numbers		Sorting	
Factor		Pretest	Posttest	Pretest	Posttest	Pretest	Posttest	Pretest	Posttest	Pretest	Posttest
Encouraged	X̄	17.923	25.885	12.692	23.577	8.212	14.154	15.827	27.173	2.288	3.750
N = 52	SD	6.483	4.427	3.649	10.744	2.858	3.589	7.120	11.224	1.258	1.595
Nonencouraged	X̄	18.722	19.667	12.667	16.667	8.167	11.000	17.611	25.333	2.222	2.889
N = 18	SD	6.927	7.562	4.379	7.483	3.792	3.464	6.705	7.769	1.003	.963

Table 5.5 (cont.)

		Variable							
		Relations		Classification		Puzzles		Grand Total	
Factor		Pretest	Posttest	Pretest	Posttest	Pretest	Posttest	Pretest	Posttest
Encouraged	X̄	8.962	12.346	11.404	16.250	2.096	3.404	75.096	119.096
N = 52	SD	3.048	2.956	3.225	4.818	1.524	1.347	18.990	31.480
Nonencouraged	X̄	9.611	10.611	10.000	11.056	1.722	2.222	77.222	94.833
N = 18	SD	2.547	2.682	4.339	3.096	1.841	1.517	23.038	25.331

Table 5.6. Description of Pretest–Posttest Learning Measures for Disadvantaged Children at California

Variable

Factor		Body Parts		Letters		Forms		Numbers		Sorting	
		Pretest	Posttest	Pretest	Posttest	Pretest	Posttest	Pretest	Posttest	Pretest	Posttest
Encouraged	X̄	20.581	26.186	15.302	27.140	10.023	13.860	19.977	31.535	2.674	3.674
N = 43	SD	7.287	5.832	7.596	12.539	3.776	3.596	9.498	12.749	1.375	1.358
Nonencouraged	X̄	18.700	24.550	15.000	20.150	8.350	12.700	17.800	26.450	1.900	3.400
N = 20	SD	5.497	4.936	6.859	11.179	2.455	3.197	8.606	11.009	1.252	1.095

Table 5.6 (*cont.*)

Variable

Factor		Relations		Classification		Puzzles		Grand Total	
		Pretest	Posttest	Pretest	Posttest	Pretest	Posttest	Pretest	Posttest
Encouraged	X̄	10.163	11.651	11.744	16.465	2.395	3.395	88.047	127.186
N = 43	SD	2.563	2.477	4.293	5.184	1.383	1.178	29.119	36.540
Nonencouraged	X̄	9.350	11.350	10.700	14.550	2.600	3.350	80.850	110.800
N = 20	SD	2.434	2.134	4.001	4.883	1.314	1.137	21.261	30.280

Table 5.7. Description of Pretest–Posttest Learning Measures for
Advantaged Children at Philadelphia

		Variable								
		Body Parts		Letters		Forms		Numbers		Sorting
Factor		Pretest	Posttest	Pretest	Posttest	Pretest	Posttest	Pretest	Posttest	Pretest	Posttest
Encouraged	$\bar{X}$	25.579	28.105	16.461	32.816	11.947	15.579	24.816	36.421	3.066	4.474
N = 76	SD	5.108	3.131	7.849	12.682	3.233	2.886	9.853	10.171	1.389	1.125
Nonencouraged	$\bar{X}$	24.630	28.926	19.778	32.926	11.185	15.481	27.704	39.000	3.000	4.370
N = 27	SD	5.520	3.385	8.078	12.105	2.923	3.239	10.080	10.884	1.271	1.245

Table 5.7   (cont.)

		Variable							
		Relations		Classification		Puzzles		Grand Total	
Factor		Pretest	Posttest	Pretest	Posttest	Pretest	Posttest	Pretest	Posttest
Encouraged	$\bar{X}$	11.316	12.408	14.461	18.553	3.092	3.513	104.908	143.658
N = 76	SD	2.526	2.155	4.087	3.814	1.277	1.064	23.119	28.096
Nonencouraged	$\bar{X}$	11.630	13.000	15.296	18.889	2.630	3.444	109.296	147.000
N = 27	SD	1.984	2.236	4.131	4.228	1.363	1.188	26.536	29.167

no stress on findings from any one site. We are looking for consistencies across sites, and replication is our watchword.

Was there Differential Attrition across Encouragement Groups?

It is important to know how many pretested children dropped out of the experiment from each treatment group. Unfortunately, we could not conduct the appropriate analyses since we did not have data on the *total* pretested sample.

Some cautious inferences can be made by going back to the plan of the original design and noting that two children were to be assigned to the encouraged group for every one child in the nonencouraged group. This implies that, if attrition were unsystematic, there should have been the same two-to-one ratio among the sample of posttested children. Table 5.8 shows the number of at-home children in each group at the five sites and gives the chi-square values that resulted when we compared the expected and obtained frequency of subjects in the two treatment conditions.

Attrition was probably not a problem in Boston, California, Philadelphia, or Phoenix. But it may have been a problem at Durham where it appeared that more nonencouraged children dropped out than encour-

Table 5.8.   Estimates of Attrition at Each Site

Site	Factor	Actual children at each site	Number of children expected according to original sampling plan	χ^2
Boston	Encouraged	69	75	1.580
	Nonencouraged	44	38	
Philadelphia	Encouraged	76	69	2.330
	Nonencouraged	27	34	
Durham	Encouraged	111	93	10.846*
	Nonencouraged	28	46	
Phoenix	Encouraged	52	47	1.806
	Nonencouraged	18	23	
California	Encouraged	41	41	.006
	Nonencouraged	20	20	

* $p < .01$.

aged children. However, we did not know if more nonencouraged children actually did drop out or whether the design was not really implemented as planned in Durham. But even if treatment-related attrition did occur at this one site, it probably was not systematically related to pretest scores, for the encouraged and nonencouraged children at Durham differed only on the pretest Sorting Test.

Although treatment-correlated attrition is a major problem in some policy-oriented field experiments, we assumed at this point that it was not a problem for the first evaluation of "Sesame Street."

Did the Encouragement Groups Differ in Viewing?

As stated earlier, it was important to check that encouraged children did, in fact, view more than nonencouraged children. Three variables were used as indicators of viewing: scores on the Sesame Street Learning Test, responses to the Posttest Parent Questionnaire viewing index, and average Viewing Log scores. (Viewing Records were not collected from nonencouraged children.)

Table 5.9 shows the means and standard deviations for each measure,

Table 5.9. Description of Viewing Measures for All Sites

Site	Factor		Posttest Parent Questionnaire	Sesame Street Test	Viewing Logs
			Variable		
Boston	Encouraged 69	N	60	69	63
		X̄	5.30	6.93	22.54
		SD	.74	2.88	5.93
	Nonencouraged 44	N	42	44	42
		X̄	5.10	6.84	20.71
		SD	1.10	3.21	5.62
Durham	Encouraged 111	N	109	111	87
		X̄	4.52	6.48	21.22
		SD	1.69	3.18	5.71
	Nonencouraged 28	N	26	28	24
		X̄	2.77	2.82	12.04
		SD	2.36	2.72	3.95

Table 5.9   (*cont.*)

Site	Factor		Posttest Parent Questionnaire	Sesame Street Test	Viewing Logs
				Variable	
Phoenix	Encouraged 52	N	49	52	40
		X̄	4.45	6.08	21.38
		SD	1.42	3.53	6.70
	Nonencouraged 18	N	17	18	17
		X̄	3.29	3.61	15.29
		SD	2.23	3.03	6.00
California	Encouraged 41	N	36	41	23
		X̄	4.56	6.93	23.04
		SD	1.98	3.37	7.03
	Nonencouraged 19	N	18	19	6
		X̄	1.56	2.63	16.67
		SD	2.09	2.57	8.17
Philadelphia	Encouraged 76	N	76	76	73
		X̄	5.00	8.93	23.49
		SD	1.34	1.75	5.63
	Nonencouraged 27	N	27	27	26
		X̄	4.78	8.44	19.50
		SD	1.37	2.33	4.72

and Table 5.10 gives the results from a one-way analysis of variance of each measure at each site. In Durham and Phoenix the encouraged group scored higher than the nonencouraged group on all the viewing measures, and the differences were all statistically significant. In California, the encouraged children scored higher on both the Sesame Street Learning Test and the Posttest Parent Questionnaire viewing index but not on the Viewing Logs. (However, these last scores were completely uninterpretable because only six nonencouraged children provided the relevant data.) It appears, then, that encouraged children viewed more than nonencouraged children at these three sites.

Table 5.10. Analyses of Variance of Viewing Measures at Each Site

Site	Factor	Posttest Parent Questionnaire		Sesame Street Test		Viewing Logs	
		MS	F	MS	F	MS	F
Boston	Encouragement	1.04	1.26	.20	.02	83.97	2.49
	Error	.82		9.07		.71	
Durham	Encouragement	64.56	19.26†	298.88	31.21†	1584.10	54.54†
	Error	3.35		9.58		.04	
Phoenix	Encouragement	16.83	6.13*	81.30	6.10*	441.13	11.41†
	Error	2.75		11.62		42.16	
California	Encouragement	108.00	26.57†	239.53	24.24†	193.50	3.68
	Error	4.06		9.88		52.60	
Philadelphia	Encouragement	.98	.54	4.78	1.30	305.70	10.44*
	Error	1.81		3.68		29.29	

* $p < .05$.
† $p < .01$.

The data for the more advantaged Philadelphia group resembled those of the Boston group in that the encouraged and nonencouraged children did not differ on the Sesame Street Test and the Posttest Parent Questionnaire. However, the encouraged mean was higher than the nonencouraged mean for the Viewing Logs at Philadelphia, although not at Boston. Despite the one Philadelphia difference, we concluded that the encouraged and nonencouraged did not differ appreciably in viewing at either Boston or Philadelphia.

It is important to consider site differences in the mean levels of viewing. Boston was the only disadvantaged site where the encouraged children did not view more than the nonencouraged. Table 5.10 indicates that the failure to obtain a difference was probably due to heavy viewing by nonencouraged children rather than to light viewing by encouraged children. This is an important point, and the evidence is strong. On the Sesame Street Learning Test, with its total of 10 points, the mean in the encouraged group in Boston was 6.93, and this was the same as, or higher than, the mean of encouraged children in Phoenix, California, and Durham. But the mean in the nonencouraged group in Boston was 6.84, and this was more than a standard deviation higher than the mean of the nonencouraged children at the other disadvantaged sites. In fact, the nonencouraged children in Boston scored (non-significantly) higher than the encouraged children at two of the other three sites!

This pattern was repeated for the Posttest Parent Questionnaire index with its total of 6 points, although the pattern there was not so pronounced as with the Sesame Street Test. The mean for the encouraged group at Boston was 5.30, and it was 5.10 for the nonencouraged. In general, the difference in viewing between Boston and the other sites was greater among the nonencouraged than the encouraged.

It is also important to note that the level of reported viewing by the encouraged children in Durham, Phoenix, and California was approximately as high as that of the nonencouraged children in Philadelphia, while the reported viewing of the nonencouraged children at these three disadvantaged sites was lower than that of the nonencouraged children in Philadelphia. One preliminary implication of this data pattern was that, without encouragement, advantaged children watched "Sesame Street" more than disadvantaged children. A second implication was that, with encouragement, disadvantaged children viewed "Sesame Street" as much as advantaged children viewed it without encouragement. However, we would be more confident of these implications if the Boston sample had been similar to the other disadvantaged samples rather than —as it was—to the advantaged sample.

Were the Assumptions of Covariance Analysis Met?

The best covariates are those that are highly correlated with the dependent variable and are not correlated with each other. This ensures that the covariates predict as much as is possible of the posttest scores. In true experiments where pretest and posttest knowledge is measured on the same scale, a reliable pretest measure will almost always be the best predictor of the posttest. It also serves as a proxy for such correlates of pretest knowledge as SES, IQ, or age, for some of the differences between children in pretest learning are related to SES, IQ, or age differences.

The power of covariance analysis is enhanced by using multiple covariates if they appreciably increase the predictability of the posttest, although some power is lost since each covariate entails the loss of one degree of freedom from the adjusted within-cell error term. In general, pretest knowledge scores were the best single predictors of posttest scores, especially with the more reliable tests like the Grand Total, Letters, and Numbers. The gain that could have been expected from multiple covariance analysis, while real, would have been of relatively small magnitude, for except in Durham the multiple correlation of posttest scores with the best linear combination of pretest scores, SES, IQ, age, and sex hardly exceeded the simple correlation of pretest and posttest. Thus, we analyzed each learning test with pretest scores on that test as the sole covariate.

A first assumption of covariance analysis is that the groups being compared should be comparable at the pretest. The random assignment procedure, and our checks on it, should inspire confidence that this assumption was met. A second assumption is that the regression of the posttest on the covariate should be homogeneous in each experimental condition. We checked this for the Grand Total by regressing the posttest on the pretest for each condition at each site, examining the scatterplots visually, and then testing the within-site difference in regression by the procedure outlined in the sixth edition of Snedecor and Cochran.[2] In no case were the regression lines different (see Table 5.11), and so we concluded that this most important assumption had been met.

EFFECTS OF ENCOURAGEMENT-AND-VIEWING ON LEARNING

The foregoing analyses indicated that the experimental groups were equivalent at the pretest, that the encouraged children viewed more than

---

[2] G. W. Snedecor and W. G. Cochran, *Statistical Methods,* 6th ed. (Ames: Iowa State University Press, 1967).

Table 5.11.   Regression Equations for Pretest Grand Total on Age
at Each First-Year Site

Site	Encouraged	Nonencouraged
Boston	$Y = 43.9 + .829X$	$Y = 46.9 + .836X$
Philadelphia	$Y = 64.8 + .752X$	$Y = 48.2 + .904X$
Durham	$Y = 48.8 + .796X$	$Y = 60.4 + .431X$
Phoenix	$Y = 60.7 + .777X$	$Y = 42.4 + .697X$
California	$Y = 39.7 + 1.007X$	$Y = 12.1 + 1.221X$

the nonencouraged, and that the assumptions of covariance analysis were met at each site. Moreover, the encouraged and nonencouraged groups differed in viewing in California, Durham, and Phoenix, although they did not in Boston or Philadelphia.

Let us now examine whether encouragement caused learning, especially in California, Durham, and Phoenix, without forgetting that the encouraged children differed from the nonencouraged children in many ways other than the extent to which they reportedly viewed "Sesame Street." It is for this reason that the treatment should be thought of as "encouragement-and-viewing" rather than as "encouragement alone" or as "viewing alone." Henceforth, we shall label the treatment "encouragement-and-viewing."

Did the Encouragement Groups Differ in Posttest Knowledge at the Separate Sites?

The Major Covariance Analyses. The unadjusted posttest means for the Boston sample were presented, along with pretest means, in Table 5.3. The analysis of covariance results are in Table 5.12. There were no adjusted posttest differences at all between the encouraged and nonencouraged children, which implied that the former did not learn (or view!) more than the latter.

The unadjusted Durham posttest means in Table 5.4 suggest that the encouraged children learned more than the nonencouraged. This was corroborated by the analysis of covariance results (see Table 5.12), for statistical significance was reached for Letters, Forms, Numbers, Classification, and the Grand Total, though not for Body Parts, Sorting, Relations, or Puzzles. In these last four cases, however, the encouraged means at the posttest exceeded the comparable nonencouraged means.

Table 5.12. Analyses of Covariance of Adjusted Posttest Learning Measures for Disadvantaged Children

		Variable									
		Body Parts		Letters		Forms		Numbers		Sorting	
Site	Factor	MS	F	MS	F	MS	F	MS	F	MS	F
Boston	Regression	1697.066	72.797†	6820.545	52.897†	466.075	32.412†	10415.528	98.979†	22.406	9.524
	Encouragement	5.548	.238	5.755	.045	13.937	.969	23.636	.225	.358	.152
	Error	23.311		127.889		14.383		105.049		2.355	
Durham	Regression	1447.363	51.314†	282.173	3.218	280.810	18.885†	4508.276	57.076†	.001	.000
	Encouragement	63.925	2.266	508.119	5.795*	118.974	8.001†	319.210	4.041*	1.925	.772
	Error	28.211		87.682		14.870		78.993		2.494	
Phoenix	Regression	379.592	15.978†	444.277	4.655*	37.904	3.086	1598.370	18.297†	3.768	1.781
	Encouragement	564.039	23.742†	635.356	6.657*	132.092	10.755†	124.622	1.427	9.612	4.543
	Error	23.757		95.442		12.282		87.331		2.116	
California	Regression	1081.534	80.121†	3475.142	37.893†	287.902	38.433†	6113.778	121.632†	17.117	12.359
	Encouragement	2.936	.217	608.918	6.640*	.123	.016	100.028	1.990	.013	.009
	Error	13.530		91.704		7.688		50.265		1.444	

* p < .05.
† p < .01.

Table 5.12 (cont.)

Site	Factor	Variable							
		Relations		Classification		Puzzles		Grand Total	
		MS	F	MS	F	MS	F	MS	F
Boston	Regression	183.681	22.756†	947.141	48.857†	28.677	16.062†	91800.714	109.909†
	Encouragement	1.859	.230	.241	.012	.021	.012	6.592	.008
	Error	8.083		20.083		1.750		824.000	
Durham	Regression	86.635	11.947†	216.693	11.072†	.722	.462	32951.804	46.766†
	Encouragement	4.481	.618	83.706	4.277*	2.534	1.518	5191.595	7.368†
	Error	7.251		19.571		1.669		704.614	
Phoenix	Regression	36.473	4.597*	23.292	1.179	32.873	22.302†	15211.207	22.042†
	Encouragement	47.676	6.009*	319.346	16.168†	13.768	9.340†	8913.002	12.915†
	Error	7.934		19.752		1.474		690.128	
California	Regression	139.762	40.995†	637.927	40.558†	8.001	6.416*	51470.202	140.198†
	Encouragement	.464	.136	16.650	1.059	.135	.108	998.401	2.720
	Error	3.412		15.722		1.250		367.059	

* $p < .05$.
† $p < .01$.

The unadjusted pretest and posttest means for the Phoenix sample are in Table 5.5 and the covariance results are in Table 5.12. There were main effects of encouragement for Body Parts, Letters, Forms, Sorting, Relations, Classification, Puzzles, and for the Grand Total, although there was no effect for Numbers.

The means for the California children, the smallest sample in the overall design, are in Table 5.6. The only difference that reached statistical significance in the covariance analysis (see Table 5.12) was for the Letters Test, although most of the other posttest trends favored the encouraged over the nonencouraged.

The unadjusted posttest means of the economically advantaged Philadelphia children were presented earlier in Table 5.7, and the covariance analysis showed no differences in learning between the encouraged and non-encouraged on any test. It should be remembered, of course, that there was no evidence that the encouraged and nonencouraged differed in viewing.

The pattern of data was fairly clear. Analyses with a conservative bias showed that the encouraged and nonencouraged children in Boston and Philadelphia did not differ in adjusted posttest learning scores and did not differ in the amount of reported viewing. Similar analyses at the other sites showed that encouraged and nonencouraged children did differ on some adjusted posttest learning scores (most consistently for the Letters Test) and also differed in reported viewing. It seems, then, that learning was related to encouragement only if encouragement was related to viewing "Sesame Street."

Were there Encouragement Group Differences between Expected and Obtained Posttest Knowledge Means?

The foregoing covariance analyses did not make clear whether children in Boston, Philadelphia, and even California, learned more from "Sesame Street" than they would have done because of maturation. This question could be answered if we could compare the obtained posttest knowledge level of these children with valid estimates of what their knowledge level would have been if there had been no "Sesame Street" and only maturation.

It is possible to use pretest learning scores in two different ways to produce good estimates of posttest knowledge levels, albeit estimates that share the following common problem. Since the pretest scores were collected at a first testing session and posttest scores at a second, the obtained posttest data included variance attributable to the treatment, to maturation, and to *repeated* testing, while the estimated posttest data derived from pretest scores included variance due to maturation and to only a *single* testing.

Estimates from the Regression Equation at Each Site. For each site we examined the scatterplot of age (in months) and the pretest Grand Total for the combined sample of encouraged and nonencouraged at-home children. (The encouragement groups were, of course, equivalent at the pretest.) The regression lines were linear except in the case of the Philadelphia sample. However, there was some heteroscedasticity, for the variance in Grand Total scores tended to be higher among older children, particularly in Boston. For each site we then calculated the regression equation so that we knew how much of a growth in information would be expected for each month of age. Knowing this, and knowing the mean age of the encouraged children at the pretest, we were able to compute how much these children would have gained in the six months between the pretest and posttest. This expected gain was then added to the mean pretest knowledge level to give an estimate of the posttest knowledge level that would be expected if cognitive maturation were the only new force affecting posttest scores. Note that this estimate is derived from pretest scores and so could not have been influenced by "Sesame Street," and note further that the estimate was of the knowledge level of children whose age was identical with that of the encouraged children at the posttest.

The estimates are in Table 5.13, in the column headed "Predicted Grand Total I." They indicate that the encouraged children *as a group* learned more than was predicted for them at each of the five sites. This implies that the encouraged children in Boston, California, and Philadelphia did learn even though there was no evidence of such learning in the covariance analysis.

The preceding analysis has two features that must detract from its definitiveness apart from the confounding of the treatment and the frequency of testing. First, it might seem surprising that the raw regression coefficient was higher in Boston (2.45) and California (2.03) than in Philadelphia (1.88), although the differences were not statistically reliable. The coefficient indicated that the Philadelphia children gained 1.88 points for every month they aged while the Boston children gained 2.45 points. (Of course, the two groups did not start from comparable pretest base lines and change may have been more difficult with high scoring children who were disproportionately represented in Philadelphia. Analyses reported in Chapter 8 indicated that there was indeed a ceiling effect operating on the highest-scoring Philadelphia sample.)

Second, there was more variability about the regression line with

Table 5.13. Obtained and Predicted Posttest Grand Total Means
for Encouraged Children

Site	Mean Pretest Age	B	Obtained Posttest Grand Total		Predicted Grand Total I	t Diff. Obtained vs. Predicted	Predicted Grand Total II	t Diff. Obtained vs. Predicted
			$\overline{X}$	SD				
Boston	47.52	2.45	114.48	37.74	99.07	3.39	101.20	2.93
Durham	52.29	1.20	106.51	31.47	79.65	8.99	79.52	9.03
California	53.73	2.03	127.19	36.54	98.62	5.13		
Phoenix	51.77	1.06	119.10	31.48	82.09	8.47	82.71	8.33
Philadelphia	50.43	1.88	143.66	28.10	116.31	8.49	118.60	7.78

older children than with younger ones, and we do not know how the slope or shape of the regression line would have changed if the pretest Grand Total means had been better estimated for older children. So, we developed a second estimate of posttest knowledge that was free of these last two problems.

Estimates from the Age-Matching Procedure. Since we knew the mean posttest age of the encouraged and nonencouraged children at each site, it should be possible to select out a sample of children whose pretest age was identical to the mean posttest age in the encouraged group. The pretest learning mean of such age-matched children could then serve as the best estimate of what the posttest learning mean would have been in the absence of "Sesame Street."

Unfortunately, this estimation procedure was not as simple as it appears, because there were so few children whose pretest age in months was the same as the mean posttest age of all the encouraged children at a particular site. To counteract this problem of sample size, we examined the distribution of pretest ages for the encouraged and nonencouraged conditions combined and selected out those children whose pretest age was higher or lower than the posttest mean age by two months (at some sites) or three months (at other sites). We chose children in equal proportions from above and below the posttest mean age until a sample of about twenty was obtained whose pretest mean age matched the posttest mean age of the encouraged children at a particular site. The pretest Grand Total mean of these twenty cases then served as the expected posttest Grand Total mean of encouraged children.

Before selecting the age-matched pretest sample we ascertained at each site that the total distribution of age in months was approximately rectangular. This is important, since if age were rectangularly distributed for the pretest sample at one site (perhaps containing an equal number of children for each month between fifty and fifty-four), and if there were fewer older than younger children in the total sample, then the posttest learning mean of the total sample would be biased downward by the younger children in a way that the posttest estimate could not be. Fortunately, the age distribution appeared to be rectangular for both the total sample and the pretest subsample at each first-year site.[3]

The estimates for the relevant sites are in Table 5.13 in the column "Predicted Grand Total II." Comparing these estimates with the "Pre-

---

[3] It was unfortunately not possible to estimate the posttest Grand Total of the California encouraged sample using this procedure since these children tended to be older than children elsewhere, and there were so few children whose pretest age matched the mean posttest age. Hence, no sensitive estimate could be ascertained.

dicted Grand Total I" values shows that the two were very close, deviating by 2.29 points at the most. The results of our comparisons of the means that were obtained and that were predicted by the second estimate are in the last column of Table 5.13. As we might expect, the results replicate those from the analyses with the regression estimate.

These age-matched estimates are not perfect, of course. The samples on which they were based were as small as seventeen in one case, and there was always considerable variability about the Grand Total mean of the age-matched pretest sample. These were not the same problems as those associated with the regression estimate, and the validity of each estimate increased because the estimates gave similar values and had dissimilar weaknesses.

But there are sources of error that the estimates shared. First, there was the possibility that something other than "Sesame Street" intervened between pretest and posttest and affected the posttest learning means in all conditions. The second possibility was that the time interval between pretest and posttest was different from six months. If it were longer, the predicted scores would have been higher and the difference between what was predicted and what was obtained would have been less. (There are reasons for suggesting that the delay period was indeed slightly longer than six months, for the first "Sesame Street" season lasted this long, and pretesting and posttesting would have had to take place before and after the season.) The third possibility was that the obtained scores reflected the effects of a double testing while the predicted scores reflected the effects of a single testing. The direction of bias from such a source cannot be definitively stated, but it is most likely to inflate the posttest mean (*via* recall of previous answers or lower anxiety on taking a second test), and an increase in the obtained posttest mean should increase the difference between what was predicted and obtained.

Unfortunately, we could not sensitively estimate the magnitude of bias from any of these sources. We merely note that the interval between pretest and posttest was probably longer than six months and that the predicted scores were not influenced by repeated testing. We should also note that the encouraged and nonencouraged children learned different amounts at Durham and Phoenix and that the analyses of the randomized experiment which established this were not subject to the particular alternative interpretations that have just been listed for the estimation analyses. Thus, the correspondence between the Durham and Phoenix findings from inferentially powerful covariance analyses and the Boston, California, and Philadelphia findings from inferentially weaker estimation analyses should make us confidently conclude that encouragement-and-viewing caused simple cognitive learning in preschool children.

THE ADEQUACY OF THE LEARNING CAUSED BY ENCOURAGEMENT-AND-VIEWING

The Magnitude of Effects

One rather arbitrary tradition of estimating whether the magnitude of effects is "socially" or "educationally" significant is to test whether the pretest-posttest mean gain within a single experimental group is at least one-half of the pretest standard deviation. An analogous test when comparing a treatment and control group in a longitudinal study where maturation is taking place might be to examine whether the difference between the adjusted posttest means in the two groups is greater than the adjusted standard deviation of the posttest group.

We therefore constructed a size of effect ratio (SER):

$$ \text{SER} = \frac{\bar{X}_E{}' - \bar{X}_{\bar{E}}{}'}{\sqrt{MS'_{wg}}} $$

in which

$\bar{X}_E{}'$ = adjusted posttest mean in the encouraged condition (the pretest being the sole covariate)

$\bar{X}_{\bar{E}}{}'$ = adjusted posttest mean in the nonencouraged condition (pretest as covariate)

$\sqrt{MS'_{wg}}$ = square root of the adjusted mean squares within groups from the covariance analysis that gave the adjusted means above.

Table 5.14 gives the SER values for the learning tests from the first-year evaluation of "Sesame Street." (Only the Phoenix and Durham samples were considered since the encouragement manipulation was most successful there and since the variances did not differ between encouraged and nonencouraged children.) The .5 limit was exceeded at each of these sites for the Grand Total, Letters, Forms, and—marginally—for the Classification tests. In general, greater adequacy was obtained at Phoenix than at Durham.

In true experiments the degree of association between a treatment and its effects can also be ascertained by means of estimated ω^2, the formula for which is:

$$ est\ \omega^2 = \frac{t^2 - 1}{t^2 + df} $$

Estimated ω^2 represents the proportion of variance accounted for by a treatment (in this case, encouragement-and-viewing). Arithmetically, it

Table 5.14.   Estimates of the Magnitude of Effects of Encouragement-and-Viewing at Durham and Phoenix

	Durham		Phoenix	
Goal	SER	Est. ω^2	SER	Est. ω^2
Body Parts	.318	.009	1.334	.253
Numbers	.425	.022	.329	.006
Letters	.510	.034	.709	.080
Sorting	.189	0	.584	.050
Forms	.599	.049	.897	.125
Relations	.166	0	.673	.069
Classification	.438	.023	1.117	.182
Puzzles	.260	.004	.840	.109
Grand Total	.574	.044	.984	.149

should have a negative value if $t < 1$, but to avoid the sign change, it is arbitrarily set at zero. It should also be pointed out that t values obtained from an analysis of covariance are computed with the denominator being an adjusted standard error of a difference rather than the more normal standard error of a difference. The former will typically be lower than the latter, implying that the value of *est* ω^2 is sensitive to the particular denominator that is used in computing a t value.

The estimated ω^2 values are also in Table 5.14. The percentage of the adjusted Grand Total posttest variance accounted for by encouragement-and-viewing is 4.4 percent in Durham and 14.9 percent in Phoenix. In no case does the treatment account for 5 percent of the variance in individual learning tests in Durham, but it does so for Body Parts, Letters, Sorting, Forms, Relations, Classification, and Puzzles in Phoenix.

The foregoing analyses compared the difference in learning between encouraged and nonencouraged children at the two sites where encouragement influenced both viewing and learning. However, the analyses had to omit three sites, and some of the nonencouraged children at Durham and Phoenix did view the show. It would be useful if we could use the data from all sites and could contrast the magnitude of encouragement-and-viewing effects with those attributable to no viewing at all.

The estimated Grand Total posttest means were computed earlier and they permitted us to do this. When we took the posttest Grand Total estimates of learning that were derived from the regression equation (pretest Grand Total on age within sites), we found that the posttest Grand Total of encouraged children differed from its predicted value by half-a-posttest-standard deviation at all sites except Boston. Even in Boston, the difference was of .43 standard deviation units, indicating that the effect was nearly socially significant by this one criterion. What is significant about these tests is that they included the sites where encouraged and nonencouraged children did not differ in viewing (Boston and Philadelphia) and where they differed in viewing but not much in learning in the covariance analyses (California).

The Range of Demonstrated Effects

One criterion for assessing the range of cognitive skills taught by "Sesame Street" is to see if the adjusted posttest mean of the encouraged group exceeded that of the nonencouraged group at the 5 percent level. If there were many such statistically significant effects, we will call the range of effects socially significant.

However, it must be realized that some effects are more important than others (e.g., Letters and Numbers), because they correspond to very high priority goals. Moreover, following this strategy involves the danger of capitalizing upon chance because so many tests were conducted without adjusting the a level. Hence, a pattern of replication across sites is more meaningful than any difference at only one site.

At the two first-year sites where the encouraged and nonencouraged children viewed and learned different amounts, Body Parts, Numbers, Sorting, Relations, and Puzzles discriminated in Phoenix, while Letters, Forms, Classification, and the Grand Total discriminated in both Phoenix and Durham. When we included the California children, where encouragement was related to reported viewing more strongly than to learning, we had a third instance of encouragement-and-viewing causing the learning of letters. Finally, when we referred to the analyses of the difference between expected and obtained scores, it was evident that the Grand Total was affected by encouragement-and-viewing at all the five first-year sites.[4]

It was not possible with the first-year data to test the effects of encouragement-and-viewing on social attitudes, information about the social world, or moral development—each of which is an aspect of "cultural growth" as we understand this term. None of them was measured in the first year.

Positive Transfer. The ETS first-year evaluation was heavily tailored, and so there were few measures of transfer—unintended but desirable side effects of a treatment.

---

[4] All these are test effects, and an analysis of subtest effects is in a discussion of the second-year evaluation in Chapter 6.

Although "Sesame Street" is basically a prereading program, it is of interest to ascertain whether encouragement-and-viewing caused an improvement in reading skills. To answer this, we went to the ETS Inferential Study in which children were first grouped by viewing quartile and their pretest-posttest gain scores were then correlated with viewing quartile. For reasons enumerated in the previous chapter, this is probably a flawed design, the bias of which should cause false treatment differences to emerge, or should inflate true differences, but should not obscure true differences.

Table 5.15 shows the relevant data from a six-item reading test in

Table 5.15. Pretest and Raw Gains for the Reading Words Subtest in the First Year—All Disadvantaged Sites Combined

	Q_1		Q_2		Q_3		Q_4	
Age	Pretest	Gain	Pretest	Gain	Pretest	Gain	Pretest	Gain
Three years old	0.06	−0.06	0.00	0.03	0.00	0.08	0.00	0.19
Four years old	0.00	0.04	0.08	−0.02	0.03	0.07	0.07	0.30
Five years old	0.00	0.00	0.08	0.28	0.05	0.55	0.31	0.61

which the child was required to read six simple words one after another. These were DOG, HAT, egg, STREET, judge, and MAIL. It can be seen that the five-year-old highest viewers (who came disproportionately from the encouraged) gained an average of .61 of a word, bringing them to the point where by the posttest they read an average of .92 of these six words. Among four-year-old heavy viewers, they read an average of .37 of the six words at the end of the "Sesame Street" season. These are not impressive figures from an analysis that capitalized upon any differences in spontaneous maturation between the four viewing groups.

Perhaps the most interesting transfer questions concern the effects of "Sesame Street" on standardized tests of achievement and IQ, but none of these was available for the first-year evaluation. They would be useful as indicators of whether the encouraged-and-viewing children had benefited in those areas which have some value as "social currency" and which would indicate whether "Sesame Street's" benefits can only be detected on measures that were tailored to the series' content.

Unintended and Negative Side Effects

The Posttest Parent Questionnaire contained items that were meant to assess the frequency of parent-child interactions of relevance to "Sesame Street." Analyses within sites showed that encouragement-and-viewing was not related to the use of art objects, the grade at which children were expected to leave school, the objects he possessed at home, the educational visits he undertook, or the hours he watched television yesterday. These single items of unknown reliability indicated that "Sesame Street" probably did not increase the "passivity" of encouraged-and-viewing children, or lower their expectations, or increase their television-watching as reported by mothers.

Items for which statistically significant results appeared in some sites are in Table 5.16. At all the disadvantaged sites except Boston, the mothers of encouraged children reported that they watched "Sesame Street" more often with their child and that they talked more often with him or her about the show. They also tended to report playing more games based on the show, although statistical significance was only reached for the California sample. These data may well have reflected parents' expectations of what they thought they were supposed to say in the encouraged condition. If they did not, and if the data reflected changes in the mother–child relationship, then this would imply that parents did not surrender their imperative to teach to the television set and that they became more closely associated with some of the child's early attempts at developing preschool skills.

However, there was some evidence that the frequency of the mother reading to her child was lower in the encouraged-and-viewing conditions. The main effect of encouragement was significant in an analysis of sites and encouragement, and the effect was statistically significant in Durham. If this effect were to be replicated in the second year (and, looking ahead, it was), we would begin to suspect that viewing and reading are countervailing forces. If so, it would be especially important to establish the immediate and long-term effects of each of these sources of acquiring preschool skills.

It can be argued that "Sesame Street" might enhance the school performance of children in the encouraged-and-viewing condition, because they will know more when they arrive at school and may stand out as good students or may be more curious to learn. Less flattering arguments can also be advanced. For example, it might be argued that "Sesame Street" graduates would be used to a fast-moving format and would be exasperated by the relative tedium of formal school learning or might find the first grade curriculum boring, because they knew so much of it.

What happens to "Sesame Street" graduates in school? Bogatz and Ball tackled this problem by first finding the at-home disadvantaged children from the first-year evaluation who had entered school the next year. Then, during the fall and spring of the child's first school year, their teachers were asked to rank them, and all the other children in their class, on

Table 5.16. Selected Item Results from the Posttest Parent Questionnaire in the First Year of "Sesame Street"

Question	Boston		Durham		Phoenix		California	
	Enc.	Non-enc.	Enc.	Non-enc.	Enc.	Non-enc.	Enc.	Non-enc.
How often child read to (1 = Never; 5 = At least once a day)	2.53	2.37	2.42	3.36	2.69	2.81	2.16	2.35
Do you watch "Sesame Street" with your child? (1 = Almost always; 4 = Hardly ever)	2.08	2.39	2.10	2.69	2.24	2.71	2.49	3.30
Do you and your child talk about "Sesame Street?" (1 = Almost always; 4 = Hardly ever)	2.27	2.27	2.27	2.75	2.09	3.07	2.11	3.20
Does your child play games based on "Sesame Street?" (1 = Almost always; 4 = Hardly ever)	2.65	3.08	2.74	3.08	3.16	3.25	3.03	3.63

scales of: general readiness for school; verbal readiness (ability to match, recognize, and label letters, etc.), quantitative readiness (recognize and label numbers, count, recognize geometric forms, etc.), general intellectual functioning (part-whole relationships, sorting, classification, etc.), attitude towards school, relationships with peers, and physical motor coordination. (The scales were presented to teachers in the general context of a follow-up study on the effects of television, and there was no mention of "Sesame Street.")

Bogatz and Ball analyzed the data by partitioning the children into viewing quartiles derived from viewing measures taken during the first season and the subsequent summer. These viewing quartiles were then correlated with the teacher's percentile rankings of the target child. However, since the ETS team reported that the heaviest viewers were younger and more able than the lightest viewers and came from homes of higher SES, the viewing groups were noncomparable and differential growth rates would be expected.

There were quartile-related differences in teacher rankings in the fall but not in the spring (i.e., there were no statistically corroborated differences at the end of the first school year). This suggested that, if there were any effects of encouragement, they did not carry over into school. However, the spring ratings did not prove this, since the test lacked power.

A more powerful analysis involves treating the teacher rankings of the encouraged and nonencouraged children as though they came from a randomized experiment. We attempted such an analysis by obtaining from ETS the names of the first-year at-home disadvantaged children who entered school in the show's second year. Unfortunately, the Boston children could not be used to assess school "carry-over effects" since the encouraged and nonencouraged samples did not differ in reported viewing. Only twenty-two of the encouraged and nine of the nonencouraged children were followed up in Phoenix by ETS, while the corresponding numbers in Durham were twenty and eight. These were not large samples. Combining the Durham and Phoenix data in an analysis by encouragement and site, we discovered that the small sample of encouraged children for whom there were second-year data had viewed more than their nonencouraged cohorts in the first year and that they had scored higher on most adjusted posttest scores at the end of the first year. But there was no relationship between encouragement and teachers' rankings in the second year when the children were in school.

Little weight should be placed on the foregoing analyses of the teachers' rankings because the data were not of high quality and the samples were small. What is important, however, is the issue of how "Sesame Street" affects the performance of children as they go through school.

The Longer-Term Effects

The second ETS evaluation included 283 children who had been in the first-year sample of at-home observed children from Boston, Durham, and Phoenix, and they were assigned to the same encouragement conditions as in the first year. Hence, it was possible to examine the effects of two years of encouragement-to-view "Sesame Street."

However, the goals of "Sesame Street" differed somewhat in the second year and, to reflect this, the second-year Grand Total contained seventy-seven items from the first-year and 137 new items that dealt with content similar to that of the first year. Thus, our analysis was of the effect of two years' encouragement on a different but overlapping Grand Total from that used in the first-year evaluation.

We separated the children who were followed up by the ETS team into their original encouragement conditions at each site. Then, we examined their first-year Posttest Parent Questionnaire viewing means and their adjusted first-year posttest Grand Total means to see if the smaller follow-up samples consisted of groups that really had differed in encouragement-and viewing. The appropriate data are in the first three columns of Table 5.17 and it was immediately apparent that the Boston data could not be used for the planned analysis since the encouraged and nonencouraged children did not differ in viewing or adjusted posttest learning. Moreover, there were only eight nonencouraged children at Phoenix for whom all the learning and viewing scores were available. This was too small a number for responsible analysis.

Fortunately, the Durham group could be analyzed since an analysis of covariance with pretest Grand Total and pretest Peabody IQ as the covariates showed that the encouraged and nonencouraged groups differed in both viewing and posttest Grand Total at the end of "Sesame Street's" first season. The issue then was: How well did the two groups perform during the next year? An analysis with these same two covariates showed that the encouraged children knew marginally more ($p < .10$) than the nonencouraged *at the second-year pretest* (i.e., at the end of the first summer during which they were not encouraged but could watch re-runs of the show). This finding indicated both a trend towards the relatively short-term persistence of the encouraged child's initial advantage and also some transfer from the first year to the second-year Grand Total measures.

As required, encouraged children viewed more than nonencouraged children during the second season. The mean of the encouraged children on the second-year Posttest Parent Questionnaire viewing measure was 4.69; it was only 3.77 for the nonencouraged ($p < .004$). In addition, the encouraged group outperformed the nonencouraged on the Sesame Street

Table 5.17. Some Long-Term Effects of Encouragement

		First Year Parents' Measure of Viewing		First Year Pretest Grand Total		First Year Posttest Grand Total		Second Year Pretest Grand Total		Second Year Posttest Grand Total	
	N	X̄	SD	X̄	SD	X̄	SD	X̄	SD	X̄	SD
Boston Encouraged	61	5.27	.757	84.87	32.18	117.38	37.17	117.38	37.12	138.23	36.84
Boston Nonencouraged	35	5.03	1.191	88.80	34.69	117.00	42.62	117.00	42.62	144.14	41.46
Durham Encouraged	74	4.63	1.39	70.88	20.52	103.95	31.50	107.41	26.60	128.69	31.18
Durham Nonencouraged	22	2.95	2.28	76.55	25.27	93.00	24.37	102.27	22.34	129.23	34.54
Phoenix Encouraged	57	4.57	1.37	76.91	18.93	122.51	34.32	142.12	22.28	161.33	23.73
Phoenix Nonencouraged	8	3.63	2.39	76.88	24.78	101.63	29.83	149.75	13.71	159.63	23.77

Test at the second-year posttest (encouraged $\bar{X} = 8.94$; nonencouraged $\bar{X} = 6.66$). Despite these required differences in viewing in Durham, there was no evidence from the statistical analysis that the encouraged-and-viewing children knew more than the nonencouraged-lighter-viewing children on the second-year posttest Grand Total.

It would not seem from these analyses of the relatively small Durham sample ($N = 96$) that two years of encouragement gave a child any learning advantage over his nonencouraged peers.[5] The same conclusion is implied by the Peabody IQ scores (which were collected both at the pretest and posttest in the second year), for there was no reliable difference in IQ between the encouraged and nonencouraged groups at the end of "Sesame Street's" second year. However, data from other sites would be required before any more definite inference could be made.

THE PROCESSES WHEREBY ENCOURAGEMENT-AND-VIEWING MIGHT INFLUENCE SHORT-TERM LEARNING

This section is divided into two parts. In the first, we examine the relationship between encouragement and a child's personal characteristic to test which groups of children learned from being encouraged to watch "Sesame Street" and to test whether children from some kinds of groups learned more than children from other groups. Such tests might provide clues as to the cognitive, maturational, or social processes that intervene between encouragement and learning and that mediate the latter. The second part of the section deals explicitly with some possible mediating processes.

Socioeconomic Status, Encouragement, Viewing, and Learning

We have previously seen how sites were the best indices of SES and how sites could be considered as three levels of SES with Philadelphia being the highest, California and Boston the next highest, and Durham and

---

[5] The small sample of Phoenix children pointed to the same conclusion with respect to the Grand Total and IQ (see Table 5.17 for the relevant Grand Total means). Moreover, if we sum across encouraged and nonencouraged children at both Phoenix and Durham an interesting main effect of site appears. The children were at approximately the same Grand Total position before "Sesame Street's" first season and were comparable on the IQ and SES indices. However, they differed on the Grand Total by more than a standard deviation at the end of the second season. This may have been due to unique characteristics of the children in the Phoenix sample or to unique learning experiences that they were undergoing and that children elsewhere were not. Whatever the origins, the difference was large and may be worth investigating.

Phoenix the lowest. It is clear from Table 5.9 that the reported level of viewing was similar among encouraged children at each site (that is, at all SES levels). For example, the Posttest Parent Questionnaire means were 5.30 in Boston, 4.52 in Durham, 4.45 in Phoenix, 4.56 in California, and 5.00 in Philadelphia; and the corresponding Viewing Log means were 22.54, 21.22, 21.38, 23.04, and 23.49. Furthermore, analyses of covariance showed that encouragement-and-viewing caused widespread learning effects in Durham and Phoenix, and an effect on the Letters Test in California, while analyses of the difference between expected and obtained posttest Grand Totals showed effects in all five sites. Thus, viewing and learning took place at all levels of SES among encouraged children.

SES is confounded with the urban-suburban-rural dimension, and it is worth noting that each of these three settings was represented in the first-year sample of sites. Moreover, SES is sometimes used as a euphemism for race, and it is also worth noting that the California and Philadelphia samples were predominantly white (90 percent and 100 percent respectively), while the Durham sample was predominantly black (88 percent). In each instance, encouragement-and-viewing caused learning. (The effects of encouragement on Spanish-speaking children will be examined in the second-year evaluation where the sample of such children was larger.)

Peabody IQ, Encouragement, Viewing, and Learning

We decided to examine the effects of Peabody in analyses within each site so as to unconfound IQ and site differences in SES. At each site we regressed the Grand Total raw gain onto Peabody IQ scores for the encouraged and nonencouraged groups and tested whether there were any group differences in slope. If there were, we would conclude that encouragement-and-viewing statistically interacted with IQ to cause learning gains; and if there were not, we would conclude that there was no such interaction. We could be relatively confident of any such conclusions because the randomized experiment implies that the encouraged and nonencouraged children were comparable at each level of IQ, including having comparable pretest scores. We could not be sure of such comparability in quasi-experiments with nonequivalent groups, and the comparison of slopes would be obfuscated by any background differences between persons with comparable IQ's. In particular, pretest Grand Total scores might differ between heavier and lighter viewers with similar IQ's.[6]

---

[6] The reader interested in the reasons for avoiding raw gain score analysis in quasi-experiments should consult L. Cronbach and L. Furby, "How We Should Measure 'Change'—or Should We?" *Psychological Bulletin* 74 (1970): 68–80; or C. E.

The results of the pertinent analysis are presented in the right-hand columns of Table 5.18, and in none of the sites was there a difference in slope, and there were no consistent trends in differences across sites. This indicated that the size of the difference in Grand Total gains between encouraged and nonencouraged children probably did not depend on Peabody IQ score.

Table 5.18 also shows how Peabody IQ and the Posttest Parent Questionnaire measure of viewing were related in the ten instances that result from factorially combining five sites with two encouragement conditions. In nine of ten cases IQ and viewing were positively related, but the relationship only reached conventional levels of statistical significance among the encouraged in California and the nonencouraged in Phoenix. There was no consistent tendency for the relationship of Peabody IQ and viewing to differ by encouragement condition across sites, except for Phoenix where the effect is not easy to interpret.

Age, Encouragement, Viewing, and Learning

We wanted to use the procedure for IQ, as outlined above, to test whether the magnitude of effects of encouragement depended on the child's age. Before doing this, we had to ascertain whether age and viewing were curvilinearly related (the three-year-olds being too young for the program and five-year-olds beyond it). Inspection of the appropriate scatterplots within encouragement conditions at each site and of the data

---

Werts and R. L. Linn, "A General Linear Model for Studying Growth," *Psychological Bulletin* 73 (1970): 17–22; or E. F. O'Connor, Jr., "Extending Classical Test Theory to the Measurement of Change," *Review of Educational Research* 42 (1972): 73–97. Our use of raw gain scores in the present analysis is not a *necessary* one. We could have partialled out the variance due to the pretest Grand Total and thus examined the relationship of the adjusted posttest Grand Total to Peabody IQ. This last procedure is often superior to using raw gain scores because of the low reliability of the latter. But in this case, with estimates of internal consistency about .96 and test–retest .72 for the Grand Total, the reliability of the difference scores is high (.86). This can be computed from the formula:

$$r_{dd} = \frac{r_{xx} - r_{xy}}{1 - r_{xy}}$$

A different kind of power consideration is more directly relevant to the analyses we conducted. The statistical test for a difference between independent slopes is not a powerful one if we can judge by the power of the related test of the difference between independent correlations (see J. Cohen, *Statistical Power Analysis for the Behavioral Sciences* [New York: Academic Press, 1969]). This means that with the small samples at our disposal for within-site analyses, we may well fail to detect true differences in slope. For this reason we comment on the consistency in slope differences *across sites*.

Table 5.18. Raw Regression Coefficients for the Effects of Encouragement on Viewing and Learning (Grand Total) at Different Levels of Peabody IQ

Site	Posttest Parent Questionnaire Measure of Viewing					Grand Total Difference Score					
	Encouraged		Nonencouraged		t-Diff in slopes	Encouraged		Nonencouraged		t-Diff in slopes
	B	S_b	B	S_b		B	S_b	B	S_b	
Boston	.017	.015	−.007	.017	1.059	−.143	.137	−.066	.244	−.275
California	.082*	.029	.043	.057	.610	.339*	.184	.264	.255	.239
Durham	.015	.009	.055	.039	−.999	.032	.114	.077	.297	−.141
Phoenix	.002	.024	.105*	.033	−2.525	−.227	.282	−.215	.245	−.032
Philadelphia	.016	.013	.009	.028	.227	.081	.180	did not enter		—

* $p < .05$ for H_0: b = 0.

presented by Ball and Bogatz (Tables 12a-c) convinced us that there was no evidence of curvilinearity.

Table 5.19 shows that viewing was not related to age at any of the sites, although there were nonsignificant trends in eight of the tests. Also, there were no differences in regression line, indicating that age and encouragement did not interact to determine raw Grand Total gains.

Sex, Encouragement, Viewing, and Learning

To examine whether encouraged boys and girls viewed "Sesame Street" in equal amounts and learned equally from it we took the Durham and Phoenix data from the at-home sample and analyzed all the learning tests in a covariance analysis in which sex and encouragement were the factors and the relevant pretest learning score was the sole covariate.

The data for the Grand Total are in Table 5.20. The disadvantaged boys lagged behind the girls in knowledge at the pretest, which is a well-documented phenomenon at this age. There were no interactions of encouragement and sex at either site for any of the tests, indicating that the effects of encouragement were similar for boys and girls, a finding that can be tested on the second-year sample also.

Encouragement, Mother-Child Interaction of Relevance to "Sesame Street," Viewing, and Learning

We saw earlier in this chapter how the mothers of encouraged children reported (1) more watching the show with their child, (2) more talking with him about the show, and (3) more playing games with him that were based on the show. This being the case, it was not clear whether the construct causing learning was viewing, the new mother-child interaction pattern attributable to encouragement, or some other correlate of encouragement.

To examine the mother-child interaction issue, we constructed a simple index of the sum of responses to the three interaction items, and these sums were then subtracted from a constant so that higher scores represented greater interaction (the ETS scoring was the other way around). This index was first used to test whether the Posttest Parent Questionnaire measure of viewing and the interaction index were correlated, as we might expect them to be if only because each measure was collected at the same time on the same test. In fact, the two variables were strongly related. The correlations are in Table 5.21, and among the encouraged, they ranged from .10 to .66, the median being .46, while among the nonencouraged, they ranged from .43 to .88, the median being as high as .80. Since reported viewing

Table 5.19. Raw Regression Coefficients for the Effects of Encouragement on Viewing and Learning (Grand Total) at Different Levels of Age in Months

	Posttest Parent Questionnaire Measure of Viewing					Grand Total Difference Score				
	Encouraged		Nonencouraged		t-Diff in slopes	Encouraged		Nonencouraged		t-Diff in slopes
Site	B	S_b	B	S_b		B	S_b	B	S_b	
Boston	−.041	.049	−.010	.040	.490	−.631	.450	did not enter		—
California	−.037	.102	−.100	.167	.322	.437	.607	.189	.766	.255
Durham	−.040	.027	.038	.083	.894	.069	.335	.663	.607	.857
Phoenix	−.029	.071	−.256	.178	1.185	−.308	.847	did not enter		—
Philadelphia	−.005	.049	.074	.090	.771	−.548	.661	did not enter		—

Table 5.20.   Pretest and Posttest Grand Totals by Sex and Encouragement at Durham and Phoenix

Site		Conditions	N	Pretest Grand Total	Posttest Grand Total
Durham	Boys	Encouraged	20	71.90	119.55
		Nonencouraged	5	74.20	81.60
	Girls	Encouraged	32	77.09	118.81
		Nonencouraged	13	78.39	99.92
Phoenix	Boys	Encouraged	60	70.32	102.43
		Nonencouraged	15	67.93	81.60
	Girls	Encouraged	51	74.92	111.31
		Nonencouraged	13	80.39	104.39

and interaction were so highly related it is impossible to unconfound adequately the effects of viewing and of the reported mother-child interaction.

A noteworthy feature of Table 5.21 is that the correlations of viewing and mother-child interaction were lower in the Philadelphia advantaged site than elsewhere. This may have been due, in part, to the restricted

Table 5.21.   Correlation between the Posttest Parent Questionnaire Measure of Viewing and the Mother–Child Interaction Index in the First-Year Evaluation

Site	Condition	Correlation
Boston	Encouraged	.65
	Nonencouraged	.59
California	Encouraged	.66
	Nonencouraged	.81
Durham	Encouraged	.10
	Nonencouraged	.88
Phoenix	Encouraged	.46
	Nonencouraged	.80
Philadelphia	Encouraged	.25
	Nonencouraged	.43

viewing variability at Philadelphia. But it may also have been due to the unexpected fact that, while Philadelphia mothers reported a higher frequency of playing "Sesame Street" games with their children than did mothers in the other sites, they also reported less watching the show with their children. In other words, the relationship between the interaction items differed at the advantaged site where mothers more often played games based on the series but viewed it less often with their children.

EVIDENCE THAT SOME SPECIAL FACTORS OPERATED IN THE ENCOURAGED CONDITION

An interesting fact emerged when comparing the total variance associated with a common set of predictors in the encouraged and nonencouraged conditions. Table 5.22 shows some results from a multiple regression analysis in which the posttest Grand Total was the criterion and the predictors were the pretest Grand Total (entered first), age, sex, the Posttest Parent Questionnaire measure of viewing, Peabody IQ, and the Home Stimulation-Affluence Index. More variance in the posttest Grand Total is associated with the predictors in the nonencouraged than in the encouraged condition, even though random assignment meant that the predictors did not differ across encouragement groups except for the fact that viewing was heavier, and viewing variance was less, among the encouraged. (However, the small differences in viewing variance [see Table 5.9] did not seem to be of a magnitude to account for the difference in R^2. Nor could encouragement-related differences in posttest Grand Total variances account for the effect since the posttest variances did not differ between encouragement groups.) Thus, the R^2 differences seemed real. They suggested to us that the encouragement-to-view treatment may have been related to unknown factors which were not included in the system of predictors that we used, and which suppressed normal associations between the predictors and learning. If discovered, such variables would be important for determining how encouragement caused learning.

Encouragement, Viewing, and Learning

Some evidence indicated that encouragement-to-view "Sesame Street" may have caused learning because encouragement increased viewing. The major reason for this was that in sites where encouragement caused higher viewing than nonencouragement (California, Durham, and Phoenix), it also caused more learning on some tests. But in sites where encouragement did not cause more viewing than nonencouragement (Boston and Philadelphia), it did not cause more learning. These last "no difference"

Table 5.22. Variance in the Posttest Grand Total (R^2) Associated with the Linear Combination of Pretest Grand Total, Viewing Measure, Age, Sex, Peabody IQ, and Home Stimulation-Affluence Index at Four First-Year Sites

| | Posttest Parent Questionnaire Measure | | | | Viewing Log Measure | | | |
	Boston	Durham	Phoenix	Phila-delphia	Boston	Durham	Phoenix	Phila-delphia
Encouraged	.56	.38	.31	.49	.55	.34	.28	.44
Nonencouraged	.62	.66	.50	.71	.59	.70	.56	.77

findings are important since they imply that encouragement had no effects other than those attributable to viewing. (If there were effects attributable to the nonviewing aspects of the complex encouragement treatment, we might have expected the encouraged children in Philadelphia and Boston to have outperformed their nonencouraged counterparts even though they did not view "Sesame Street" any more heavily.)

Such a pattern of site differences does not prove that encouragement caused viewing and that viewing alone caused learning. The pattern could have emerged for any of three reasons. First, encouragement and viewing might have interacted in such a fashion that encouraged and nonencouraged children learned different amounts only if they were light viewers. Second, the pattern could have emerged, because encouraged parents knew they were expected to say on the posttest questionnaire that their children had viewed the program and because the testers knew which children were encouraged and treated these children differently from nonencouraged children at the posttest. Finally, it might have been that viewing did indeed cause learning but that in some sites other correlates of encouragement inflated the encouragement-learning relationship above and beyond the relationship due to viewing and learning. In other words, it is possible to have a relationship:

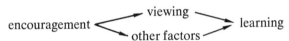

Encouragement, Tester Biases, and Learning

Testers could bias responses either by inadvertently making some types of respondents more anxious than others or by selectively reinforcing respondents for the correct response. In the case of "Sesame Street" we know that Ball and Bogatz had the foresight to select testers from the local community, which probably attenuated the bias that occurs when middle-class adults test economically disadvantaged children. However, we know from comments by Ball to us that testers were also responsible for implementing the encouragement manipulation in an unknown number of cases. These testers knew the treatment that a child was receiving and the effects it was meant to bring about; and they could relate these effects to specific responses to posttest items. Thus, they were in an excellent position to bias the learning responses of encouraged children, however careful and conscientious they may have been. In addition, the viewing scores of encouraged children could have been inflated either because parents knew they were supposed to make their children view more frequently or because, in the case of the Sesame Street Test, the encouraged children had access to nonbroadcast information about "Sesame Street" characters as part of the treatment. If these factors operated, encouraged children would have scored higher on tests of both viewing and posttest learning.

A different source of tester bias may have operated as high viewers were tested, and this bias is also related to the encouragement treatment since encouraged children viewed more heavily. Testers could have learned how much children viewed through inspection of the continuously collected Viewing Logs or Viewing Records data or because posttest learning was assessed *after* administering the Sesame Street Test or the Posttest Parent Questionnaire. Either of these tester artifacts is possible and should influence only the scores of high viewing children at the posttest, thereby causing a correlation between viewing and learning among encouraged children.

We do not know whether tester artifacts could account for all or part of the encouragement-learning or encouragement-viewing-learning relationships. Future evaluations should take pains to employ testers who are ignorant of the treatment, whether it is defined as an experimenter-controlled treatment such as encouragement-to-view or as a treatment that is defined from ratings by respondents (e.g., as viewing would be among nonencouraged children). Such blind testing is often difficult to accomplish in the hurly-burly of field experiments when resources are limited and a heavy reliance has to be placed on field staffs whose difficult task makes them quite content if they manage to collect any data at all—blind or not blind. Nonetheless, blind testing is crucial if the construct validity of the treatment is to be strengthened by ruling out that the effect is caused by tester bias.

CONCLUSION

We have demonstrated that learning was caused as a result of ETS staff members distributing promotional material about "Sesame Street" to parents and children and then visiting the children once a week in their homes in order to encourage them to watch the program. Learning occurred on a variety of cognitive tests and was of a magnitude that is traditionally considered educationally significant. It affected black and white children; urban, suburban and rural children; three-, four-, and five-year-old children, and children of both sexes. The only possible negative side effect that we discovered in the data was that parents reported reading less to encouraged than nonencouraged children.

However, the large effects of encouragement-to-view in the first year of "Sesame Street" may not persist over two years, although the data are not definitive. In the one site where the test was possible, children encouraged to view for a second year watched the program more than children who were not encouraged in either year. But the encouraged and nonencouraged groups had similar posttest knowledge scores at the end of the second year.

In the three sites where encouragement was related to viewing "Sesame Street," encouragement was related to learning; but at the two sites where there was no association of encouragement and viewing, there was no association of encouragement and learning. This suggested that viewing "Sesame Street" mediated the relationship between encouragement and learning. However, the possibility cannot be ruled out with the evidence on hand that tester biases or other unknown factors caused or inflated the encouragement-learning relationship.

Chapter 6
The Effects of Encouragement-and-Viewing in the Second Season of "Sesame Street"

THE SECOND-YEAR EVALUATION

The second-year evaluation was very much like the first with some important exceptions. As in the first year, children were randomly assigned to treatments where they were or were not encouraged to view the program. Also, a battery of learning tests was given to children before and after the program, and the majority of the tests were simple cognitive ones with the same names as the measures used in the first year. Moreover, the children came from poor neighborhoods in Winston-Salem and Los Angeles, and both boys and girls between three and five years old were included. And as in the first year, the sample was composed of children who had not seen the program previously.

One important difference was the second-year procedure for increasing the likelihood that encouraged children would watch "Sesame Street" more than nonencouraged children. Bogatz and Ball creatively chose two sites where "Sesame Street" was available on a restrictive basis. It was only available on cable in Winston-Salem, and so the ETS team arranged for households with a target child to be provided with a cable if they had been assigned to the encouraged condition. As a matter of fact, all the target households within a block were assigned to the same treatment in order to reduce discussion among neighbors about why some homes were provided with cable and others were not. "Sesame Street" was only available in Los Angeles on UHF, and so the ETS team provided adaptors to target households and withheld them from others. Once again, assignment to conditions was on a neighborhood block basis.

However, the treatment involved more than merely providing children with the opportunity to view the show. The second-year report described the full treatment as follows:

> All children who were encouraged to view the show were visited once a month by testers who told the parents and children about the show and its importance for all preschool-aged children. The testers distributed CTW publicity materials to all encouraged parents and gave *Sesame Street* buttons and other souvenirs to the children. In Los Angeles and Winston-Salem, the homes of encouraged children were given the capability of receiving the show, if the capability was not already there (p. 34).

Another important difference between the evaluations was the omission of the at-school sample in the second year. This was altogether a wise move, since there was less urgency in generalizing to children who view at school than there was to children who view at home,[1] and since it was difficult—although not impossible—to carry through a randomization procedure in schools where teachers insisted on deciding whether "Sesame Street" should or should not be part of their curriculum.

There were no economically advantaged children at all in the second-year sample, *and this was a severe loss.* Without them it was impossible to ascertain whether economically advantaged children learned from the show and whether their gains were larger, smaller, or comparable to those of disadvantaged children. In this sense, omitting the advantaged children made the second-year evaluation irrelevant both to the issue of whether all children learned from the show and also to the issue of whether the achievement gap was narrowed by "Sesame Street." The only way that learning and SES could be related was within the economically disadvantaged. But this involved relatively restricted variability in SES, and it also involved classifying children on the basis of SES measures of only moderate validity.

Although many of the measures in the second year had the same name as measures in the first year, there were differences both in the items within tests and in the number of tests. In general, the second-year measures put relatively greater emphasis on prereading skills (Initial Sounds of Words; Decoding; Left-Right Orientation; Reading Simple Words) and on more difficult numerical skills (Counting to Twenty; Addition and Subtraction; Conservation) and less emphasis on simple associative items

---

[1] The special importance of the at-home sample, with which we have exclusively worked in this study, is pointed out by Bogatz and Ball who wrote that "the show was meant primarily for at-home preschoolers" (p. 22).

(18 percent for the Prereading Test which closely resembles Letters and 13 percent for Numbers). Moreover, there were some measures of learning about the social environment (Functions of Mailmen and Firemen) and some measures of the child's ability to recognize simple emotions (happy and sad) and of his attitude towards school and race. However, though each of these was given more weight in the second year than in the first, the absolute weight was still small in the second year. For example, the Grand Total in the second year was composed of 214 items of which only eight were from the Emotions Test and four were from the test on knowledge of community members. Finally, Peabody Picture Vocabulary IQ was measured at both the pretest and posttest in the second year, so that the transfer of learning to IQ can be examined. (This was not possible in the first year because there was only a pretest Peabody measure.)

The differences between the first- and second-year evaluations were not large, but they were important. The absence of an economically advantaged group was probably the most important loss, and it would have been preferable had there been many more measures of social and personal development as well as measures of more complex cognitive skills (problem-solving was omitted in the second year). These extra measures might have been substituted for many of the items that could only replicate findings from the previous year. Technically, the second year was superior to the first year in the use of cable and adaptors to create groups that differed in the amount of viewing; in the exclusive use of children who viewed at-home; and in the presence of at least some measures of social learning and emotional development. It was also superior in terms of the analysis, for the ETS team analyzed the second-year data as coming from a randomized experiment, as we did with the first-year data.

The second-year evaluation also involved a follow-up of some of the Boston, Durham, and Phoenix children from the first year. The purpose of the follow-up was to see if the gains from the first year persisted over time, particularly after the child entered school. We are not concerned with the follow-up children in this chapter. Instead, we focus exclusively on the sample of new viewers of "Sesame Street"—the New Study as Bogatz and Ball called it.

DESCRIPTIVE ANALYSES OF THE NEW STUDY

Design Balance

Table 6.1 shows the number of boys and girls of different ages in each of the two treatment conditions at Winston-Salem and Los Angeles. All the children had English as their first language. (The data from the sixty-six

Table 6.1.   Cell Sizes in the Second-Year Study

	Winston-Salem						Los Angeles						
	Encouraged			Not Encouraged			Encouraged			Not Encouraged			
	3	4	5	3	4	5	3	4	5	3	4	5	
Male	0	6	7	3	7	7	18	19	7	27	20	7	
Female	7	4	13	6	5	8	21	18	10	24	26	13	283

Spanish-speaking children in Los Angeles are discussed later.) It was striking that only seventy-three of the 283 children came from Winston-Salem and that, when they were divided by age and sex, the resulting cell sizes were very low (range = 0 to 13). Moreover, there were some minor imbalances in the Winston-Salem sample: about 54 percent of all the encouraged children were five years old, while only about 42 percent of all nonencouraged children were; and all the encouraged three-year-olds were female. In general, however, the Winston-Salem design was reasonably balanced, and the Los Angeles design was very well balanced as Table 6.1 shows.

The Learning Tests

There were tests of knowledge of Body Parts, Forms, Prereading (much like what was termed "Letters" in the first year), Numbers, Object Relations, Object Classification, Object Sorting, Parts of the Whole, Emotions, and the Grand Total of all the preceding tests. Seventy-seven of the 214 second-year items were identical to first-year items, and in general much the same area was covered. However, the Emotions Test, which required children to label how happy or sad they would be at certain events (e.g., when physically hurt, eating ice cream, etc.), was new; and the vocabulary-based Peabody IQ test could be used as an index of transfer. Thus, including the Emotions and Peabody tests, there were eleven areas of learning tapped by the second-year tests.

The measurement in the second year was of the same high technical quality as the first year with respect to internal reliabilities, and in the second year reliability estimates were not inflated by being computed across both economically advantaged and disadvantaged samples. The reliability data are reported in Table 8 of Bogatz and Ball, and our Table 6.2 briefly summarizes their results for the test totals. It was obvious that, with the exception of the Parts of the Whole, the tests had high internal consistency both at the pretest and posttest. For example, the Kuder-Richardson reliability for the Grand Total (a sum of all individual items) was

Table 6.2. Reliability Estimates from the Second-Year Study

	Pretest	Posttest	Test–Retest	
			Los Angeles	Winston-Salem
Body Parts	.90	.86	.36	.44
Forms	.79	.78	.45	.19
Prereading	.86	.91	.50	.52
Numbers	.88	.90	.53	.57
Relations	.76	.72	.34	.48
Classification	.82	.73	.30	.27
Sorting	.71	.72	.36	.20
Parts of the Whole	.44	.51	.26	−.01
Emotions	.80	.85	.23	.04
Grand Total	.96	.97	.57	.73

.96 at one time, and .97 at the other. Moreover, the posttest reliabilities were not higher than the pretest reliabilities.

The picture presented by the test-retest correlations (see also Table 6.2), adjusted for the effects of the encouragement manipulation, was quite different, and the test-retest correlations were not strikingly high. For example, the Grand Total was .57 at Los Angeles and .73 at Winston-Salem, and for Parts of the Whole and Emotions the correlations were strikingly low (average across sites .13 and .14 respectively). It is noteworthy that, as in the first-year evaluation, the reliability estimates were higher for the measures of simpler processes (Prereading or Letters, Numbers, Body Parts) than they were for measures of more complex processes (Object Sorting, Object Classification, Parts of the Whole).

We examined the distributions of the dependent variables at both the pretest and posttest in much the same way as for the first year. In general, the distributions were slightly positively skewed at the pretest, thereby leaving room for growth, and at the posttest they were more normal or skewed negatively within each encouragement condition. The only deviant learning test distributions were for the pretest Emotions Test at both Winston-Salem and Los Angeles, where the distributions were rectangular.

The distribution of Sesame Street Test scores was shaped like a reversed letter J at the pretest, and nearly all the children were low scorers.

At the posttest, the distributions for nonencouraged children remained the same while the distributions for encouraged children approached normal. Such a posttest difference in distribution strongly indicated that, by the posttest, encouraged children at each site recognized more characters from "Sesame Street" than did nonencouraged children.

Moderator Variables

The moderator variables were very differently related to each other in the second-year study. Whereas we had examined the pattern of correlations from the Posttest Parent Questionnaire in the first year and had derived two SES indices (one weighted toward education and the other toward affluence), when we intercorrelated the same items from the second-year sample, the correlations did not differ from zero within sites and so we were not justified in creating the two SES indices. This suggested that much of the variance in the first-year indices came from differences between sites rather than from differences between households within sites. Since we cannot compute SES indices, we are forced to rely on single items for classifying children into SES groups. These items were the same as were collected in the first year.

Viewing Measures

Three viewing measures were collected: the Sesame Street Test from children at the posttest, the Parent Questionnaire viewing measure from mothers at the posttest, and Viewing Records from parents during the viewing season. We computed our Posttest Parent Questionnaire index in the same way as for the first-year evaluation (see Chapter 4), and we divided the sum of each child's Viewing Records score by the number of monthly records collected. At Los Angeles, fourteen of the 210 children could not be assigned a score on the Posttest Parent Questionnaire measure, and there were forty-four children without Viewing Records.

Our strategy with respect to these measures was similar to that of Bogatz and Ball. They used the Sesame Street Test when analyzing whether encouraged and nonencouraged children differed in viewing, and they classified children as high or low viewers on the basis of an equally weighted composite derived from both the Posttest Parent Questionnaire and the Viewing Records. They therefore avoided the problems associated with classifying children as viewers on the basis of the Sesame Street Test.

The distribution of viewing scores deviated markedly from normal in all of the nonencouraged groups at the posttest. For example, 69 percent of the Los Angeles children scored zero on the Posttest Parent Questionnaire measure, while 97 percent did in Winston-Salem. This corroborated

Bogatz and Ball's reason for choosing these particular sites since it was possible to create a control group of children who, presumably because of restricted access to "Sesame Street," did not watch the show.

The grossly non-normal distributions detract from the value of any simple correlational analysis. Nonetheless, it was instructive to note that for the Los Angeles nonencouraged sample neither the pretest Grand Total, nor the education of either parent, nor Peabody IQ was correlated with the amount of viewing (as indexed either by the Posttest Parent Questionnaire or by Viewing Records or by an equally weighted composite of both). The highest of these twelve correlations was .08. This was not at all the case in the first year where, among the nonencouraged, viewing was significantly correlated with the pretest Grand Total and with indicators of SES, although none of these first-year correlations was high.

It is possible, then, that the criteria for self-selection into different levels of viewing were not the same in Los Angeles as they had been in the first year. It may well be that among nonencouraged children possession of a UHF set, or access to a home with such a set, was not as systematically related to indicators of economic advantage as was the amount of viewing "Sesame Street" in the first-year study when the program was freely available to all.

PRELIMINARY ANALYSES OF THE LOS ANGELES SAMPLE

Pretest Differences

Table 6.3 presents descriptive statistics for the eleven pretest learning measures. One-way analyses of variance showed that the encouraged and nonencouraged children did not differ at the 5 percent level on any of the tests. Nor did they differ on a number of individual SES items. Furthermore, the obtained frequencies of ninety-three encouraged and 117 nonencouraged children did not differ from the expected frequencies based on Bogatz and Ball's sampling plan of one nonencouraged child for every encouraged one. We were confident, therefore, that random assignment was successfully implemented and maintained at Los Angeles.

One other feature of these pretest data deserves mention. There was considerable incidental evidence that the Los Angeles children were very economically deprived. First, there was the ghetto location that Bogatz and Ball deliberately selected. Next, the children's measured IQ was low ($\overline{X} = 72$). And finally, their mothers were relatively poorly educated (on a five-point scale, the mean fell between "less than high school graduate" and "high school graduate").

Table 6.3. Pretest Learning Scores for Winston-Salem and Los Angeles

			Variable					
Site	Factor		Body Parts	Forms	Pre-reading	Numbers	Relations	Classifi-cation
Winston-Salem	Encouraged	$\bar{X}$	10.486	2.189	7.676	15.486	8.676	5.919
	N = 37	SD	4.794	1.681	4.302	7.827	3.127	3.328
	Nonencouraged	$\bar{X}$	13.944	2.778	10.167	13.528	10.278	7.056
	N = 36	SD	3.189	2.113	4.469	5.396	3.716	3.153
Los Angeles	Encouraged	$\bar{X}$	9.677	2.731	8.860	14.280	8.376	6.075
	N = 93	SD	5.046	2.237	6.324	8.530	3.629	4.312
	Nonencouraged	$\bar{X}$	10.598	2.974	8.812	14.744	8.547	6.769
	N = 117	SD	5.094	2.476	6.872	8.201	3.597	5.035

Table 6.3 (cont.)

		Sorting	Parts of the Whole	Emotions	Grand Total	Peabody IQ
Winston-Salem						
Encouraged	X̄	7.432	3.216	4.432	67.811	77.432
N = 37	SD	1.980	1.512	2.734	23.566	11.720
Nonencouraged	X̄	5.667	4.250	3.472	77.917	75.278
N = 36	SD	2.280	1.680	2.384	18.443	13.298
Los Angeles						
Encouraged	X̄	3.753	4.108	3.914	67.108	69.914
N = 93	SD	2.816	2.019	2.796	31.539	16.767
Nonencouraged	X̄	4.325	3.726	3.855	69.846	74.085
N = 117	SD	3.101	1.846	2.324	31.038	16.934

Variable

Encouragement and Viewing

There was heavier viewing by encouraged children than by nonen-couraged ones. At the pretest, only .41 of the "Sesame Street" characters were recognized by encouraged children and this rose to 6.00 by the posttest. The corresponding means among nonencouraged children were .49 and 2.21. It is possible, of course, that the information about "Sesame Street" left by ETS staff in the homes of encouraged children caused these children to recognize more characters. If so, print media rather than television might have been responsible for the differences on the Sesame Street Test. Hence, the Posttest Parent Questionnaire measure of viewing was also analyzed. It showed that 86 percent of the encouraged children reported viewing the show at least once while only 31 percent of the non-encouraged children did. There can be no doubt that encouragement was successfully manipulated.

Meeting the Assumptions of Covariance Analysis

It is clear that the encouraged and nonencouraged groups were com-parable at the pretest. Moreover, regressing the posttest onto the pretest Grand Total resulted in a regression equation $Y = 56.5 + .51X$ among the encouraged and $Y = 32.8 + .75X$ among the nonencouraged. The Snedecor and Cochran test failed to disprove the null hypothesis of homo-geneous regression.

The Effects of Encouragement-and-Viewing on Learning

We attempted to discover whether encouragement-and-viewing was related to learning by conducting analyses of covariance in which each post-test was analyzed with its own pretest as the sole covariate. The pretest and unadjusted posttest means are presented in Table 6.4, and the results of the covariance analyses are in Table 6.5. The encouraged children outper-formed the nonencouraged children on all the cognitive learning tests. The only exceptions were for the Emotions Test—the ability to label situa-tions as happy and sad—and for the Parts of the Whole Test—the ability to select an object that could be made from a set of parts. The data from the Los Angeles sample provided a striking and easily comprehensible analysis of the effectiveness of being encouraged to view "Sesame Street."

PRELIMINARY ANALYSES OF THE WINSTON-SALEM SAMPLE

Pretest Differences

Table 6.3 gives the pretest data provided by the Winston-Salem chil-dren. Analyses of variance showed that the encouraged and nonencouraged

Table 6.4. Pretest–Posttest Learning Means for Los Angeles Children

		Body Parts		Forms		Prereading		Numbers		Relations	
Factor		Pretest	Posttest	Pretest	Posttest	Pretest	Posttest	Pretest	Posttest	Pretest	Posttest
Encouraged N = 93	X̄	9.677	14.054	2.731	4.656	8.860	13.699	14.280	22.957	8.376	11.634
Nonencouraged N = 117	X̄	10.598	13.214	2.974	3.752	8.812	11.333	14.744	19.026	8.547	10.453

Table 6.4 (cont.)

		Classification		Sorting		Parts of the Whole		Emotions		Grand Total		Peabody IQ	
Factor		Pretest	Posttest	Pretest	Posttest	Pretest	Posttest	Pretest	Posttest	Pretest	Posttest	Pretest	Posttest
Encouraged N = 93	X̄	6.075	8.419	3.753	6.140	4.108	5.097	3.914	5.591	67.108	99.806	69.914	72.720
Nonencouraged N = 117	X̄	6.769	7.299	4.325	4.615	3.726	4.692	3.855	4.838	69.846	85.897	74.085	70.333

Table 6.5. Covariance Analyses of Posttest Scores for Los Angeles Children

| Factor | Variable | | | | | | | | | |
| | Body Parts | | Forms | | Prereading | | Numbers | | Relations | |
	MS	F	MS	F	MS	F	MS	F	MS	F
Regression	373.895	30.227†	211.458	52.275†	3665.342	68.550†	4723.293	81.372†	226.461	26.755†
Encouragement	60.331	4.877*	52.416	12.958†	282.515	5.284*	911.654	15.706†	78.439	9.267†
Error	12.370		4.045		53.466		58.045		8.464	

Table 6.5   (cont.)

| Factor | Variable | | | | | | | | | |
| | Classification | | Sorting | | Parts of the Whole | | Emotions | | Grand Total | | Peabody IQ | |
	MS	F	MS	F	MS	F	MS	F	MS	F	MS	F
Regression	293.374	19.783†	231.000	30.537†	57.361	15.151†	88.424	11.948†	68731.016	101.896†	2855.392	12.238†
Encouragement	86.363	5.824*	153.101	20.239†	4.633	1.224	28.262	3.819	12427.055	18.423†	557.066	2.387
Error	14.829		7.565		3.785		7.400		674.540		233.375	

* $p \leq .05$
† $p < .01$

groups were not equivalent at the pretest. The nonencouraged children scored higher than the encouraged (at the 5 percent level) for Body Parts, Prereading, Object Relations, Object Sorting, Parts of the Whole, and the Grand Total. Only the Forms, Numbers, Object Classification, and Emotions tests showed no effects. The Winston-Salem data have to be analyzed, therefore, as coming from a quasi-experiment.

It is important to note that the direction of bias was conservative. The lower pretest scores of the encouraged children implied that these children were less advanced maturationally than the nonencouraged children. They might therefore be expected to mature at a slower rate and to be further behind the nonencouraged group at the posttest. Hence, we would be especially confident in asserting that encouragement to view "Sesame Street" was effective if, despite a probable bias against the encouraged children growing more, they did in fact grow more and outperformed the nonencouraged children by the end of the television season.

Before we proceed to such an analysis we must rule out one interpretation of why encouraged children might start below their nonencouraged counterparts and might finish above them. This would be plausible if the encouraged children were younger (and so scored lower at the pretest) and brighter (and so they matured more quickly). This was not the case. The chronological age of the encouraged children was 56.4 months, and it was 54.1 months for the nonencouraged, a statistically nonsignificant difference. Furthermore, the mean pretest IQ of encouraged children was 77.4, while it was 75.3 among nonencouraged children, which was also nonsignificant.

Before attempting to analyze the effectiveness of encouragement we have to ask if the encouraged viewed more than the nonencouraged. They did. Encouraged children recognized .62 characters from "Sesame Street" at the pretest and 5.22 at the posttest, while nonencouraged children recognized .50 and .28 characters respectively. The Posttest Parent Questionnaire measure corroborated this impression, for 97 percent of the encouraged children reported viewing the show at least once, while only 3 percent of the nonencouraged did.

The Effects of Encouragement-and-Viewing on Learning

A rigorous conservative analysis of a longitudinal study where the treatment group starts below the control group at the pretest involves (1) checking whether the experimental and control time trends "crossover" between pretest and posttest, and then (2) establishing that the posttest difference favors the experimental group and is significant while the pretest difference favors the control group and is also significant.

Table 6.6 presents the pretest and posttest means for all eleven tests. Visua inspection shows "cross-over" effects for Body Parts, Forms, Prereadin; Relations, Classification, Sorting, and the Grand Total. Analysis of th simple posttest differences between encouraged and nonencourage groups showed that the encouraged group with its heavier viewers wa superior at the posttest ($p < .05$) for Body Parts, Forms, Prereadin; Relations, Sorting and the Grand Total, and was marginally superic ($p < .10$) for Numbers and Classification. Since the encouraged and view ing children had been inferior at the pretest on five of these same test (Body Parts, Prereading, Relations, Sorting, and the Grand Total), w concluded that these posttest effects that are in the opposite direction t pretest effects were not artifacts of group differences in maturational rate statistical regression, or scaling.

The preceding analysis was a stringent one. Nonetheless, effects c encouragement-and-viewing emerged. But the findings must be interprete with caution, because the means indicated that the Winston-Salem non encouraged group did not mature at all between the pretest and posttes Indeed, to judge by the Grand Total, there was a nonsignificant tendenc for scores to decline! This was surprising because the children aged mor than six months between tests, because they were better acquainted with th tests at the second session, and because they were presumably less anxiou by then about strangers coming into their homes and testing them. W would expect some growth among the control children for any of thes reasons. Yet there was no growth, and this suggested that an unknow part of the apparent learning of Winston-Salem encouraged children wa due to the inexplicable absence of change between the pretest and posttes among the nonencouraged. Were it not for the unambiguous data from th Los Angeles sample, the Winston-Salem results alone would be less thar definitive.

The breakdown by research site allows us to explain why Bogatz anc Ball were able to analyze the second-year study as a randomized experi ment even though no randomized experiment was achieved at Winston Salem. Bogatz and Ball combined the data from each site, analyzed th pretest scores, found no significant differences, concluded they probabl had a randomized experiment, and then analyzed the pretest–posttest dif ference scores using multiple covariates. Because there were three Los Angeles children for every one Winston-Salem child, the effect of non random assignment at the latter site was obscured both by the relatively greater weighting of the Los Angeles scores and by the increased error var iance that was contributed by analyzing the scores from two different popu lations as though they belonged to the same population. Despite this one

Table 6.6 Pretest–Posttest Learning Means for Winston-Salem Children

		Variable									
		Body Parts		Forms		Prereading		Numbers		Relations	
Factor		Pretest	Posttest	Pretest	Posttest	Pretest	Posttest	Pretest	Posttest	Pretest	Posttest
Encouraged N = 37	$\overline{X}$	10.486	14.081	2.189	3.541	7.676	14.216	15.486	21.649	8.676	11.081
Nonencouraged N = 36	$\overline{X}$	13.944	11.528	2.778	2.500	10.167	8.833	13.528	18.167	10.278	9.250

Table 6.6 (cont.)

		Variable										
		Classification		Sorting		Parts of the Whole		Emotions		Grand Total		Peabody IQ
Factor		Pretest	Posttest	Pretest	Posttest	Pretest	Posttest	Pretest	Posttest	Pretest	Posttest	Pretest	Posttest
Encouraged N = 37	$\overline{X}$	5.919	8.054	3.432	4.973	3.216	3.865	4.432	5.622	67.811	95.324	77.432	76.405
Nonencouraged N = 36	$\overline{X}$	7.056	6.556	5.667	3.944	4.250	4.333	3.472	4.889	77.917	75.694	75.278	71.667

critique, the randomized experiment part of the New Study by Bogatz and Ball stands as a real accomplishment in evaluation research.

AN ANALYSIS OF EXPECTED AND OBTAINED POSTTEST MEANS

Estimates from the Regression Equation

We used the total sample of pretest children at each site to compute the regression equation for the pretest Grand Total on age in months. Then we obtained the mean posttest age of the children in each combination of site and encouragement condition and used this in the regression equations to predict the Grand Total that would have been expected from children of identical age to the mean posttest age. These predicted scores are in Table 6.7, and they illustrate that the encouraged children at each site had obtained significantly higher posttest means than would have been predicted for them.

However, there was no such effect among the nonencouraged who, as a group, viewed considerably less than the encouraged. However, 39 percent of the Los Angeles children did report some viewing.

Estimates from the Age-Matching Procedure

We also computed the predicted posttest scores by the age-matching procedure outlined in Chapter 5. Table 6.7 shows that the encouraged children in Winston-Salem learned significantly more than expected whereas the nonencouraged did not.

A problem arose with the Los Angeles sample because the total age distribution was skewed. This indicated that younger children were over-represented in computing the obtained learning means whereas, with the age-matched sample, children would be taken in equal proportions around a pretest age identical to the age of the total sample at the posttest. The skewness in the total sample would lower the obtained mean, thereby inflating the difference between the obtained and the predicted means.

Hence, we selected out all the children who fell in the part of the total age distribution that was most rectangular (Rectangular Total Sample) and we computed their pretest and posttest Grand Total means together with their average age. Then we isolated a sample of children whose pretest age matched that of the new posttest average ± two months, and compared this Grand Total with the obtained posttest Grand Total of the Rectangular Total Sample. The predicted mean of the encouraged group ($N = 63$) was 85.93 and the obtained posttest Grand Total of the Rectangular Total Sample was 101.78 ($SD = 28.18$). This difference was

Table 6.7. Obtained and Predicted Posttest Grand Total Means
in the Second-Year Study

Site	Condition	Mean Pretest Age	B	Obtained Posttest Grand Total		Predicted Grand Total I	t diff. Obtained vs. Predicted	Predicted Grand Total II	t diff. Obtained vs. Predicted
				X̄	SD				
Winston-Salem	Encouraged	56.35		95.32	27.29	80.82	3.23	79.65	3.49
			1.10						
	Nonencouraged	54.11		75.69	23.94	78.35	-.67	76.14	-.11
Los Angeles	Encouraged	47.34		99.81	31.39	80.68	5.87	See text for analysis of total rectangular sample	
			1.99						
	Nonencouraged	47.33		85.90	31.85	80.66	1.78		

statistically significant at the 5 percent level. The predicted mean of the nonencouraged was 85.34 and their obtained mean ($N = 82$) was 85.31 ($SD = 28.51$). Such a difference is obviously not statistically significant. It seems clear, then, that as a group the encouraged children viewed "Sesame Street" and learned while the nonencouraged viewed less as a group and, as a group, could not be demonstrated to have learned.

THE ADEQUACY OF EFFECTS OF ENCOURAGEMENT-AND-VIEWING

The Magnitude of Effects

Following the same procedure outlined in Chapter 5 for the first-year data, we computed the size of effect ratio (SER) for the Los Angeles and Winston-Salem samples. However, it should be noted that the covariance adjustments were strictly legitimate only for Los Angeles children since the initial nonequivalence of experimental groups and the absence of growth among control children made the Winston-Salem results suspect. However, the Winston-Salem data were included, first, because we know that only 3 percent of the nonencouraged children ever saw "Sesame Street," and so the difference in viewing between encouragement groups was greater than elsewhere, and second, because the covariance adjustment removes some, but not all, of the initial nonequivalence between groups.

Table 6.8 shows that SER for the second-year Grand Total exceeded .5 at each site. However, none of the individual learning tests met this criterion, although Object Sorting, Forms, and Object Relations exceeded the level at one site and approached it at the other. Only Parts of the Whole and Emotions failed to meet the criterion at any site.

The foregoing analysis compared the difference in learning between encouraged and nonencouraged children, and some of the latter watched "Sesame Street." It would be advisable, therefore, to compare the effects of encouragement-and-viewing with the effects of no viewing at all. When we took the estimates derived from the regression equation (age and pretest Grand Total) computed on the basis of *pretest* scores within each site, we found that the encouraged posttest Grand Total differed from its predicted value at each site by more than half-a-posttest-standard deviation.

The estimated ω^2 values for the second year are also in Table 6.8, and the percentage of adjusted Grand Total posttest variance associated with encouragement-and-viewing is 7.7 percent at Los Angeles and 37.9 percent at Winston-Salem. Each of these obviously exceeds the arbitrary 5 percent criterion, although the Winston-Salem figure is probably inflated by the inexplicable absence of pretest-posttest growth among nonencouraged children.

Table 6.8.   Size of Effect Ratios (SER) and Variance Accounted for at Los Angeles and Winston-Salem

	Los Angeles		Winston-Salem	
Goal	SER	Est.ω^2	SER	Est.ω^2
Body Parts	.308	.018	1.134	.209
Numbers	.551	.066	.313	.001
Prereading	.319	.020	1.353	.296
Sorting	.481	.085	.557	.046
Forms	.499	.054	.628	.078
Relations	.422	.038	.844	.137
Classification	.336	.023	.538	.055
Parts of the Whole	.155	.001	−.266	.002
Emotions	.272	.013	.322	.001
Grand Total	.597	.077	1.603	.379

It might be helpful if we summarized the findings from the first and second years. If we consider the Durham and Phoenix first-year sites (where encouragement was most strongly related to viewing and learning), and the two second-year sites (glossing over the fact that some tests had the same name each year but differing items), the size of effect ratio exceeds .5 at four sites for the Grand Total, and it averages .5 or more for Body Parts, Letters, Forms, Relations, and Classification. The average for Numbers and Sorting was below .5, but these tests were significant at two of the sites. However, there was no indication at all that Parts of the Whole or the recognition of emotions were taught by the show. When we turned to the estimated ω^2 criterion, the results were similar—as might be expected. The Grand Total exceeded 5 percent at three of the four sites, and the highest percentages were obtained for Prereading or Letters (range = 30 percent to 2 percent), Body Parts (25 percent to 1 percent), Classification (18 percent to 2 percent), Relations (14 percent to 0 percent), and Forms (13 percent to 4 percent).

The Range of Intended Effects in the Cognitive Domain

When we began analyzing the effects of encouragement-and-viewing on test totals, taking the 5 percent confidence limit as the criterion for statistical significance, it turned out that Body Parts, Prereading, Sorting, Forms, Relations, and Classification discriminated at both second-year sites while Numbers discriminated only at Los Angeles.

When we summed across the two years in impressionistic fashion, we concluded that encouragement-and-viewing was particularly successful in the area of Letters (Prereading), Forms, and Classification, where it discriminated in four out of five sites (California is included for this analy sis because viewing did vary with encouragement); was moderately suc cessful with Body Parts, Relations, and Sorting, where it discriminated at three sites; was less successful with Numbers, where it discriminated at only two of five sites; and was hardly successful at all with more abstract prob lem-solving tasks, where, considering the first year Puzzles Test and the second year Parts of the Whole Test together, encouragement-and-viewing only discriminated at one site.[2]

We have not put much stress on *subtests* in our previous analyses for two reasons. First, the treatment by Bogatz and Ball in the second year was splendid. It was comprehensive and should have been informative to the producers of "Sesame Street." Second, subtests are not as important in summative as in formative evaluation research. The major importance of subtests results lies in showing producers where the program might be strengthened. For policymakers, however, it is usually more important to provide knowledge of more general results. For example, policymakers are concerned about whether "Sesame Street" is an adequate prereading program; and so, for them, assurances about the quality of the prereading measures and information about the prereading total results are more help- ful than data on the program's particular strengths and weaknesses within the prereading area.

We shall content ourselves, therefore, in presenting the results that Bogatz and Ball obtained in their analysis of the second-year data. They pooled the Los Angeles and Winston-Salem children, took pretest-posttest difference scores, and then analyzed these as a function of the encourage- ment treatment. This was similar to the strategy we used earlier except that we separated the sites and analyzed adjusted posttest scores. Nonethe- less, there is a high correspondence between the two analyses. In their gain score analysis, Bogatz and Ball reported significant differences in the following subtests:

Body Parts:	Naming body parts; knowing the function of body parts
Forms:	Naming forms
Matching:	Matching by form
Prereading:	Naming letters, making letter sounds, reading words
Numbers:	Recognizing numbers, naming numbers, counting from one to thirty

---

[2] These tests were the least reliable and so should be the least likely to demon- strate true differences.

Relations   Knowledge of degree, e.g., more, most, less, first, last, be-
                  tween, on, heaviest, lightest
Classification: Single classification
Sorting: Recognizing differences among objects, e.g., shape, size,
                  number, letters, and class

Using the same general design but adding pretest score, Peabody IQ,
and SES as covariates, the following additional tests revealed significant
adjusted gain score differences due to encouragement-and-viewing:

Letters: Knowledge of initial sounds and adopting a left-right orienta-
                  tion; (the latter discriminated for counting but not reading)
Numbers: Counting strategies, number/numeral correspondence (e.g., how
                  many frogs are there in the picture, adding and subtracting)

These subtest results are based mostly on the large Los Angeles sample where the Numbers posttest was related to encouragement-and-viewing.
However, Numbers did not discriminate at Winston-Salem and it only
discriminated at one first-year site.

It is worthwhile documenting the magnitude of what seemed to us to
be some of the more important and comprehensible effects. For example,
the "reading words" subtest of nine mostly monosyllabic words showed
that the encouraged children could read an average of 1.1 of these words
at the pretest and 1.9 at the posttest, while the corresponding values among
the nonencouraged children were 1.3 and 1.6. This effect, while statistically significant, seemed to be small in magnitude and may have had little
practical significance, especially in the light of an item analysis to follow.
Even restricting ourselves to the five-year-old children who showed the
greatest gains on this subtest revealed that the encouraged read 1.3 words
at the pretest and 2.4 at the posttest while the nonencouraged read 1.6 and
1.8 respectively.

When we considered counting from one to thirty (enlarged from one
to twenty in the first-year evaluation), the total second-year encouraged
sample counted up to 5.5 on the average at the pretest and 13.8 at the
posttest. The corresponding nonencouraged means were 5.2 and 10.9. In
essence, then, encouragement-and-viewing had the effect of teaching children to count up to fourteen instead of up to eleven as would be expected
of them in the course of their spontaneous maturation. This estimate of
eleven may not have been entirely accurate because some nonencouraged
children did view in the second year, thereby underestimating the effects
of encouragement-and-viewing relative to nonencouragement-and-no-view-
ing. But, on the other hand, the Bogatz and Ball analyses of subtests included the nonencouraged children from Winston-Salem who, quite surprisingly, did not mature at all as measured by the ETS tests, and this
led to a probable *overestimate* of the effects of encouragement-and-

viewing. Unfortunately, the net effect of these countervailing trends cannot be established.

It is important to list the subtests that, according to Bogatz and Ball, definitely did not discriminate between encouragement conditions in the second year. These were: recognizing geometric forms, matching objects by position, reciting the alphabet, enumerating (counting how many objects were in a group), conservation (selecting a picture with as many objects as a different configuration of the same number of objects), and parts of the whole (selecting an object that could be made from a set of parts). There were other subtests for which no statistically significant effects were obtained either with or without covariance analysis. These were: recognizing letters (selecting a letter named by the tester from a group of letters); decoding (reading words, associating words with a picture, and classifying by word rhyme), double classification (classifying objects into groups on the basis of two attributes rather than one), and knowledge of emotions.

It is not clear whether encouragement-and-viewing failed to affect learning on the preceding subtests, because less programming time was spent on these goals, or because these subtests were less well tailored to the program content than other subtests, or because the subtests had fewer items and these were lower in potential discriminability, or because these subtests were less reliable than others. Table 6.9 gives data pertinent to some of these issues. The subtests are divided into two groups: those demonstrating an unambiguous effect in each of the ETS analyses with and without covariance, and those not demonstrating any effect after covariance.

Column 1 gives the percentage of total viewing time spent on the goal area relevant to a particular subtest. There was no noticeable difference between the subtests that did or did not discriminate with respect to the mean percentage of time per viewing season spent teaching each set of goals ($\bar{X}s=$ 1.87 and 1.60 respectively). But the mean number of items in each kind of subtest differed, with the more successful tests being longer ($\bar{X}s = 11.33$ and 8.60 respectively). The mean pretest reliabilities also differed ($\bar{X}s = 72.9$ and 54.0 respectively), as did the posttest reliabilities (69.2 and 51.1). These data suggested that the "effectiveness" of encouragement-and-viewing may not be as strongly related to the amount of time per goal as to the reliability of subtests, and longer tests were typically more reliable than the shorter ones.

Range of Intended Effects in the Social and Affective Domains

The second-year evaluation assessed knowledge of the social world by asking children four questions about the function and artifacts of a

Table 6.9.   Time Spent Teaching Various Subtests, Number of Items
per Subtest, and Pretest and Posttest Reliabilities

	Time	Items	Pretest Reliability	Posttest Reliability
Subtests showing a clear effect of encouragement-and-viewing				
Naming body parts	2.1	10	.87	.77
Function of body parts	2.1	8	.82	.81
Matching by form	.3	9	.58	.52
Naming letters	2.1	8	.85	.90
Making letter sounds	.9	4	.84	.83
Reading words*	1.9	9	.52	.52
Recognizing numbers	1.5	4	.41	.44
Naming numbers	.8	6	.85	.81
Counting	3.3	30	none reported	none reported
Relations	4.8	17	.76	.72
Single classification	1.7	15	.81	.77
Sorting	1.2	16	.71	.72
$\bar{X}$	1.87	11.3	72.9	69.2
Subtests showing no effect of encouragement-and-viewing				
Recognizing geometric forms	.8	4	.70	.71
Matching by position	?	3	.25	.13
Reciting the alphabet	2.4	26	none reported	none reported
Enumeration	.2	7	.76	.77
Conservation	.5	7	.41	.32
Parts of the whole	1.2	10	.44	.51
Recognizing letters	2.7	4	.50	.53
Decoding	2.6	8	.48	.48
Double classification	.5	9	.52	.30
Recognizing emotions	3.5	8	.80	.85
$\bar{X}$	1.60	8.6	54.0	51.1

mailman and fireman. In Bogatz and Ball's analysis of the Los Angeles and Winston-Salem samples combined, the mean for encouraged children at the pretest was 2.0 and 3.1 at the posttest, while the corresponding means for nonencouraged children were 2.1 and 2.4. The difference was statistically significant. No other items about knowledge of the social world were asked although this was a goal and 2.3 percent of the total programming was devoted to social roles and functions.

We previously classified the Emotions Test as cognitive on the grounds that children were called upon to recognize and label happiness and sadness. Our classification was rather arbitrary, of course, and it may be worthwhile noting in this section that encouragement-and-viewing was not related to knowledge of emotions.

This last fact was methodologically important since the Emotions Test was used as a filter for assessing children's attitudes towards race, school, and other children. Bogatz and Ball reasoned that attitudes were related to affect and that only those children who could correctly label six out of eight behavioral situations as happy or sad could make valid discriminations about affect, and so only children reaching this criterion were given the attitudes test. Forty-one encouraged and thirty-seven nonencouraged children met the criterion at the pretest, and seventy-nine encouraged (61 percent) and seventy-seven nonencouraged (50 percent) at the posttest. The differences in these posttest percentages was not quite statistically significant ($\chi^2 = 3.09$, $df = 1$), implying, first, that encouragement-and-viewing was not strongly related to the ability to discriminate emotions and, second, that there was not much of a selection artifact between the kinds of encouraged and nonencouraged children who provided attitude data.

Children were asked whether they would be happy or sad reading a book, being in class at school, writing on paper, etc., and these items were constructed to make three scales: attitude towards race, school, and other children. Unfortunately, encouragement-and-viewing was not related to any attitude in the Bogatz and Ball posttest-only analysis of the reduced samples of encouraged and nonencouraged children. The relevant means for the encouraged group were 6.1 for attitude towards school, 2.9 for attitude towards others, and 4.5 for attitude towards the race of others. The corresponding means for the nonencouraged were 5.8, 2.9, and 4.5.

The Range of Intended and Unassessed Effects

According to Bogatz and Ball's content analysis of the second year of "Sesame Street," 4.8 percent of the time was spent teaching Reasoning and Problem-solving (down from the 8.6 percent of the previous year).

This time was divided into knowledge of inferences and of antecedent and consequent events and teaching the ability to generate and evaluate solutions to problems. No tests were made of this domain. A further 4.8 percent of the program was devoted to social interaction (differing perspectives, cooperation, division of labor, combining skills, reciprocity, conflict resolution), and no tests were made of this domain.[3] About 2.8 percent was designed to induce knowledge of the man-made environment (machines and tools, buildings and structures), and no tests were made of this. About 6.7 percent was concerned with knowledge of the natural environment (land, sky, and water; city and country; plants and animals; natural processes). This was down from 10.9 percent the previous year, and no tests were made of this domain either year. Finally, 20.1 percent was devoted to entertainment, and possible effects of this were not assessed, although entertainment was not, of course, part of the instructional curriculum.

The research evidence indicated that encouragement-and-viewing has a broad effect in the cognitive domain which was the area of highest priority to CTW. But encouragement-and-viewing cannot be demonstrated to have had any broad impact on affective development or knowledge of the social world, and there has not yet been any adequate test of its effects on higher-order concepts like double classification, problem-solving, understanding of causality, or knowledge of the man-made and natural worlds.

The Effects of Encouragement-and-Viewing on Transfer Items

The number of individual transfer items was greater in the second-year evaluation than in the first. Some of the major ones having to do with prereading and knowledge of numbers are in Table 6.10. It was obvious that encouragement-and-viewing had no effect on reading the number 27 or on naming "+" and "=" signs. Moreover, if there was any gain in recognizing the number 32, it was restricted only to Los Angeles children, and if there was enhanced learning of the superlatives "heaviest" and "lightest," it was more apparent in Winston-Salem than in Los Angeles.

---

[3] CTW has commissioned tests to measure the child's learning of justice and co-operation, and these have been in the construction stage for several years. Plans were made to test the child's learning of cooperation (e.g., helping others build a structure of blocks that one child cannot build alone) at the end of the program's second season since cooperation was explicitly taught at the end of that season. But it is not clear whether the plans were carried out or what has become of the long-awaited and patiently developed tests. Details of some tests can be obtained from D. L. McDonald and F. L. Paulson, "The Evaluation of Sesame Street's Social Goals," a paper presented at the annual meeting of the Association for Childhood Education, Milwaukee, Wisconsin, Apr. 1971. Copies can be obtained from the authors at Teaching Research Center, Monmouth, Oregon.

Table 6.10. Proportion of Children Correctly Answering Major Transfer Items in the Second Year

	Los Angeles				Winston-Salem			
	Encouraged		Nonencouraged		Encouraged		Nonencouraged	
	Pretest	Posttest	Pretest	Posttest	Pretest	Posttest	Pretest	Posttest
Recognition of No. 32	.151	.323	.222	.291	.216	.189	.333	.222
Naming No. 27	.032	.022	.051	.043	.000	.054	.028	.000
Naming + sign	.022	.043	.017	.060	.000	.000	.000	.000
Naming = sign	.011	.054	.009	.060	.000	.000	.000	.000
Knowing heaviest	.538	.613	.632	.667	.568	.703	.639	.583
Knowing lightest	.204	.280	.239	.214	.135	.595	.333	.167

The major transfer item in the first year was the ability to read words, and we saw in Chapter 5 that the gains in this area were small. Reading was more of a learning goal in the second year than a transfer test because some of the test words were explicitly taught. Nonetheless, it is instructive to examine the reading data. Table 6.11 is taken from

Table 6.11. Percentage of Children at Winston-Salem and Los Angeles
Who Correctly Answered the Reading-Related Items

Item	Encouraged		Nonencouraged	
	Pretest	Posttest	Pretest	Posttest
Which is "BIRD"	25	51	29	39
Which is "SUN"	18	26	23	24
Which is "MOP"	30	45	37	36
Read "stop"	12	25	13	22
Read "exit"	0	2	1	2
Read "TELEPHONE"	57	67	52	71
Read "SCHOOL BUS"	8	28	16	12
Read "STREET"	2	2	7	1
Read "met"	1	2	1	1
Read "love"	2	2	3	1
Read "THE"	2	8	3	3
Read "MAN"	2	2	1	1
Read "IS"	2	2	2	2
Read "BIG"	2	1	1	3
Total Read	8	13	9	11
Write name correctly	0	5	3	7

Bogatz and Ball's item analysis and gives the percentage of children from Los Angeles and Winston-Salem combined who correctly read a series of words. It was clear from these data that the encouraged children outperformed the nonencouraged in picking out the words "bird," "sun," and "mop" from several other words. But it was not clear that they outperformed the nonencouraged in any significant way on items which required reading a word as opposed to picking one out. The mean percentage of children correctly reading a word was 8 percent in the encouraged condition at the pretest and 13 percent at the posttest, while the corresponding figures were 9 percent and 11 percent in the nonencouraged condition. Moreover, most of this trend was due to reading the one word "SCHOOL

BUS," where 20 percent of the encouraged learned the word and –40 percent of the nonencouraged did!

Given the sensitivity of the mean to extreme cases, some of which are clearly evident in Table 6.11, the median may be a more appropriate measure of central tendency. The median percentages of correctly read words at the pretest were 2 percent and 3 percent in the encouraged and nonencouraged conditions respectively and did not differ from these values at the posttest.

We had to suspect, therefore, that the reading test results were statistically significant in the second-year ETS evaluation, because only four of fifteen items discriminated between encouragement conditions and three of these involved word recognition rather than reading words. There was no convincing evidence that encouragement-to-view "Sesame Street" caused such an advance in literate skills that the average disadvantaged child in the second-year study learned to read monosyllabic words.

The second-year study included both pretest and posttest measures of the Peabody IQ, so that it is possible to ask whether encouragement-and-viewing affected IQ scores. The pertinent data are in Table 6.12. The

Table 6.12. Mean IQ at Pretest and Posttest in the Encouragement Conditions at Los Angeles and Winston-Salem

	Los Angeles		Winston-Salem	
	Pretest	Posttest	Pretest	Posttest
Encouraged	69.914	72.720	77.432	76.405
Nonencouraged	74.085	70.333	75.278	71.667

effect of encouragement was not quite statistically significant at either site in our analyses of covariance, but it was marginally significant when both sites were combined.

The nature of the IQ effect has to be carefully noted. There was less indication of a gain in IQ by the encouraged children than there was of a decrease in IQ by the nonencouraged. It seemed, then, that encouragement might prevent decay rather than cause gain. It should also be noted that the magnitude of the encouragement effect was not large. The SER index for the Los Angeles sample was .227 and .344 at Winston-Salem. Thus, the effect was not larger than a gain of one-half a standard deviation and by this criterion was inadequate. However, it should also be remembered that it was not a goal of "Sesame Street" to modify even a vocabulary-based measure of IQ, and any effects in this domain were a bonus. While the Peabody Test requires children to select named objects and is a vocabulary test rather than a test of higher-order cognitive functioning, it was at least one measure in the ETS evaluations that had been used with other preschool programs. Thus, it permitted a first, coarse comparison between programs.

The Possible Negative Side Effects of Encouragement-and-Viewing

Analysis of the Posttest Parent Questionnaire showed no differences between encouraged and nonencouraged parents in their expectations for the child, including how long they thought he would remain in school; no difference in the use of artifacts of presumed educational relevance, including art objects; and no differences in attitude about the child's spontaneous desire to learn. Moreover, there were no reported differences in the number of hours the child watched television yesterday, implying that viewing "Sesame Street" is associated with a change in preferences for television programs rather than with an increase in the preference for television in general.

These results were similar to the first year, as was the only important difference to reach conventional levels of statistical significance. Table 18 of Bogatz and Ball showed that the parents of encouraged-and-viewing children reported less reading to their child than did the parents of nonencouraged children.[4] Of nonencouraged parents at Los Angeles and Winston-Salem combined, 18 percent reported reading to their child once per day, and 43 percent, several times a week. The corresponding percentages among encouraged parents were 12 percent and 32 percent. It may be remembered that this pattern was obtained at three of the disadvantaged first-year sites (although it was only statistically significant at one of them), and such replication across sites and seasons enhances the likelihood that encouragement-and-viewing decreased the amount a mother reported reading to her child.

The number of unexplored possible side effects outweighed the number of explored ones. For example, we did not know how encouragement

---

[4] Bogatz and Ball cautioned against interpreting this effect since they "were computed on small expected cell frequencies." This is a valid caution in that their analysis involved four degrees of freedom (two encouragement conditions by five meaningful independent response alternatives), and none of the nonencouraged parents reported never reading to their child while only two of the encouraged did. Thus, there are very low expected values for the "never read to child" response alternatives. However, when we omit this alternative and compute χ^2 on the basis of two encouragement conditions and four response alternatives about reading to the child "less than once a week," "once a week," "several times a week," "once a day," the value of χ^2 is 9.08, which with $df = 3$ is significant at the .05 level. The mothers of encouraged children did indeed report less reading to their child.

affected school performance—did "Sesame Street" graduates find school simple, dull, or unimaginative, and did this influence their performance or achievement motivation? Did "Sesame Street" make the children into passive learners who expected to be provided with information rather than finding it themselves and regulating their own learning? What were the opportunity costs of viewing "Sesame Street"? How did children of four pass their time before "Sesame Street" came along, and what did they gain from their previous experiences that they were not now gaining?

The Long-Term Effects of Encouragement-and-Viewing

The second-year ETS sample has not yet been tested to see if the advantages conferred by the encouragement-and-viewing treatment persisted over time, and there was obviously not enough time for the ETS team to do this for their second-year report. The issue is important, and the only available data of relevance come from the single Durham site in the first year that we analyzed in the previous chapter.

PROCESSES RELATED TO THE EFFECTIVENESS OF ENCOURAGEMENT-AND-VIEWING

Socioeconomic Status, Encouragement, Viewing, and Learning

As already noted, the second-year evaluation did not include an economically advantaged site, and there was little difference between Los Angeles and Winston-Salem in SES indicators. Thus, we could not use site as a locator variable for SES. Nor could we use either of the first-year SES indices, since there was no empirical evidence that the same SES-relevant items intercorrelated in the second year as in the first. Thus, we were constrained to use the reported years of mother's education as the best, imperfect indicator of SES, and our analysis has to involve the relatively restricted variability in mother's education that was found within economically disadvantaged sites. This was far from being an optimal procedure for assessing whether SES interacts with encouragement to determine learning gains.

We regressed Grand Total pretest-posttest difference scores onto mother's education for the encouraged and nonencouraged groups and tested whether the resulting slopes differed. Since the two encouragement groups in Los Angeles were comparable at each level of mother's education, the selection artifacts were avoided that typically plague the use of raw difference scores in quasi-experiments.

At Los Angeles, the value of the slope (B) was 3.46 $(S_b = 2.98)$ in the encouraged group and 1.43 $(S_b = 2.34)$ in the nonencouraged, implying that the encouraged children tended to gain more if their mothers had had a longer education. However, the difference was not reliable, though the statistical test is not powerful. Hence, the only justified conclusion was that encouragement and mother's education did not interact to determine Grand Total gains, though the nonsignificant trend hinted that encouragement may have had larger effects among the better educated.

An interesting fact emerged in relating the encouragement conditions to the Posttest Parent Questionnaire measure of viewing. The regression of viewing on mother's education resulted in a slope of .83 ($S_b = .26$) in the encouraged group at Los Angeles, and a slope of $-.11$ ($S_b = .26$) in the nonencouraged. This difference was statistically reliable, indicating that encouragement and mother's education interacted to determine viewing with the relationship among the encouraged being positive and with there being no relationship among the nonencouraged.

Over 90 percent of the Los Angeles children we examined previously were black, indicating once again that encouragement-and-viewing facilitated growth among these children. It is less clear whether encouragement-and-viewing caused learning in Spanish-speaking children. The best test of this was to take the sixty-six Spanish-speaking children from Los Angeles and examine whether the encouraged and nonencouraged groups were comparable in learning at the pretest but not at the posttest. The pretest analysis showed that the encouraged outperformed the nonencouraged (at the 5 percent level) on Body Parts, Numbers, Parts of the Whole, Emotions, and the Grand Total. Thus, a randomized experiment was not successfully implemented, and the more able Spanish-speaking children received encouragement to view.

The encouraged children did recognize more "Sesame Street" characters than the nonencouraged at the posttest ($\bar{X}s = 5.58$ and 3.62 respectively, $p < .05$), and their mothers reported higher viewing on the Posttest Parent Questionnaire ($p < .05$). Because viewing differed and because the problem was an important one, we conducted covariance analyses that should *approximate* a test of the program's effectiveness among Spanish-speaking children. Using pretests as covariates did not eliminate all bias; it merely reduced the magnitude of bias and left some of the pretest difference in the adjusted posttest difference. The covariance results indicated that the adjusted posttest scores of encouraged children were only significantly higher for Parts of the Whole Test, a single effect that may well have been due to chance. Since no other effects were significant, it was unlikely that the Spanish-speaking children at Los Angeles benefited from encouragement-to-view "Sesame Street" over and above any advantages that might have been conferred on nonencouraged children by viewing the show to the restricted extent they did.

The first-year evaluation of "Sesame Street" included a small sample of forty-three children from Phoenix who were designated by community leaders as being Spanish-speaking. Ball and Bogatz divided these children into viewing quartiles, and their learning gains were examined as a function of the level of viewing. The analyses showed a statistically significant correlation between viewing and raw gains ($Q1$ gain $= 24.36$; $Q2 = 29.64$; $Q3 = 49.86$; $Q4 = 75.55$). This "effect" was difficult to interpret. A selection-maturation interaction was especially likely with these children since it might have been the Spanish-speaking children in English-speaking environments who were most likely to watch "Sesame Street" and most likely to gain more on tests that relied on knowledge of the English language.[5] In addition, the first-year results from Spanish-speaking children were based on a small sample. We had to conclude, therefore, that there was no unambiguous and consistent evidence to date that Spanish-speaking children benefited from being encouraged to view "Sesame Street."

Peabody IQ, Encouragement, Viewing, and Learning

We followed the same within-site regression strategy as the first year for determining whether encouragement and Peabody IQ interacted to determine viewing or Grand Total difference scores. There was no indication of any type of relationship between viewing and Peabody IQ. The slope for the Grand Total difference on IQ was $-.51$ ($S_b = .19$) in the encouraged group and $-.44$ ($S_b = .16$) in the nonencouraged. Neither of these values differed, indicating no support for an interaction of encouragement and IQ.

Age, Encouragement, Viewing, and Learning

We repeated this procedure regressing the Grand Total difference and viewing onto age in months for the encouraged and nonencouraged children at Los Angeles. Age was not related to viewing, either as a main or interaction effect. Unlike the first year, age marginally interacted with encouragement to determine learning gains ($t = 1.67$, $p < .10$), and the difference in gains between encouraged and nonencouraged children tended

---

[5] Ball and Bogatz indicate (p. 223) that there was considerable heterogeneity in the extent to which the children's background was Spanish and in the extent to which they spoke Spanish during the day. Also, some of the children were tested in English and others in Spanish. We think it likely that the heaviest viewers were best in English and did better in terms of raw gains either because they were maturing faster in the English language or because the posttests had a higher correspondence with the program's content for persons tested in English (who would be heavier viewers) or because the testing situation is anxiety-arousing when a tester talks to the child in Spanish about the test, yet has to conduct some of the testing about the English alphabet and number sounds.

to be larger among younger than older children. (Bogatz and Ball presented a trend in the same direction, p. 121.) The relevant B value for the encouraged was $-.71$ ($S_b = .36$) and for the nonencouraged, $.08$ ($S_b = .30$), indicating also that gains tended to be greater with younger children among the encouraged and tended to be independent of age among the nonencouraged. However, these effects are marginal and are not replicated across the first- and second-year evaluations. The most reasonable conclusion at this time is that encouragement-and-viewing caused learning in three-, four-, and five-year-old children and that the size of the difference in gain between encouraged and nonencouraged children was similar in each age group.

Sex, Encouragement, Viewing, and Learning

Bogatz and Ball analyzed their second-year data with sex, encouragement, and age as the relevant factors in an analysis of variance design. Their results showed that girls tended to outperform boys at the pretest but that the gains made by each group did not differ either with or without covariance analysis except for one triple interaction for Classification that may well have been due to chance. It did not seem, therefore, that encouragement-and-viewing affected boys and girls differently.

Encouragement, Mother-Child Interaction of Relevance to Sesame Street, Viewing, and Learning

Table 18 of the Bogatz and Ball report showed that encouraged children in the second year talked more with their parents about "Sesame Street" than did nonencouraged children, played more games based on the show, and watched it more with their parents. This outcome is hardly surprising since nonencouraged children in the second year were unlike those in the first year in that they had limited access to television sets capable of receiving the show. Thus, watching in the second year was probably determined more by the availability of an appropriate television set than by the desire to watch the show. The consequence of encouragement-related differences in mother-child interaction of relevance to "Sesame Street" was that we could not be sure whether the effects of encouragement were due to viewing, the new interaction pattern, both of these forces, or to both of these forces plus other correlates of encouragement.

As in the first year, we correlated the Posttest Parent Questionnaire measure of viewing and the three-item interaction index for the Los Angeles sample. The correlations were .55 among the encouraged and .83 among the nonencouraged. Once again, these correlations of items from the same test were high, and they precluded a sensitive analysis to unconfound the encouragement-related differences in viewing and in reported mother-child interaction patterns.

Evidence that Special Factors Operated in the Encouragement Condition

We conducted multiple regression analyses to examine the relative magnitude of R^2 in the encouraged and nonencouraged conditions at Los Angeles. The posttest Grand Total was the criterion in these analyses, and the predictors were the pretest Grand Total, sex, age, Peabody IQ, the mother's years of formal education, and viewing. The viewing variable differed by analysis, being the Posttest Parent Questionnaire measure in one analysis and Viewing Records in the other. Thanks to randomization, the encouragement groups were comparable in most ways, except for posttest Grand Total means (but not variances!) and for the level of viewing on the Posttest Parent Questionnaire measure. Mean viewing was 3.46, $s = 1.83$ among the encouraged and was 1.13, $s = 1.79$ among the nonencouraged. The corresponding values for Viewing Records were 9.47, $s = 2.77$, and 1.48, $s = 2.93$.

In the Posttest Parent Questionnaire analysis, R^2 among the encouraged was .41, and .53 among the nonencouraged, while in the Viewing Records analysis the corresponding R^2 values again were .41 and .53. These relative differences replicate what was found at the first-year sites; and are all the more surprising since, as is apparent later, some of the variables (age, viewing, and mother's education) were curvilinearly related to the posttest Grand Total in the nonencouraged but not in the encouraged condition. Such curvilinearity should have reduced R^2 for the nonencouraged, but it did not do so to a degree that made it less than for the encouraged.

Once again, it appeared that some factor or factors operated in the encouraged condition to depress the correlation of posttest knowledge and our set of predictors. This factor or factors, if known, would probably help understand how encouragement caused learning.

Encouragement, Viewing, and Learning

The second-year evaluation threw no extra light on whether encouragement caused learning because it caused viewing and nothing else. While encouragement, viewing, and learning varied together at Los Angeles and Winston-Salem, there were no sites where, fortuitously, encouragement and viewing failed to vary with each other and with learning. In Chapter 7, we test whether viewing caused learning independently of encouragement.

Encouragement, Tester Biases, and Learning

The same correlation of encouragement and tester knowledge of the child's treatment occurred in the second evaluation and may have influenced the tester's posttest behavior with encouraged children. If so, part of the encouragement-learning relationship may be due to tester bias. We had no way of testing if this bias operated and, if it did, how strong it was.

CONCLUSIONS

Most of the second-year results replicated those of the first year, and instead of listing the second-year results alone we list the results obtained by considering all the sites in each of the years. To do this, we sometimes have to make impressionistic judgments of the extent of replication across sites, years, and tests. No positive results are claimed for relationships where a replication was possible and failed to emerge in the data analysis. In ordering the conclusions about the effects of encouragement-and-viewing, the outline listed in Chapter 3 is followed.

Performance. Encouragement-to-view was a factorially complex treatment involving both periodic visits to the home or telephone calls from members of a research team and attempts by the researchers to have the child view "Sesame Street." This treatment caused encouraged children at five of the seven sites (all of them classified as disadvantaged) to view the show more, but it did not have this effect at the one clearly advantaged site or among disadvantaged children in Boston who were among the most advantaged of the total ETS disadvantaged sample. However, encouragement-to-view is not representative of the context in which most American children view "Sesame Street," and it has only been made available to children in the ETS research samples. We could not, therefore, extrapolate from the effects of encouragement to effects of viewing. Encouragement is more complex than viewing and, at most disadvantaged sites, it increased the level of viewing to a level that was not obtained without encouragement.

Efficiency. Encouragement-to-view unambiguously caused learning.

Adequacy. The magnitude of most cognitive learning gains met conventional criteria of pedagogical significance at most sites. Statistically significant effects were consistently obtained on tests requiring recognition of letters, forms, body parts, and (sometimes) numbers, as well as on tests requiring single classification, sorting objects, knowing elementary spatial and temporal relationships, and knowing the function and equipment of mailmen and firemen. There were no demonstrated relationships between encouragement and problem-solving, double classification, conservation, reading, recognition of emotions, social attitude development, social or emotional growth, or knowledge of the man-made world. Some of these relationships were not tested at all, while others were tested with measures of lower reliability than for the effects which were statistically significant. It is not clear, therefore, whether the absence of encouragement-and-learning effects for the more complex processes of problem-solving, double classification, etc. are due to the program's inability to teach, the children's inability to learn at this age, or to the lower quality of the measures.

As far as unintended effects are concerned, encouragement prevented a slight decrease in IQ as measured by the Peabody Picture Vocabulary Test, but it did not cause knowledge of numbers above twenty or of arithmetic operations. Moreover, there have not yet been tests with standardized preschool tests of reading readiness. Encouragement had only one demonstrated negative side effect in that the mothers of encouraged children reported less reading to their child. However, encouragement did not seem to cause an increased preference for television in general nor a decline or increase in parents' desires or aspirations for their child or in the education-relevant items they had in the home. What is still unknown is how encouraged children fared in school. What advantages, if any, did encouragement-and-viewing confer?

There were no entirely adequate data on the effects of two seasons of encouragement. Only at Durham could any test be made, and it did not seem from the analysis we made that two years of encouragement conferred any special knowledge or IQ advantage over no years of encouragement. (Encouraged children viewed demonstrably more than nonencouraged children in each season.)

Process. Effects of encouragement-and-viewing were obtained across boys and girls in various IQ, age, race, and socioeconomic groups, as well as with urban, suburban, and rural children in the North, South, East and West of the continental United States. (Some of these factors were understandably confounded, and effects of encouragement have not been replicated across SES levels within the South, for example.) In addition, the pretest-posttest differences in knowledge gains due to encouragement were approximately equal across sex, age, and IQ groups. The only social group for which benefits from encouragement could not be demonstrated were Spanish-speaking children.

It was not absolutely clear how encouragement caused learning. The most likely possibility was that encouragement caused increased viewing of "Sesame Street" and that this increased viewing caused learning. But we were not able to establish how much, if any, of the relationship between encouragement and learning was due to elements of the encouragement treatment other than viewing, or was due to consequences of encouragement like mothers watching the show with their children, playing games based on the show with them, or discussing with them what they had seen. Nor were we able to establish how much, if any, of the encouragement-learning relationship is due to testers knowing the child's experimental condition, knowing the evaluation hypothesis, and treating encouraged and nonencouraged children differently at the posttest. We have to unconfound encouragement-to-view and actual viewing, and we have to examine the effects of viewing on nonencouraged children because these children could not have been influenced by the encouragement manipulation.

Efficiency. The encouragement treatment that the ETS team implemented is in part a face-to-face social intervention, and we could not sensitively estimate the costs of visiting children and parents on a weekly or monthly basis as in the first and second years. However, it is obvious that encouragement-to-view is a considerably more expensive treatment than viewing on a *per capita* basis. After all, it requires a large field staff to reach the large viewing audience that is necessary for making an expensive technological innovation like "Sesame Street" inexpensive on a *per capita* basis.

It is our opinion that encouragement-to-view illustrated what might result from "Sesame Street" if it were available to the mass of American children in the way it was available to the ETS research sample. But encouragement-to-view does not illustrate what resulted from "Sesame Street" as it was available to American children in their own homes in 1969, 1970, and 1971.

Chapter 7
The Effects of Viewing "Sesame Street" Without Encouragement-to-View

THE MAJOR QUESTIONS

The ETS evaluations were designed to test whether encouragement-to-view teaches. They were not designed to test whether "Sesame Street" taught, which is the focus of the present chapter. Because the central question to Ball and Bogatz differs from our present one, it is not surprising that the ETS data were more suited to answering their question than ours. This does not mean that the ETS team totally neglected the question of whether "Sesame Street" taught independently of encouragement, for each ETS report contained analyses in which encouragement and viewing were treated as independent factors to test whether they affected learning uniquely and in interaction. Nonetheless, the emphasis on encouragement rather than viewing created major difficulties for probing the questions that interested us in this chapter, difficulties that could easily have been avoided if children, especially in the second year, had been randomly assigned to receiving the capability of seeing "Sesame Street" rather than to encouragement-to-view the series.

The first question that we probed was whether encouragement-to-view had effects on learning over and above the gains attributable to viewing. If it did, it would be misleading to label effects of encouragement as effects of viewing. We primarily reviewed the first- and second-year ETS reports to answer this question.

A second question concerned whether viewing "Sesame Street" was related to learning gains among nonencouraged children. This was the most important question since nonencouraged children viewed the program in conditions which best approximate how most American children view it. To answer the question, we conducted a number of different data analyses. Some used the Posttest Parent Questionnaire measure of viewing and others used either Viewing Logs (for the first year) or Viewing Records (for the second year). The basic analysis plan was to use two viewing measures with the first- and second-year data in each of three types of data analysis. One type of analysis used regression adjustments to take partial account of the pretest differences between viewing groups among the nonencouraged; another involved correlating viewing scores with pretest and then posttest learning scores; while the third involved dividing children into pretest and posttest groups of comparable maturational level who had either differed in viewing by the posttest or who were going to go on and differ later but had not yet differed by the pretest. (More details of these analyses will be given later.)

We conducted so many analyses, because we did not want to have to rely on a single viewing measure and because we assumed that there is no "correct" mode of data analysis that statistically adjusts for initial group differences if heavier viewers knew more than lighter viewers at the pretest and if it could be plausibly assumed that the heavier viewers were maturing at a faster rate. We are not unique in making this pessimistic assumption about quasi-experiments with nonequivalent groups. Lord,[1] Cronbach and Furby,[2] and Campbell and Erlebacher[3] have also made it. Since we knew we had to live with imperfection our strategy was to conduct two kinds of data analysis in which we presumed the bias to inflate a viewing-learning relationship (i.e., the multiple regression and, probably, the pretest-treatment *versus* posttest-treatment correlational analyses) and one analysis in which we presumed that there was a conservative bias (the design with maturationally equivalent groups). We wanted to use the analyses to create

---

[1] The important work of Lord on this topic can be found in F. M. Lord, "Large-Sample Covariance Analysis When the Control Variable Is Fallible," *Journal of the American Statistical Association* 55 (1960): 309–321, and in F. M. Lord, "A Paradox in the Interpretation of Group Comparisons," *Psychological Bulletin* 68 (1967): 304–305.

[2] L. J. Cronbach and L. Furby, "How We Should Measure 'Change'—or Should We?" *Psychological Bulletin* 74 (1970): 68–80.

[3] D. T. Campbell and A. E. Erlebacher, "How Regression Artifacts in Quasi-Experimental Evaluations Can Mistakenly Make Compensatory Education Look Harmful," in J. Hellmuth, ed., *Disadvantaged Child,* Vol. 3, *Compensatory Education: A National Debate* (New York: Bruner-Mazel, 1970).

a sort of confidence interval in which the "true effect" of viewing on learning will probably lie.[4]

Such a strategy will seem strange to readers who are used to seeing questions answered by a single adequate statistical test. But in many quasi-experiments there is simply no such test. Moreover, in the present context conservatively biased tests initially showed what we interpreted to be few and weak effects of "Sesame Street" on learning, and so the positively biased analyses were conducted to check whether the paucity of effects could be plausibly attributed to the bias in the conservative analyses rather than to a weak relationship between viewing "Sesame Street" and gaining from it.

It would be desirable if our question about the effects of viewing among nonencouraged children could be examined with a body of data provided by someone other than the ETS team. Hence, we also considered an evaluation of "Sesame Street" by Judith Minton.[5] This was useful in several respects other than coming from an independent source. These respects included: The children in her sample did not have to be classified into viewing groups on the basis of fallible viewing measures; her samples were larger than those for the nonencouraged at-home children in either of the ETS evaluations; her quasi-experimental design was a particularly strong and ingenious one for making causal inferences; and finally, she used a well-known test of school readiness for assessing possible effects of "Sesame Street" on American children.

However, Minton's major research question was whether children, nearly all of whom had viewed "Sesame Street" but in different amounts, increased their knowledge *as a group*. She did not ask whether children who viewed different amounts gained different amounts. The question of group gains by nonencouraged children provided the third question for this chapter, and to answer it, we used both Minton's study and our own reanalyses of the ETS data from all the nonencouraged children at each first-year site. Thus, we included nonviewers and infrequent viewers together with frequent viewers for the analysis. This might seem unfair to some readers

---

[4] Actually, the basic plan for reporting twelve analyses (two viewing measures × two years × three modes of analysis) was not fully carried out. This was largely because the number of children with Viewing Logs or Records was lower than that with Posttest Parent Questionnaire viewing measures. Thus, only nine of the analyses are reported. The other three were conducted, had some cell entries as low as five, and resulted in no statistically significant effects which imply that viewing caused learning among the economically disadvantaged.

[5] J. H. Minton, "The Impact of 'Sesame Street' on Reading Readiness of Kindergarten Children" (Ph.D. diss., Fordham University, 1972).

since nonviewer and lighter viewers could not have been influenced much by "Sesame Street." We acknowledge this, but think several points pertinent. First, we did probe whether nonencouraged children who viewed different amounts learned different amounts; second, our concern with the impact of "Sesame Street" on the knowledge level of various social groups required us to estimate how the program affected group knowledge levels; and third, combining the data of all nonencouraged children avoided classifying them into viewing groups on the basis of imperfect measures of viewing.·

EXAMINING THE TWO ETS REPORTS

The First-Year Report

The major analysis in the first-year ETS evaluation (the Inferential Study) involved four classification variables that were treated as independent variables. These were: the child's sex, viewing quartile (derived from the ETS four-item composite), encouragement condition, and school/home locality factor. The major dependent variables were raw gain scores from the individual learning tests.

A multivariate analysis of variance with these four independent variables resulted in a marginally significant interaction of encouragement and viewing ($p < .07$). This implied that viewing might have been differently related to learning gains among the nonencouraged than it was among the encouraged. Unfortunately, the report did not give any details about univariate tests of the interaction.

We examined the ETS report in order to discover the pattern of means associated with this marginal interaction. However, there was no table of the gains broken down by encouragement and viewing for the total sample. There were, however, tables for the disadvantaged at-home and disadvantaged at-school children which involved the breakdowns we desired. Table 7.1 gives details from the at-home sample in which we were most interested. It should be firmly noted, however, that viewing was indexed by the flawed ETS composite; that the pattern of pretest attainments was systematically related to gains; that three cell sizes fell below twenty-five; and—as will be explained later—site was complexly confounded with encouragement and viewing. Hence, we use the ETS tables to explore the data and not as a means of definitively testing the three questions that interest us.

The first question concerns the possible statistical interaction of encouragement and viewing. Table 7.1 shows that the gains of encouraged and nonencouraged children were similar in the quartiles corresponding to the lightest and heaviest viewers. However, the encouraged groups tended to differ in the second and third quartiles, and the encouraged appeared to

Table 7.1. Grand Total Pretest and Raw Gain Score Means for the
First-Year At-Home Children by ETS Viewing Quartile and
Encouragement Condition

	Nonencouraged			Encouraged			
	N	Pretest $\bar{X}$	Gain $\bar{X}$	Gain S	N	Pretest $\bar{X}$	Gain $\bar{X}$	Gain S
Q_1	53	72.17	18.92	20.34	52	65.98	20.83	20.48
Q_2	24	78.08	18.63	20.03	83	76.30	29.36	24.84
Q_3	18	99.50	26.33	38.16	71	79.54	40.20	25.76
Q_4	21	93.48	53.86	29.57	67	90.54	50.39	25.52

gain more than the nonencouraged. This suggests that encouragement might have facilitated learning independently of viewing, *if and only if* the viewers were neither the heaviest nor the lightest.

The second question concerns how viewing and learning gains were related among the nonencouraged. It can be seen from Table 7.1 that the gains of the children in the first two quartiles (and perhaps the third) were relatively slight, especially when compared to the gains of the children in the heaviest viewing quartile. Moreover, there did not seem to be the same simple linear relationship between viewing and learning gains among the nonencouraged as there was among the encouraged. (We are not trying to suggest, of course, that the quartiles represented equal intervals. We are at this stage only reporting impressions in order to develop hypotheses for exploration.)

The third question concerns learning by nonencouraged children as a group. Table 7.1 shows that nonencouraged children were systematically overrepresented in the lowest viewing quartiles and that only twenty-one of 116 were in the heaviest viewing quartile where gains were most dramatic. The net effect of these trends might have been relatively "low" levels of learning by the total sample of nonencouraged at-home children in whom we were most interested.

Ball and Bogatz did not comment in detail about the possible interaction of encouragement and viewing and its implications. Their reluctance was to a large extent understandable. First, the interaction was after all only marginally significant in the multivariate analysis. Second, it is true, as Ball and Bogatz pointed out, that encouragement was confounded with site in such a way as to make the California children overrepresented among the encouraged children. However, a more germane issue to the marginal interaction was whether children with high gains were disproportionately represented at different levels of viewing within the encouraged and nonencouraged groups. Also, the viewing variable was not an independent variable in a strict experimental sense, and the use of raw difference scores did not totally control for the fact that children who viewed equal amounts in the encouraged and nonencouraged groups may have been cognitively maturing at different rates over time. The nonencouraged child who viewed four times per week on his own initiative was probably different in many ways from the encouraged child who viewed the same amount in response to pressure from outsiders or parents.

The Second-Year Report

The report by Bogatz and Ball contained an analysis explicitly designed to unconfound viewing and encouragement. Table 7.2 gives the posttest Grand Total means for 283 Winston-Salem and Los Angeles children who were divided into the six groups formed by factorially combining two levels of encouragement-to-view and three levels of viewing. The data were taken from page 115 of Bogatz and Ball, and viewing was computed from an ETS index that weighted equally scores from the Posttest Parent Questionnaire and the Viewing Records.[6] The first viewing group was composed of nonviewers; the second, of children whose viewing was described by Bogatz and Ball as "two or three times a week and about half an hour of each show"; and the third of children whose viewing was described as "about four times a week and almost all of each hour" (p. 111).

Several details of the table stand out. First, the design was heavily imbalanced, and among the encouraged there are fewer nonviewers (nine of 108) and more heavy viewers (seventy-eight of eighty-six). This was to be expected, since the encouragement manipulation successfully increased viewing.

Second, the pretest means among the encouraged children increased with viewing level, but this was not the case among the nonencouraged where the impression left by Table 7.2 is that viewing was curvilinearly related to pretest knowledge.

Third, the very small sample of nonencouraged-heavy viewers appeared to gain less than the larger sample of nonencouraged-lighter viewers! This did not imply that heavy viewers gained more than lighter viewers among the nonencouraged, although it must be pointed out that the two groups did not start out at the same pretest position.

---

[6] Viewing Records were collected from all encouraged and nonencouraged children in the second year, meaning that "Sesame Street" must have been somewhat obtrusive in the nonencouraged condition. Ball and Bogatz specifically refrained from collecting Viewing Records data from their first-year sample because of this (see Ball and Bogatz, p. 41).

Table 7.2. Grand Total Pretest and Raw Gain for Second-Year At-Home
Children by ETS Viewing Groups and Encouragement Condition

| | Nonencouraged | | | | Encouraged | | | |
	N	Pretest $\overline{X}$	Gain $\overline{X}$	Gain S	N	Pretest $\overline{X}$	Gain $\overline{X}$	Gain S
Nonviewers	99	74.4	7.8	26.9	9	56.9	22.0	36.1
Lighter Viewers	46	64.0	19.8	25.8	43	63.6	27.8	30.0
Heavy Viewers	8	83.1	13.9	25.0	78	70.6	34.2	24.9

Fourth, the encouraged-heavy viewers appeared to gain more than the small sample of nonencouraged-heavy viewers. Indeed, when we computed a weighted mean of all viewers, thereby combining the heavy and light viewers, the pretest mean of encouraged viewers was 68.1 and the pretest mean of nonencouraged viewers was 66.8. Yet the raw gain of encouraged viewers was 31.9, while that of nonencouraged viewers was 18.9. These means suggest, and at this stage they do nothing more than suggest, that the encouraged and nonencouraged viewers were not markedly different at the pretest and that the gains of encouraged viewers may have been greater than those of nonencouraged viewers.

Bogatz and Ball reported computing "a univariate analysis of covariance" which was designed "to examine the effects of encouragement and viewing on the total gain score." The table they present is included as Table 7.3.[7] One conclusion drawn from the table was that encouragement

Table 7.3. Analysis of Variance Table Presented by Bogatz and Ball in their Attempt to Unconfound Encouragement and Viewing in the Second Year

	df	MS	F	p
Error	174	732.43		
Encouragement	1	7640.10	11.13	.001
Viewing	1	3114.87	4.54	.05
Error	172	686.66		
Encouragement × Viewing	1	1613.66	2.37	.13
Error	171	680.93		

and viewing did not interact to cause learning gains (interaction $p < .13$). This implied that viewing did not have different effects on learning in the two encouragement-to-view conditions. Another conclusion was that encouragement-to-view caused learning gains independently of viewing—a conclusion that is germane to our first question. Another conclusion was that viewing caused learning gains independently of encouragement, which is germane to our second question. Finally, they concluded that the viewing main effect appeared less strong than the encouragement main effect, which is germane to an understanding of the relative strength of the viewing and encouragement effects.

---

[7] We have corrected the *F* and *p* values. They are reported in Bogatz and Ball to be 5.54 and .03, but they are 4.54 and .05.

The ETS conclusion that viewing caused equal amounts of learning at each level of encouragement merits discussion, for our simple visual inspection of the unadjusted gains in Table 7.2 suggested that heavier viewers may only have learned more than lighter viewers among the encouraged where heavy viewers gained 34.2 points and lighter viewers, 27.8. Among the nonencouraged, the relationship was reversed: the small sample of heavier viewers gained 13.9 points and the lighter viewers gained 19.8!

Tables 7.2 and 7.3 give us a clue to the statistical analysis that Bogatz and Ball actually conducted. They reported 174 degrees of freedom. This suggests that their analysis did not involve the total sample of 283 New Study children. Moreover, since viewing had only one degree of freedom associated with it, and since the total sample of light and heavy viewers from Table 7.1 is 175, the 174 degrees of freedom indicated to us that the analysis was restricted to heavy and light viewers and that the nonviewers were omitted. If so, it was unlikely that an analysis of covariance was conducted since the appropriate number of degrees of freedom for the error term would have been 173 and not 174. Let us assume, then, that a simple analysis of variance was conducted on all the children who reportedly watched "Sesame Street," with the nonviewers omitted.

When we collapsed across encouragement conditions to see if viewing caused learning, the *unweighted mean gain* of heavy viewers was 24.1 ([34.2 + 13.9]/2). The corresponding value for lighter viewers was 23.8. How could the trivial difference between 24.1 and 23.8 have resulted in a main effect of viewing in the ETS analysis?

A likely possibility is that the analysis of variance was computed using a procedure that weighted the heavy and light viewing means according to sample size. If so, the *weighted raw gain* among heavy viewers would have been 32.32 and among lighter viewers, 23.67. This difference between weighted and unweighted means arose because only eight of the eighty-six heavy viewers were nonencouraged. They counted relatively little, therefore, in determining the weighted mean of all heavy viewers. Bogatz and Ball were justified in computing the main effect this way since the mean of the eight nonencouraged-heavy viewers may not have been a good estimate of the population mean and, if unweighted, would have altered the findings considerably.

However, the procedure of weighting by sample size indicates that the main effect of viewing was primarily due to encouraged children who were heavy viewers and is little affected by nonencouraged children who were heavy viewers. Hence, it is not justified to conclude from the ETS analyses that heavy viewers gained more than lighter viewers *irrespective of encouragement level*. If this were true, how could a raw gain of 13.9

points by nonencouraged-heavy viewers be more than a raw gain of 19.8 points among nonencouraged-lighter viewers in the absence of any discussion of adjustments for group pretest differences?

The tentative conclusions we drew from visual inspection of Tables 7.2 and 7.3 with respect to our three guiding questions were these: If there was any interaction of encouragement and viewing at all, the greatest difference in learning gains between encouraged and nonencouraged children was among the heaviest viewers and the least difference was among the lighter viewers; if there was any relationship at all between viewing and learning among nonencouraged children, it may not have been a linear relationship and heavier viewers may have gained less than lighter viewers even if all viewers gained more than nonviewers. (The issue of whether nonencouraged children gained as a group has little relevance to the second-year samples since they were deliberately chosen from sites where "Sesame Street" was not readily available.)

An Impressionistic Combination of the Two ETS Reports and Some Methodological Problems

The relationship of viewing to learning among the nonencouraged seemed to differ across seasons. In the first year, the greatest gains seemed to have been made by the heaviest viewers; in the second year, the greatest gains seemed to have been made by the lighter viewers. However, the sample sizes were low (less than twenty-five) in certain of the cells involved in these comparisons, and better hypotheses about "Sesame Street's" effects are gained by collapsing across viewing cells.

Table 7.1 can be rewritten with $Q1$ and $Q2$ combined (the lower viewing quartiles) and with $Q3$ and $Q4$ combined. When this is done the weighted mean gain of nonencouraged children is 18.83 in $Q1$ and $Q2$, and is 38.58 in $Q3$ and $Q4$. The corresponding gains of encouraged children are 26.07 and 45.15. There is no indication here of an interaction of encouragement and viewing; and it seems that learning was related to both viewing and encouragement separately.

When we summed across the two viewing groups in the second-year analysis, the mean gain of nonencouraged nonviewers was 7.8 and of nonencouraged viewers, 18.9.[8] The corresponding gains of encouraged nonviewers were 22.0 and of encouraged viewers, 31.9. Once again, there was no indication of an interaction of encouragement and viewing; and

---

[8] Obviously, the gain in sample size from pooling across quartiles obscures possible curvilinear effects. This loss is presumably not so crucial in the present instance since the very different patterns of curvilinearity in each ETS evaluation suggest that the observed curvilinearity may be due to unstable means rather than to curvilinear effects of viewing.

once again learning seemed to be related to both viewing and encourage-ment separately.

The size of the relationship of viewing to raw learning gains did not seem to be large within the nonencouraged. In the first year, the heaviest viewing quartile differed from all others in raw gains at the 5 percent level, but none of the other quartiles differed from each other. In the second year, the heaviest viewers did not differ from the nonviewers ($t = .66$), and all of the viewers combined did not differ from the non-viewers ($t = 1.68$), though they tended to.[9] This negative impression would have had important implications if it had been corroborated in more ade-quate analyses.

The relationship between viewing and pretest knowledge levels dif-fered between the first- and second-year nonencouraged children. While viewing and pretest knowledge were positively correlated the first year, the attainment of nonviewers in the second year (74.4) was not differ-ent from, and tended to be less than, the pretest attainment of all viewers combined (66.8). This may have been due to the absence of the Sesame Street Test in the second-year viewing composite or to the possibility that viewing *among children who did not have access to a set with UHF trans-mission* was determined by different factors than those which governed the watching of "Sesame Street" where the program was easily available. (Note from Table 7.2 that viewing in the second year seemed to be related to pretest attainments among both encouraged and nonencouraged children who had access to a television set with UHF reception.) The point to be noted for our present purposes is that a comparison of nonviewers *versus* all viewers in the second year avoided the problem of comparing non-equivalent groups whose pretest differences increased the likelihood that different rates of intellectual maturation could masquerade as an effect of viewing.

Each of the previous analyses involved confounds relating to research site. It was clear from the first-year data that the nonencouraged Boston children viewed more heavily than nonencouraged disadvantaged children from other sites and that their raw gains were also larger. Hence, they were more likely to be overrepresented among nonencouraged children in the heaviest viewing quartile. Furthermore, since encouragement had the ef-fect of raising viewing levels at other sites, Boston children were less likely

---

[9] We have used two-tail tests in all the comparisons reported in this chapter. Since it is conceivable that "Sesame Street" could inhibit learning by distracting a child from the learning opportunities in his environment, it is also conceivable that heavy viewers could gain less than light viewers or nonviewers. We are, therefore, in-terested in the possibility that viewing may be positively or negatively related to learn-ing gains. To conduct one-tail tests would imply that we would only interpret positive relationships.

to be overrepresented among encouraged children in the heaviest viewing quartile. Thus, if Boston children gained more than other children for reasons totally unrelated to "Sesame Street," their effect would have been to inflate the gains of nonencouraged-heavy viewers. This might then have been falsely interpreted as an effect of viewing "Sesame Street."

As far as the second year is concerned, it is noteworthy that only one nonencouraged child from Winston-Salem ever viewed "Sesame Street." Hence, there were proportionately fewer Winston-Salem children among the nonencouraged-viewers than among the nonencouraged-nonviewers. Since the nonencouraged children from Winston-Salem did not measurably grow between the pretest and posttest (see Chapter 6) their overrepresentation among nonviewers presumably reduced the raw gain of nonencouraged-nonviewers and inflated the difference in gains between nonencouraged-nonviewers and nonencouraged-viewers. This also meant that a site confound could be falsely interpreted as an effect of viewing "Sesame Street."

Another problem with the ETS analyses concerned their implicit assumption of comparability between individual viewing groups across the encouraged and nonencouraged treatments. The viewing groups were formed by collapsing viewing scores into categories, and no evidence was presented to test whether there were mean differences in viewing between encouraged and nonencouraged children within particular viewing categories. Given that encouragement increased viewing at most of the ETS sites, it would seem that this same relationship could have also held within viewing categories. In other words, it was possible that the level of viewing by encouraged-heavy viewers was heavier than that of nonencouraged-heavy viewers. If so, encouragement and viewing would not have been fully independent of each other in the first- or second-year ETS analyses.

These three problems precluded our using the ETS reports in any but an impressionistic manner. We wanted, therefore, to explore the issues they raised with a series of quasi-experimental analyses, and we decided to concentrate on probing the direction and size of any relationships between viewing and learning gains among nonencouraged children. This was, after all, the most important question of policy relevance, and our reading of the ETS reports raised doubts about whether the viewing-learning relationship was either consistently positive or consistently "large" in magnitude.

VIEWING "SESAME STREET" AND LEARNING GAINS IN A SINGLE SEASON: MULTIPLE REGRESSION ANALYSES

It is sometimes erroneously believed that multiple regression analyses can equate the pretest means of nonequivalent groups, thereby permitting a statistical control for what randomization is meant to accomplish. The evidence clearly indicates that this is not the case when predictor variables are imperfectly measured.

The extent to which multiple regression reduces initial group differences depends on the multiple correlation of the predictors with the posttest scores and on the magnitude of the initial group differences. A major determinant of the multiple correlation is the reliability of the predictor variables, and it is appropriate to claim, as Campbell and Erlebacher among others have done, that multiple regression analyses will decrease in sensitivity as measures become more unreliable. This causes a special problem when groups are not equivalent at the pretest and a group receiving an ameliorative treatment scores higher than another group receiving no treatment. We would run the risk of making a serious inferential error if we were to use fallible predictors in this situation and found that viewing was still related to posttest learning after the effects of pretest scores, SES, Peabody IQ, age, etc., had been purportedly partialled out of the posttest scores. We might want to ascribe the remaining correlation of viewing and posttest learning to the treatment in the mistaken belief that the multiple regression analysis had adjusted for all the group nonequivalence at the pretest. But it will not have made such a total adjustment, and any remaining posttest differences could alternatively be interpreted in terms of the partial presence at the posttest of pretest differences between the nonequivalent groups.

These comments also hold for covariance analysis with nonequivalent groups since covariance is, after all, merely a special case of multiple regression. In covariance analyses, two or more nonequivalent viewing groups are established as independent variables, the posttest learning scores are the dependent variables, and pretest scores, SES, IQ, age, etc., are covariates. Since the covariates are fallible, not all of their influence is partialled out of the posttest scores. Hence, any adjusted posttest differences between viewing groups can be composed of two factors: the effects of viewing, which are of interest to us, and pretest differences which have not been adjusted away and which are not of interest to us.

Setting Up the First-Year Multiple Regression Analyses

Multiple regression analyses require a precise definition of the purpose of the analysis and a rigorous specification of the model that is to be followed for achieving the purpose. Our aim was to see if viewing was related to posttest Grand Total scores (the most reliable indicator of learning) among nonencouraged children.[10] To do this, we constructed a model in

---

[10] Only the Grand Total results are presented at this point since less reliable tests will tend to produce statistically significant but spurious results because some of the pretest difference between nonequivalent groups will remain in the "adjusted" posttest

which the first two predictors of the posttest Grand Total—the pretest Grand Total and a viewing measure—were fixed to enter the analysis in that order. Two analyses were carried out. In one, the viewing measure was derived from the Posttest Parent Questionnaire, and in the other it was obtained from the Viewing Logs. The other predictors, which were free to enter the analysis, were age, sex, pretest Peabody IQ score, and the Home Stimulation-Affluence Index.

The pretest Grand Total was entered into the analysis first because it is an antecedent of viewing. Viewing was entered next to give it the maximum opportunity to reveal a relationship with the posttest. Predictors that enter an analysis first will account for their unique relationship to the criterion and for any variance due to their interaction with the predictors that enter after it. Thus, any interaction effects of viewing with age, sex, Peabody IQ, and the Home Stimulation-Affluence Index would have to appear as correlates of viewing, and we would expect the bias to be positive in any analysis like the one described, both because of the order in which the variables entered the analysis and because all the pretest differences favoring heavier viewers would not be removed from the posttest scores.

But warning is required about the analysis. It is an assumption of the method that the regressions of the first-order correlations be linear. We examined plots of the relationship between the posttest Grand Total and the predictor scores at each site. There was noticeable curvilinearity at Philadelphia involving some measures. The relationship to the pretest Grand Total is depicted in Figure 7.1 where the curvilinearity is obvious. There was also weaker evidence of curvilinearity at Boston (see Figure 7.2) but nowhere else. Since it was clearly not as easy for the advantaged Philadelphia children to gain as it was for disadvantaged children, we therefore decided to restrict the analyses to children from the four economically disadvantaged sites.[11]

---

group means. Some of the difference will also remain with the tests that were more reliably measured, but the effect of such "under-adjustment" of pretest differences will be slight. We did not attempt to adjust scores for unreliability, in part because it is not yet clear which reliability estimate should be used when, and mostly because our analysis strategy was to conduct at least one analysis that should overestimate the effects of viewing "Sesame Street." A simple covariance analysis should overestimate effects, and restricting the analysis to more reliable measures should minimize the extent of overestimation. For a simple discussion of the problems associated with covariance analysis—with and without corrections for unreliability—see A. C. Porter and T. R. Chibucos, "Selecting Analysis Strategies" in G. Borich (ed.), *Evaluating Educational Products and Programs,* Educational Technology Press, 1974.

[11] We did, in fact, compute all the within-site analyses to be reported here on the Philadelphia children. Viewing was not related to adjusted posttest knowledge levels at that site except in one analysis using the Viewing Logs index of viewing.

Figure 7.1.   Scatterplot of the Pretest and Posttest Grand Total Scores of Nonencouraged At-Home Children from Philadelphia

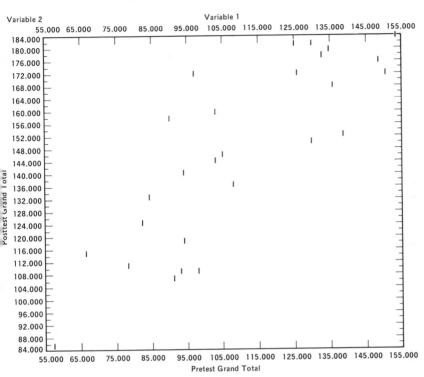

Results of the Analyses

We first analyzed the data from each site both with the Posttest Parent Questionnaire measure of viewing and with the Viewing Logs. Then, we pooled across sites. The within-site analyses should not be given much weight, since the bias from the mode of analysis was positive; the samples were so small; and only three of the forty-three Boston children scored less than 5 on the six-point viewing scale derived from the Posttest Parent Questionnaire measure. This meant that the three Boston children could have had a disproportionate effect on correlations involving viewing.

Tables 7.4 and 7.5 give the analysis results from each disadvantaged site except California where only six children had Viewing Logs data. Each viewing measure significantly added to our ability to predict posttest knowledge at Boston and Durham; and neither measure predicted at Phoenix. In fact, the nonsignificant trend at Phoenix was for heavier viewers to know less at the posttest.[12]

---

[12] An analysis using the Posttest Parent Questionnaire measure with the California sample was not statistically significant.

Figure 7.2.   Scatterplot of the Pretest and Posttest Grand Total Scores of Nonencouraged At-Home Children from Boston

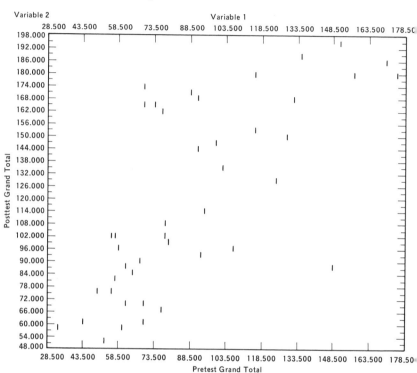

The preceding analyses did not pool the data across sites, and there were no results for the less reliable individual learning tests. We therefore asked whether viewing was related to various indicators of posttest learning among nonencouraged-disadvantaged children in general. To answer this we pooled the data across the first-year disadvantaged sites, including the California sample when using the Posttest Parent Questionnaire and omitting it when using the Viewing Logs. Although viewing and learning were not related in Phoenix as they were elsewhere, we nonetheless included the Phoenix sample because it was part of the total disadvantaged sample and because its seventeen children formed less than 20 percent of the total sample. To conduct the analysis we defined three "dummy" variables corresponding to the four sites after the manner outlined in Draper and Smith.[13] These dummy variables were useful in partialling the site variance out of the posttest.

---

[13] N. C. Draper and H. Smith, *Applied Regression Analysis* (New York: John Wiley & Sons, 1966), p. 136.

Table 7.4. Multiple Regression Analysis within the Nonencouraged Condition at Three First-Year Sites: Posttest Parent Questionnaire Viewing Measure

	Boston				Durham				Phoenix		
Variable	R^2	Increase in R^2	β	Variable	R^2	Increase in R^2	β	Variable	R^2	Increase in R^2	β
Pretest Grand Total	.49	.49	.49*	Pretest Grand Total	.15	.15.	−.03	Pretest Grand Total	.38	.38	.49
Viewing	.56	.07	.32*	Viewing	.41	.26	.41*	Viewing	.38	.00	−.12
Age	.58	.02	.28	Age	.59	.18	.48*	Sex	.46	.08	−.39
Home Affluence	.61	.02	−.13	Peabody IQ	.64	.05	.21	Peabody IQ	.48	.02	.22
Sex	.62	.01	.10	Sex	.65	.01	.17	Home Affluence	.49	.01	.08
Peabody IQ	.62	.00	.04	Home Affluence	.66	.01	.13	Age	.50	.00	.08

* p < .05.

Table 7.5. Multiple Regression Analysis within the Nonencouraged Condition at Three First-Year Sites: Viewing Logs Measure

	Boston				Durham				Phoenix		
Variable	R^2	Increase in R^2	β	Variable	R^2	Increase in R^2	β	Variable	R^2	Increase in R^2	β
Pretest Grand Total	.49	.49	.43	Pretest Grand Total	.15	.15.	−.12	Pretest Grand Total	.38	.38	.68*
Viewing	.51	.03	.27*	Viewing	.22	.07	.53*	Viewing	.46	.08	−.41
Age	.54	.03	.36	Sex	.42	.20	.46*	Sex	.54	.08	−.33
Sex	.58	.04	.19	Peabody IQ	.57	.15	.48*	Peabody IQ	.56	.02	.15
Home Affluence	.58	.00	−.06	Age	.67	.11	.39*	Age	.56	.00	−.09
Peabody IQ	.59	.00	.08	Home Affluence	.70	.03	.18	Home Affluence	.56	.00	−.05

* $p < .05$.

The general model for the analysis was similar to the previous one in that the pretest of a particular measure was forced into the analysis first, the viewing measure was forced in next, and the dummy variables were left free to enter along with age, sex, Peabody IQ, and the Home Stimulation-Affluence Index.

The results of the analysis are summarized in Table 7.6. Each viewing

Table 7.6.   Relationships Involving Two Measures of Viewing* and Posttest Learning Scores from Stepwise Multiple Regression Analyses of the Pooled First-Year Disadvantaged Data

Individual Tests	Posttest Parent Questionnaire			Viewing Logs		
	R^2	Increase in R^2	β	R^2	Increase in R^2	β
Body Parts	.43	.00	.11	.43	.01	.18
Letters	.47	.08	.30†	.46	.07	.27†
Forms	.39	.04	.20†	.37	.05	.27†
Numbers	.55	.05	.31†	.49	.01	.10
Sorting	.28	.00	.04	.31	.02	.20
Relations	.34	.01	.20	.31	.00	.11
Classification	.45	.01	.15	.47	.03	.19
Puzzles	.37	.00	.19	.40	.03	.30†
Grand Total	.57	.05	.29†	.54	.04	.21†

* The California sample is only included for the Posttest Parent Questionnaire analysis where N = 101. Otherwise, N = 83.
† $p < .05$.

measure was related to adjusted posttest knowledge levels for the Grand Total, Letters, and Forms. In addition, the Posttest Parent Questionnaire measure was also uniquely related to posttest Numbers, while the Viewing Logs measure was uniquely related to posttest Puzzles. Body Parts, Sorting, Relations, and Classification were not related to viewing in either of these positively biased analyses.

Setting Up the Second-Year Multiple Regression Analysis

Because of the low incidence of viewing by nonencouraged children at Winston-Salem, we decided to restrict our analyses to the larger Los An-

geles second-year sample. Because we suspected that viewing was curvilinearly related to pretest learning scores across the whole range of nonencouraged at-home children (although not within the group of children who
watched the show more than once), we decided to conduct covariance
analyses rather than stepwise multiple regression. And because covariance
analysis is more sensitive with reliable measures, we restricted our multiple
regression analyses of Los Angeles children to the Grand Total.

It might not be obvious why covariance analyses can be conducted in
some situations where stepwise multiple regression cannot. The crucial
assumption of covariance analysis is that the regression of the posttest on
the covariates be homogeneous *within each viewing group*. Unlike multiple
regression, no assumption is required about the form of the relationship
of the classification variable (viewing) and the dependent variable (posttest knowledge levels).

We divided children into three viewing groups within each of the
encouraged conditions. One group consisted of children who were reported
as not viewing; a second group included children who scored from 1 to 3
on the Posttest Parent Questionnaire (1 corresponded to viewing one-quarter of an hour once a week and 3 corresponded to viewing all of one program once a week, or viewing about one-half of each program two or three
times a week, or viewing very little of each program four or five times
per week); and the third group consisted of children scoring from 4 to 6
(6 corresponded to viewing more than once per day and for almost all of
the program each time, while 4 corresponded to viewing most of the program two or three times per week, or viewing about half of each program
four or five times per week, or viewing very little of each program more
than once a day).[14] Then, with the potential covariates being the pretest
Grand Total, pretest Peabody IQ, years of mother's education, and child's
age, we examined the appropriate regression lines to test the homogeneity
of regression assumption. Unfortunately, cell sizes were small, especially
with the two categories of nonencouraged viewers (see Table 7.7), and
this precluded a sensitive test. But visual inspection of the data did not

---

[14] The purpose of this particular partitioning was to create approximately equal-
sized viewing groups. This does not mean that the resultant samples are as large as we
would like, but it does mean that the sample of designated heavier viewers is larger
than in the ETS analysis of the nonencouraged. Taking a Posttest Parent Questionnaire
cutting point of three entails creating heavier viewers whose absolute level of viewing
is slightly less than in the ETS analysis. But this is not a great loss in the present context since the ETS analysis reported heavier viewers making smaller gains than lighter
viewers.

Table 7.7. Some Means from the Nonencouraged and Encouraged Samples at Los Angeles after Partitioning into Three Viewing Levels on the Basis of the Posttest Parent Questionnaire Viewing Measure

	Nonencouraged			Encouraged		
	Nonviewers (0) N = 72	Light Viewers (1–3) N = 16	Heavy Viewers (4–6) N = 17	Nonviewers (0) N = 13	Light Viewers (1–3) N = 32	Heavy Viewers (4–6) N = 46
Pretest Grand Total	73.22	59.75	73.76	66.46	55.12	75.48
Posttest Grand Total	85.38	81.25	94.26	90.08	91.72	108.95
Adjusted Posttest Grand Total	83.80	88.67	93.90	98.03	94.53	104.76
Pretest Peabody IQ	76.03	70.56	74.82	76.69	65.56	71.02
Mother's Education	2.43	2.25	2.41	1.49	2.69	2.46
Age in Months	48.06	45.16	48.00	47.00	43.66	49.91
Home Stimulation-Affluence	5.90	5.00	6.59	5.31	5.78	6.11
Sesame Street Test	1.36	3.50	4.65	1.69	5.91	7.52

reveal any gross violations of the homogeneity assumption and so we proceeded with the analysis.

Results of the Analysis

The results of the analysis are in Table 7.7, and we would like to point out how viewing is curvilinearly related to most of the pretest moderator variables. Moreover, there is consistent evidence that Sesame Street Test scores were higher for the encouraged than the nonencouraged within viewing categories. While this may merely have reflected greater knowledge of nonbroadcast "Sesame Street" materials because of the encouragement treatment, it may have alternatively reflected heavier viewing by encouraged children within the categories formed by collapsing across some viewing scores. If so, encouragement and viewing would not have been independent.

Our major purpose was to test whether nonencouraged-heavy viewers differed from light viewers or nonviewers at the posttest. Analyses within the nonencouraged group failed to show an overall difference in adjusted posttest means. Even the contrast of the heaviest viewers and nonviewers failed to reach acceptable levels of statistical significance ($t = 1.64$). However, the ordering of the adjusted posttest means was as we would have expected if viewing "Sesame Street" caused learning. That is, the adjusted mean of nonviewers was 83.80; of lighter viewers, 88.67; and of heavier viewers, 93.90.

Three other aspects of the data deserve mention. First, there was a close correspondence on all the background variables between the nonviewers and heavier viewers among the nonencouraged. Hence, it was not likely that these groups initially differed, although we did not, of course, have measures of all the variables on which they could have differed and which might have been correlated with posttest knowledge. This seeming group comparability facilitated making causal inferences about effects of viewing. But all we could conclude was that, while the relevant group means were in the direction that a viewing effect would take, their difference was not statistically reliable.

Second, there was a trend, albeit statistically nonsignificant, for viewing to be positively related to learning in the encouraged group, and this served as a replication of the findings from the analysis of the nonencouraged.

And finally, there appeared to be a main effect of encouragement on learning since the encouraged gained more than the nonencouraged by at least eleven raw Grand Total points in all viewing categories, including nonviewers.

VIEWING "SESAME STREET" AND LEARNING GAINS IN A SINGLE SEASON: TREATMENT-OUTCOME CORRELATIONS

We explained in Chapter 4 how a quasi-experiment can be conceptualized as a situation where there is a correlation between a treatment and the pretest values of some potential outcome variable. If the treatment influenced the outcome, we would expect a higher posttest-treatment than pretest-treatment correlation. Translated into the "Sesame Street" context, cause would be implied if viewing and posttest knowledge were more highly correlated than viewing and pretest knowledge.

Campbell,[15] has advocated the use of treatment-outcome correlational analysis with the particular ETS data on "Sesame Street" that we examined. This was because the typical drawback to using the technique can be avoided with some of the present data. The drawback is that treatments are usually measured *at the same time* as either the pretest or posttest outcome measure, and variables which are measured at the same time tend to be more highly correlated than variables which are measured at different times. One reason for this is that simultaneously measured variables share common measurement error, especially if similar kinds of tests are used for assignment to treatment conditions and for measuring outcomes. A second reason has been advanced by Campbell who claims that correlations typically "erode" with time so that, if *A* is correlated both with *B* which is measured four weeks after *A* and with *C* which is measured eight weeks after *A,* the correlation of *A* and *B* will be higher than the correlation of *A* and *C* if all other things are equal. Thus, if viewing were measured at the posttest, Campbell would claim that there is a force attenuating the value of the pretest-viewing correlation relative to the posttest-treatment correlation.

Some of the ETS viewing measures (Viewing Logs and Viewing Records) were extremely useful for treatment-outcome correlational analysis since they were collected *between* the pretest and posttest from parents rather than from children. However, the problems should be particularly acute with the Sesame Street Test since it was collected from children at the posttest and since, as a recognition test, it was factorially similar to the learning tests. The general problem should also exist with the Posttest Parent

---

[15] D. T. Campbell, "Temporal Changes in Treatment-Effect Correlations: A Quasi-Experimental Model for Institutional Records and Longitudinal Studies," in E. V. Glass, ed., *The Promise and Perils of Educational Information Systems,* Proceedings of the 1970 Invitational Conference on Testing Problems (Princeton, N.J.: Educational Testing Service, 1971).

Questionnaire measure of viewing since it too was collected at the posttest. But it should be less pressing with this measure since it was not a recognition measure collected from the children themselves.

There are other threats to the interpretation of treatment-outcome correlations. If posttest measures are more reliable than pretest measures, this will inflate correlations involving the posttest over those involving the pretest. It is not likely, however, that this source of bias seriously affected the "Sesame Street" data, for we saw in Chapter 4 that estimates of internal consistency were scarcely higher at the posttest. Moreover, we shall report analyses by Kenny that involved adjustments for shifts in reliability.

The most serious problem with the treatment-outcome correlations to be reported is that they may not have controlled for all the effects due to the children in different viewing groups maturing at different rates. While multiple regression analyses attempt to control statistically for the growth rate problem by equating pretest groups that are nonequivalent, treatment-outcome correlations take the pretest differences as they are and do not attempt to adjust them away. Instead, group differences in growth rates are reduced as validity threats because the increase in covariation due to maturation is to some extent counterbalanced by an increase in posttest learning variability that arises, because the different viewing groups are further apart at the posttest than at the pretest.

This can perhaps best be understood in terms of the definition of r as $\frac{\Sigma xy}{NS_xS_y}$ where $\Sigma xy =$ the sum of the products of viewing and learning and $S_y =$ posttest variability in knowledge. If there were no treatment effects and only group differences in growth rates, the higher viewers would have had higher posttest than pretest scores, thereby increasing the numerator. But this very "spreading out" of persons who viewed different amounts should increase the variability in posttest knowledge. If the increase in the numerator (Σxy) is proportional to the increase in the denominator, then group differences in growth rates are controlled for.

The problem is to ascertain when such proportionality holds. Both Seaver[16] and Kenny[17] have claimed that it will hold when nonequivalent groups are maturing at different rates and when the ways in which the nonequivalent treatment groups differ are similarly related to the pretest and posttest. This is called the "stationarity assumption," and it requires that one group should not suddenly spurt in its cognitive growth or should not suddenly cease to grow. Instead, the differences between the groups

---

[16] L. B. Seaver, "College Impact on Student Personality as Reflected by Increases in Treatment-Outcome Correlation" (M.A. thesis, Northwestern University, 1970).

[17] D. A. Kenny, "A Quasi-Experimental Approach to Assessing Treatment Effects in the Non-Equivalent Control Group Design," *Psychological Bulletin* (forthcoming).

should follow a stationary pattern over time, and variables defining the nonequivalence of groups should be related in similar ways to pretest and posttest outcome measures. Clearly, discontinuities in cognitive growth are possible. Thus, while we can assume that treatment-outcome correlations will attenuate biases due to group differences in maturational rate, we should not assume that they will eliminate all biases if the stationarity assumption is not met.

Setting Up the First-Year Analysis

Our strategy in presenting the treatment-outcome correlations is two-fold. First, we present the raw correlations and test their difference using the Pearson-Filon test for the difference between correlations that share one array (viewing in this case).[18]

Then, in order to control for possible spurious effects that may be related to group differences in maturational pattern over and above those controlled for in the analysis of raw correlations, we examine the difference between the pretest-viewing and posttest-viewing correlations with some of the effects of age, sex, Peabody IQ, and SES removed. To accomplish this, we regress pretest learning scores on the moderator variables and repeat this for posttest scores. Then, we compute the difference between each child's resulting standardized scores and examine the regression of these standardized scores on age, sex, Peabody IQ, and an indicator of SES. In this way, we are testing the difference between two partial correlations.[19]

The Results of the Analysis

We wanted to pool the data from nonencouraged children across the disadvantaged sites, in order to both increase statistical power and examine

---

[18] The test is reproduced in the text by C. C. Peters and W. R. Van Voorhis, *Statistical Procedures and Their Mathematical Bases* (New York: McGraw-Hill, 1940). Its power is not yet known. However, we do know that the power of the test between the difference of two *independent* correlations is low (see J. Cohen, *Statistical Power Analysis for the Behavioral Sciences* [New York: Academic Press, 1969]). Our guess is that the Pearson-Filon test of the difference between *correlated* correlations will also have relatively low power despite the advantage that is gained by the correlational factor and the partialing strategy we followed in order to remove the variance attributable to some extraneous sources. This power consideration countervails against the basic assumption we have made that the treatment-outcome correlations have positive biases. However, Kenny has used a more powerful test in subsequent analyses of the present data and they only increased the *t* values to be reported here by amounts up to .10.

[19] We are grateful to D. A. Kenny for suggesting this way of removing the effects of moderator variables and for conducting the statistical tests.

the less reliable individual tests. Hence, we computed the average within-site correlations between the various viewing and learning indices weighted by sample size. The results of the analysis are in Table 7.8.

Table 7.8. Raw Treatment-Outcome Correlations Involving Average
Within-Site Correlations from First-Year Disadvantaged Sites*

	Posttest Parent Questionnaire N = 101			Viewing Logs N = 83		
	Treat-ment-Pretest	Treat-ment-Posttest	*t* diff.	Treat-ment-Pretest	Treat-ment-Posttest	*t* diff.
Body Parts	.22	.19	− .27	.20	.16	− .36
Letters	.01	.28	2.71†	.02	.21	1.72
Forms	.15	.30	1.33	.14	.19	.45
Numbers	.06	.29	2.80†	.08	.09	.18
Sorting	.11	.08	− .26	.04	.14	.77
Relations	.11	.23	1.09	−.01	.03	.32
Classification	.05	.16	1.09	.07	.13	.53
Puzzles	.08	.17	.73	.14	.25	.87
Grand Total	.11	.30	2.25†	.11	.17	.70

* The California sample was only included for analyses with the Posttest Parent Questionnaire measure of viewing.
† p < .05.

The pretest-viewing correlations were generally small but positive at the first-year sites. The posttest-treatment correlations were larger than the pretest-treatment correlations for six of the eight independent tests when the Posttest Parent Questionnaire measure of viewing was used, and for seven of the eight when the Viewing Logs were involved. Statistical tests demonstrated that the difference in correlations was statistically reliable for Letters, Numbers, and the related Grand Total when the Posttest Parent Questionnaire was used as the viewing index, and that none of the differences were statistically significant when the Viewing Logs were used.

The results of the analyses when some variance due to age, sex, Peabody IQ, and the Home Stimulation-Affluence Index were removed from the analysis are in Table 7.9. The addition of these variables made no major difference to the conclusions that we drew from the analysis of raw correlations.

There was some indication from within-site analyses that at Boston

Table 7.9. β and t Values for the Adjusted Treatment-Outcome Correlations from the First-Year Pooled Disadvantaged Sites*

	Posttest Parent Questionnaire		Viewing Logs	
	β	t	β	t
Body Parts	—.02	— .19	—.06	— .52
Letters	.28	2.71†	.18	1.51
Forms	.15	1.20	—.01	— .04
Numbers	.28	3.20†	—.01	— .05
Sorting	—.09	— .64	.04	.26
Relations	.17	1.54	.04	.30
Classification	.14	1.20	.05	.42
Puzzles	.12	1.03	.10	.72
Grand Total	.23	2.76†	.04	.42

* The California nonencouraged children are included in the analysis using the Posttest Parent Questionnaire measure and are omitted in the Viewing Logs Analysis.
† p $<$ .05.

and perhaps Durham the correlation of the Posttest Parent Questionnaire measure of viewing may have been higher with the posttest than the pretest Grand Total. Tables 7.10 and 7.11 give the appropriate results from the analyses of raw and adjusted correlations. It is noteworthy, however, that the relationship was restricted to one index of viewing, that the within-site sample sizes were small, and that at Phoenix the difference in correlations tended to be in the opposite direction to the difference at Boston and Durham.

Table 7.10. Raw Treatment-Outcome Correlations Involving Grand Total Scores from Nonencouraged Children at Three First-Year Sites

	Posttest Parent Questionnaire				Viewing Logs			
	N	Pretest	Posttest	t diff.	N	Pretest	Posttest	t diff.
Boston	41	.12	.35	2.00*	42	.06	.20	1.22
Durham	26	.22	.58	1.94*	24	.06	.28	1.05
Phoenix	17	.22	.10	— .58	17	.35	—.04	—1.95*

* p $<$ .10.

Table 7.11.   β and *t* Values for the Adjusted Treatment-Outcome Correlations
(Viewing and Grand Total) for Nonencouraged Children at
Three First-Year Sites

	Posttest Parent Questionnaire		Viewing Logs	
	β	*t*	β	*t*
Boston	.29	2.42*	.19	1.54
Durham	.34	1.33	.25	.85
Phoenix	−.08	− .26	−.56	−2.03†

* p < .05.
† p < .10.

Kenny's Treatment-Outcome Correlational Analysis of the First-Year Data

Kenny analyzed the first-year "Sesame Street" data in preparing a methodological paper designed to point out the assumptions of treatment-outcome correlations. His analysis strategy differed from ours in six respects. First, he chose to include the Philadelphia sample; second, he computed correlations across all the sites rather than taking the weighted average of the sites; third, he omitted the Peabody IQ test from the control variables used in his partialing analyses; fourth, he omitted the Grand Total from the list of outcome measures; fifth, he made statistical adjustments for any possible differences between pretest and posttest reliabilities,[20] and these adjustments are referred to as "communality corrections" in the tables that follow; and sixth, he conducted treatment-outcome correlations within both the encouraged and nonencouraged conditions.

The results of Kenny's correlational analyses of nonencouraged children are in Table 7.12. In general, the findings closely mirrored those from our analysis. The Posttest Parent Questionnaire measure was more strongly related to posttest than to pretest scores for the Letters and Numbers tests, in each analysis, while Viewing Logs were related to Letter gains in one of these analyses. The communality corrections had the general effect of slightly decreasing *t* values. The major exception was for the Puzzles Test where a statistically significant viewing effect emerged with each viewing measure when, and only when, the correction was made for higher posttest reliabilities. However, the Puzzles finding was not obtained among encouraged

---

[20] The nature of these adjustments is outlined in D. A. Kenny, "PANAL: Panel Data Analysis Computer Program" (Unpub. paper, Department of Psychology and Social Relations, Harvard University, 1974).

Table 7.12. Treatment-Outcome Correlations from Kenny's Analysis of All the First-Year At-Home Nonencouraged Children

| | Posttest Parent Questionnaire | | | | | | Viewing Logs | | | | | |
| | Analysis with Partialing | | | Partialing plus Communality Correction | | | Analysis with Partialing | | | Partialing plus Communality Correction | | |
	Pretest r	Posttest r	t	Pretest r	Posttest r	t	Pretest r	Posttest r	t	Pretest r	Posttest r	t
Body Parts	.226	.234	.08	.226	.234	.09	.320	.170	−1.67	.323	.168	−1.72
Forms	.217	.353	1.19	.232	.331	.87	.197	.340	1.26	.211	.316	.92
Letters	.071	.296	2.41*	.076	.277	2.14*	.111	.307	2.10*	.119	.286	1.77
Numbers	.099	.300	2.34*	.098	.303	2.38*	.178	.187	.10	.179	.186	.08
Relations	.103	.275	1.59	.102	.278	1.62	.154	.071	−.76	.162	.068	−.87
Classification	.110	.221	1.05	.114	.214	.94	.160	.244	.79	.165	.237	.68
Sorting	.064	.139	.64	.087	.103	.12	.012	.153	1.20	.016	.116	.78
Puzzles	.077	.246	1.55	.061	.314	2.15*	.104	.265	1.48	.083	.329	2.12*

* $p < .05$.

children, and we were therefore not inclined to attach much weight to it. Table 7.13 gives the results from Kenny's analysis of the encouraged first-year children. Once again, the Letters and Numbers tests were significantly related to viewing, as also were Relations and Sorting when the Posttest Parent Questionnaire measure was used. Using these last two findings as a cue, we examined the Relations and Sorting effects in previous analyses. From Table 7.12 it is clear that the Relations effect approached marginal levels of statistical significance when the Posttest Parent Questionnaire measure was used, as is also apparent from Tables 7.6 and 7.9 where the effect was again restricted to the one viewing measure. These almost marginal effects among the nonencouraged, the statistically significant effect among the encouraged, plus the second-year findings to be reported, all lent support to the proposition that viewing caused gains in Relations.

However, the same could not be said of Object Sorting since the effect was not consistently indicated at even marginal levels when a different data analysis technique was used, or when communality corrections were made, or when a different viewing measure was involved.

Setting Up the Second-Year Analysis

The curvilinear relationship of viewing to both pretest and posttest learning precluded a sensitive correlational analysis of the Los Angeles data, even though the same variable—viewing—was part of both the pretest and posttest correlations, and it might have been presumed that the weaker curvilinear relationship with the posttest (see Table 7.7) would have inflated the correlation between viewing and the posttest more than it would have inflated the correlation between viewing and the pretest.

The raw correlations are in Table 7.14 and the adjusted correlations are in Table 7.15. Seven of the nine independent differences in raw correlations were in the direction that would have been expected if viewing, as indexed by the Posttest Parent Questionnaire, were causing learning. Eight of the nine independent differences were in the same direction for the Viewing Records. However, only the Relations Test attained conventional levels of statistical significance in the analyses of both raw and adjusted correlations, and this effect was restricted to the Posttest Parent Questionnaire measure. No emphasis should be placed on these analyses except in the context of the other, and better, analyses of the Los Angeles data.

VIEWING "SESAME STREET" AND LEARNING GAINS IN
A SINGLE SEASON: AGE COHORTS ANALYSES

A problem with our earlier multiple regression analyses of the first-year data was that they did not make the viewing groups equivalent on meas-

Table 7.13. Treatment-Outcome Correlations from Kenny's Analysis of All the First-Year At-Home Encouraged Children

	Posttest Parent Questionnaire						Viewing Logs					
	Analysis with Partialing			Partialing plus Communality Correction			Analysis with Partialing			Partialing plus Communality Correction		
	Pretest r	Posttest r	t	Pretest r	Posttest r	t	Pretest r	Posttest r	t	Pretest r	Posttest r	t
Body Parts	.102	.149	.83	.102	.149	.82	.052	.112	1.03	.053	.112	1.02
Forms	.144	.206	.98	.147	.201	.85	.060	.059	−.03	.062	.057	−.08
Letters	.116	.287	2.79*	.139	.239	1.56	.149	.182	.54	.179	.151	−.48
Numbers	.150	.257	2.15*	.154	.252	1.97*	.155	.172	.35	.159	.169	.20
Relations	.036	.172	2.05*	.037	.165	1.92	.053	.120	1.01	.055	.114	.86
Classification	.133	.199	1.01	.141	.188	.70	.039	.154	1.72	.042	.144	1.55
Sorting	.015	.180	2.23*	.018	.152	1.75	.004	.106	1.39	.004	.089	1.10
Puzzles	.135	.075	−.89	.128	.079	−.72	.056	.129	1.08	.052	.140	1.29

* $p < .05$.

Table 7.14. Raw Treatment-Outcome Correlations at Los Angeles

	Posttest Parent Questionnaire N = 105			Viewing Records N = 91		
	Treat-ment-Pretest	Treat-ment-Posttest	*t* diff.	Treat-ment-Pretest	Treat-ment-Posttest	*t* diff.
Body Parts	—.09	.03	1.08	—.00	.06	.53
Forms	—.12	.08	2.01*	—.09	.06	1.36
Letters	.15	.10	— .57	.05	.02	— .38
Numbers	—.01	.02	.34	—.02	.10	1.32
Relations	—.06	.18	2.20*	—.07	.10	1.66
Classification	—.05	.07	1.18	—.07	—.02	.40
Sorting	—.09	.07	1.40	—.21	—.01	1.76
Parts of the Whole	—.03	—.11	—.65	—.11	—.06	.40
Emotions	.11	.13	.15	—.02	.08	.82
Grand Total	—.02	.08	1.19	—.06	.06	1.41

* $p < .05$.

ured or unmeasured variables that could be associated with differences in growth rate. Moreover, the position of viewing in the analyses probably capitalized upon any correlations viewing might have had with the other predictors of posttest knowledge. The treatment-outcome analysis had presumably less positive bias than the multiple regression analysis, because our partialing strategy should have reduced, but not entirely eliminated, any artifacts related to the different viewing groups maturing at different rates.

Ball and Bogatz developed a unique quasi-experimental design for dealing with the problem of differential maturation. It is called the "Age Cohorts" design, and we use it now for examining whether viewing caused learning, especially among nonencouraged children. The Age Cohorts design has less statistical power than the previous analyses, and so it is biased against obtaining statistically significant effects. But it is stronger than the earlier analyses in that it more adequately rules out the problem of differential growth.

As used in the first-year evaluation, the design required viewing and *pretest* learning scores from all economically disadvantaged children who were between fifty-three and fifty-eight months old at the pretest. It also required viewing and *posttest* learning scores from all disadvantaged chil-

Table 7.15. β and t Values for the Adjusted Treatment-Outcome Correlations for the Nonencouraged Children in Los Angeles

	Posttest Parent Questionnaire		Viewing Records	
	β	t	β	t
Body Parts	.02	.17	.03	.21
Forms	.16	1.53	.13	1.18
Letters	−.10	−1.00	−.04	− .44
Numbers	−.01	− .08	.10	1.08
Relations	.24	2.13*	.15	1.32
Classification	.05	.39	.01	.12
Sorting	.25	2.32*	.19	1.72
Parts of the Whole	−.09	− .72	.07	.51
Emotions	.06	.45	.13	.95
Grand Total	.06	.65	.09	1.11

* $p < .05$.

dren who were fifty-three to fifty-eight months old at the posttest. (The latter group had therefore been forty-seven to fifty-two months old at the pretest.) The maturational stage of these pretest and posttest groups, called cohorts, should have been equivalent since they were of equivalent age when one group gave its pretest data and the other gave its posttest data. Moreover, using *all* children within these ages should have eliminated any systematic selection differences.

The logic behind the design was to partition each of the cohort groups into heavy and light viewers so that, if "Sesame Street" were teaching, we would then expect the difference in knowledge between heavy and light viewers in the posttest cohort to be greater than the difference between heavy and light viewers in the pretest cohort.

It is particularly important to note that heavy viewers in the pretest cohort were children who went on to view heavily but whose pretest data were the only ones used. Likewise, the heavy viewers in the posttest cohort were children who had viewed heavily and whose posttest data were the only ones used. In other words, the pretest and posttest cohorts were independent. The only differences between the cohorts should have been: First, only the posttest cohort members could have watched "Sesame Street"; second, the posttest cohort was tested twice and the pretest cohort only once; and third, it was possible that some historical event correlated with learning occurred during the six months that the pretest group was alive and the posttest group unborn. This last possibility hardly seems plausible.

Ball and Bogatz divided each of their two cohort groups into four viewing groups on the basis of scores from their flawed viewing composite. They then conducted a multivariate analysis of the independent pretest and posttest scores (*not* gain scores), and this resulted in a statistically significant interaction of viewing quartile and cohort group. In general, the difference between heavy and light viewers was greater in the posttest cohort than in the pretest cohort, just as would be expected if heavy viewers gained more than light viewers because of "Sesame Street." Given maturationally equivalent cohorts, it was impossible to attribute such an interaction pattern to group differences in maturational rate.

There are two major problems with most studies using an Age Cohorts design. One involves the possibility that the pretest and posttest cohort groups are not equivalent. If there are nonmaturational differences between the cohorts, the kind of person who was a heavier viewer in the posttest cohort may be different from the kind of person who was a lighter viewer. Most importantly of all, this difference may be different from the way in which heavy and light viewers differed in the pretest cohort. Thus, a simple selection process could alternatively explain an interaction of cohort and viewing groups.

The second difficulty is more likely and concerns the reduction in statistical power that can occur because of (1) decreasing degrees of freedom through omitting children whose ages do not lie within the time interval between pretest and posttest (i.e., in the ETS Age Cohorts Analysis this would be all children whose pretest age was less than forty-seven months or more than fifty-eight); (2) the between-subjects error term that goes with an analysis of independent pretest and posttest cohorts; (3) the general difficulty of removing the variance due to extraneous variables from the error term for testing effects; and (4) the difficulty of defining groups which differ so much in viewing that the rigorous interaction criterion for testing causal propositions can be met. For example, if viewing caused learning and we were only able to form groups of heavy viewers and less-than-heavy viewers, the heavy viewers might well have outscored the less-than-heavy viewers at the posttest by more than they did at the pretest. But the difference would have presumably been even larger if we could have contrasted heavy viewers with nonviewers.

Setting Up the First-Year Analysis

We decided to replicate the Age Cohorts analysis that Ball and Bogatz conducted of their first-year data, but using different measures of viewing than the ETS composite. Thus, we partitioned the at-home, disadvantaged sample (excluding California but including encouraged and nonencouraged children) into pretest and posttest cohorts. Our sample sizes differed slightly from theirs (117 pretest and 110 posttest children as opposed to 114 and 101). We could discover no reason for this discrepancy, and we confirmed from Ball that we had indeed used identically designated samples. Since the pretest and posttest cohorts had to be subdivided into encouragement and viewing groups, the small sample sizes precluded within-site analyses, and we were forced to pool across sites.

We would have liked to have had multiple levels of viewing and a large difference between nonviewing and heavy viewing groups. This did not prove feasible. The only way to achieve any kind of decent design balance was to dichotomize the children into lighter viewers (0–4 on the Posttest Parent Questionnaire) and heavier viewers (scores of 5 and 6 on the same scale where 5 corresponds to reports of viewing four or five times per week and almost all of each show, or more than five times a week and about one-half of each show).

After forming our encouragement, viewing, and cohort groups, we inspected how these variables were related to site and discovered that Boston children were overrepresented among heavier viewers in general and among posttest-heavy viewers in particular. Since the Boston learning means were higher than at the other disadvantaged sites, this site confound implied that the mean of posttest-heavy viewers would be inflated because of the overrepresentation of Boston children. Such inflation would contribute to an interaction of viewing and cohort groups that might be incorrectly attributed to viewing "Sesame Street."

We attempted to reduce this site confound by separately standardizing the pretest and posttest learning scores. For each test, each site was given a mean of ten and a standard deviation of one both at the pretest and at the posttest. Then these standardized scores were used to compute the learning means and standard deviations for each of the eight groups in our basic Age Cohorts design. These eight groups resulted from factorially combining encouragement, viewing level, and cohort group.

The standardization procedure eliminates site confounds and has two other advantages. First, it reduces the error term for testing effects by taking out the extraneous variance due to sites. And second, it puts the data from each site onto the same scale, thereby eliminating problems that might emerge because the children from different sites scored at different parts of the learning scale and because the size of learning intervals might vary with scale location.

However, the rescaling *via* standardization is no panacea. Its major drawback is that it renders all absolute differences meaningless. In particular, the pretest and posttest means of a heavy or light viewing group cannot be compared to determine how much gain there had been since the pretest and posttest grand means were set at ten. Hence, we urge readers to treat the mean pretest and posttest knowledge values we give in relative fashion to establish only whether the difference between heavy and lighter viewers at the posttest was larger than the corresponding pretest differences.

Results of the Analysis

Table 7.16 gives the standardized means for the cohort and viewing groups within both the encouraged and nonencouraged conditions. Scores were, of course, left free to vary within viewing and encouragement levels.

If we look first at the pattern within the nonencouraged, it can be seen that cell sizes vary between only twelve and seventeen. Hence, no firm conclusions could be expected if we restricted ourselves to this sample. This is why the encouraged sample has been included and why, if the relationship of viewing and cohort groups was similar within each encouragement condition, we could then pool across encouragement treatments.

Statistical analyses within the nonencouraged showed only one statistically significant interaction, and that was for the Letters Test. The mean differences for the Grand Total, Numbers and Puzzles tests also indicated larger differences between viewing groups at the posttest than the pretest, but these interactions were not statistically reliable at the 5 percent level.

Analysis within the encouraged condition revealed no statistically significant interactions, although for all the independent tests the pattern of mean differences was as we would expect if "Sesame Street" were teaching disadvantaged children.

The low power of the analyses within the nonencouraged, and the similarity between the data patterns between the encouraged and nonencouraged—at least with respect to the more reliable Letters, Numbers, and Grand Total—prompted us to conduct a least-squares analysis of variance in which encouragement, viewing, and cohort groups were the factors. No three-way interactions emerged, but the interaction of viewing and cohort groups reached the 5 percent level and was in the anticipated direction for Letters and Numbers and reached the marginal 10 percent level for the Grand Total. No other tests reached even the 10 percent level.

We would have liked, following our normal strategy, to have replicated the Age Cohorts analyses using the Viewing Logs or Viewing Records. But cell sizes were low in these Age Cohorts analyses, and because of the higher frequency of missing Viewing Logs data, they would have fallen below ten in several cells of the first-year Age Cohorts design. However, it is perhaps worth noting that effects of viewing were stronger in other analyses

Table 7.16. Transformed Means for Heavy and Light Viewers at Pretest and Posttest within the Encouraged and Nonencouraged Conditions—Age Cohorts Analysis: First-Year Sites

	Encouraged				Nonencouraged			
	Pretest Cohort		Posttest Cohort		Pretest Cohort		Posttest Cohort	
	Light Viewers (N = 33)	Heavy Viewers (N = 50)	Light Viewers (N = 18)	Heavy Viewers (N = 52)	Light Viewers (N = 16)	Heavy Viewers (N = 12)	Light Viewers (N = 14)	Heavy Viewers (N = 17)
Body Parts	9.79	9.88	9.63	10.09	9.65	9.94	9.65	9.61
Letters	9.73	9.79	9.74	10.26	10.14	9.70	9.35	10.09
Forms	9.70	9.82	9.56	10.10	9.61	9.94	9.57	9.68
Numbers	9.72	9.79	9.52	10.16	10.02	9.72	9.67	10.07
Sorting	9.67	9.89	9.64	10.22	9.76	9.78	9.66	9.44
Relations	9.99	9.73	9.87	10.15	9.67	10.06	9.81	10.06
Classification	9.77	9.93	9.64	10.12	9.85	9.59	9.40	9.68
Puzzles	9.86	9.78	9.42	9.96	9.98	9.96	9.52	9.77
Grand Total	9.69	9.76	9.55	10.19	9.85	9.75	9.46	9.90

with the Posttest Parent Questionnaire measure than with the Viewing Logs.[21]

Setting Up the Second-Year Analysis

Instead of taking only children who were fifty-three to fifty-eight months old at the pretest or posttest, it is possible to take advantage of the relatively high age variability in the Los Angeles sample and to take one set of cohorts who were between forty-one and forty-seven months old, a second set of cohorts who were between forty-eight and fifty-four months old, and a third set of cohorts who were between fifty-five and sixty-one months old. In this way, a Multiple Age Cohorts design can be formed in which statistical power is higher than in the first-year analysis.

To achieve multiple cohort groups with the present data, it is necessary to have some children whose pretest scores appeared in one set of cohorts and their posttest scores in another. For example, a child who was fifty-two months old at the pretest and fifty-eight months old at the posttest could have had his pretest score represented in the second set of cohorts (forty-eight to fifty-four months) and his posttest score in the third set (fifty-five to sixty-one months). This meant that some pretest cohort scores were not independent of posttest cohort scores. However, other pretest cohort scores were independent since some older children would have fallen outside the specified age range by the posttest and some younger children would have fallen outside the age range at the pretest. Thus, a completely within-subjects design was not possible. The only increase in statistical power came through the increase in sample size afforded by multiple cohort groups.

Once the children were in cohorts they were divided into six groups: the encouraged and nonencouraged who were nonviewers (score of 0 on the Posttest Parent Questionnaire), lighter viewers (score from 1 to 3), and heavier viewers (score from 4 to 6). Since some cell sizes were small, particularly for the light and heavy viewers (see Table 7.17), it would have been advantageous if we could have collapsed across levels of viewing and formed a single viewing group. The danger in this was that we might have had a weak test of the effects of viewing "Sesame Street," for comparing nonviewers and heavy viewers was presumably more sensitive than comparing nonviewers with the combined category of light and heavy viewers.

---

[21] We actually did compute the analyses with Viewing Logs, and the interaction of encouragement and cohort groups did not reach conventional levels of statistical significance. We also computed the second-year analysis with Viewing Records, and no effects were significant.

Table 7.17. Balance of Design and Raw Means for Unconfounding Viewing and Encouragement among Los Angeles Children

Cohort	Time of Testing	Encouraged						Nonencouraged					
		Non-viewers		Low Viewers		High Viewers		Non-viewers		Low Viewers		High Viewers	
		N	$\bar{X}$	N	$\bar{X}$	N	$\bar{X}$	N	$\bar{X}$	N	$\bar{X}$	N	$\bar{X}$
41–47 Month Cohorts	Pretest	5	53.80	9	68.67	8	56.62	25	57.88	8	47.25	4	57.75
	Posttest	3	80.00	14	91.07	10	91.80	17	70.29	3	72.00	5	79.60
48–54 Month Cohorts	Pretest	3	60.00	5	56.00	10	91.70	9	75.00	3	77.00	4	73.75
	Posttest	5	91.20	9	107.22	8	93.13	25	69.96	8	73.88	4	77.25
55–61 Month Cohorts	Pretest	2	122.50	3	67.00	14	84.71	16	91.19	2	63.50	2	107.50
	Posttest	3	75.00	5	73.40	10	115.20	9	80.67	3	99.00	4	95.50

Fortunately, there was some justification for summing across levels of viewing. We computed the raw learning means for the pretest and posttest cohorts after each had been partitioned into nonviewers, lighter viewers, and heavier viewers. Then, we visually inspected the pretest-posttest differences of the resulting six groups (see Table 7.17). In four of these six cases the gains of lighter viewers were greater than those of heavier viewers, just as they were in the ETS analysis of the second year (see Table 7.3). We felt justified, therefore, in pooling the lighter and heavier viewers.

Let us reexamine the balance of the design after making a single category of viewers. There was obviously a strong confounding of viewing and encouragement. This confounding had two aspects. First, more nonencouraged children were nonviewers; and second, encouraged viewers may have viewed more than nonencouraged viewers, for we saw earlier how the Sesame Street Test mean of encouraged viewers was 6.86, while that of nonencouraged viewers was 4.09. Thus, the viewing groups may not have been equivalent in viewing.

A second imbalance concerned the confounding of age and pretest-posttest cohort group within the nonencouraged condition. Of the twenty-three *nonencouraged viewers* in the pretest cohort, twelve (52 percent) are in the forty-one to forty-seven month group, 28 percent in the forty-eight to fifty-four month group, and 20 percent in the fifty-five to sixty-one month group. Of the twenty-seven nonencouraged viewers in the posttest cohort, 30 percent are in the forty-one to forty-seven month group, 44 percent in the next age group, and 26 percent in the oldest group. This implied that the pretest group had proportionately more younger children; that the pretest learning means were deflated thereby; and that the difference in knowledge between the pretest and posttest cohorts of nonencouraged viewers was inflated.

A different relationship between age and pretest-posttest group held among the *nonencouraged nonviewers.* Of the fifty such children in the pretest cohort, 50 percent were in the youngest group, 18 percent in the next youngest, and 32 percent in the oldest; while of the fifty-one nonencouraged nonviewers in the posttest cohort, 33 percent were in the youngest group, 50 percent in the next youngest, and only 17 percent in the oldest group. This indicated that the posttest cohort had more younger children which should lead to the posttest mean being deflated relative to the pretest mean. Thus, the relationship of age and cohorts among nonviewers was the exact opposite of the relationship among viewers: Among nonviewers the pretest mean should have been elevated and among viewers the posttest mean should have been. This would lead to exactly the interaction pattern which indicated that viewing "Sesame Street" caused learning among nonencouraged children!

Because of the age confounds and the error variance due to age we transformed the scores of the pretest and posttest cohorts at each of the three age levels, giving each of these six groups a mean equal to ten and a standard deviation equal to one. The effects of encouragement and viewing were left to vary freely with the imposed constraints. In this way, the variability due to age differences was removed from the error term for testing effects, and the effects of age were removed from the learning means.

Results of the Analysis

Table 7.18 gives the transformed means for all the learning tests. Among encouraged children, the difference between the posttest groups of heavy and light viewers was greater than the difference between the corresponding pretest groups on seven of the nine independent learning tests. But the interaction of cohort groups and viewing was not statistically significant for the Grand Total or any other measures in least-squares analyses within the encouraged.

Consider next the important nonencouraged group. Here, for some inexplicable reason, the interaction pattern on many of the tests reflected larger pretest than posttest differences between viewing groups. The interaction of viewing and cohort groups was marginally significant ($p < .10$) for the Grand Total and for the Relations Test, and in each of these cases the posttest superiority of viewers over nonviewers was greater than the unexpected pretest superiority of nonviewers over viewers. (The interaction of viewing and cohort groups was significant at the 5 percent level for the Forms Test. But this effect was in part due to the pretest difference between nonviewers and viewers [.50] being larger than the posttest difference [.42]. Since the data pattern that would be expected if "Sesame Street" were effective involves finding slight differences at the pretest favoring heavier viewers and considerably larger differences at the posttest favoring heavier viewers, the Forms Test presented at best marginal conceptual evidence for an effect of viewing among the nonencouraged.)

Table 7.18 implies that viewers tended to know more than nonviewers at the posttest but not at the pretest, and that this relationship held for both encouraged and nonencouraged children. Hence, we conducted a three-way analysis of variance (least-squares) with encouragement, viewing, and cohort groups as the independent variables. There were no three-way interactions, and the interaction of viewing and cohort groups was significant at the 5 percent level for Forms and at the 10 percent level for the Grand Total.

Table 7.18. Transformed Means for Learning from the Age Cohorts Analysis of Los Angeles Children

	Encouraged				Nonencouraged			
	Pretest Cohort		Posttest Cohort		Pretest Cohort		Posttest Cohort	
	Nonviewers (N = 10)	Viewers (N = 49)	Nonviewers (N = 11)	Viewers (N = 56)	Nonviewers (N = 50)	Viewers (N = 23)	Nonviewers (N = 51)	Viewers (N = 27)
Body Parts	9.68	9.98	9.74	10.27	10.15	9.74	9.81	9.94
Forms	9.93	10.02	10.29	10.34	10.17	9.63	9.60	10.02
Letters	10.17	10.13	10.04	10.41	9.95	9.88	9.66	9.89
Numbers	9.86	10.04	10.01	10.49	10.02	9.91	9.62	9.86
Relations	9.70	10.13	10.17	10.29	10.03	9.82	9.55	10.04
Classification	10.55	9.95	10.23	10.30	10.00	9.94	9.73	10.00
Sorting	10.06	9.88	10.10	10.42	10.11	9.91	9.68	9.78
Parts of the Whole	9.92	10.09	9.61	10.33	9.91	9.96	9.93	9.70
Emotions	9.96	10.10	9.68	10.33	9.87	10.11	9.80	10.18
Grand Total	9.99	10.05	10.00	10.50	10.04	9.81	9.58	9.90

Once again, we would have liked to replicate the foregoing analysis with the Viewing Records measure of viewing. But to do so would have entailed prohibitively low cell sizes within the encouraged Los Angeles sample of nonviewers.

A SUMMARY OF THE EFFECTS OF VIEWING AMONG NONENCOURAGED CHILDREN

The preceding presentation was complicated, but it reflects the difficulties of making causal inferences in situations where a randomized experiment has not been conducted. The major problem with the first-year data was that viewing was related to pretest knowledge levels among the nonencouraged and that the sample sizes were low for analyses within sites. The second-year data from nonencouraged children were fortunately not plagued with selection differences between viewers and nonviewers, but there was a problem of sample size when considering any partitioning among viewers. There were further problems with each year's data in that the analyses were restricted to children from disadvantaged sites and in that the quality of the viewing measures could be questioned. Viewing Logs and Viewing Records were presumably better than the Posttest Parent Questionnaire in that they were collected during the viewing season and not after it. There were, however, greater problems of reliability with the logs and records since, as we saw in Chapters 4 and 6, there were many children with no or few observations on these single-item measures.

Where we could and did replicate analyses across viewing measures, relationships with posttest learning were stronger with the Posttest Parent Questionnaire than with Viewing Logs or Records, even though most of the trends were in the same positive direction for all viewing measures. This comparability in direction, plus the low reliability and missing scores for Viewing Logs and Viewing Records, inclined us to put greater faith in the Posttest Parent Questionnaire measure than any other, and the following summary is based upon that measure.

The summary is also based upon the analyses which pooled across the four first-year disadvantaged sites. Tables 7.4, 7.5, 7.12, and 7.13 indicate that viewing may have been differently related to posttest learning across sites, and the evidence for a positive relationship among nonencouraged children was stronger at Boston and Durham than at Phoenix or California, although the Boston and Durham effects were limited to one viewing measure and could only be performed with tests of presumed positive bias. However, we could see no conceptual rationale for pooling across only two sites, particularly since the Phoenix and California samples were the smallest in the first-year evaluation and since we attempted to remove some of the site variance from the analyses that we conducted. Hence, the analysis from pooled disadvantaged sites should give a better composite picture of "Sesame Street's" global effect, although it does lose some of the finer-grained analysis that goes with both demonstrating and explaining unique site effects.

Table 7.19 gives the results from our six analyses using the Posttest Parent Questionnaire measure. The first column gives results for the Grand Total as a convenient index of "Sesame Street's" general effectiveness. It can be seen that the index was related to viewing in the two first-year analyses that were most likely to be positively biased and was marginally related in the one most likely to be conservatively biased. (Hence, we have reported Age Cohorts results from the analysis of the combined encouraged

Table 7.19. A Summary of the Statistically Significant Relationships between the Posttest Parent Questionnaire Measure of Viewing and the Posttest Grand Total and Individual Posttest Knowledge Levels*

Analysis	Statistically Significant Grand Total Results		Statistically Significant Individual Test Results	
	Pooled First-Year Disadvantaged Sites	Los Angeles Second Year	Pooled First-Year Disadvantaged Sites	Los Angeles Second Year
Multiple Regression	statistically significant	not statistically significant but in the required direction	Letters Numbers Forms	Relations
Treatment-Outcome Correlation	statistically significant	not statistically significant but in the required direction	Letters Numbers	Relations (Forms)‡
Age Cohorts† Design	marginally statistically significant	marginally statistically significant	Letters Numbers	Relations (Forms)‡

* Use of Viewing Logs and Viewing Records in the appropriate years would not have revealed these differences, but for reasons explained in the text, these are probably less adequate measures of viewing.

† These results are from the analysis with the encouraged and nonencouraged combined.

‡ This Forms effect may not be attributable to "Sesame Street." For an unknown reason, the correlation of pretest and viewing was negative for this test at the pretest ($r = -.12$) in the treatment-outcome analysis, and the difference between light and heavy viewers was greater in the pretest cohort than the posttest one.

and nonencouraged samples.) The third column gives results for the individual tests, and it can be seen that Letters and Numbers (the two principal discriminators within the Grand Total) are consistently related to learning. But no other tests were. It is worth pointing out, however, particularly in the light of the Los Angeles results, that the Relations Test was nearly marginally related to the Posttest Parent Questionnaire measure of viewing in most analyses. (Almost marginally means $.20 > p > .10$.)

The Los Angeles data had lesser problems associated with the pretest nonequivalence of viewing groups but greater problems with securing an adequate sample of nonencouraged heavy viewers. The Grand Total was not significantly related to learning gains at the 5 percent level in any analysis. But it was positively related in all analyses, and in the Age Cohorts analysis with the combined encouraged and nonencouraged groups, the relationship was marginally significant (i.e., $> 5\% < 10\%$). Of the individual tests, Relations was the only one which was consistently related to viewing in a manner indicating that viewing might have caused learning.[22] However, it is worth pointing out, particularly in the light of the first-year results, that the Letters and Numbers tests were the major discriminators within the Grand Total.

Although the major focus in the preceding analyses was on the effects of viewing "Sesame Street" on the learning gains of nonencouraged children, it is instructive also to consider the results of the less systematically conducted analyses of the effects of watching the program among children who were encouraged to view by the ETS field staff. This is of interest, first, because there were twice as many encouraged as nonencouraged children in the first year; and second, because the relationship of viewing to learning gains could be the same within the encouraged and nonencouraged groups even if the encouraged were to gain more than the nonencouraged at all levels of viewing.

Kenny's treatment-outcome correlational analysis of the total first-year sample of encouraged at-home children indicated that viewing-posttest correlations tended to be higher than viewing-pretest correlations for all tests and that the Letters, Numbers, Relations and Sorting tests were statistically significant at the 5 percent level when the Posttest Parent Questionnaire measure was used. None was statistically significant using Viewing Logs, and only Numbers remained significant after corrections were made for higher posttest reliability. Our own Age Cohorts analyses of the encouraged children ($N = 153$) produced comparable results insofar as all the individual learning tests implied effects of viewing and none of the

---

[22] This result comes from the covariance analyses of individual test data in the second year that have not been previously reported.

viewing by cohort interactions was statistically significant when the Posttest Parent Questionnaire measure was used.

Turning to the second-year tests of the encouraged children, the appropriate Grand Total means are in Table 7.7, and, although the effect was in the direction that would be required if "Sesame Street" were teaching, the adjusted posttest means were not reliably different from each other. The Age Cohorts analyses in Table 7.18 suggest the same non-significant trend as the covariance analyses for seven of the nine independent tests.

Taken all in all, and restricting ourselves to the Posttest Parent Questionnaire viewing measure, we concluded that the direction of mean differences in all analyses suggested that viewing caused learning among both encouraged and nonencouraged children. There were eight tests in the first-year evaluation and nine in the second-year work. It seems that, in the first year, some Letter and Number skills were enhanced by viewing while in the second year the ability to understand Relationships was improved. Since the Relations effect was consistently present in the first-year data at "nearly marginal" levels of statistical significance, and since the Letters and Numbers effects were indicated by the second-year data insofar as these tests were the major discriminators within the Grand Total, it is warranted to conclude that the evidence from one viewing measure suggested that "Sesame Street" taught some Letter and Number skills and some knowledge of comparative relationships to a statistically significant degree. If the series taught other cognitive skills, these have not yet been measured or have not resulted in effects that were strong enough to have attained conventional levels of statistical significance with tests of the power of those that we conducted.

DID THE NONENCOURAGED CHILDREN AT EACH SITE GAIN FROM "SESAME STREET" AS A GROUP?

If we are prepared to believe that heavier viewers learn more than lighter viewers or nonviewers on a minority of learning tests, then it becomes an academic issue as to whether the nonencouraged gained as a group. If any subgroup of the nonencouraged gained on any test (e.g., heavier viewers), then the population mean of all nonencouraged children must inevitably increase on that test. Although this may sound paradoxical, the purpose of analyzing whether the nonencouraged gained as a group was not to test whether they gained as a group. Rather, the purpose was to test whether effects of viewing would be obtained in analyses where children did not have to be partitioned into viewing groups on the basis of fallible viewing scores.

Setting Up the Analysis of the Nonencouraged Children

We used two procedures in Chapters 5 and 6 for estimating what the posttest Grand Total mean would have been in encouraged groups had there been no "Sesame Street." One procedure required regressing the pretest Grand Total scores onto age in order to predict what the scores of encouraged children would have been when they were six months older at the posttest. This resulted in what we called "Predicted Grand Total I." The other took a subsample of children whose pretest age was similar to the mean posttest age of all encouraged children at a particular site. The pretest Grand Total mean of this subsample was then used as an indicator of what the Grand Total mean of all the children would have been at the posttest. We called this "Predicted Grand Total II."

Each procedure has the common weakness that estimated posttest means came from tests that children were seeing for the first time while the obtained posttest means came from tests that the children had seen once before. Moreover, the regression-based estimate was not a strong one with Philadelphia children because the ceiling effect at that site depressed estimates of linear slope. In addition, and somewhat unfortunately, an estimate from the pretest scores of older children was not possible with the Philadelphia sample since there were so few children there whose pretest age was fifty-nine months. As a consequence, no sensitive estimate of the expected posttest Grand Total was possible with the nonencouraged children from the single advantaged site. Finally, it must be noted that we did not analyze the gains of the second-year nonencouraged children as a group since the second-year sites were deliberately chosen so that nonencouraged children would not have easy access to a television set capable of receiving "Sesame Street."

Results of the Analysis

The results of the analyses are in Table 7.20. It can be seen that at Boston and Phoenix there was a close correspondence between the two posttest Grand Total estimates. However, there was a discrepancy of 6.4 Grand Total points at Durham. This was the largest single discrepancy in our estimates of either the encouraged or nonencouraged samples.

It can also be seen from the *t* tests that the difference between the obtained mean and that predicted from the regression equation (Predicted Grand Total I) was reliable at the 5 percent level at Philadelphia and Phoenix, and was reliable at the 10 percent level at Boston, Durham, and northern California. At the three sites where the second estimate was possible, the Phoenix difference was reliable at the 5 percent level, the Boston

Table 7.20. Obtained and Predicted Posttest Grand Total Means for
Nonencouraged At-Home Children at the First-Year Sites

Site	N	Mean Pretest Age	B	Obtained Posttest Grand Total		Predicted Grand Total I	t Diff. Obtained vs. Predicted	Predicted Grand Total II	t Diff. Obtained vs. Predicted
				X̄	SD				
Boston	43	50.23	2.45	119.39	44.94	105.71	2.02	105.73	2.01
Durham	28	54.07	1.20	92.18	27.10	81.78	2.03	88.21	.78
California	19	53.55	2.03	110.80	30.28	98.26	1.85		
Phoenix	18	50.78	1.06	94.83	25.33	81.04	2.31	81.05	2.31
Philadelphia	27	52.96	1.88	147.00	29.17	121.06	4.62		

difference at the 10 percent level, and the Durham difference was not reliable.

There is consistent evidence, then, that the nonencouraged groups gained more than was expected between the pretest and posttest. Unfortunately, the relative contribution of viewing and test familiarity to this effect could not be established, and it is possible that the effects of viewing were overestimated. Such is not the case with the following analysis.

MINTON'S NEW YORK EVALUATION OF "SESAME STREET"

Our Purpose in Using Minton's Evaluation

The ETS evaluation designs tested the effects of encouragement-to-view "Sesame Street" rather than the effects of viewing the program. The difference between the ETS purpose and our purpose in this chapter meant that the ETS data were not entirely suitable for assessing whether viewing caused learning gains and that our quasi-experimental analyses did not have the definitive stamp that would have resulted if children had been randomly assigned in the second year to having or not having the capacity to receive "Sesame Street" *and if nobody had been encouraged.*

We wanted, therefore, to find data from an independent evaluation of "Sesame Street" with a strong design to test whether its conclusions about viewing corroborated ours. The only convincing summative evaluation with a sample of American children from different social backgrounds that we found was a doctoral dissertation by Judith Minton at Fordham University.

Research Design

Minton set out to evaluate whether "Sesame Street" increased the reading readiness of kindergarten children who were aged between fifty-eight and seventy months at the end of the first season of the series. She used the Metropolitan Readiness Test (MRT) as her outcome measure. The MRT can be divided into six subtests. One is a test of *Word Meaning* in which the child selects a picture that corresponds to a word given by the examiner. This subtest has sixteen items. The second is a test of *Listening* (sixteen items), and the child is required to select a picture that corresponds to a situation that the examiner describes. This taps into comprehension of phrases and sentences rather than words. The third subtest is of *Matching* (fourteen items), and the child is required to match one picture with another or one group of letters with another. The fourth subtest is of the *Alphabet* (sixteen items), and the child is asked to recognize lowercase letters by choosing a named letter from among four alternatives. The fifth subtest is of *Numbers* (twenty-six items), and this tests number concepts and knowledge of numbers. The final subtest is of *Copying* (fourteen items), and this measures visual perception and motor skills that are germane to handwriting. The MRT is meant to measure the extent to which a child is ready for first grade and is often given in kindergarten. It is therefore particularly suited to the five-year-olds in Minton's study. It is perhaps especially important to note that the Matching, Letters, and Numbers tests closely correspond to the behavioral objectives of "Sesame Street." They thus provide the best opportunity of testing whether the series had any effect on tests measuring what it was meant to teach without these tests having been deliberately tailored to the series' content.

In May 1970 Minton obtained the MRT scores of all the children who had attended a particular kindergarten in a New York state school district as well as school records of the scores of children who had attended the kindergarten in 1968 and 1969 before "Sesame Street" went on the air. We shall call this her Total Sample, and it consisted of 482 children in 1968, 495 in 1969, and 524 in 1970.

She was also able to divide some of the 1968, 1969, and 1970 children into three groups: those who were economically advantaged and came from an all-white, affluent suburb; those who had been enrolled in Headstart the previous summer and were economically disadvantaged (over 50 percent were black; about 10 percent were Spanish-speaking; and the remainder were white); and those who were to go on later to a Catholic parochial school in the area. All the children in the last category were white and were described as coming from "working-class middle-income families but all socioeconomic levels were represented." We shall call these her "Socioeconomic Samples," although it is noticeably difficult to classify the parochial school group in this respect since they are designated as "working-class" and "middle-income" and representing "all socioeconomic levels."

The basic design for evaluating "Sesame Street" was simple. Minton compared the knowledge levels of the 1970 kindergarten group with those of the 1968 and 1969 groups. If "Sesame Street" were effective, she maintained that it would result in knowledge means for 1970 children that were higher than for previous years. Of course, other explanations of such an outcome were possible. The two major contenders were (1) that the kind of child entering kindergarten in 1970 differed from the child entering in 1969 or 1968 and (2) that some historical event other than "Sesame Street" intervened between 1969 and 1970 and affected reading readiness.

Fortunately, Minton was able to rule out the first objection by a clever subsidiary design in which she analyzed the readiness scores of all 1969 and 1970 kindergarten children for whom there were data from a sibling. Let us explain the rationale behind this. The 1969 kindergarten children could not have watched "Sesame Street" since it was not on the air when they were in kindergarten and when their MRT scores were recorded. Nor could their older siblings have watched it when they were in the kindergarten. Thus, any differences in MRT scores between these groups, who came from the same homes, would have presumably been due to being older versus younger siblings. However, the 1970 kindergarten children could have watched "Sesame Street," although their older siblings could not have done so when they were in kindergarten. Hence, if the 1970 group knew more than their siblings had at the same age, *and if this difference were larger than the difference between the 1969 group and their siblings,* this would be strong presumptive evidence that "Sesame Street" caused learning.

Findings for the Total Sample

Minton was able to show that the means for the 1968, 1969, and 1970 samples did not differ for the word meaning, listening, number or copying subtests. However, the matching and alphabet tests resulted in statistically significant difference, although only the alphabet test means were in the direction indicating the effectiveness of "Sesame Street" (1968—$\bar{X}$ = 9.00; 1969—$\bar{X}$ = 8.49; 1970—$\bar{X}$ = 10.45). Furthermore, Newman Keuls tests of the alphabet means showed that the 1970 mean differed from the other two means, which did not differ from each other.

The analysis with siblings resulted in a similar pattern of findings. It was only for the alphabet subtest that the 1970 kindergarten group differed from their siblings by more than was the case with the 1969 group. The mean of the 1969 group ($N = 132$) was 8.63 and that of their siblings at the same age was 8.27; the mean of the 1970 group ($N = 122$) was 10.42 and that of their siblings was 8.00. The interaction of year and sibling groups was statistically significant at the 1 percent level.

These data provided corroboration for the earlier findings that "Sesame Street" taught letter skills (particularly recognition) better than other aspects of school readiness. Indeed, according to the Minton results, "Sesame Street" did not teach other aspects of readiness to an extent which raised the mean of the total sample of children.

It is important to note that Minton's major research question was whether the total group gained. This is presumably less sensitive a test of "Sesame Street's" effectiveness than an analysis of nonviewers versus daily viewers would be. Nonetheless, it is worth noting that only thirteen children out of her total 1970 sample of 491 who provided viewing data did not watch the program at all and that about 54 percent reported daily viewing (see Table 8.11 in the next chapter). It is not easy, therefore, to argue that the group comparisons tested the effectiveness of a program that was rarely watched.

Findings for the Separate Socioeconomic Samples

Minton reported analyses of the 1968, 1969, and 1970 means within each of her separate samples. For economically advantaged children she found that the 1970 group outperformed the other two groups only on the alphabet subtest (1968—$\overline{X}$ = 11.13; 1969—$\overline{X}$ = 10.38; 1970—$\overline{X}$ = 13.58). The variance was lower in 1970 than in earlier years, suggesting that the 1970 mean value was deflated because of a ceiling effect on the sixteen-item test. Indeed, one-quarter of the advantaged children achieved a perfect score. For the economically disadvantaged group she found no statistically significant differences to support the effectiveness of "Sesame Street" in teaching aspects of reading readiness. But for the parochial school group she found the same pattern as with the economically advantaged. The alphabet subtest mean for the 1968 group was 9.30, while it was 8.88 for the 1969 group, and 11.32 for the 1970 group. (Newman Keuls tests showed that the 1970 mean differed significantly from the other two means.) It seems, then, that the 1970 group outperformed the earlier groups only in letter recognition and that this effect was obtained for advantaged children and for white children who were described as "working-class middle-income" and representing "all socioeconomic levels," and who were later to go on to parochial schools. The effect was not obtained for economically disadvantaged children.

Minton's analyses of the separate groups would have been inferentially stronger if she had also conducted her siblings design with each of the three separate samples. Without the design it is not possible to be definitive in ruling out the alternative interpretation that for one or some of the separate samples the 1970 experimental group differed in composition from the 1968 and 1969 groups. Such a difference might explain, for example, why the alphabet test failed to discriminate among the economically disadvantaged sample. However, this fact does not threaten the interpretation from the siblings analysis of the total sample where it was established that viewing "Sesame Street" was associated with statistically significant group gains in letter recognition and in no other preschool skills. The siblings design is an elegant one that deserves wider usage and that is conducive to confident causal inference-making. Moreover, it does not entail the problem that arose with our analyses of group gains by the nonencouraged, for the children in Minton's study who watched "Sesame Street" were presumably tested as often as their siblings who had not watched the show when they were in kindergarten.

Taken together, our analyses and Minton's study indicated that learning gains can be attributed to "Sesame Street" even when children did not have to be partitioned into viewing groups on the basis of fallible viewing measures. However, Minton's data suggested that learning gains on the MRT are restricted to letter recognition skills.

THE ADEQUACY OF GAINS FROM VIEWING WITHOUT ENCOURAGEMENT

The Magnitude of Gains

We saw in Chapters 5 and 6 how an increase in variance of 5 percent or gains of one-half a standard deviation are conventionally considered criteria for concluding that gains are pedagogically rather than statistically significant. We now report the results of relevant variance tests from the multiple regression and Age Cohorts analyses of the nonencouraged. The first-year multiple regression analyses were presumably the most biased toward demonstrating large effects of viewing while the Age Cohorts analyses had low statistical power in that the error term is computed from the difference among children rather than the difference between pretest and posttest scores within children.

Table 7.6 shows that R^2 increased by 7 percent or more for the Letters Test in the first-year pooled sites analysis when either the Posttest Parent Questionnaire or Viewing Logs were used to index the level of viewing. In addition, Numbers and the related Grand Total were associated with increases of 5 percent when the first of these measures was used. Given the presumed positive bias in the analysis, it is not likely that the real increase is this high. As a matter of record, the obtained increase was 4.8 percent in the case of Numbers, and so the 5 percent level in Table 7.6 was only reached because of rounding.

If we turn now to the Age Cohorts analysis of the pooled first-year sample of economically disadvantaged children, we can compute the estimated ω^2 which corresponds to the interaction of viewing and cohort groups within the nonencouraged condition. The values from this analysis are in Table 7.21, and it can be seen that the Letters Test exceeded the 5 percent criterion but no other test did. (It should be recognized that $est.\omega^2$ is not a measure of associative strength which is independent of the error term. Indeed, it is directly dependent so that, in a between-subjects design like the Age Cohorts, a given mean difference tends to produce a lower estimate of ω^2 than would be the case if it were obtained in a within-subjects design.)

The multiple covariance design for estimating the effects of viewing among nonencouraged children at Los Angeles produced nonviewers and heavier viewers who had comparable pretest Grand Total attainments and background characteristics (see Table 7.7) and whose posttest averages

Table 7.21. Estimated ω^2 Associated with the Interaction of Viewing and Cohort Groups from the Separate Analyses of All Learning Tests within the Nonencouraged in the First and Second Years

	First-Year Pooled Disadvantaged Sites	Los Angeles
Body Parts	0	1
Letters	8	0
Forms	0	3
Numbers	2	0
Sorting	0	0
Relations	0	2
Classification	0	0
Puzzles	0	—
Parts of the Whole	—	0
Emotions	—	0
Grand Total	1	2

tended to differ in a direction indicating an effect of viewing. But the effect was not statistically reliable. We took the adjusted posttest difference between the nonviewers and heavier viewers, and it was not larger than one-half a standard deviation when the latter was computed from the adjusted standard error of the difference between the two means. In addition, neither the adjusted Letters nor Numbers means of these groups differed significantly at the posttest, and none of them met the criterion of gains larger than one-half a standard deviation.

The same conclusions were evident from the Age Cohorts analysis of nonencouraged Los Angeles children where it can be seen from Table 7.21 that the most variance that the interaction of encouragement and viewing caused on any test was 3 percent for Forms.

A quite different perspective on the magnitude of learning from "Sesame Street" can be gained by asking how much of the alphabet children learned and how well they learned to count. These are well-known simple skills; they were explicit goals of the show in the second year; and many individual readers will have an intuitive grasp of what they represent. For this reason these outcomes were selected for special presentation before we knew how the data looked. Table 7.22 is abstracted from Tables 33a and 33b of Bogatz and Ball and comes from their analysis of second-year chil-

Table 7.22. Mean Pretest and Gain by Encouragement and Viewing Groups of Second-Year Children on Tests of Knowledge of the Alphabet and Counting to Thirty*

		Nonencouraged				Encouraged		
	N	Pretest X̄	Gain X̄	Gain S	N	Pretest X̄	Gain X̄	Gain S
Knowledge of the alphabet								
Nonviewers	99	3.4	5.8	6.7	9	3.1	3.2	3.5
Lighter viewers	46	2.8	5.2	4.9	43	4.3	5.1	6.9
Heavy viewers	8	2.9	4.4	5.2	78	5.5	7.2	8.0
Counting from one to thirty								
Nonviewers	99	5.3	5.7	7.8	9	3.1	6.9	5.0
Lighter viewers	46	5.0	6.0	7.5	43	5.1	6.4	7.5
Heavy viewers	8	5.3	3.5	7.3	78	5.9	8.6	7.4

* This table is abstracted from Tables 33a and 33b of Bogatz and Ball.

dren who were broken down into encouragement and viewing groups.[23] The latter were formed using a composite of the Posttest Parent Questionnaire and Viewing Records.

The first thing to note about the table is that among nonencouraged children the pretest means did not vary with viewing groups. On the average, nonencouraged children knew the alphabet as far as the third letter— C—before the season began. By its end, nonviewers knew the alphabet to I; lighter viewers knew it to H; and heavier viewers knew it to G! As far as counting is concerned, the average nonencouraged child knew up to five by the pretest. Nonviewers knew up to eleven by the posttest; lighter viewers knew up to eleven; and heavier viewers knew up to nine. Once again, there is no evidence that viewing caused learning gains.

The situation is different among encouraged children where pretest attainments were related to viewing level. Thus, nonviewers knew up to C at the pretest and F at the posttest; lighter viewers went from knowing D to I; and heavier viewers went from E or F to M. In counting, nonviewers went from three to ten; lighter viewers from five to eleven or twelve; and heavier viewers from six to thirteen or fourteen. The pattern of pretest data implies that an unknown part of these viewing-related differences in alphabet (but not counting) gain may have been due to nonequivalent groups of children maturing at different rates.

For our final analysis of the magnitude of effects, we computed whether the predicted Grand Total posttest mean for nonencouraged children from the regression equation differed by more than one-half a standard deviation from the obtained mean at the first-year sites. Using the posttest Grand Total standard deviation of nonencouraged children, the Boston mean differed from the predicted mean by .30 standard deviation units, the California mean by .41, the Durham mean by .38, the Phoenix mean by .54 and the Philadelphia mean by .89. We must repeat once again that test familiarity may have inflated these estimates and that a ceiling effect may

---

[23] It was more difficult with the first-year sample to capitalize upon our intuitive understanding of the magnitude of counting and alphabet recitation effects. We did not conduct subgroup analyses ourselves, and the tests in the Ball and Bogatz report are from the flawed Inferential Study which used the Sesame Street Test for determining the viewing composite. Unfortunately, no alphabet recitation means were reported for the disadvantaged at-home samples of encouraged and nonencouraged children. There are means, however, for a test of counting up to ten. To judge by the ETS Tables 18b and 18c, viewing quartiles were not related to counting gains. However, since pretest counting was positively related to viewing score, a ceiling effect may have been inhibiting growth among the higher scorers on the viewing composite. For these reasons, the first-year data are not helpful for testing to what extent nonencouraged viewers learned to count or to recite the alphabet.

have especially inflated the Philadelphia estimate. Thus, only at Phoenix was the criterion of a gain of one-half a standard deviation met.

The Generality of Learning Gains

We earlier established that statistically significant effects of viewing were demonstrated for two of eight tests in the first year (Letters and Numbers); that one of nine tests was statistically significant in the second year (Relations); that the Grand Total, a measure in which Letters and Numbers predominated, was marginally related to viewing in the second year; and that Relations was almost marginally related to viewing among nonencouraged children in the first year. This led us to conclude that "Sesame Street" was probably teaching some letter, number, and relationship skills. Minton's study produced corroboration of the Letters effect but not the Numbers effect.

The second-year evaluation included both pretest and posttest measures of Peabody IQ. Hence, we conducted the same multiple covariates analysis that we listed earlier, and Peabody pretest IQ, the pretest Grand Total, age, and mother's education were the covariates. Viewing was not related to adjusted posttest Peabody scores, either across all three viewing groups or in the contrast of nonviewers and the heaviest viewers (see Table 7.23) or even in the contrast of nonviewers and lighter viewers.

Table 7.23. Peabody IQ as a Function of Level of Viewing*
Among Nonencouraged Children from Los Angeles

	Nonviewers (N = 72)	Lighter Viewers (N = 16)	Heavier Viewers (N = 17)
Pretest Peabody IQ	76.03	70.56	74.82
Posttest Peabody IQ	69.08	71.56	68.76
Adjusted Posttest Peabody IQ	68.83	73.70	67.82
Standard Error of Adjusted Mean	1.57	3.41	3.27

* The viewing measure is the index derived from the Posttest Parent Questionnaire.

(The adjusted posttest differences were larger for this last comparison than in the comparison of nonviewers and heavier viewers.) Thus, it cannot be demonstrated that viewing affected a vocabulary-based measure of IQ in the second-year evaluation.

Since there were no posttest measures of Peabody IQ in the first year, it was not possible to conduct a similar analysis on the first-year samples. However, a second possibility to explore the effects of viewing on Peabody IQ is provided by the fact that a group of the first-year children from Boston, Durham, and Phoenix were followed into the second year where Peabody IQ was measured both at the pretest and posttest. Thus, there were three IQ measures for these children: one at the pretest of the first year, a second at the pretest of the second year, and a third at the posttest of the second year. We took the nonencouraged Boston sample that was followed through the second year and for which there was a Posttest Parent Questionnaire measure of viewing from the first year. They were a particularly good sample because viewing was related to Grand Total posttest knowledge in the multiple regression analysis of first-year data at this site. We then constructed the same multiple regression model that was frequently used earlier in the chapter. The predictors were pretest Grand Total, pretest Peabody IQ, age, sex, Home Stimulation-Affluence Index, and the viewing measure. The pretest Grand Total was forced into the analysis first, the pretest Peabody IQ score from the first year second, and the viewing measure third. The other variables were left free to enter. The relationship of viewing to IQ at the second-year pretest was not statistically significant after adjustments were made for the other predictors. By itself, this would not mean much since only a sample of thirty-one children was involved. However, in the context of the previous analysis from the Los Angeles sample, it raised doubts as to whether viewing increased IQ.

Since IQ gains have a special importance as indices of a gain in general cognitive ability rather than some specific skill, and since the ETS conclusions about "Sesame Street's" influence on Peabody IQ seemed more positive than ours, it is important to examine the major evidence for the ETS conclusions other than the second-year difference between encouraged and nonencouraged children in posttest Peabody IQ.[24] (See Chapter 6.) The auxiliary ETS evidence came from a design which Bogatz and Ball freely admitted "is quite insufficient to allow a causal relationship between viewing and gain in Peabody IQ." In essence, the ETS team divided the first-year sample which was followed through the second year into six groups: (1) children who were relatively heavier viewers in the first year, the intervening summer, and the second year; (2) those who were heavier viewers the first year and summer but not the second year; (3) those who were

---

[24] Caution is, of course, required before generalizing from scores on a vocabulary-based measure of IQ for preschoolers, like the Peabody, either to the results of more problem-solving IQ tests for older school children or to some construct like intelligence.

heavier viewers the first year but not the summer or second year; (4) those who were lighter viewers the first year but heavier viewers the summer and second year; (5) those who were lighter viewers the first and second years but not the summer; and (6) those who were lighter viewers at each of the three times. Then, these six groups were related to IQ scores at the first- and second-year pretests and the second-year posttest.

The ETS results are illustrated in Table 7.24. Note, first of all, the prob-

Table 7.24.   Peabody IQ Means at Three Time Intervals for Some First-Year Encouraged Children Who Were Followed into the Second Year

Group	Pretest Year I	Pretest Year II	Posttest Year II	Overall Gain
$H_1 H_s H_2$	82.0	88.8	94.5	15.5
$H_1 H_s L_2$	84.5	86.0	95.8	11.3
$H_1 L_s L_2$	88.8	91.8	98.0	9.2
$L_1 H_s H_2$	71.9	80.1	86.8	14.9
$L_1 H_s L_2$	76.9	83.0	86.0	9.1
$L_1 L_s L_2$	75.8	81.4	89.9	14.1

H = heavy viewer; L = light viewer; the subscript 1 refers to the first year; s refers to summer, and 2 to the second year.
* The data in this table are taken from Bogatz and Ball, p. 145.

able statistical regression. Among first-year heavy viewers Peabody IQ gains were positively related to the amount of viewing over summer and the next year, but they were also negatively related to the Peabody IQ level of the first-year pretest. This means that the effects of viewing and statistical regression were confounded. Among first-year lighter viewers, those who viewed more in summer and the second season also manifested both the largest gain and the lowest pretest starting point so that once again, viewing and regression were confounded. Second, it should also be noted that one of the largest (regression-inflated) gains is registered by the group which viewed least of all over the two years! The differences in gain by children who viewed different amounts were not clearly interpretable as effects of viewing: first, there was the regression confound; next, there was the apparently large gain of the lowest viewers; and finally, all the children in the ETS analysis were encouraged.

What does require interpretation is why Peabody IQ increased with time for all the viewing groups in Table 7.24. Since almost all the children viewed "Sesame Street" to some extent, one might be tempted to attribute this overall increase of about twelve IQ points to watching the show. There are, of course, other possible interpretations: increased test familiarity; better tester rapport as the child gets used to testing; poor norming of the test; and nonviewing correlates of the complex encouragement treatment. The norming explanation loses some credence when we remember that the IQ scores did not increase as the second-year children grew older (see Table 7.23), which we would expect if the test was particularly badly normed for low-scoring younger disadvantaged children. The familiarity explanation also loses credence when we remember the decrease over time in IQ for the second-year nonencouraged group whose familiarity with the test had increased by the posttest. However, it is not possible to rule out the explanation that the results are due to nonviewing aspects of the encouragement treatment (e.g., testers giving more feedback about correct responses to encouraged children when they tested them).

The incidental evidence is not strong that the increase of twelve IQ points was due to "Sesame Street" in that (1) the powerful true experiment with the Los Angeles children produced an absolute gain of only two points; (2) the Word Meaning subtest of the MRT is a vocabulary test like the Peabody, and it was not related to learning gains in Minton's analysis of group learning from "Sesame Street"; and especially (3) since most preschoolers who had access to "Sesame Street" viewed it, we would expect the IQ of disadvantaged children throughout the nation to have been raised by twelve or more points on the widely used Peabody. This would be a newsworthy event and easy to document because it should show up in all preschool and even first-grade surveys that have been conducted since 1970. But we have not yet heard of surveys reporting unexpectedly higher IQ means than were found before 1969. An analysis of IQ gains by nonencouraged viewers is urgently required in the light of the difference between our tentative results and those reported by Bogatz and Ball.

The Long-Term Effects of Viewing "Sesame Street"

We would have liked to examine whether heavy viewers in the first season knew more at the end of the second season than lighter viewers. But the second-year follow-up was not conducted on a large sample of nonencouraged children. The largest single sample was at Boston where a total of only thirty-one children provided usable data. This was not enough for conducting sensitive quasi-experimental analyses in the absence of a possible replication from another year. The long-term effects of viewing "Sesame Street" remain an important problem to be pursued in future research.

The second-year ETS report included an analysis of whether the first-year sample of children learned from "Sesame Street" in their second season of viewing. The analysis developed to answer this question was a modified Age Cohorts design. It was an Age Cohorts design since there was a pretest cohort of children whose age was between sixty-three and sixty-eight months at the beginning of the second year, and a posttest cohort whose pretest age was between fifty-seven and sixty-two months and whose posttest age was between sixty-three and sixty-eight months. It was a *modified* Age Cohorts design because, unlike the Age Cohorts analysis in the first-year report, there was no partitioning of pretest and posttest cohorts into viewing groups. The reason for this was probably the restricted sample size of first-year children who had not entered school during the second year: namely, twenty-nine in the pretest cohort and thirty-one in the posttest cohort. These small samples meant that the ETS team could not test whether the cohort and viewing groups interacted to determine learning (as in the first-year report); instead they had to test whether the posttest cohort knew more than the pretest cohort. This placed a special burden on Bogatz and Ball to demonstrate that the cohort groups were comparable in all ways other than that (1) the posttest cohort had viewed "Sesame Street" during its second season whereas the pretest cohort had not; and that (2) the posttest cohort had been tested once more than the pretest cohort.

Analyses in the second-year report indicated that the pretest and posttest cohorts did not differ in age, Peabody IQ, viewing in the first year or in the summer between the first and second years, or in sex, parental education, or research site. Furthermore, all the children had been encouraged and observed in the first year, and so all were encouraged in the second year. Though it is logically possible for the cohorts to have differed on unmeasured variables related to knowledge, this does not seem likely. The only possibility of a difference on *measured* variables stems from perusal of Table 7.25, which is a reproduction of Bogatz and Ball's Table 53. The table indicates that variances for most learning tests and subtests tended to be higher in the posttest than the pretest cohorts. Whether this is a result of group differences in background variables or a result of the posttest group's second-year viewing is not clear.

We chose to analyze the data in Table 7.25 differently from the ETS team whose analysis capitalized upon chance and required making some difficult distinctions between "old" and "new or revised" tests.[25] We began by asking if the Grand Total differed between the pretest and posttest cohorts. A simple *t*-test for unequal variances (given the trend in the tabu-

---

[25] P. 151. The ETS analysis was designed to classify subtests as "old" goals (those in the first-year but not the second-year evaluation) and "revised and new" goals.

Table 7.25.   Follow-Up Age Cohorts Study*
(Cohort 1 = Children who were 63–68 months at pretest Year II
Cohort 2 = Children who were 63–68 months at posttest Year II)

Test and Subtest	Maximum Possible Score	Cohort 1 N = 29 Pretest		Cohort 2 N = 31 Posttest	
		Mean	SD	Mean	SD
Naming Body Parts	10	9.2	1.6	9.4	1.1
Function of Body Parts	8	6.4	1.4	6.7	1.4
Body Parts Total	18	15.6	2.7	16.1	2.1
Naming Forms	4	2.5	1.3	2.6	1.4
Recognizing Forms	4	3.0	1.2	2.9	1.4
Forms Total	8	5.5	2.2	5.5	2.6
Roles of Community Members	4	2.9	1.1	3.5	1.0
Matching by Form	9	6.1	1.3	6.1	1.5
Matching by Position	3	1.6	.8	1.5	.8
Recognizing Letters	4	2.3	1.2	2.6	1.1
Naming Letters	8	1.9	2.5	3.5	3.1
Letter Sounds	4	.7	1.2	1.6	1.7
Initial Sounds	6	1.6	1.3	1.6	1.7
Decoding	8	2.1	1.5	2.9	2.0
Reading	9	2.0	1.3	2.9	2.0
Left-Right Orientation	4	1.8	1.4	2.2	1.3
Alphabet (A to Z)	26	10.2	9.2	16.5	10.1
Prereading Total	48	15.6	7.9	20.4	10.2
Recognizing Numbers	4	1.9	1.1	2.3	1.2
Naming Numbers	6	.7	1.0	2.0	1.9
Enumeration	7	5.6	1.1	5.7	1.4
Conservation	7	4.0	1.5	4.5	1.2
Counting Strategies	8	6.7	1.1	6.4	1.5
Number/Numeral Agreement	3	2.0	.9	2.0	.9
Addition & Subtraction	13	4.0	1.6	4.8	2.8
Counting (1–30)	30	13.8	6.5	18.6	9.8
Numbers Total	54	28.6	6.3	32.1	8.0
Relational Terms Total	17	13.3	2.3	14.3	2.5
Classification	15	11.0	3.8	10.9	3.5
Double Classification	9	3.9	1.4	4.6	2.1
Classification Total	24	14.8	4.7	15.5	5.0
Sorting Total	16	8.9	4.0	8.4	5.0
Parts of Whole Total	10	5.8	1.7	6.5	1.8
Emotions Total	8	6.4	1.5	6.1	1.5

Table 7.25   (*cont.*)

Test and Subtest	Maximum Possible Score	Cohort 1 N = 29 Pretest		Cohort 2 N = 31 Posttest	
		Mean	SD	Mean	SD
Attitude to School†	7	4.9	1.8	5.8	1.2
Attitude to Others†	4	2.8	1.0	3.1	1.0
Attitude to Race of Others†	6	3.8	1.7	4.9	1.4
Grand Total	214	122.8	26.5	133.6	34.0
Peabody Raw Score	—	45.1	8.1	48.4	10.7
Peabody Mental Age in Months	—	54.9	12.7	61.3	19.2
Peabody IQ	—	85.3	14.5	88.9	19.8
Chronological Age in Months	—	65.4	1.9	65.5	1.6

* The data in this table are taken from Bogatz and Ball, Table 53.
† *N*'s for these subtests: Cohort 1 N = 24; Cohort 2 N = 17.

lated data) did not reach the 10 percent level. We next asked if the cohorts differed on any of the individual learning tests. The only comparison to reach the 5 percent level was for Letters or Prereading ($t = 2.05$), although Numbers reached the 10 percent level ($t = 1.89$). Exploring subtest differences ran an even greater risk of capitalizing upon chance. But using the 1 percent level of statistical significance as our decision criterion, the posttest cohorts knew more than the pretest cohorts with respect to knowledge of the Alphabet ($t = 2.53$) and naming Numbers ($t = 3.36$). There were more differences at the 5 percent level, particularly within the Letters Test, some of which may be due to chance. The differences were in Naming Letters, Letter Sounds, and Reading (this is likely to be recognizing words; note the low means and the fact, remarked upon earlier, that there were four word recognition items in the Reading subtest), Counting, Attitude toward Race, and Knowledge of Community Members. Thus, of twenty-nine subtests (excluding Attitude), seven reached conventional levels of statistical significance, though only one of the tests did, and the Grand Total did not. What is perhaps most noteworthy is that, once again, it was the Letters Test and its subtests which most obviously showed effects.

However, the modified Age Cohorts analysis is hard to interpret. Since it was restricted to children who were encouraged-to-view by the ETS staff in two seasons, its most serious problem is that the analysis was of the effects of encouragement-and-viewing rather than of viewing without encouragement. This makes the analysis more akin conceptually to the problems we analyzed in Chapter 6 rather than to those we are examining in this chapter. A second problem is that the samples were small. Small samples are considerably less of a problem when replication across different sets of data is possible and when each replication provides similar outcomes. Small samples are more of a problem, however, when replication is possible but the results of the small sample analysis conflict with those of other analyses of the same issue. For instance, the Alphabet and Counting subtests discriminated in the second-year modified Age Cohorts study, but they did not discriminate either in the analysis of the effects of encouragement-and-viewing from the second-year randomized experiment, or in the analysis of the effects of viewing without encouragement in the second year, or in the ETS analysis of the effects of viewing on counting in the first year (see our footnote 23). Why should this one small sample analysis have produced different results from the other analyses, some of which seem to be more powerful than the modified Age Cohorts design?

These were not the only problems; others were that the posttest cohort was tested once more than the pretest cohort (four times *versus* three) and that the basic design depended on the ultimately untestable assumption that the cohort groups were equivalent. However, the first two problems were the most serious, and because of them we were not inclined to put much weight on the ETS modified Age Cohorts analysis for its relevance to testing whether children who viewed for a second season gained more than children who viewed a first season but not a second. In any event, it was in no way a test of the long-term effects of viewing; it was a test of the effects of one season's encouragement-and-viewing following a previous season's encouragement-and-viewing.

Adequacy Questions That Could Not Be Probed

In the absence of the strongest possible design where children were randomly assigned to viewing groups *without encouragement,* there were other questions of adequacy that could not be tackled, because there were no relevant data on hand. These included issues relating to the effects of viewing "Sesame Street" on academic motivation, academic self-concept, and on generalized self-concept or the learning of interpersonal cooperation. They also included issues relating to whether children adopted new sources from which they hoped to receive information, whether they read more or less, and whether they became more active or passive as information-seekers.

RAISING QUESTIONS ABOUT PROCESS

The Problems of Answering the Major Process Questions

With the available data, it was extremely difficult, if not impossible, to conduct sensitive analyses of whether children of specific IQ, SES, racial, age, or sex groups learned from viewing and whether children at some specific level on one of these moderator variables gained more than children at some other level even when they reportedly viewed "Sesame Street" for the same amount of time. One major source of difficulty arose because of the small sample sizes which result if any attempt is made to partition children into more groups after they have already been partitioned into encouragement and viewing groups. Another problem occurred because of the restricted range of some variables. Indicators of SES were a case in point since the ceiling effect at Philadelphia meant that analyses would have to be restricted to the SES range found in the economically disadvantaged neighborhoods which comprised the rest of the ETS sample.

We decided, therefore, to place major stress on assessing whether the moderator variables interacted in simple multiplicative fashion with viewing to determine posttest learning. To do this, we restricted ourselves to the first-year disadvantaged sites (because of the curvilinearity problem at Los Angeles and the ceiling effect problem in Philadelphia) as well as to the Posttest Parent Questionnaire measure of viewing (which had produced stronger relationships with posttest learning than the continuously collected Viewing Logs measure). Then, in separate analyses, we took Peabody IQ, age, sex as a dummy variable, and the indices of Home Stimulation-Affluence and Home-Education, and multiplied each child's score on these moderator variables by his viewing score. Following this, we conducted multiple regression analyses at each site and at the pooled disadvantaged sites (with site as a dummy variable). In all cases nonencouraged children formed the sample, the posttest Grand Total was the criterion, the pretest Grand Total was forced into the analysis first, and the score representing the interaction of viewing and a particular moderator variable was forced in next. The remaining variables were left free to enter. This analysis permits the detection of gross multiplicative interactions of viewing with particular moderator variables.

As far as the SES indicators were concerned, there were ten relevant analyses (four sites $\times$ two SES indicators plus one pooled site analysis for each indicator). Only one of these was significant at the 5 percent level and that was at Phoenix where children from more education-conscious homes gained at a faster rate. However, this single effect may have been due to chance. Neither the sex, age, nor Peabody IQ analyses produced significant p values associated with the interaction scores. We do not consider it likely, therefore, that viewing interacted with the moderator variables we have analyzed to cause learning gains. However, the analyses were not sensitive ones, and the issue is not closed.

Race is another indicator of SES, and it is likely that black children can gain from viewing without encouragement. This conclusion can be gleaned from the fact that the conservative Age Cohorts analysis of Los Angeles children resulted in a marginal interaction of cohort groups and viewing, and 90 percent of the children from that site were black. In addition, the difference between estimated and obtained posttest Grand Totals was statistically reliable among the nonencouraged children at Durham where the sample was also about 90 percent black. Though this last analysis may have inflated effects because of the confound with test familiarity, it is worth noting that even a weaker trend at Durham would have independently corroborated the finding from the Los Angeles Age Cohorts Study. Unfortunately, sample sizes precluded an analysis of the effects of viewing on nonencouraged Spanish-speaking children.

DO ENCOURAGEMENT AND VIEWING INTERACT TO DETERMINE LEARNING GAINS?

Although we feared that the amount of viewing might have differed between supposedly comparable viewing groups in the encouraged and non-encouraged conditions, we nonetheless explored whether encouragement and viewing were multiplicatively related. We used two strategies for this. One was based on the approximation to a factorial experiment which resulted when children were classified into naturally occurring viewing and cohort groups. The other was based on multiple regression analyses with the encouragement treatment as a dummy variable.

"Factorial" Experiments

In Table 7.18 we reported the transformed means for the entire English-speaking Los Angeles sample. A three-way analysis of variance of the transformed scores (encouragement, viewing, and cohort groups) resulted in a statistically significant interaction of viewing and cohort groups for Forms and a marginal interaction for the Grand Total. Let us consider only the Grand Total and work with the difference between the means of pretest and posttest cohorts who were or were not encouraged and who did or did not report viewing "Sesame Street." The gain of encouraged viewers from the pretest to the posttest was .45 transformed units, and the gain of non-encouraged viewers was .09, while the gain of encouraged nonviewers was .01 and that of nonencouraged nonviewers was —.48. There were obvious trends here for main effects of both viewing and encouragement, and no indication that the greater gains of viewers over nonviewers was larger among encouraged or nonencouraged children.

When we turned to the transformed Grand Total data from the pooled first-year sites, a similar pattern emerged. In the three-way analysis of variance, the interaction of viewing and cohort groups was marginally significant for the Grand Total ($p < .10$) and was significant for the Letters and Numbers tests. The difference between the transformed pretest and posttest cohort means for the Grand Total was .44 among encouraged heavy viewers and .12 among nonencouraged heavy viewers, while it was —.06 among encouraged light viewers and —.45 among nonencouraged light viewers. This pattern was very similar to that for the Los Angeles sample and indicated that learning may have been related to both viewing and encouragement. It did not indicate that effects of viewing were increased or decreased if there was encouragement.

Interpretation of the first-year data was hindered because of the pretest noncomparability of viewing groups. It is worthwhile in this respect reconsidering Table 7.7 for its implications about whether encouragement caused learning among encouraged and nonencouraged children with comparable pretest attainments. It will be remembered from that table (which is based on the second-year sample) that encouraged and nonencouraged children in each of three viewing groups had similar background characteristics and pretest knowledge levels but that at each level of viewing—*including nonviewing*—the encouraged gained more than the nonencouraged by at least eleven Grand Total points.

Multiple Regression Analyses

In the previous analyses, viewing and encouragement may have been correlated, not only because encouraged children viewed more than nonencouraged children, but also because encouraged children may have viewed more than nonencouraged children within the viewing categories we constructed by collapsing across certain viewing scores. Multiple regression skirts the problems associated with the noncomparability of supposedly identical viewing groups. This is because each child is given his or her own viewing score rather than being placed in a viewing category defined by a certain range of scores.

To examine the interaction possibility we created a dummy encouragement variable by assigning encouraged children a one and nonencouraged children a zero. Then we multiplied each child's encouragement score by his exact score on the Posttest Parent Questionnaire viewing measure and assigned each child the resulting viewing-encouragement interaction score. These scores were naturally highly correlated with both viewing and encouragement, especially the latter, so that in any multiple regression analysis there is a problem of multicollinearity.

We then constructed a model in which the posttest Grand Total was the criterion, the first predictor to enter the analysis was the pretest Grand Total, the second was the viewing-encouragement interaction score, and the next predictors were viewing and encouragement for which no order was specified. Our interest lay in ascertaining whether the interaction scores were related to posttest knowledge after most of the variance due to viewing and encouragement was removed, and we computed the appropriate statistical tests at each first-year site.

A statistically significant β weight for the interaction variable was only obtained at Phoenix where, as we saw earlier, viewing and knowledge level tended to be negatively related among nonencouraged children and positively related among the encouraged. There were no observable relationships at Boston, California, or Durham. It would seem, then, that encouragement and viewing are not generally related in multiplicative fashion.

The Philadelphia and Boston Puzzle

There is one major stumbling block to accepting the implied conclusion that encouragement and viewing did not interact to cause learning gains. We saw in the previous chapter that the randomly created groups at Boston and Philadelphia differed in encouragement but did not differ either in reported viewing or adjusted posttest knowledge. Now, if encouragement-to-view did affect learning gains and had the same effect at all levels of viewing, the encouraged children at Philadelphia and Boston should have known more than the nonencouraged at the posttest even if they had viewed "Sesame Street" for comparable amounts of time. How might we explain the apparent discrepancy between the absence of a main effect of encouragement in these particular Boston and Philadelphia analyses and the presence of a main effect of encouragement in our Age Cohorts analyses of disadvantaged children as well as in the ETS analyses reported in Tables 7.1 and 7.2?

A possibility which immediately springs to mind is that the Philadelphia and Boston children were the highest scorers of all at the pretest and that there was probably restricted room for posttest growth at these sites on these particular scales. Figures 7.1 and 7.2 seem to support this possibility at first glance. However, it is probably not correct to suggest that ceiling effects at these sites may have obscured any additional gains that encouraged children made because of nonviewing aspects of the global encouragement treatment. If it were correct, we would expect the encouraged children who scored lower at the pretest to have outscored their nonencouraged counterparts while the higher pretest scorers could not have done. This being so, we would expect the slope of the regression of the posttest on pretest to differ between the encouraged and nonencouraged groups in Philadelphia and Boston. More specifically, we would expect the posttest scores of encouraged children to be higher than those of nonencouraged children if pretest scores were low but not if they were high. However, we saw in Chapter 5 when we tested the assumptions of covariance analysis that the relevant slopes were not different. The reader might be able to corroborate this for himself visually by examining the scatterplots of pretest and posttest Grand Total scores in Figures 7.3 and 7.4 which came from encouraged children at Philadelphia and at Boston and which correspond to Figures 7.1 and 7.2 for nonencouraged children.

A second possibility is that encouragement and viewing might have statistically interacted in a specific nonlinear way which our first-year analyses were not sensitive enough to have detected. In particular, Table 7.1 im-

Figure 7.3. Scatterplot of the Pretest and Posttest Grand Total Scores of Encouraged At-Home Children from Boston

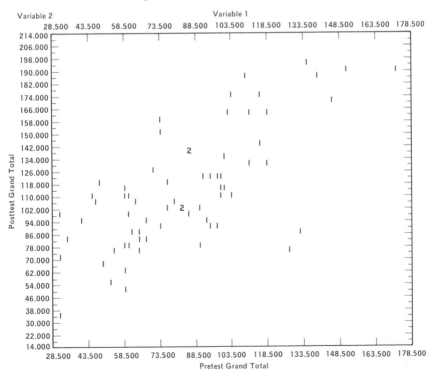

Figure 7.4.   Scatterplot of the Pretest and Posttest Grand Total Scores of
Encouraged At-Home Children from Philadelphia

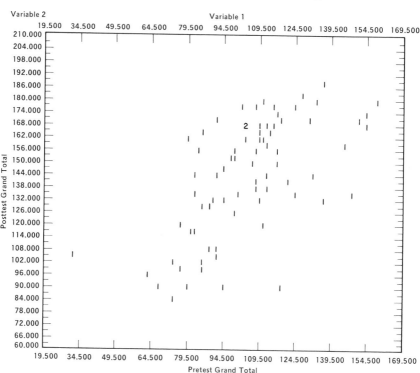

plies that encouraged children might have gained more than nonencouraged children only when viewing was relatively light and that, when it was heavy, roughly four or more times a week, encouragement may have made little difference in learning. One way of approximately analyzing this issue would have been to take the regressed gain scores of encouraged and nonencouraged children at Philadelphia and Boston and plot them as a function of the level of viewing. Unfortunately, this was not possible because the level of viewing was absolutely so high that there was little within-site variability in viewing (see Table 4.10). In fact, on the Posttest Parent Questionnaire measure of viewing, thirty-nine of forty-two nonencouraged children at Boston scored 5 or 6 on the six-point scale!

A third possibility was that our attempts to unconfound encouragement-to-view and viewing resulted in viewing categories that were not equivalent in the mean level of viewing across encouragement conditions. If this were so, the encouraged-heavy viewers would have been heavier viewers than the nonencouraged-heavy viewers, so that any differences in gains between these groups might have been due, not to differences in encouragement, but to differences in viewing. We attempted to rule out this possibility by the regression analysis in which children were given a score that was computed by multiplying a "dummy" encouragement value with their exact score on the Posttest Parent Questionnaire measure of viewing. However, it was possible that these analyses using six viewing intervals were not sensitive enough to detect subtle interaction effects or that the interaction was of a more complicated form than the simple multiplicative model that we tested. It is unclear, therefore, why there was a main effect of encouragement on learning in most of our analyses and those of the ETS team even though there was no such effect in our analyses of the randomly created Boston and Philadelphia samples.

CONCLUSION

Effects of Viewing without Encouragement

Our analysis and Minton's dissertation suggested that one season's viewing of "Sesame Street" taught nonencouraged children. If we consider only the Posttest Parent Questionnaire measure of viewing, statistically reliable gains were found in the first year for the Letters and Numbers tests and marginally reliable gains were found for the Relations Test. The Relations Test was significantly related to gains in the second-year evaluation, as was the Grand Total, a composite which was heavily weighted in terms of Letters and Numbers. Moreover, in an evaluation not using ETS data, Minton found that children learned letter recognition skills from the programs, although she failed to find that they learned number skills. Thus, statistically significant Letter, Number, and Relations effects have been demonstrated, though only the first effect could be demonstrated to have met conventional statistical criteria of social significance.

For five of the eight individual first-year tests, and six of the nine second-year tests, we were unable to demonstrate that "Sesame Street" had statistically significant effects that were replicable enough to be found across modes of data analysis. However, most of the effects in most of the analyses were in a direction indicating that "Sesame Street" might have taught the skills in question. As with all no-difference findings, these present us with a dilemma. If we had been able to increase power by controlling for more sources of extraneous variance, by increasing sample size, or by more powerful statistical tests, would these non-significant effects have become statistically significant? And if they had done so after even more controls had been instituted than were available to us with the ETS data (which were, after all, not collected to establish whether "Sesame Street" teaches nonencouraged children), how educationally significant would such statistically significant effects have been, given that they could only be obtained after much naturally occurring variability had been controlled?

The data we have reviewed about statistically significant effects suggested to us that one season's viewing of "Sesame Street" was not causing as generalized or as large learning gains as those that were attributed to "Sesame Street" in the two ETS reports. When we considered effects that met statistical criteria of social significance, the series seemed to have practical consequences only for gains in letter-related skills. To judge by Table 7.22, these skills may not have included learning to recite the alphabet any more quickly than would have happened in the course of the child's spontaneous maturation. It may well have been that the new letter skills are most pronounced in areas relating to letter recognition.[26]

Nine points need to be noted about these less-than-comforting conclusions. *First* of all, there were indeed some demonstrable effects. This has not always been the case when other preschool programs were evaluated.

Second, the conclusions applied only to economically disadvantaged children who watched "Sesame Street." They cannot logically be extrapolated to children from more affluent homes.

Third, the effects were for only one six-month season of viewing the series. Many children view it for longer, and their gains may be larger over the longer time period.

Fourth, the analyses were limited to the 1969–1970 and 1970–1971 viewing seasons and to the particular programming broadcast in these years.

Fifth, many—*but not all*—of the analyses depended upon a valid measure of viewing, and it is not known to what extent the Posttest Parent Questionnaire measure was valid nor to what extent it was more valid than the Viewing Logs or Viewing Records. If it were less valid, our conclusions about "Sesame Street's" effectiveness would have had to be even more pessimistic, since the analyses using Viewing Logs and Viewing Records produced even fewer effects.

Sixth, the samples of nonencouraged children were not more than 110 in either year. This precluded extensive and sensitive analysis of whether learning gains were larger with some kinds of children or at some sites than others, although the latter possibility was indeed suggested by the data. The small samples and the low power of some statistical tests also necessitated occasional examination of the effects of viewing within the encour-

---

[26] This conclusion is also suggested by the fact that Letters had a stronger relationship with viewing in the first year than the second and that the test was composed of more associative type recognition items in the first year than the second.

aged and, in the case of the conservative Age Cohorts analyses, it even necessitated pooling the encouraged and nonencouraged samples.

Seventh, though the ETS learning tests seemed to be of high reliability, the tests that showed effects were the more reliable ones. The implication of this is that the failure to obtain effects or larger effects might have been due to the quality of the measures rather than the impact of "Sesame Street." Of course, this possibility exists whenever effects are disappointingly narrow in range and corrections for unreliability have not been made.

Eighth, to demonstrate a failure to obtain large and consistent learning gains does not mean that a program failed to teach. It merely means that the program failed to teach more than a child would otherwise have learned. A child might well have learned from "Sesame Street" in all areas of cognitive development. But if he did, our analyses suggest that in many areas he only learned from the program in six months what he would otherwise have learned from other sources. Learning from "Sesame Street" does not necessarily imply gaining from it, and it seemed to us that gaining is an outcome of greater policy relevance than shifting the source from which a child learns.

Finally, it is worth noting that the somewhat pessimistic conclusions about watching "Sesame Street" that we have drawn are implied by two sources independent of our work. Minton's study was one obvious source of corroboration. The other came from the second-year ETS evaluation itself. We have already referred to the only explicit test in the ETS reports of the effects of viewing *independently of encouragement,* and the tables relevant to this test are 7.2 and 7.3.[27] They indicated that viewing was just related to learning gains at the 5 percent level for the Grand Total (no individual test analyses were reported), and that encouragement was more strongly related to gains than viewing. It should also be noted that the main effect of viewing in that analysis capitalized upon the fact that there were many more encouraged-heavy viewers than nonencouraged-heavy viewers. Hence, the mean of all heavy viewers was disproportionately influenced by the mean gain of encouraged-heavy viewers which was larger than the gain of nonencouraged-heavy viewers.

Effects of Encouragement without Viewing

Table 7.7 implies that encouraged children in the second year gained

---

[27] Both the first- and second-year ETS reports contained analyses in which encouragement and viewing were treated as independent variables. It was, however, only in the second year that the analysis was conducted for the explicit purpose of examining the unique effects of encouragement and viewing. Hence, their relative contribution to learning gains was not discussed in the first-year report.

more than nonencouraged children who supposedly watched "Sesame Street" in equal amounts or did not watch it at all. Table 7.1 implies the same relationship for three of four viewing levels in the first year. Moreover, Tables 7.16 and 7.18 report the means from Age Cohorts analyses in each year, and it seems that at each level of viewing the encouraged children outperformed the nonencouraged by more at the posttest than at the pretest. All of this evidence implies that encouragement caused learning gains for reasons that have nothing to do with viewing "Sesame Street."

But the conclusion cannot be accepted as definitive with the evidence on hand. The major reason for this is that, if encouragement had effects over and above those attributable to viewing, the Boston and Philadelphia encouraged children should have known more than the nonencouraged children at the posttest. Our Chapter 5 analyses, however, revealed that they did not.

If encouragement had the effect of increasing viewing but not of causing learning gains, this would imply that the ETS evaluations produced more positive conclusions about "Sesame Street," because they concentrated on what the series could accomplish if disadvantaged children were stimulated to view it more than they would otherwise have done. Thus, the ETS team may have evaluated "Sesame Street's" potential rather than its typical accomplishments; they may have demonstrated how much economically disadvantaged children could have learned under special conditions and not how much they did learn under normal conditions.

If encouragement had the dual effect of stimulating viewing and of causing learning gains over and above those attributable to viewing, this would imply that equating encouragement and viewing is especially misleading because effects would be attributed to viewing which are due both to nonviewing aspects of the encouragement treatment and to an atypical level of viewing. Unsuspecting persons might thereby be lulled into believing that the effects of normal viewing are as large and as consistent as the effects of encouragement-to-view by the ETS field staff.

Chapter 8
The Probable Effects of "Sesame Street" on the National Achievement Gap

EXPLICATING THE WIDENING ACHIEVEMENT GAP

Some Background Description

Figure 8.1 would result if one took a heterogeneous group of pre-schoolers of equal age and charted their development through the school years on a general knowledge test that had no ceiling effects. One can see from the figure that children would become increasingly more knowledge-able in general; that the variability in knowledge would increase with the years; and that there would also be an increase over time in the difference in knowledge between children who originally scored high and low. It would seem from this that the absolutely more knowledgeable children acquire rela-tively more knowledge as they mature.

The eight lines in Figure 8.1 should be thought of as groups of children that were formed by using pretest scores as a stratification variable. When the trends are thought of in this way, it should become clear that the figure oversimplifies what is in nature since nature does not recognize arbitrary cutting points such as those that were responsible for making the eight groups. A more exact way of portraying the relationship in Figure 8.1 would have been to redraw it in terms of distributions of scores for chil-dren at different ages. If we imagine the distributions to be normal, those at the earlier ages would have had a mean of X and a standard deviation of Y

Figure 8.1.   Typical Cognitive Growth Patterns for Eight Groups of
              Children of Different Initial Ability Levels

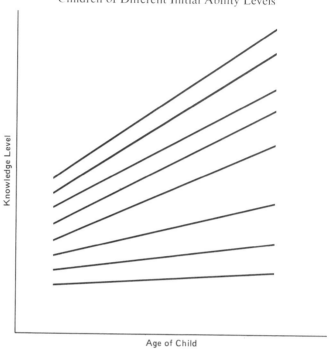

and those at a later age would have had a mean of $X + n$ and a standard deviation of $Y + m$ (n and m are positive).

Just as it is possible to simplify the situation and draw eight groups that mature at different rates, so it is also possible to simplify the eight and arrive at two. To do this, one would merely average the top four means at each time interval and then the bottom four. This would result in two diverging trend lines that represent the achievement growth of children at two levels of initial ability. The point of this is merely to illustrate on the one hand that the number of trend lines is arbitrary, and on the other hand that the knowledge means and variances will typically be correlated because there will be less variability about the knowledge mean at an earlier age than about the higher knowledge mean at a later age.

The Explanation Problem

The fact that the more able mature cognitively at a faster rate than the less able tells us nothing about why this is so. Typically, explanations focus upon both genetic and environmental factors, and it is not yet clear how much of the variance in learning is related to each of these and their interaction.[1]

The importance of our current ignorance stems from the possibility that the variance related to environmental factors may be so small that considerable amounts of environmental change or stimulation might be required for relatively small cognitive gains. However, since genetic engineering is not yet at hand, and since the technically most feasible means of genetic change—systematic breeding—is ethically distasteful, environmental changes are all we have at present for increasing what children know.

Some environmental factors related to learning are easier to manipulate than others. If one were to conceptualize learning as being associated with home factors (e.g., parental reinforcement practices, books in the home, SES level, etc.), peer factors (e.g., how knowledge is valued, which other time-consuming activities are available, etc.), and school factors (e.g., teachers' skill, school resources, etc.), then it is clear that the school factor may be technically and politically easier to change than the home factor. However, within the home factor, some things can be changed relatively more easily than others. The availability of books or a television set is one modifiable aspect of home life, as are the television programs which a child could watch. A particular problem is to conceptualize and assess how learning might be related to environmental forces that can be easily changed or easily introduced into settings where they were not formerly present.

The foregoing suggests that it might be useful to set up models of how the widening gap between children of high and low initial ability is related to genetics and to a variety of environmental forces. Moreover, it might be especially useful to see how variables that can be easily manipulated are related to the widening gap. But we do not develop such models here because our aim is not to explain the widening gap between persons of high and low ability or to see how this gap might be narrowed. Rather, our aim is to test how one environmental input—viewing "Sesame Street"—affected the mean learning gain of groups of different SES levels and race. However, with the limited knowledge that is currently available about relationships between learning and both genetic and environmental inputs, we cannot be sure of the upper bound limiting the extent to which children of different abilities can be influenced by a program like "Sesame Street."

---

[1] This problem is discussed in A. R. Jensen, "How Much Can We Boost IQ and Scholastic Achievement?" *Harvard Educational Review* 39 (1969): 1–123. It is also discussed in C. Jencks et al., *Inequality: A Reassessment of the Effects of Family and Schooling in America* (New York: Basic Books, Inc., 1972).

The Gap between Whom?

The example in Figure 8.1 illustrates *an* achievement gap but not *the* achievement gap. This is because the gap of greatest interest to most policymakers in education is the gap, widening with age, between economically advantaged and disadvantaged children and not the widening gap between the more and less able.

In an ideal world, initial ability would not be correlated with measures of economic advantagement, and Figure 8.1 would merely reflect the process whereby children of different ability take advantage of their natural differences in talent and so learn in different amounts. But in our world, initial ability is correlated with indices of both socioeconomic status and race so that, if we conceive of eight SES groups for the moment, their relationship to learning is as depicted in Figure 8.1 for the eight groups of children of different ability. But in the case of the eight SES groups we could not assume that these group differences in maturational rate are due to natural differences in talents between children of different backgrounds. Rather, one would have to entertain the hypothesis that the different social backgrounds are totally or partially responsible for the differences in growth rates which make for a widening gap.

Conceptualizing *the* gap as a social phenomenon does not mean that all children of the highest SES group or of the highest-scoring race are high scorers. Individual differences in ability are measurable within each social and racial group. Hence, there are examples of low-scoring sons of white professors from Massachusetts and of high-scoring sons of black day laborers from Mississippi. The gap is defined in terms of the *average* knowledge level of various groups at various times, and the number of groups involved depends on how finely the researcher wants to categorize the various SES levels or racial groups he is working with. Certainly, it is an oversimplification to talk of the economically advantaged and disadvantaged in such a way as to imply that advantagement is dichotomous. Rather, advantagement is a continuum that could be sliced many ways, just as initial ability could be stratified into two, eight, twelve, or more categories.

A more important issue than the number of groups is the nature of the groups. We have used the phrase "economic advantagement" as a global catchall to refer to the extent to which persons have access to the goods produced by our economic system, and we have assumed that children from social groups with greater access develop intellectually at faster rates. The reason for this assumption is that access to economic goods is related to socioeconomic status (a composite of education, income, and occupation), and it is well known that children from different SES groups mature at different rates on the average. Economic disadvantagement and lower socioeconomic status are sometimes used as euphemisms for race, and are used for referring to black Americans in particular. It should be no surprise, therefore, to note that there is also a widening gap between various racial groups. And finally, there is a distinct difference in income between rural, urban, and suburban Americans so that the possibility emerges of an achievement gap that affects the relationship of these three groups. In short: There is no one widening gap. There are probably as many gaps as there are conceptualizations of what advantagement means—SES, race, residence, access to societal goods, and even patterns of interaction between the parent and child.

Which Gaps?

Just as there are widening gaps between several social groups, so there are several kinds of gap. On the one hand, it is naive to think that there is only an achievement gap. We know, for example, that children from poorer homes are less well fed, may be exposed to fewer models of academic excellence, and may have more distractions from learning. And on the other hand, within the narrower academic sphere, there are widening gaps with respect to reading, writing, arithmetic, algebra, etc. Thus, it is overly simple to conceive of a single gap even though, in evaluating "Sesame Street," we are primarily concerned with the academic gap in prereading skills rather than in other areas of development. Moreover, it is also overly simple to believe that the economically advantaged outperform the relatively more disadvantaged in all spheres of intellectual or social life. There are undoubtedly areas where the more affluent are the "underachievers," though these areas have not been as publicized as those which imply the reverse relationship.

An Absolute or Relative Widening Gap?

Joan Cooney mentioned in her original proposal for funding "Sesame Street" that there was a national problem of a widening achievement gap. The problem only has dramatic proportions if it is viewed in terms of the absolute difference between group achievement means. If one thinks in terms of a ratio of group means or in terms of standard deviation units, then there is a problem in the United States today of a gap that persists as children grow older, but there is no problem of a gap that dramatically widens. This point is made clearly by the Coleman Report with respect to the difference between absolute mean values and standard deviation units:

> Negroes in the metropolitan Northeast are about 1.1 standard deviations below whites in the same region at grades 6, 9, and 12. But at grade 6 this rep-

resents 1.6 (school) years behind; at grade 9, 2.4 years; and at grade 12, 3.3 years.[2]

If we assume that white children in the Northeast are performing at their grade level, then the black children are performing (with rounding) at 73 percent of the white level in the sixth grade, 73 percent in the ninth grade, and 73 percent in the twelfth grade. There is simply no dramatic national problem of a widening achievement gap when we conceive of the problem as a ratio of group means.

There is an even more compelling reason for conceptualizing the problem of the achievement gap as the absolute difference in group means at different points in time. Blaug makes this clear in his analysis of the financial earnings caused by education. The problem in this respect is whether we should analyze the absolute difference in earnings between persons with different education or whether we should take a ratio of group means.

> What we have been discussing is the contribution that education makes to the earnings differentials between people with different amounts of education, and not to the absolute level nor to the percentage distribution of these earnings. If we were interested in explaining the demand for graduates, the fact that this is a function of the relative price of graduates—relative, that is, to the wages and rentals of other kinds of inputs—would have impelled us to recognize the *ratio* of the earnings of college graduates to those of high-school graduates rather than the absolute difference between them. However, from the point of view of education as a private or social investment, what is relevant is in fact the absolute differentials between more and less educated people. Clearly, the high-school graduate who is contemplating the pecuniary sacrifice that is involved in attending college cares about how much he will earn, not whether he will learn a certain percentage more if he went to work immediately. Likewise, a government, evaluating a given expenditure for the sake of a future increase in national income, must compare like with like the fact that an increase in the supply of highly educated people may reduce their relative advantage over the less educated is neither here nor there.[3]

The implication of Blaug's statement is that, if in one year the average member of a particular group knows A and B while the average member of another group knows A, B, C, D, and E, it is the three items C, D, and E that make a difference. Moreover, if in the next year the average member of the first group knows four items (A, B, C, and D), while a

---

[2] J. S. Coleman et al., *Equality of Educational Opportunity* (Washington: U.S. Government Printing Office, 1966), p. 21.

[3] M. Blaug, *An Introduction to the Economics of Education* (Middlesex, England: Penguin Books, 1970), p. 46.

member of the other group knows ten (*A, B, C, D, E, F, G, H, I,* and *J*), then the ratio of the two group means is the same each year (40 percent), but by the second year a member of the second group has an even greater advantage because he or she knows *E, F, G, H, I,* and *J* that are not in the repertoire of a person from the other group. Absolute differences in knowledge are much more important than relative differences, and for this reason we shall conceptualize the problem of the widening national achievement gap as a problem of increasing absolute mean differences between the economically advantaged and disadvantaged.

Summary

The widening achievement gap describes a pattern of data that results when the mean absolute knowledge level or the grade equivalent means of children of different SES, race, or residential groups are plotted over time. What results is that less economically advantaged groups score lower at the early measures and are further behind at later ones. However, it is not yet clear how this pattern of data can be explained, and we do not attempt to explain it. Rather, we test whether an environmental input like "Sesame Street" can affect the gap that separates the absolute knowledge levels of the three SES groups that we have abstracted from the ETS data. The tests to be used relate to prereading skills and they were developed by ETS to reflect the content of "Sesame Street."

PREVIOUS RESEARCH CLAIMS OF RELEVANCE TO "SESAME STREET'S" EFFECTS ON THE ACHIEVEMENT GAP

Minton's Dissertation

We have previously seen how Minton's dissertation obtained findings which suggested that the white children she labelled as "advantaged" and as "working-class, middle-income [representing] all socio-economic levels" seemed to have gained from the program on a test of knowledge of letters, while it could not be demonstrated that the "disadvantaged" learned anything.

However, we also saw that there were inferential problems associated with Minton's analysis of the differential gains of various social groups. In particular, she did not compare the different social groups directly and her sample sizes did not permit the sophisticated sibling control design that was possible with the combined sample of all children. Hence, Minton's work suggested that "Sesame Street" may have been widening the achievement gap with respect to simple alphabet skills, but was by no means definitive.

The Relevant Claim in the First-Year ETS Report

The conclusion of the first-year ETS report on "Sesame Street" describes the findings from the Philadelphia sample in the following way:

> There were 169 children in the study (at-home and at-school) who were considered advantaged, all of them from suburban Philadelphia. These children watched more of the show on the average than any of the groups of disadvantaged children. As expected, they scored higher on the pretest than any other children in the study. Their mental ages were also the highest of any subgroup. Among the advantaged, children in all viewing quartiles made significant gains from pretest to posttest, and those who viewed more of the show gained more. The biggest difference in gains . . . was between Q1 and Q2, indicating that relatively small amounts of viewing produced relatively large gains in this sub-sample. However, and most importantly, gains of high viewing (Q4) advantaged children were somewhat less than gains of high viewing disadvantaged children. In addition, advantaged children who watched little or none of the show (Q1 and Q2) were surpassed at posttest time by disadvantaged children who watched a lot. Thus, in terms of attainments, Sesame Street helped to close the gap between advantaged and disadvantaged children (pp. 357–358).

All of these claims were based on the flawed Inferential Study in which the bias-prone ETS viewing composite was used to partition children into viewing groups, after which viewing group and raw gains were correlated. Not surprisingly, they correlated highly, and an unknown part of the correlation is determined by group differences in maturational rate and by a higher rate of statistical regression from the viewing measure to the pretest than to the posttest.

But it is more important to note that the difference in raw gains favoring the heaviest viewers among the disadvantaged over the heaviest viewers among the advantaged was trivial in magnitude (2.11 Grand Total points). In addition, the ETS analysis did not compensate for the ceiling effect problem which presumably restricted the growth of the advantaged more than the disadvantaged children. Furthermore, the comparison of the raw gains of advantaged light viewers with disadvantaged heavy viewers was irrelevant to the gap issue. This was because the underrepresentation of disadvantaged children among heavy viewers and of advantaged children among light viewers entailed that disadvantaged-heavy viewers and advantaged-light viewers contributed relatively little to the mean gain of their respective disadvantaged and advantaged groups. Hence, even if some disadvantaged children who were particularly able overtook some advantaged children who were less able, it did not mean either that "Sesame

Street" caused the overtaking—different rates of maturation might have—or that, if "Sesame Street" did cause the overtaking, the achievement gap was narrowed.

The Relevant Claim in the Second-Year ETS Report

For their encouraged sample, Bogatz and Ball reported a correlation of —.24 between raw Grand Total gains and a measure combining mother's and father's education. This correlation was used to suggest that the children with less well educated parents may have benefited more from "Sesame Street" than children with better educated parents. But since the relationship only appeared among encouraged children, it would have been more exact to infer that the less advantaged may have benefited more from "Sesame Street" only if they were encouraged.

Yet even this last inference was not possible from the correlation reported by Bogatz and Ball. When measures are fallible, statistical regression ensures that high pretest scorers will be associated with relatively lower posttest scores while low pretest scorers will be associated with relatively higher posttest scores. Thus, low pretest scorers will seem to gain more than high pretest scorers, and the correlation of initial scores with gains will be negative, *as will any correlation involving a correlate of initial scores.*[4] And we have previously seen in Table 7.7 that the home educational climate was one correlate of initial knowledge among the encouraged Los Angeles sample who made up most of the second-year children.

Two facts indicated that the regression explanation may have accounted for at least part of this negative correlation. First, the Los Angeles children predominate in the second-year sample and the test-retest reliability for the Grand Total was low at that site when compared to other sites ($r = .53$), suggesting that more statistical regression would have taken place there than elsewhere. Second, and most importantly, there was no evidence of a statistically significant negative slope at any of the first-year sites where we examined the regression of the pretest-posttest Grand Total gain scores on Home Education Index scores. We can therefore be confident that the ETS analyses did not unambiguously demonstrate that less educationally advantaged children were more responsive to the encouragement treatment than were more advantaged children. And since there was no statistically significant negative correlation of raw gains and parental educational attainment among nonencouraged children, we can also be confident that the ETS analyses did not demonstrate that less advan-

---

[4] For a discussion of the frequency of negative correlations, see E. L. Thorndike, "The Influence of Chance Imperfections of Measures upon the Relationship of Initial Score to Gain or Loss," *Journal of Experimental Psychology* 7 (1924): 232–255.

taged children gained more from "Sesame Street" than did advantaged children.

STRATEGIES FOR COPING WITH PROBLEMS IN THE ETS DATA

The ETS evaluations were designed primarily to answer the question of whether children who were encouraged to watch "Sesame Street" gained from it. This may explain why the ETS conclusions about narrowing the achievement gap did not come from a design or from analyses that were explicitly set up to probe the gap issue. Rather, they were incidental conclusions drawn from analyses exploring other issues.

Probing the gap question required comparing children from intact social groups, and Ball and Bogatz wanted to avoid such comparisons as much as possible. Hence, they concentrated on analyses of the effects of viewing within social groups rather than between them and were largely successful in their efforts. However, a salient exception occurred in the second-year evaluation where an analysis of the relative gains by black and white children appeared. What is interesting to note is that Bogatz and Ball conducted this analysis, because some persons had reportedly reacted to their first-year report by wondering how "Sesame Street" affected blacks relative to whites. In short, the desire by the ETS team to avoid comparisons between intact groups had to give way in the face of public curiosity about such comparisons. We suspect that such public curiosity existed because many persons define some social problems (like the achievement gap) in group terms, so that a comparison of intact groups was absolutely required if the problem was to be analyzed at all.

Special difficulties faced us in exploring the gap issue with the ETS data, and these stemmed from the fact that the gap was not the major issue around which the ETS evaluations were designed. We want now to outline these problems and to detail how we propose to deal with them. Unfortunately, none of our solutions is perfect, and the ETS data could not be used for a definitive test of the gap issue.

Proxies of Economic Advantagement

It would be optimal for probing the gap issue if the ETS evaluations had included children of different races and if for each race there had been considerable variability in SES and in the suburban, urban, rural location of homes. With such data, one would have been able to explore how the racial, SES, and geographic location gaps are affected by "Sesame Street." But there were no such data. Moreover, there was not even a measure of SES that would satisfy hardheaded sociologists that could have been used for validly stratifying children.

The major indicator of advantagement in the ETS evaluations was site. In the first-year evaluation, the Philadelphia children were considered advantaged, and the children from the four other sites as disadvantaged. Our analyses of pretest learning scores, IQ, and two SES indices corroborated the relative difference that the ETS team tried to achieve. More importantly, our analyses indicated that three levels of SES could be conceptualized, thereby escaping from the limitations imposed by a simple SES dichotomy based on sites and from the limitations of having a single instance of a relatively more advantaged site. Hence, since the Boston and California children scored systematically higher than the Phoenix and Durham children with respect to pretest knowledge, IQ, Home Affluence-Stimulation, and Home Education, we considered the Philadelphia children as the most advantaged, the Boston and California children as the next most advantaged, and the Phoenix and Durham children as the least advantaged.[5]

The problems with such a trichotomy can be illustrated by describing the kinds of sites and children involved. The Philadelphia children were white suburbanites from the East; the Boston children were black and white inhabitants of poor districts in an East Coast city; the northern California children were white inhabitants of a rural district in the West; the Durham children were black inhabitants of a poorer district in a southeastern city; while the Phoenix children were black and white inhabitants of a poorer district in a southwestern city. As we can see from this list, there was a complex confounding of race, SES, and geographic location.

We have to accept these confoundings and reconcile ourselves to not examining the gap between blacks and whites, or between high and low SES groups. Instead, we have to accept the three levels of site advantagement as they stand. We need not be too defensive about our trichotomy, since the confounds we have just outlined are not fortuitous ones. They describe the social stratification of American society today, for suburban, white, East Coast children are among the very most advantaged, while urban, black, Southern children are among the very least advantaged. In other words, the confoundings reflect the complexities of the American social system and are thus useful for assessing differential patterns of cognitive growth among some of the very most and very least advantaged children in the nation.

The Absence of Replication across Sites and Years

One of the strengths of our previous analyses was that we were able to replicate relationships across sites and years, thereby permitting con-

---

[5] The absolute differences in SES indices between sites are not meaningful as indicators of how far apart the sites are in SES. This is because the items in our SES composites are not all standard measures that make up traditional SES indices.

clusions about the generality of effects and also freeing us from concerns about the error rate problem that arises when comparisons are made on many tests and some statistically significant "results" appear by chance.

In considering the Philadelphia sample as one level of SES, the Boston and California samples as a lower level, and the Durham and Phoenix samples as the lowest level, we preclude replicating relationships across sites since we are in fact interested in differences between sites. Moreover, there can be no replication of relationships across years, since the second evaluation of "Sesame Street" did not include a high SES site, and the SES variability within sites was relatively slight. Thus, we cannot follow our normal strategy of replicating across the two ETS data sets.

However, we can use a modified replication strategy. If "Sesame Street" were narrowing or widening the achievement gap, we would expect its effects on group learning means to follow a systematic pattern. There would have to be a difference in gain between the Philadelphia and the combined Boston and California samples that was in the same direction as the difference in gain between the combined Boston and California sample and the combined Durham and Phoenix sample. Such a pattern of differences could hardly be explained by chance, if it were replicated across several of the ETS first-year learning tests.

However, it must be pointed out that our analysis strategy makes a social class distinction between ghetto-living in Boston and ghetto-living in Durham or Phoenix! This would clearly be a preposterous basis for drawing any conclusions about the gap if it were the only social class comparison available to us. We want to stress, therefore, that we are only using this particular comparison to check whether the data patterns from the comparison of Philadelphia with Boston and California children were similar to patterns from the comparison of Boston and California children with Durham and Phoenix children.

The Ceiling Effect

The children from different sites had different pretest attainments on the ETS tests. This suggested that there might have been ceiling effects in the raw data which would have disproportionately affected the sites where scores were highest and so might have restricted the range of raw gains at these sites. It was with this possibility in mind that we plotted the distributions of posttest Grand Total scores for the nonencouraged at-home children at each first-year site and, after inspecting them, computed indices of skewness. These are in the first column of Table 8.1, and it can be seen that there is negative skewness at Philadelphia. (This same effect was visually apparent in Figure 7.1.) Skewness was also the case with the separate Letters and Numbers tests, although the ceiling effect may have been

Table 8.1.   The Degree of Posttest Skewness for Selected Learning Tests among the Nonencouraged, At-Home Children from Each First-Year Site

	Grand Total	Letters	Numbers
Philadelphia	−.38	− .22	−.68
Boston	.17	.61	.06
California	.62	1.59	.87
Durham	.42	1.33	−.38
Phoenix	.64	2.92	.87

less with the former than the latter. It is nonetheless a problem with all three tests, and they might underestimate the true cognitive growth of the most advantaged children.

Correlated Means and Variances

There are many contexts in which means and variances are correlated. In growth situations, posttest knowledge means will be higher than pretest means and higher variances will typically be associated with these higher posttest means. Indeed, if we consider the Grand Total means and standard deviations from the encouraged and nonencouraged children at each of the five first-year sites, it turns out that the posttest means and variances were higher than the pretest means and variances in all ten instances. (See Tables 5.3 through 5.6.)

Means and variances can also be associated because of site differences. It is clear from Tables 5.3 through 5.6 that the Grand Total means and variances were lower at Durham and Phoenix than they were in California and Boston. This holds true for the pretest as well as the posttest. The relationship of means, standard deviations, and sites is graphically presented in Figure 8.2, where for each site the pretest and posttest Grand Total means of encouraged and nonencouraged groups are plotted against their respective standard deviations. The resulting relationship is essentially linear and positive for the four disadvantaged sites in that sites with higher means have higher variances. However, the Philadelphia data provided an exception, since the learning means were higher there than elsewhere but the variances were not. This one anomaly is probably due to a ceiling effect.

Means and variances can also be correlated if multiple tests are administered to children and there is more variability on longer tests than shorter ones. Figure 8.3 shows the relationship of pretest and posttest means to their standard deviations for all nine tests from the combined sample of first-year children. The pattern of linear correlation is most striking.

Figure 8.2.   The Relationship of Raw Grand Total Means and Standard
Deviations for Encouraged and Nonencouraged At-Home Children
at Each First-Year Site (The pretest and posttest values are
presented but not distinguished.)

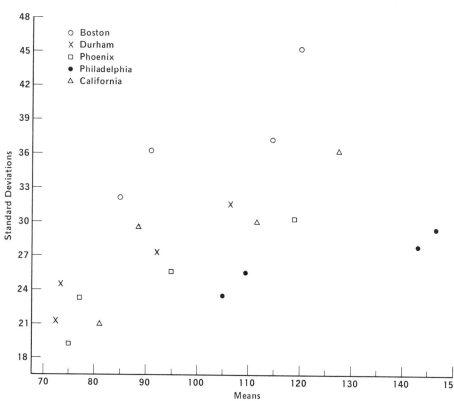

Rescaling is required when means and variances are correlated. One
frequently used procedure in such situations involves a logarithmic transformation of the raw data. But this was not suitable in the present instance.
Logs have the effect of pulling in deviantly high scores and so are particularly useful when distributions are positively skewed (e.g., when dealing
with income or reaction time). Since there is a ceiling effect operating on
the Philadelphia children and since this manifests itself as a negatively
skewed distribution, a log transform would exacerbate the ceiling effect
problem and would make the transformed distribution even more skewed
than the raw data. This is, in fact, what we found when we used a logarithmic transform and then plotted the frequency distribution of transformed
posttest Grand Total scores for the Philadelphia sample. Indeed, when we
computed the degree of skewness, it was −.67 for the transformed data
whereas it had only been −.38 for the raw data.

Figure 8.3.   The Relationship of Means and Standard Deviations for
Nine Learning Tests at Both Pretest and Posttest—All Nonencouraged,
At-Home, First-Year Children Combined

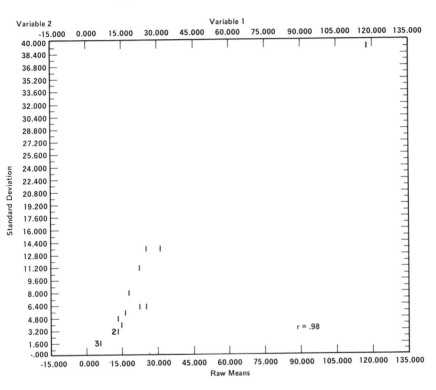

A better transformation involved separate standardization at the pretest and posttest for each learning measure. We first took the pretest scores
on a particular test for all the at-home nonencouraged children at all five
first-year sites combined and then transformed these raw scores to z scores.
After this, the transformed mean and variability in knowledge computed
for each site, and of course the Philadelphia children scored highest; the Boston and California children, next highest; and the Durham and Phoenix
children, lowest. The identical procedure was then carried out on the posttest
scores, so that for each test the pretest and posttest grand means were equal.

We then plotted the transformed means against the transformed
standard deviations for the nine tests using the total sample of nonencouraged children. The resulting Figure 8.4, which should be compared with
Figure 8.3, shows little of the linear relationship that was so obvious in the
latter figure. Finally, we computed the degree of skewness for the posttest
Grand Total of the Philadelphia nonencouraged at-home children, and its

Figure 8.4.   The Relationship of Standardized Means and Standard
Deviations for Nine Learning Tests at Both Pretest and Posttest—
All Nonencouraged, At-Home, First-Year Children Combined

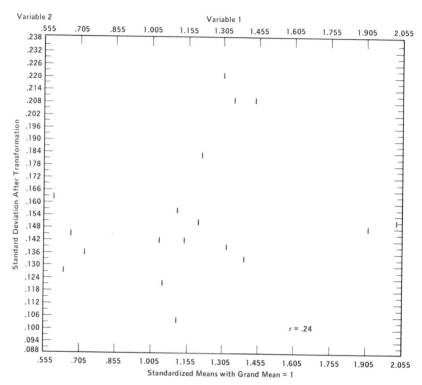

value (—.38) was of course the same as with the raw data and was less than
when the log transform had been used.

AN ANALYSIS OF THE GAP ISSUE
USING THE FIRST-YEAR DATA

Strategy of Analysis

We followed a two-stage strategy in attempting to use the ETS data to
test whether any aspects of the achievement gap were being affected by
"Sesame Street," the viewing of which was heavier in the advantaged Philadelphia site than at all the disadvantaged sites except Boston. First, we
computed measures of central tendency for standardized gain scores (each
child's standard score at the posttest *minus* his standard score at the pretest). We then examined these gains across all five sites to test whether the
difference in gains between the Philadelphia and the Boston and Califor-

nia samples was in the same direction as the difference in gain between the Boston plus California samples and the Durham plus Phoenix samples. The purpose of this was to see if we could collapse the data into three sets of sites corresponding with three SES levels. The second stage was to combine the Boston with the California data and the Durham with the Phoenix data to examine how the gains of these groups differed from each other and from the gains of the Philadelphia sample.

The median presumably provides a better description of group gains than the mean because the mean is more sensitive to any ceiling effects operating at Philadelphia. However, the median is not perfect since it only eliminates all ceiling problems if there is no ceiling below the fiftieth percentile. Moreover, the statistical tests of median differences are less powerful than tests of mean differences, and this can be simply illustrated by noting that the standard error of a median is equal to the standard error of a mean multiplied by 1.25[6] Since we could not estimate whether the better descriptive power of median differences in gain would be offset by the lesser statistical power of mean differences in gain, we decided to compute standardized gains using each measure of central tendency. We did this even in the case of the Letters Test where the ceiling effect was less than on the other tests. Indeed, this fact, plus the high reliability of Letters, gives it a special status as the most sensitive of all tests for examining the gap issue.

Both the mean and median tests are biased against obtaining a widening of any achievement gaps. The reason for this is that we standardized scores to scale the data. The formula for a standard score is $z = \frac{X-\bar{X}}{s}$. Now, if the gap were widened by "Sesame Street," this would increase s and so decrease the z values of raw scores (X) which deviated from the mean ($\bar{X}$) of all nonencouraged at-home children. Hence, if the gap were widening, the relative gain of the highest scoring group (Philadelphia) would be underestimated, as would the relative loss of the lowest scoring group (Durham and Phoenix), and the net effect of these forces would be to decrease the difference in gain of the highest and lowest scoring sites. We should not forget this source of bias nor the ceiling effect problem in the analyses which follow.

Analysis of Five Sites

Table 8.2 gives the standardized mean and median gains at the five first-year sites, and a constant of ten has been added to the gains for con-

---

[6] This is discussed in S. J. Armore, *Introduction to Statistical Analysis and Inference for Psychology and Education* (New York: John Wiley & Sons, 1967).

Table 8.2. Mean and Median Standardized Gains at Each First-Year Site
(a constant of 10 is added to all gains)

		Philadelphia (N = 27)	Boston (N = 43)	California (N = 19)	Durham (N = 28)	Phoenix (N = 18)
Body Parts	Median Gain	9.92	9.88	10.40	9.88	9.58
	Mean Gain	10.08	10.01	10.34	9.97	9.56
	S	.66	.72	.61	.88	1.32
Letters	Median	10.26	9.87	9.81	9.74	9.95
	$\bar{X}$	10.23	10.08	9.86	9.81	9.89
	S	.74	1.15	.60	.89	.60
Forms	Median	10.26	9.51	10.31	9.80	10.01
	$\bar{X}$	10.21	9.79	10.36	9.87	10.02
	S	.90	1.08	.66	1.28	1.03
Numbers	Median	10.08	9.98	9.96	9.84	10.11
	$\bar{X}$	10.15	9.95	10.06	9.88	10.03
	S	.64	1.01	.64	.78	.44
Sorting	Median	10.07	10.07	10.81	9.53	9.67
	$\bar{X}$	10.19	10.06	10.45	9.53	9.83
	S	1.08	1.19	.52	1.44	.83

Table 8.2 (cont.)

		Philadelphia (N = 27)	Boston (N = 43)	California (N = 19)	Durham (N = 28)	Phoenix (N = 18)
Relations	Median	9.75	10.32	10.09	10.05	9.89
	$\bar{X}$	9.88	10.06	10.11	10.13	9.73
	S	.73	1.18	.93	1.21	.90
Classification	Median	10.08	9.93	10.06	9.78	9.63
	$\bar{X}$	10.01	10.12	10.18	9.86	9.70
	S	.85	1.03	.72	.95	1.00
Puzzles	Median	10.25	9.97	9.75	9.73	9.61
	$\bar{X}$	10.14	10.03	10.01	9.90	9.89
	S	1.09	1.26	1.06	1.08	1.04
Grand Total	Median	10.18	10.00	10.02	9.96	9.86
	$\bar{X}$	10.11	10.05	10.10	9.87	9.82
	S	.49	.90	.41	.82	.62

venience only. Except for the Body Parts and Sorting tests, there is a consistent tendency for the Philadelphia gains to be larger than the Boston gains, and for the Durham and Phoenix gains to be less than elsewhere and more like each other than they are like the gains at other sites. For instance, the median Grand Total gains are 10.18 at Philadelphia, 10.00 at Boston, and 10.02 at California, while they are 9.96 and 9.86 at Durham and Phoenix. The corresponding mean values are 10.11, 10.05, 10.10, 9.87, and 9.82.

The most surprising single site is California where both the mean and median gains for Body Parts, Forms, and Object Sorting seemed surprisingly high (the means being 10.34, 10.36 and 10.45 respectively, and all of these differences are significant at the 5 percent level from a base line of ten [i.e., no change]). Such absolute gains are not registered on psychometrically better tests like Letters, Numbers, and the Grand Total (mean gains = 9.86, 10.06, and 10.02), and we are at a loss to understand why such gains were made on some tests at California but not on others.

Although the California data did cast some doubt as to whether the Boston and California data were more like each other than they were like the Philadelphia or Durham and Phoenix data, we went ahead with the planned analysis of three sites since they did differ on proxies of SES in a way that is meaningful to examining the gap issue. But we also decided to place greatest stress on statistical comparisons of the Philadelphia children and the Durham plus Phoenix children since this (1) maximizes the SES-site differences; and (2) avoids the uncertainty associated with combining the California and Boston sites even though—on the psychometrically superior tests—the California and Boston data did appear comparable.

Analysis of Three Sets of Sites

The mean and median standardized gains for the analysis of three sets of sites are in Table 8.3. On four of the eight independent learning tests (i.e., excluding the Grand Total), the Philadelphia gain was numerically greater than the Boston and California gain which was greater than the Durham and Phoenix gain. This was true for the Letters, Forms, Numbers, and Puzzles tests in analyses of both the means and medians. It was also true of the Grand Total. Moreover, of the four other learning tests, the Philadelphia gain appeared larger than the Durham and Phoenix gain in three instances. But the Philadelphia gain was less than the Boston-California gain for each indicator of central tendency involving Body Parts and Relations and for one of the indicators involving Sorting and Classification.

Table 8.3. Standardized Gains by Tests at Three SES-Level Sites
(a constant of 10 has been added to all gains)

		Philadelphia (N = 27)	Boston and California (N = 62)	Durham and Phoenix (N = 46)
Body Parts	Median Gain	9.92	10.11	9.88
	Mean Gain	10.08	10.11	9.81
	S	.66	.70	1.08
Letters	Median	10.26	9.89	9.85
	X̄	10.23	10.02	9.84
	S	.74	1.01	.78
Forms	Median	10.26	10.11	9.90
	X̄	10.21	9.96	9.93
	S	.90	1.00	1.18
Numbers	Median	10.08	9.97	9.95
	X̄	10.15	9.98	9.94
	S	.64	.88	.67
Sorting	Median	10.07	10.11	9.56
	X̄	10.19	10.18	9.64
	S	1.08	1.12	1.24
Relations	Median	9.75	10.10	10.03
	X̄	9.88	10.07	9.97
	S	.73	1.06	1.11
Classification	Median	10.08	10.00	9.70
	X̄	10.01	10.14	9.80
	S	.85	.94	.96
Puzzles	Median	10.25	9.92	9.59
	X̄	10.14	10.02	9.89
	S	1.09	1.19	1.05
Grand Total	Median	10.18	10.00	9.88
	X̄	10.11	10.07	9.85
	S	.49	.78	.74

Thus the pattern of the gains generally is: Philadelphia, highest; Boston-California, next highest; and Durham-Phoenix, least of all. And there is a particularly consistent trend of differences between the Philadelphia and the Durham-Phoenix samples.

We analyzed the difference in *median gains* between the Philadelphia and Durham *plus* Phoenix children for each test and the Grand Total. No differences were significant at the 5 percent level, although Letters and the related Grand Total were at the 10 percent level. The differences in *mean gains* were in general smaller than the differences in median gains. However, the difference between the two sets of sites was significant at the 5 percent level for Letters and the 10 percent level for Sorting and the Grand Total.

Concluding Remarks

The direction of mean and median gains suggests that the achievement gap may have been widening because of "Sesame Street." However, the statistical corroboration of the widening is marginal at best, and it does not seem likely from the present analysis that, in a single season, "Sesame Street" was widening any gaps to a socially significant extent. However, it was not clear whether the weak effect of site differences in learning gains when there were site differences in viewing was due to the weak effects of viewing on learning in a single season (as was demonstrated in Chapter 7), or to the presumed bias of the analysis of mean and median gains, or to the poor estimate of gain derived from the small samples. In any event, there were no indications in the ETS data as we analyzed them to suggest that "Sesame Street" was narrowing any preschool achievement gaps. Indeed, the very opposite conclusion was marginally indicated by the data.

The present data are similar to Minton's for she found that economically advantaged children may have learned letter recognition skills from "Sesame Street" while disadvantaged children probably did not. The implication of this is that "Sesame Street" may have been widening a gap in letter skills rather than in other areas of preschool competence where the series' demonstrable effects were weaker anyway. The same conclusion is implied by the present data inasfar as the two extreme groups reliably differed on the Letters Test in the analysis of mean standardized gains and marginally differed in the less powerful test of medians. However, it is unclear whether the more reliable findings for the Letters Test in the present analyses were due to the gap widening being restricted to this one cognitive area or to the Letters Test having had less of a ceiling effect problem than the other tests (see Table 8.1). If it was the latter, widened gaps in other domains would have been all the more difficult to obtain.

THE SOCIAL COMPOSITION OF "SESAME STREET'S" VIEWING AUDIENCE

It is important to establish the social composition of "Sesame Street's" viewing audience because, if it were systematically related to indices of socioeconomic status, this would have implications for whether the program was likely to be narrowing, widening, or not affecting the achievement gap. In particular, an overrepresentation of lower SES children in the viewing audience would be a clue that the gap was narrowing (provided, of course, that higher SES viewers did not learn more than lower SES viewers who spent equivalent amounts of time watching the program). And an overrepresentation of higher SES children in the viewing audience would be a clue that the gap was widening (provided this time that lower SES viewers did not learn more than higher SES viewers who spent equivalent amounts of time watching the program). It is important to stress once again that we are asking whether different SES groups viewed the show in different amounts. We are not asking whether children of different SES groups learned different amounts when they viewed equally.

Our probing of the issue falls into six sections. First, since "Sesame Street" is available on educational television channels in most areas of the country, we enquire about who can receive the show. Next, we examine the relationship between indicators of SES in three audience surveys conducted by Harris,[7] two Nielsen audience surveys,[8] the ETS studies, Minton's dissertation, and some survey reports by Daniel Yankelovich, Inc.[9]

Once again we are in the position where none of the surveys is perfect, even though CTW has used some of them in its publicity to illustrate both the total audience size for "Sesame Street" and the size of particular subgroup audiences, especially blacks. Indeed, only two of the surveys (Nielsen and Harris) made any claim to being representative of the nation, and we place greater interpretative stress on the better of these (Harris) than on any other audience survey. However, each of the studies had weaknesses, and we have to detail these and to probe whether they had common or different biases. It would be especially useful, of course, if the studies had different biases but common results.

THE NATIONAL VIEWING AUDIENCE OF
EDUCATIONAL TELEVISION

Since its inception "Sesame Street" has been shown primarily on public television. Public television is not available in all areas of the coun-

---

[7] Louis Harris and Associates, Inc., "The Viewers of Public Television," Nov. 1969; "The Viewing of Public Television," Nov. 1970; and "The Viewing of Public Television," Nov. 1971.

[8] These are reported in B. Samuels, "The First Year of Sesame Street: A Summary of Audience Surveys" (New York: Children's Television Workshop, Dec. 1970).

[9] The surveys are reported in Daniel Yankelovich, Inc., "Survey Results on Viewing of Sesame Street by Preschool-aged Children," Mar. 1970, and "A Report of Three Studies on the Role and Penetration of Sesame Street in Ghetto Communities— Bedford Stuyvesant, East Harlem, Chicago, and Washington, D.C.," June 1971.

try, however, and this necessarily restricts the potential audience of the show. A second restriction arises because public television is only available on UHF in some parts of the country, and some sets cannot pick up the UHF signal. We need, therefore, to estimate the percentage of American households where public television is available and whether this audience is biased in favor of any particular socioeconomic groups.

Louis Harris and Associates conducted audience surveys for the Corporation for Public Broadcasting in 1969, 1970, and 1971. These surveys used a multi-stage area probability sampling procedure[10] in which the United States was divided into a small number of strata (usually four), and smaller areas or clusters were chosen within these strata proportionate to population size. In the 1969 survey, for example, there were 200 such clusters. Then, blocks or comparable dwelling units were randomly selected within clusters, and specific households were randomly selected within blocks. Then, the households were contacted. In some cases, a person was at home at the time of contact, and an interview was made; in other cases, a person was home, but the interview was refused; and in yet other cases, no one was home when the interviewer called. The crucial issues then become: What percentage of the households could not be contacted after the first call, and how many callbacks were required to raise the percentage of completed interviews to an acceptable level? A single attempt to interview normally involves a completion rate of only about 40 percent of the originally selected households, while three callbacks could raise this to more than 80 percent. Unfortunately, none of the Harris surveys indicated the rate of completed interviews nor the number of callbacks, and we could not therefore estimate the accuracy of the Harris estimates of viewing rates in general or of viewing rates in different social groups in particular.

However, there was one fact that added to the power of the Harris surveys. The major analyses that we shall eventually report concerned viewing in households where there was a child under six. Having a child of this age in the home restricts the physical mobility of parents so that one of them, or an adult baby sitter of some kind, is likely to be at home when the interviewer comes. Thus, the rate at which interviews were completed was probably higher for households with a young child than for other households. However, it is difficult to estimate how much higher the rate was or what the final completion rate was in the Harris surveys if only households with a child under six are considered.

_____

[10] We are in Peter Rossi's debt for explaining technical aspects of the Harris surveys, as well as for estimates of the difference in response rates when no or three callbacks are used for contacting households that were chosen to be in the sample.

The 1969 Harris poll differed in a significant way from the 1970 and 1971 polls. The first was conducted on a random sample of 4,102 persons from 200 different sample areas representing all of the United States, and results from the poll could be generalized to the United States in 1969, if the completion rate for interviews were high enough. However, results for the second and third polls could only be generalized to those parts of the United States where educational television was available. This was because officials of the Corporation for Public Broadcasting inspected the initial sample of areas representing all of the country and selected for study only those where public television was available. This meant that only 214 of 300 sampling points were polled in 1970 and 149 of 200 in 1971. As a consequence, only the 1969 data can be used to assess the nationwide availability of public television.

There was no attempt made in the Harris audience surveys to oversample various national subgroups. All were represented in the percentage with which they occurred in the American population. For example, in the 1969 survey 11 percent of the respondents were black ($N = 445$), while 12 percent ($N = 352$) were in 1970 and 11 percent ($N = 217$) in 1971. This means that our confidence in findings was especially low for groups that were represented in the survey by few cases. Blacks (11 percent) and town-dwellers (10 percent) were categories with particularly small sample sizes, especially since important analyses were based on subsamples within the black sample. In particular, analyses were made of black households with a child from zero to six years of age, and, as we see later, our best estimate is that there were only about sixty such families in the 1971 survey which was smaller than the two others (total $N = 2,036$ in 1971; 3,040 in 1970; and 4,102 in 1969).

According to Louis Harris and Associates, the percentage of American homes in areas capable of receiving educational television was 72 percent in 1969, 71 percent in 1970, and 72 percent in 1971. In some areas of the nation, public television is only available on UHF. The Harris estimates are that this was the case for 35 percent of the homes in 1969 and 31 percent in both 1970 and 1971. There were some older sets in these UHF areas that were not capable of receiving UHF signals, and a more accurate estimate of the potential audience of public television must take this into account. Louis Harris and Associates calculated that 42 percent of all households who only had access to public television on UHF channels did not have a UHF adapter in 1969, while the percentages were 42 percent in 1970 and 28 percent in 1971.

We can estimate the potential audience for 1971 quite easily. Seventy-two percent of the nation lived in areas where public television was available either on VHF or UHF. However, 28 percent of the households in areas reached only by UHF could not receive these signals, and this percentage was about 9 percent of the nation (28 percent of the 31 percent in UHF areas). Thus, in 1971 the potential audience was 63 percent of the nation's households. Using the same procedure, it can be computed that percentages were 59 percent in 1969 and 57 percent in 1970. It is likely, therefore, that "Sesame Street" was available in over 60 percent of the nation's homes and that this percentage was increasing over the years.

The breakdowns of the data in Table 8.4 reveal a number of interest-

Table 8.4.   Percentage of Households Where a Public Television Signal Can Be Received (Base: Total United States)

	1969	1970	1971
Total	*59*	*57*	*63*
East	57	68	78
Midwest	51	52	55
South	64	48	50
West	69	72	73
Cities	74	77	81
Suburbs	70	78	83
Towns	51	44	44
Rural	38	31	39
White	58	57	*
Black	64	50	*
Less than high school	52	52	*
High school graduate	62	61	*
College graduate	67	67	*
Under $5000	47	45	*
$5000 to $9999	58	57	*
$10,000 and over	69	69	*

* The breakdown of these data was not reported in 1971.
SOURCE: Louis Harris and Associates, "The Viewing of Public Television" (1969, 1970, and 1971 surveys).

ing aspects of the availability of public television. Availability in 1971 was highest in the East and West and lowest in the South. City and suburban households were twice as likely as town or rural households to receive public television; and availability was 6 percent higher for blacks than for whites in 1969 but was 7 percent higher for whites in 1970. Finally, public television was more available in homes with a larger income and more education than in homes of lesser advantagement. Thus, the viewing audience was biased in favor of more advantaged homes when we define these in terms of income, education, or geographic region. There did not seem to be any bias with respect to race—we are considering the 6 percent and 7 percent differences in opposite directions as sampling error—even though race is confounded with income and education. Our guess as to this anomaly is that blacks are overrepresented among urban dwellers and that this fact countervails against, and even eliminates, the relationship between access to public television and indicators of economic advantagement.

Viewing Estimates from Louis Harris and Associates

Respondents to the Louis Harris audience surveys in 1970 and 1971 were asked to name the television programs they had watched during the last three or four months. The percentage of persons with access to public television who spontaneously mentioned "Sesame Street" was broken down by various demographic characteristics. Twenty percent of the homes capable of receiving public television had a child under six years of age, and it is this population that is of interest to us. Table 8.5 gives the percentage

Table 8.5.   The Penetration of "Sesame Street" in Public TV Areas
(Base: all households with children under six = 20% of the
total households in public television areas)

	1970	1971
Total	*47%*	*56%*
East	52	59
Midwest	49	58
South	38	49
West	48	59
White	49	57
Black	41*	56*
Less than high school graduate	31	44
High school graduate	51	57
College graduate	61	80

* The sample size is very small for these estimates.
SOURCE: Louis Harris and Associates, "The Viewing of Public Television" (1970 and 1971 surveys).

of these households where "Sesame Street" was viewed at least once in the last three months.

Several features of the table stand out. First, the number of parents who spontaneously mentioned tuning in to "Sesame Street" increased from

47 percent in 1970 to 56 percent in 1971, and this rate of growth was approximately similar in all parts of the country. Second, there was a positive correlation between years of education and viewing "Sesame Street." In 1970, 31 percent of the households where no one had graduated from high school reported viewing, while the corresponding percentage was 61 percent in households where someone had had college experience. In 1971, these percentages were 44 percent and 80 percent. Third, there was no indication that the gain in viewers between 1970 and 1971 was greater for the less educated. Indeed, if we compare the college group and the non-high school graduates, it appears that the gain of the college educated (19 percent) was larger than the gain of the non-high school graduates (13 percent).

If we examine the data on race and viewing in Table 8.5, it appears that whites with a child under six years of age living in areas where educational television could be received reported more frequent viewing than blacks in 1970 (49 percent *versus* 41 percent). However, the difference was smaller by 1971 (57 percent *versus* 56 percent). Two points must be noted about these data. On the one hand, the percentage of blacks and whites who lived in public television areas was approximately the same (see the relevant Harris data presented in Table 8.4). And on the other hand, if we assume that the percentage of black families with a child under six years of age was similar to the national percentage (27 percent), then the number of blacks with a young child in the Harris sample was 27 percent of 217, which was about sixty.[11] This sample was so small that we could have little confidence in any estimate of viewing in black households with a child under six years of age that was derived from it. Furthermore, if we were only interested in the viewing of the target group of three- to five-year-olds, the sample size would decrease by about 50 percent, since the Harris survey dealt with younger children too!

The Harris survey results had several other problems which limited their usefulness. First, the surveys did not cover the seventy communities where "Sesame Street" was available on commercial television stations. As we later learn, "Sesame Street" is probably more popular among economically disadvantaged viewers when it is shown on commercial stations than when it is shown on public television. Hence, the Harris surveys missed a number of young viewers. Secondly, the Harris surveys dealt with house-

---

[11] The number may be higher or lower depending on how the probability sampling was carried out. From his experience, Rossi estimated the range to be from twenty-five to eighty-five. Even if the sample is as high as eighty-five, it would still be too small for generalizing to all black households in the nation with a child from two to five years of age.

holds and not with individuals, and so they did not give us the exact information we needed on the number of children who viewed. Moreover, the survey did not distinguish between occasional and regular viewing except to note that 65 percent of all homes watching "Sesame Street" watched "almost every day." It was therefore impossible to examine how regular viewing is related to indicators of SES. In addition, the Harris survey included all households with a child under six years of age, including those with infants and very young children under two years of age. Despite all these weaknesses, the Harris surveys were the best available to date.

The Harris report for 1971 included a table where the percentage of households viewing "Sesame Street" was computed against a base of *all the households who viewed public television* (rather than against a base of all households in areas where public television could be received). Table 8.6 reproduces part of the Harris table, and it is noteworthy that the

Table 8.6.   Percentage of Public Television Households Where "Sesame Street" Was Viewed at Least Once in the Past Three or Four Months

	1970	1971
Total	*81*	*85*
White	85	85
Black	64	85
Less than high school graduates	65	84
High school graduate	83	86
College graduate	88	90

SOURCE: Louis Harris and Associates, "The Viewing of Public Television" (1971 survey).

largest gain in viewers appeared to be among the less educated and among blacks. These data were not very useful to us. Quite apart from considerations of sample size, we were more interested in the size of "Sesame Street's" national audience than in its audience among persons who viewed public television. Using the latter base line for computing "Sesame Street" audience capitalizes upon any selection factors that make members of different social groups view public television and inflates the percentage of viewers of "Sesame Street." This is why the Harris report mentioned that it was "self-serving" to use such data to compute "Sesame Street's" audience.

Nonetheless, the CTW newsletter of January 12, 1972, reported that "Sesame Street's" audience was growing and claimed, on the basis of evidence from homes where public television was watched, that "the show apparently picked up much of its new audience from among black viewers and homes where adults have not completed high school." However, the sample size precluded any such conclusions about viewing among blacks, and the references to the audience size and gains among the less educated were based on homes where public television was watched and not on all the homes in the nation or in areas where "Sesame Street" can be received.

Nielsen Data

Data from the A. C. Nielsen Company were relevant to the question of the relationship of viewing and socioeconomic status. They were not as relevant as we would have liked for two major reasons. First, we could not obtain breakdowns of the data to reveal the relationship of viewing and race. Second, and more importantly, the Nielsen data were probably not of high quality for our purpose, since they were collected by means of an obtrusive mechanical device that monitors viewing in a sample of homes in the United States. Systematic bias probably enters into the surveys, because some inhabitants refuse to collaborate with Nielsen and have their television set obtrusively monitored. Moreover, the purpose of Nielsen surveys is to sell information about the size and social composition of the audience reached by televised advertisements. There is probably, therefore, more interest in maintaining a large and somewhat representative sample of affluent homes than of less affluent ones. Indeed, we suspect that when Joan Cooney referred to the "middle-class biases of audience surveys" she primarily—and rightly—had Nielsen in mind.

The figures in Table 8.7 are based on nationwide Nielsen data for a two-week period in late November and early December, 1969, shortly after "Sesame Street" first went on the air. The data indicate, first, that only 9 percent of homes with a child under six years of age were tuned in to "Sesame Street" in the average viewing minute and second, that viewing and family income were positively related. Less than 1 percent of all households with an annual income of $5,000 or below were tuned into the program in the average viewing minute, while 2.7 percent of homes in the middle-income range were tuned in and 3.2 percent of the most affluent homes were. (These last figures do not refer, of course, to households with a child under six years of age. They refer to all households.)

Data are also available for a four-week period later in the first season (late January and early February, 1970) when "Sesame Street" was better known. The data are in Table 8.8, and two facts stand out. First, the audience of "Sesame Street" grew between November and February from 9 percent to 15 percent per viewing minute. Second, there was still a posi-

Table 8.7. Average Audience: Percent of Households Tuned to
"Sesame Street" During the Average Minute
(Based on 58.5 million television households)

	Percent
Composite	2.3
Household Income	
Lower (under $5000)	0.7
Middle	2.7
Upper	3.2
Age of Child	
No children	0.2
Youngest child under 6	9.0
Youngest child 6–17 yrs.	0.6
Children 6–11 (age not a factor)	4.0

SOURCE: Bruce Samuels, "The First Year of Sesame Street: A Summary of Audience Surveys" (New York: Children's Television Workshop, Dec. 1970), p. 17.

tive relationship between viewing and income with 11.7 percent of the audience viewing, when the household income was under $7,999 and 17.4 percent when the income was over.

A. C. Nielsen Company conducted an audience survey from January 18 to January 22 during "Sesame Street's" second year. During this period the program penetrated at least once into 48 percent of the homes in areas where it could be received, into 53 percent of the homes with a set to receive it, and into 36 percent of all the nation's homes. Unfortunately, the Nielsen report of the second year did not break down the viewing data by

Table 8.8. Average Audience: Percent of Total Population

	Percent
Total United States	3.8
Total homes with children ages 2–6	15.1
Children ages 2–6 by income	
Under $7,999	11.7
Over $8,000	17.4

SOURCE: Bruce Samuels, "The First Year of Sesame Street: A Summary of Audience Surveys" (New York: Children's Television Workshop, Dec. 1970), p. 19.

income. We are therefore unable to estimate the relationship of viewing and socioeconomic status in the second year.

Viewing Estimates from the ETS Reports

The ETS reports were only marginally relevant to the problem of estimating audience size, because no attempt was made to draw a random sample of the nation's children or even of the inner-city black children who were the primary target audience for the evaluation. Moreover, the sites in the second-year study were deliberately chosen because public television was not available. Hence, we would expect viewing to be atypically low among the nonencouraged children in the second-year study, as it was. Fortunately, an indirect estimate of the program's audience can be calculated from the first-year evaluation. However, it must be stressed that any estimate based on these economically disadvantaged children is only a rough approximation to the national audience, and we encourage readers to consider the estimates only in the context of the other surveys (particularly Harris).

Table 8.9 gives the percentage of non-Spanish children from the five different sites for the first year ($N = 900$) who fell into each of the ETS viewing quartiles ($Q1 = 231$ children; $Q2 = 242$; $Q3 = 235$; $Q4 = 235$). The most outstanding feature of the table is the way in which the percentage of economically disadvantaged viewers decreased as viewing increased (from 27 percent in $Q1$ to 22 percent in $Q4$), while the percentage of advantaged viewers increased with viewing level (from 9 percent in $Q1$ to 38 percent in $Q4$). A second feature of the table is that the Boston children viewed less than the advantaged Philadelphia children but more than the children from the other disadvantaged sites.[12]

An alternate way of examining the same data is to use a different measure of viewing that has none of the defects of the ETS viewing index and to restrict the analysis to the nonencouraged, at-home children to whom we most want to generalize. We used the Posttest Parent Questionnaire viewing measure trichotomized into nonviewers, viewers who scored between 1 and 4, and viewers who scored either 5 or 6. The last of these groupings was equivalent to daily viewing, and the second covered the whole spectrum from minimal viewing to viewing about four times a week. The results for this analysis are in Table 8.10. About 29 percent of the nonencouraged disadvantaged children were nonviewers, and 21 percent of them were children who viewed less than once a day. By contrast, the percentage of nonviewers was lower among the nonencouraged Philadel-

---

[12] These data are based on all non-Spanish children in the ETS evaluation and so include encouraged as well as nonencouraged and at-school as well as at-home children.

Table 8.9. Percentage of Non-Spanish Children in Each ETS Viewing Quartile by Research Site

	Boston	Durham	Phoenix	California	Dis-advantaged Combined	Advantaged (Philadelphia)
Q_1	16.19	27.42	44.97	37.70	27.09	9.47
Q_2	31.43	23.12	24.85	26.23	26.95	18.34
Q_3	24.76	28.49	18.93	13.11	23.53	33.73
Q_4	27.62	20.97	11.24	22.95	22.44	38.46
N for 100% =	315	186	169	61	731	169

Table 8.10.   Percentage of At-Home Disadvantaged and Advantaged Children
in Each Viewing Group by Encouraged and Nonencouraged Condition

	Disadvantaged		Advantaged	
	Encouraged	Non-encouraged	Encouraged	Non-Encouraged
Nonviewers	9.29	28.70	1.78	5.66
Middle Level Viewers	28.62	21.30	16.96	33.96
Heaviest Viewers	62.08	50.00	81.25	60.37
N =	269	108	112	53

phia children (6 percent), and the percentage of daily viewers was noticeably higher (60 percent).

Bogatz and Ball reanalyzed some of their first-year data and demonstrated that black and white children from economically disadvantaged
districts in Boston and Phoenix did not differ in the amount they viewed
"Sesame Street." When Bogatz and Ball correlated viewing (using the four-
test ETS composite) and race, they found equal proportions of black and
white children in each viewing quartile. They therefore concluded "that
black and white children viewed 'Sesame Street' about the same amount"
(p. 12). We examined the same issue for only the Boston children (who
comprised most of the ETS sample of Boston plus Phoenix children),
using the least biased measure of reported viewing, the Posttest Parent
Questionnaire. In our analysis there were no differences in mean viewing
between the black and white children from Boston. We must caution, of
course, that these samples were not representative of any meaningful universe, and that they were based on small samples. The ETS report was not,
after all, conducted as an audience survey.

Minton's Dissertation

The same problems that beset the ETS studies as viewing surveys also
pertained to Minton's dissertation. Indeed, the problems were exacerbated
because her samples were even smaller (N of advantaged, white suburban
children $= 33$; N of Headstart enrollees who served as the disadvantaged
$= 94$; N of working-class, middle-income children bound for parochial
school $= 83$). In addition, the children were taken out of class and into
a separate room for testing. We do not know how this procedure, or the
social class of the testers, may have affected children's responses.

Minton had three measures of viewing. One of them involved asking the 1970 children about their viewing habits and classifying children as everyday viewers of "Sesame Street," sometime viewers, and nonviewers. When the child did not mention the frequency of viewing in response to indirect probes, he or she was asked outright. Very few children were non-viewers (six out of 210), and so we collapsed the data into daily viewers and less-than-daily viewers. Twenty-two of the thirty-three advantaged children reported themselves to be daily viewers (67 percent); fifty-three of the ninety-four disadvantaged children reported daily viewing (56 percent); while forty of the eighty-three parochial children did (48 percent). The overall difference between these percentages was not statistically significant; nor was the simple contrast of the most economically advantaged and disadvantaged.

The second measure required children to recognize six photographs of characters from "Sesame Street." Table 8.11 presents the percentage of children who correctly recognized from zero to six characters. It is noteworthy that only 6 percent of the disadvantaged recognized all the characters while 58 percent of the advantaged did, and that 21 percent of the disadvantaged recognized no characters whereas none of the advantaged recognized no characters. A chi-square test of the difference between the advantaged and disadvantaged was statistically significant ($\chi^2 = 44.56$, $df. = 6$, $p < .05$). An alternate test would have been to compute the mean number of characters recognized based on the obviously skewed distributions within each of the groups of children. The mean for advantaged children was 4.79; for disadvantaged, 2.26; and for the parochial children, 3.87.

Her third test required children to identify the function of the various characters (e.g., what does Mr. Hooper do?). The percentage of children giving correct responses to the items is also in Table 8.11. Once again, there was a tendency for the advantaged ($\bar{X} = 3.76$) and parochial children ($\bar{X} = 3.64$) to outperform the disadvantaged ($\bar{X} = 3.30$), although the difference was not statistically significant.

These admittedly imperfect viewing measures all indicated that advantaged children tended to view "Sesame Street" more than the disadvantaged, although for two measures the difference was not statistically significant. Moreover, although the disadvantaged reported heavier viewing than the parochial school group, this effect was not replicated across measures and was indeed not even statistically significant. This presumption of no-difference in viewing is important since the group that had been in Headstart was largely composed of black children while the group that was to go on to parochial school was composed of whites who were described as being from working-class, middle-income homes.

Table 8.11.   Viewing Data from Minton's Dissertation

	Advantaged Children	Headstart Children*	Parochial School Children†	Total Kindergarten Sample
	N = 33	N = 94	N = 83	N = 491
Watches "Sesame Street": Sometimes	11 (33%)	41 (44%)	43 (52%)	266 (54%)
Everyday	22 (67%)	53 (56%)	40 (48%)	225 (46%)
Number of characters identified correctly: 6	19 (58%)	6 (6%)	28 (34%)	154 (31%)
5	3 (9%)	8 (9%)	12 (14%)	58 (12%)
4	3 (9%)	9 (10%)	8 (10%)	51 (10%)
3	3 (9%)	14 (15%)	10 (12%)	63 (13%)
2	3 (9%)	21 (22%)	11 (13%)	61 (12%)
1	2 (6%)	16 (17%)	9 (11%)	49 (10%)
0	0	20 (21%)	5 (6%)	55 (11%)
Number of functions of characters identified correctly: 6	8 (24%)	17 (18%)	20 (24%)	112 (23%)
5	8 (24%)	11 (12%)	10 (12%)	85 (17%)
4	3 (9%)	15 (16%)	13 (16%)	72 (15%)
3	3 (9%)	17 (18%)	20 (24%)	84 (17%)
2	6 (18%)	18 (19%)	5 (6%)	59 (12%)
1	3 (9%)	6 (6%)	9 (11%)	38 (8%)
0	2 (6%)	10 (11%)	6 (7%)	41 (8%)

* These were children who had been enrolled in Headstart the summer before attending kindergarten.
† These were children who later went on to a Catholic parochial school.

Viewing Estimates from Daniel Yankelovich, Inc.

In 1970 and 1971 CTW, feeling that "rating services tend to reflect the viewing preferences of the more affluent middle class," commissioned Daniel Yankelovich, Inc., to conduct an audience survey in the New York neighborhoods of Bedford-Stuyvesant and East Harlem, as well as in Chicago and Washington, D.C. A detailed report of the 1970 results is available for the Bedford-Stuyvesant study,[13] and some of the 1970 results for the other three sites are contained in the full report of the 1971 findings from all sites.

The Yankelovich surveys were primarily designed to see if economically disadvantaged children in the four areas were viewing "Sesame Street" in the numbers that CTW hoped to attract through their local public relations campaigns—the utilization programs. The need for such programs, especially in economically disadvantaged areas, was recognized even before the first season of "Sesame Street" began. Months before the first broadcast, articles in local minority newspapers and magazines across the country dealt with the participation of black people in the planning and execution of the show:

> These utilization projects were supplemented with special advertising programs in key black newspapers and on ethnic radio stations in the New York City area and elsewhere. Likewise, ads in Spanish language papers and on foreign-language radio were also placed during the weeks surrounding the launching of the series. Follow-up ads announcing inner-city distribution points for the "Parent/Teacher Guide" have maintained visibility for the series in black neighborhood publications.[14]

In addition, there were efforts directed toward persuading ghetto residents to watch their public broadcasting station, since two-thirds of the stations broadcasting "Sesame Street" were UHF channels.

In the CTW proposal for the 1971–1972 season, the utilization efforts of the first year were judged "generally successful in large cities, such as New York and Chicago, where 'Sesame Street' was not broadcast on UHF." For the second year, utilization projects were increased by opening CTW field offices in twelve large cities, including Washington. Commenting on the utilization component during the second season, CTW noted a change in focus:

> The goal of the operation remains, when it is still a need, the introduction of the program to inner-city families. Increasingly, however, the utilization pro-

---

[13] Yankelovich, "Survey Results."

[14] "Children's Television Workshop in 1970–1971: A Proposal" (New York: Children's Television Workshop, April 1970), p. 40.

grams have been able to turn toward goals with a more substantive educational content which extend the value and uses of "Sesame Street." . . .[15]

The fact that CTW no longer felt it especially necessary to increase audience size suggested that penetration of the series had reached an acceptable plateau by the middle of the second year.

Daniel Yankelovich was contracted by CTW to measure the results of these utilization efforts during both the first and second seasons. Any results obtained about the size of the viewing audience were not representative of national viewing habits. There are several reasons for this: At each of the sites, there was a utilization campaign underway when the study was conducted; each site was in a large city, and it is known that public television is most easily available in such areas; at three of the sites, "Sesame Street" was available on both VHF and UHF channels (at Bedford-Stuyvesant, "Sesame Street" was even available on commercial channels in the first year); and, in addition, the studies were conducted in northern cities in winter months when children stay indoors. Hence, the bias in the Yankelovich sample probably led to an overestimate of "Sesame Street's" audience, and it is impossible to compute the magnitude of such bias.

In conducting their study, the Yankelovich firm sent out trained black or Spanish-speaking interviewers who lived in, or adjacent to, the areas being studied. Each interviewer was assigned to a different starting point in the neighborhood and was then given a route to follow in search of adult respondents from households with a working television set and a child between two and five years of age who was not in a day-care center or nursery school. Alternatively, the respondent could be someone who cared for two- to five-year-old children on a daily basis.[16] Data available for the 1970 Bedford-Stuyvesant studies showed that, of 1,676 households contacted, 544 met the criteria, and 502 interviews were completed. Thus, about 30 percent of the households contacted were used in the Bedford-Stuyvesant study. In the 1971 studies, 1,222 interviews were completed in the four communities combined. No information was given about the breakdown of this figure by site nor was there any indication of the total number of households contacted.

Similar content and format were used in the 1970 and 1971 inter-

---

[15] "Sesame Street in 1971–1972: A Proposal" (New York: Children's Television Workshop, June 1971), p. 9.

[16] There is evidence that children of different SES levels attend day-care centers in equal percentages. However, the children from higher SES homes are more likely to attend proprietary day-care centers, while children from lower SES homes in large cities are more likely to be cared for in other neighborhood homes. Thus, the Yankelovich surveys were designed to pick up the fact of multiple viewing in neighborhood homes that served as informal day-care centers.

views. The interviewers began by asking the parents whether the children viewed a daytime program on television called "Sesame Street" (the unaided question). They followed this with an aided question:

> Let's make sure we're talking about the same program. Here's a picture with some of the characters they show on "Sesame Street." Now do you recall whether the children (two to five) ever watch this program?[17]

We judge it to have been fairly obvious from the question format that respondents expected a "Yes" answer would please the interviewer more than a "No" answer.

Table 8.12 gives the results for the aided question at each of the four sites in 1970 and 1971. Consider, first, the Bedford-Stuyvesant data. The percentage of *occasional viewers* was 91 percent in 1970 and 77 percent by 1971. (The drop probably occurred, because the program was available on commercial channels in 1970 but not in 1971.) Consider, now, the other sites. At all of them the percentage of occasional viewers increased between 1970 and 1971—from 78 percent to 86 percent in East Harlem, from 88 percent to 95 percent in Chicago, and from 32 percent to 59 percent in Washington, D.C. The absolute percentage of viewers was noticeably lower in Washington, D.C., than in New York and Chicago, and this was probably because "Sesame Street" was only available on UHF in Washington. However, the increase in viewers in Washington between 1970 and 1971 was large, and this may have been due—in part—to the new utilization campaign there.

The Yankelovich reports also contained estimates of the *regular viewing audience—children who view at least four times per week*—and these children are important since they are in a good position to learn from "Sesame Street." The data on regular viewers are in Table 8.13. It is noteworthy that there was a gain in regular viewers at these sites—from 65 percent to 68 percent in East Harlem; 60 percent to 70 percent in Chicago; and 22 percent to 34 percent in Washington—but that there is a decrease in Bedford-Stuyvesant—from 73 percent to 45 percent. This decrease may have been due to the loss of "Sesame Street" from commercial channels, for we can see no other reason why viewing in Bedford-Stuyvesant should have dropped so precipitously to below the East Harlem and Chicago levels.

The Yankelovich data were better than those of other surveys in that the unit of analysis was the child rather than the household. Nonetheless, the exclusive use of ghetto samples make the Yankelovich data inadequate

---

[17] Daniel Yankelovich, Inc., "Memorandum of March 1970 to Robert Hatch, Children's Television Workshop," p. 4.

Table 8.12. Percentage of Eligible Households with Children Who Have or Have Not Viewed "Sesame Street": Results for the Aided Question Only

	Bedford-Stuyvesant*		East Harlem*		Chicago†		Washington‡	
	1970	1971	1970	1971	1970	1971	1970	1971
Yes	91	77	78	86	88	95	32	59
No	8	16	18	4	8	2	59	18
Not sure	1	7	4	10	4	3	9	23

* "Sesame Street" available on VHF commercial and educational channels and UHF commercial channels.

† "Sesame Street" available on VHF educational channel.

‡ "Sesame Street" available on UHF educational channel.

SOURCE: Daniel Yankelovich, Inc., "A Report of Three Studies on the Role and Penetration of Sesame Street in Ghetto Communities—Bedford-Stuyvesant, East Harlem, Chicago, and Washington, D.C.," June 1971, p. 13.

for answering questions about the relationship of viewing to race or socioeconomic status since only one SES level was represented. Moreover, we strongly suspect that the Yankelovich data overestimated the number of viewers in the nation, and even the number of ghetto children who were viewers. The urban sites, the utilization programs, the VHF transmissions, the winter testings, the demand characteristics of the questions, and the unknown number of children who viewed during the day in a babysitter's home where "Sesame Street" was used in a way that it might not have been in the child's own home, all may have accounted for the high estimates of regular viewers in the Yankelovich surveys.

Table 8.13. Percentage of Children Who Watch "Sesame Street" Four or More Times per Week: Based on All Households Interviewed at Each Site

Bedford-Stuyvesant		East Harlem		Chicago		Washington	
1970	1971	1970	1971	1970	1971	1970	1971
73	45	65	68	60	70	22	34

SOURCE: Daniel Yankelovich, Inc., "A Report of Three Studies on the Role and Penetration of Sesame Street in Ghetto Communities—Bedford-Stuyvesant, East Harlem, Chicago, and Washington, D.C.," June 1971, pp. 20, 34, 50, 64.

The Suggestion of Regional Differences in Viewing "Sesame Street"

It will be remembered that the ETS viewing data indicated heavier viewing in the northern cities of Boston and Philadelphia than in Durham, Phoenix, or rural California. In addition, the Yankelovich data suggested heavier viewing in northern cities than in Washington, D.C. Moreover, educational television is more available in the North and in cities than in the South, in towns, or in rural areas. These data do not prove that voluntary viewing is heavier in the North and in cities than elsewhere, since we do not know how children were chosen for inclusion in the ETS study and since "Sesame Street" was only available on UHF stations in Washington, D.C. Hence, there is only a suggestion of regional differences.

This raises the question of whether the relationship of viewing and indicators of SES may be inflated, or totally explained, by regional differences in viewing. We cannot estimate whether any inflation of a possible relationship occurred because of regional differences. But we do not consider it likely that regional differences could have accounted for all the correlation. This is because viewing was correlated with indicators of SES—the Home Education Index, pretest learning scores, and IQ—*within* the first-year ETS sites (see Chapter 4). Such within-site correlations cannot be due to regional differences.

Race and Viewing "Sesame Street"

The Harris surveys were the only national studies which broke down viewing data by race and by homes with a child under six years of age. The data indicated slightly higher viewing rates by whites than blacks in one year and comparable viewing rates the next. Unfortunately, the number of relevant black homes in the sample was so low that these estimates were not very reliable for extrapolating to blacks in the nation at-large. Thus, these are not "hard" data about race and viewing "Sesame Street."

Since viewing was correlated with income and education, and since race is correlated with both income and education, it may be surprising to some persons that viewing was not more obviously correlated with race even with the small Harris samples. Let us assume, for the moment, that the Harris estimates were not biased by some obvious factor like an over-representation of black families from northern cities. How, then, could the data we have be made relevant to the propositions: (1) viewing is related to income and education; (2) race is related to income and education; but (3) viewing is not related to race?

For all three of the above propositions to be true we would have to assume that black children viewed more heavily than white children at some

SES level. If they did not, and viewed equally at all levels, then blacks must have viewed less than whites in the nation at-large, because blacks are over-represented among the less affluent and less educated in the nation. It does not seem plausible to assume that the black middle class outviewed the white middle class, since the white middle class viewed so much that there was little room in which the black middle class could have outviewed them and since there are relatively so few blacks who are middle class. It would be more plausible to assume that the black lower class outviewed the white lower class since the relatively large number of blacks in the lower class would have raised the average viewing level of all blacks by an appreciable amount. Yet we saw from analyses of the ETS samples that blacks prob-ably did not outview whites among the lower class. Thus, the scanty and low quality viewing data that are available do not suggest that black lower class children viewed more than their white counterparts. Given this, it is difficult to understand how viewing can be related to income and education in the nation without being related to race. The issue of the relationship between race and viewing is still open, and a sophisticated audience survey is required. Samples of children from Latin homes also need to be included in the survey.

CONCLUSION

The data that we have examined were not of high quality for ascer-taining how one season's viewing of "Sesame Street" is affecting the na-tional preschool gap in prereading skills. The data consistently suggested, however, that (1) "Sesame Street" is not narrowing the gap; (2) if it is affecting the gap at all, it is widening it, especially in letter-related skills; but that (3) the magnitude of gap-widening may not be of great social signif-icance in a single season. There were three bases for these conclusions.

Social Class Correlates of Viewing

The best audience surveys were by Harris and they consistently indi-cated that viewing was related to the education level of the home; Nielsen surveys indicated that viewing was related to the income level of the home; the ETS first-year report—which was not intended as an audience survey—indicated that viewing was related to the SES level of sites and to SES indicators within sites; while the Minton experiment—which was also not intended as a survey—suggested a relationship of viewing with whether a child had previously been enrolled in Headstart or lived in an affluent suburb. Thus, in all four studies with an SES breakdown of view-ers, viewing was positively related to the particular SES indicator used.

The implication of these data is that "Sesame Street" will have great difficulty in narrowing any achievement gaps between groups of different income or education levels. However, it must be stressed that the size of group differences in viewing could not be realistically estimated for the nation at large with the quality of data available at the time. The most we can conclude is that viewing was probably correlated positively with income and education.

The data on the nationwide relationship of viewing and race were particularly bad. The only available data came from Harris surveys, one of which indicated that whites viewed slightly more than blacks (eight percentage points in 1970), and the other indicated comparable levels of viewing (one percentage point more by whites in 1971). The major problem with interpreting these data was that the samples of black homes with a child under six years of age were so small (about sixty in 1971, which was less than in the large sample 1970 study). Even if the number were twice as high, it would still be too small—even in a well-designed and executed audience survey—for generalizing to the national population of black homes with a child under six years of age.

Reanalyses of the First-Year ETS Data

The ETS data were not collected to examine the gap issue and were consequently of low quality for answering the relevant questions. In particular, only the first-year data were appropriate; there was only a single advantaged site that year; this one site had only twenty-seven nonencouraged at-home children; and the learning scales were relatively less sensitive to changes by the economically advantaged children than to changes by the disadvantaged. Thus, the nature of the research design and the scales entailed that only a weak test would be possible of whether the learning gain of all advantaged children was greater than the gain of all disadvantaged children. More importantly, the scales entailed that the growth by the advantaged would be artifactually inhibited, thereby biasing the data against demonstrating a widening of the gap.

Our analyses indicated that the most advantaged as a group tended to gain more than the most disadvantaged as a group on most of the learning tests. But only one of eight differences reached conventional levels of statistical significance. What is not clear at this time is whether the failure of the other tests to reach conventional levels of significance was due (1) to the gap really not widening despite heavier viewing by the advantaged (this would presumably be because viewing is not strongly related to learning—see Chapter 7); or (2) to the inadequacies of the data. In any event, the conclusion is evident from our analyses that "Sesame Street" was not demonstrably narrowing the gap in prereading skills.

Minton's Dissertation

It will be remembered from Chapter 7 that Minton found no evidence of learning from "Sesame Street" by disadvantaged children on any of the tests from the Metropolitan Readiness Test. However, she did find that the show probably caused gains in letter-related skills among the advantaged and among "working-class middle-income" white children from "all socioeconomic levels." For reasons elaborated upon in Chapter 7, her study was not definitive, particularly with respect to subgroup analyses. But it did support the general conclusions implied by the audience survey data and the ETS data.

The issue of "Sesame Street's" effects on the national academic achievement gap has not been solved in this chapter. However, there seems to be no empirical corroboration for the incidental conclusions of the ETS team to the effect that "Sesame Street" has narrowed some part of the academic achievement gap. All the evidence, weak as it is, points in the opposite direction and suggests that "Sesame Street" is likely to be widening gaps in those areas that it teaches best, though the magnitude of such widening was probably low in either 1969–1970 or 1970–1971 when the seasons are considered singly.

Chapter 9
The Dollar Costs of "Sesame Street"

THE DIFFICULTIES OF ASSESSING COSTS, BENEFITS, AND THE RELEVANT AUDIENCE UNIT

Conceptualizing Costs and Benefits

It is desirable to establish the ratio of any program's costs to its benefits. Four items of information are necessary to do this: an index of costs; an index of benefits; a unit of persons or aggregates that incurs the costs and enjoys the benefits; and a time interval during which the costs and benefits become apparent. Although we would like to be able to conclude with a statement that "Sesame Street" costs X units for a benefit of Y units per child per year, there are a number of reasons why we will not be able to make such a sophisticated statement.

First, there are a multitude of costs that any program incurs. Dollar costs to the program's sponsors are the most obvious example. But it cannot be forgotten that the development of "Sesame Street" was at the expense of other programs that were never developed; that the probable widening of the achievement gap "by Sesame Street" may involve social costs which cannot yet be measured; and that there may be side effects of the program that we do not yet know about. There are difficulties, then, of drawing up a universe of costs. We must add to these the problems of quantifying costs other than dollars and of scaling each kind of cost so as to make a single index. Finally, since the difficulties of quantifying, scaling, and defining a universe of costs also apply to benefits, it is unrealistic to expect that we could perform a rigorous cost-benefit analysis with the information that was available to us at the time we conducted this study.

We decided instead that we would estimate the dollar costs of "Sesame Street" in its first and second years. This was a much simpler goal, although not one that could be attained without making several untested assumptions. Unfortunately, estimating the dollar costs per child per year is not as useful as a good cost-benefit analysis, because a "low" level of dollar costs is necessary but not sufficient for declaring an educational program successful. Money is merely the means to learning, an important point made by Daniel P. Moynihan: "The test of a program, when this program is part of a policy, is not input but output. It is interesting, and at times important, to know how much money is spent on schools in a particular neighborhood or city. But the crucial question is how much do the children learn. Programs are for people, not for bureaucracies."[1] Moynihan's point takes on special meaning in the context of "Sesame Street" since we believe that one can reasonably doubt whether the program is causing large and generalized learning gains in one season except among the very few children in the nation who were encouraged to view the show by ETS field staffs or among children whose parents have spontaneously created a process that is akin to the ETS encouragement process.

Conceptualizing Dollar Costs per Child

To compute the dollar cost of "Sesame Street" required establishing the total expenditures on the program. The CTW budget that we cited in Chapter 2 gave an estimate of the organization's expenditures. But it did not include CTW's additional income from nonbroadcast materials and overseas sales of "Sesame Street," and it did include the costs of developing "The Electric Company" in CTW's second broadcast year. Unfortunately, we could not estimate the magnitude of these last two factors, one of which inflated the costs attributable to "Sesame Street" and the other of which deflated them. Hence, we assumed that the budget reported in Chapter 2 represented CTW's total expenditure on "Sesame Street."

We also needed to decide whether we were interested in the number of children reached by "Sesame Street" at least once in a season, or the number reached at least once a week, or the number reached four or more times a week (regular viewers). We also needed to decide whether we were interested in four-year-olds, children between three and five years of age, or those between two and five years of age. Since benefiting from the series required that children learned from it, and since it was only likely

---

[1] Daniel P. Moynihan, "Policy vs. Program in the '70's" *Public Interest*, Summer 1970, pp. 90–100.

that regular viewers learned, we decided to compute the dollar cost per regular viewer (viewing four or more times per week). Since there is some evidence from Yankelovich[2] that two-year-old children also viewed the show we therefore decided to try and estimate the number of regular viewers in the nation between two and five years of age inclusive.

ESTIMATING THE DOLLAR COST PER REGULAR VIEWER PER YEAR IN 1970 AND 1971

The Size of "Sesame Street's" National Audience

To estimate the cost per regular viewer required a valid estimate of the size of the series' regular viewing audience of children between the ages of two and five. It is difficult to make such an estimate with the available information from viewing surveys. First, the ETS, Minton, and Yankelovich data could not be used on their own for estimating the viewing audience, because the samples were not representative of any meaningful universe. Second, the Nielsen sample was better, but it was presumably far from adequate because of the biases that are associated both with individuals' agreeing to have their television sets monitored and with Nielsen's relative lack of interest in poorer segments of the economy. Third, the Harris data were the best we had, but we did not know the percentage of planned interviews that were actually completed, and, like the Nielsen surveys, the Harris studies were of the number of households viewing the show as opposed to the number of children. Hence, no cognizance was taken of homes with more than one target child, of group viewing in day-care centers, or of neighbor's homes serving as informal day-care or baby-sitting centers. Fourth, there was a difference between the surveys in the age of the sampled children. Harris reported data for homes with a child under six and Nielsen for homes with a child from two to five. The two to five range obviously seemed more appropriate for "Sesame Street" than the zero to five range.

And finally, most of the available data was on "occasional" viewers —once per week in the ETS studies and Nielsen; once at any time in Yankelovich; and once in the past "three or four months" in Harris. However, we were interested in regular viewers, and so we needed to convert the available data for occasional viewers into data on children who watched "Sesame Street" four or more times per week. The Harris surveys included a direct question about the frequency with which "Sesame Street" was watched, and in 1970, 65 percent of the American households in public

---

[2] Daniel Yankelovich, Inc., "Survey Results on Viewing of Sesame Street by Preschool-Aged Children," Mar. 1970.

television areas where "Sesame Street" was watched at all and where there was a child under six reported viewing the program "almost every day." Since an estimate of regular viewing was absolutely crucial for our purpose, we attempted to use the ETS, Minton, and Yankelovich data to validate this 65 percent figure that we took as our best single estimate of the proportion of all viewers who were regular viewers.

The ETS data that we reported in Table 8.10 indicated that 50 percent of the disadvantaged and 60 percent of the advantaged fell into the "heaviest viewing" category that roughly corresponded with daily viewing, and the unweighted mean was 55 percent.[3] Viewing increased by about 20 percent between the first and second seasons according to Harris, though the increase in regular viewers was presumably less than this. In any event, an increase of 12 percent to 18 percent in regular viewers would bring the ETS estimate for the second season to the 61 percent to 65 percent range for children from three to five years of age.

Minton found that 67 percent of the advantaged were daily viewers, 56 percent of the disadvantaged, and 48 percent of the lower class white children who were destined for parochial schools. The unweighted mean was 57 percent. When we corrected this for the gain in regular viewers between the first and second seasons (between 12 percent to 18 percent), the estimate of regular viewers in the second season became 62 percent to 66 percent. These were mostly four-year-old viewers.

Finally, Yankelovich found that in 1971 the percentage of disadvantaged regular viewers from two to five years old was 45 percent in Bedford-Stuyvesant, 68 percent in East Harlem, 70 percent in Chicago, and 34 percent in Washington, D.C. There was no way to estimate the second-year national audience of regular viewers from these figures which probably overestimated the national disadvantaged audience because of the utilization campaigns in the sampled cities, the winter testing when children were more likely to be at home, the demand characteristics of the questions, and the availability of "Sesame Street" on VHF instead of UHF. Nonetheless, they indicated a range of 45 percent to 70 percent when we omitted the Washington sample where "Sesame Street" was only available on UHF.

Each of these studies involved children of different ages. The best single estimate (by Harris) was based on the 81 percent of homes in areas where public television could be received where the program was in fact

---

[3] If we had any confidence that the figures derived from the ETS, Minton, and Yankelovich data represented the population of children implied by the descriptive labels, we would have weighted the composite viewing estimate so as to reflect differences in population size. But it is not clear what "disadvantaged" means in each of these studies and how the samples were obtained.

watched. Hence the 65 percent estimate became 53 percent when computed against the more appropriate base line of all households in public television areas with a child under six years of age. However, 53 percent may have been an underestimate, because it was also based on homes where there was at least one child in his first or second year and where there were no two- and five-year-olds. The ETS and Minton studies omitted two-year-olds, who might plausibly be assumed to be less frequent viewers than older children. Hence their estimates of 60 percent to 65 percent may have been overestimates. Since there was no way of determining the audience of regular viewers as a point estimate (i.e., as a single figure), we think it reasonable to conclude that the audience of regular viewers from two to five years of age in public television areas was between 55 percent and 70 percent of all children whom the program reached. Since about 60 percent of all American children lived in public television areas in 1970 or had UHF sets in exclusively UHF areas, between 33 percent and 42 percent of the nation's children would have been regular viewers.

There were about 16,000,000 children between the ages of two and five so that the estimated number of children in the audience of regular viewers for the 1970–1971 season was probably between 5,250,000 and 6,750,000 children. This is a wide range, but it is probably unrealistic with data of the quality we had to expect more sophisticated estimates.

Our Estimate of Dollar Costs per Regular Viewer per Year

The dollar costs per regular viewer can be easily computed with the information we have, especially for the program's second year. The dollar outlays we assumed from the CTW budget for 1970–1971 to have been $6,500,000, while the number of regular viewers was probably between 5,250,000 and 6,750,000. Hence the dollar costs per regular viewer were probably between .96 and $1.24. (Since we have had to make so many assumptions the two decimal places should not be taken seriously.) However, it should be noted that these dollar costs per regular viewer in the second year were to an unknown extent contingent on the previous year in that equipment from that year was used the next. Hence, the costs should be summarized as having been between $1 and $1.25 per regular viewer contingent upon some costs having been carried over from the previous year.

The estimate of dollar costs for the first year was slightly more difficult, because we did not know the size of the 1969–1970 audience. Harris found that the audience of occasional viewers increased by 20 percent between the two seasons, and we assume that the audience of regular viewers increased by 15 percent. This being so, our estimates of the first-year audience were 4,500,000 and 5,750,000. Since $7,200,000 was spent in the first year, our estimates of dollar costs fell into the $1.25–$1.60 range.[4]

When he was federal commissioner for education, Sidney Marland quoted the per capita cost of "Sesame Street" as being $1.29 for the program's first season.[5] This estimate was of all viewers between the ages of three and five rather than regular viewers between two and five, and it seemed to have been computed against an estimated audience of 5,400,000 children. While we think that a point estimate of per capita cost to two decimal places implies an unrealistic belief in the accuracy of available audience surveys, it is nonetheless noteworthy that our financial estimate for the first year ($1.25–$1.60) and the former commissioner's ($1.29) were not very discrepant, although ours was slightly higher. "Sesame Street" is remarkably inexpensive on a per capita basis irrespective of the estimate used!

Some Implications of the Cost Data

It is a monumental achievement, we feel, for a program like "Sesame Street" to have captured such a large percentage of the available audience and to have both held and increased it. What is all the more noteworthy is that the program is voluntary and that few children are presumably forced to watch it. Since capturing and holding a voluntary audience is a necessary condition for mass instructional campaigns to work, it is important to know why a program like "Sesame Street" is as popular as it is.

The absolute capital outlay for a program like "Sesame Street" does not depend on audience size, and we should not forget that other programs could have been funded for the same amount of money. However, a large

---

[4] It should be noted that this figure would decrease if the initial capital costs of equipment were amortized over the whole span of their useful life rather then being completely absorbed in the first-year estimates. It should also be noted that the average cost of reaching a child does *not* represent the marginal cost of reaching each new child. We might surmise that it will cost more to reach children who do not avail themselves at present of the chance to watch "Sesame Street" than it will cost to reach children who spontaneously tune in to the program.

[5] "But here (with the "Sesame Street" program) creative people . . . have produced for $7 million, a program that is reaching about 80 percent of the disadvantaged population that it was meant to serve. Broadcast authorities say it is overwhelming, if not impossible, to reach 80 percent of the audience that is served by television. There is a substantial part of our audience in this country still not reached by television, but even in the total population of the three-, four-, and five-year-olds we are reaching something in the neighborhood of 60 percent at a cost-benefit of $1.29 per child, per year," Hearings before a subcommittee, Committee on Appropriations, House of Representatives, 92nd Cong., 1st Sess., 1970, p. 24.

audience can have a dramatic effect on per capita costs. In fact, the per capita dollar cost of a popular mass instructional program can be so low as to put it in a quite different category from traditional face-to-face educational programs with similar aims to the mass program. Traditional efforts with their relatively high salary costs for professionals and their relatively small audiences of children turn out to be much more expensive on a per capita basis, and perhaps this is why "Sesame Street" symbolizes to some persons the great financial savings that can be made by introducing effective technology into education.[6]

Actually, the per capita costs of a program like "Sesame Street" might be expected to decrease even more in the future for reasons that go beyond a growth in audience size. Film technology permits re-runs; it also means that parts of old films can be spliced into new programs and that some old films can be dubbed with a new sound track in a different language. In other words, production costs per television program are likely to decrease once a library of filmed shows is built up and a store of technical experience is developed.

COST DIFFERENCES IN REACHING ECONOMICALLY ADVANTAGED AND DISADVANTAGED CHILDREN IN 1970 AND 1971

Utilization Centers

It costs less money to reach each economically advantaged viewer than it costs to reach each disadvantaged viewer. The major reason for this is that the staffs of the CTW utilization centers concentrated their efforts on the economically disadvantaged, and the costs of their salaries, buildings, and efforts were costs incurred in reaching the disadvantaged rather than the advantaged. The same bias may have also been present in CTW's advertising expenses, and it was certainly present in the organization's research expenses. Nearly all the formative, summative, and audience research commissioned by CTW was research on the less affluent.

We are not in a position to estimate the expenditure by CTW that was directed at disadvantaged children and that was caused by "Sesame Street" alone (as opposed to "The Electric Company"). But it is likely that the per capita cost for disadvantaged children was several times higher than for more advantaged children. We do know that $600,000 of CTW's $7,200,000 budget was allocated for utilization centers in 1969 and that their allocation

---

[6] Lawrence P. Grayson, "Costs, Benefits, Effectiveness: Challenge to Educational Technology," 175 *Science* (1972): 1216–1222.

in the 1970 budget was $1,000,000 out of $6,500,000.[7] Thus, at least 8.6 percent of the first year's budget was aimed exclusively at the less affluent sections of society while the percentage doubled to 15 percent in 1970. This certainly makes it appear as though the per capita dollar cost of "Sesame Street" is decreasing when we consider the nation as a whole, while the cost of reaching more and more economically disadvantaged children is likely to be increasing.

There are several reasons why more has to be spent on trying to reach the economically disadvantaged. Etzioni and Remp[8] have pointed out that technological innovations become more and more expensive if face-to-face programs are required to complement technological delivery systems. Utilization centers were such face-to-face costs. Then again, we have seen from audience surveys that economically advantaged children were more likely to view "Sesame Street." It generally costs less to reach those who want to take part in a new program than those who are more indifferent about it or are less well informed about it. As far as the budget for contacting the potential recipients of a service is concerned, it costs more per capita to reach out to potential recipients than it costs to be sought out by them. Moreover, expanding the number of recipients costs even more per capita if the expansion has to come from among those who have consistently failed to avail themselves of the service when they had a chance to receive it. Expanding the audience of "Sesame Street" among economically disadvantaged children may well involve per capita costs for these children that go beyond the $2 or less per year that has been computed on the basis of all the nation's children, most of whom spontaneously viewed without much encouragement from CTW's own staff or public relations consultants.

"Sesame Street" as a Compensatory Educational Program

The fact that CTW was prepared to spend more money reaching the average disadvantaged child in 1969, 1970, and 1971 implies that "Sesame Street" should be conceived of as a compensatory educational program.

Actually, the situation is slightly more complicated than this. Since it is broadcast over the public airwaves, "Sesame Street" is potentially available to all children in public television areas who choose to tune in. In this sense, it is a universally available program. However, use has to be stimulated, and the attempt to stimulate viewing involves higher per cap-

---

[7] "The First Year of Sesame Street: A History and Overview" (New York: Children's Television Workshop, Dec. 1970), p. 11.

[8] Amitai Etzioni and Richard Remp, "Technological 'Shortcuts' to Social Change," *Science* 175 (1972): 31–38.

ita costs among the economically disadvantaged than the advantaged. Hence, the series is universal in availability but selective as to who is stimulated to view, and this selectivity favors the economically disadvantaged and is thus compensatory. However, the series is quite the opposite to compensatory in its outcomes in that economically advantaged children are probably heavier viewers of the show than the disadvantaged and so stand to gain more from it as a group. Thus, the framework within which the program is broadcast is universal; the financial costs of stimulating children to view are selectively spent in a traditional compensatory way that favors the disadvantaged; while the program is used by children in a selective way that stands to favor the advantaged.

COST-BENEFIT AND ENCOURAGEMENT-TO-VIEW

We saw earlier how encouragement-to-view "Sesame Street" caused learning gains of a magnitude that can be considered socially important and how the nature of the causal treatment could not be specified. Encouragement-to-view may be confounded with: viewing; enhanced parental interest in the child's development; testers' interest in the child's development; children's desire to please the tester or parent; testers' knowledge of the child's encouragement condition and/or level of reported viewing; or children's enhanced use of nonbroadcast "Sesame Street" materials. It is simply not clear which of these variables—or which combination of them —was responsible for the effects of encouragement-to-view the show. The issue is an important one, for if variables like tester–child rapport accounted for the encouragement effect, it is difficult to attribute the effect to "Sesame Street," and it is meaningless to compute the dollar cost of encouragement. This last exercise only has sense if one can assume that encouragement caused the acquisition of new information rather than the development of social relationships which facilitated the expression of information that had been learned before viewing "Sesame Street."

Hence, if we are prepared to assume that encouragement had desirable learning effects, it is of interest to ask how much it cost to encourage each child each year. To do this, we would have to take the costs of the ETS evaluation, divide them by the proportion of children who were encouraged (to get the amount of money spent on encouraged children), and then divide this figure by the number of encouraged children. This would give an approximate index of the dollar cost per encouraged child.

We only had a detailed breakdown on the evaluation budget for the first-year study (actually a thirteen-month budget). We took the cost of all the field staffs and added to this the ETS overhead charge. (The latter was included to represent the inevitable costs of coordinating any encouragement program in the field.) This gave a total of $93,500. To this, we added the costs of paying disadvantaged parents for their time ($6,480) and the costs of office rental at two sites ($5,600).[9] This gave us a total expenditure of just over $105,000. Many of the children were encouraged at school in the first year, and we assumed that the costs of reaching the at-home sample were 70 percent of the total cost (testing children at home is more expensive per child than testing them in intact classes at school). Thus, we calculated the costs of reaching at-home children to be just under $74,000, which was $68,400 when computed on a twelve-month basis.

This $68,400 figure needs to be adjusted for the fact that some of it was spent on nonencouraged children. These formed one-third of the total first-year sample, and it seems reasonable to assume that the per capita costs of nonencouragement were less than those of encouragement. Hence, we arbitrarily decided to reduce the $68,400 by 20 percent to give $54,700. Since there were 341 encouraged children in the first year, this was about $160 per child per year *in excess of the costs of producing and distributing "Sesame Street."* However, we cannot attach any realistic assessment of variability to this figure and the assumptions we have made may be incorrect to an extent which decreases the estimate to $100 or increases it to $220. We simply do not know.

COST-EFFECTIVENESS AND "SESAME STREET"

Cost-effectiveness involves comparing the ratio of costs to benefits of different programs that are aimed at the same objectives. It is a way of trying to determine which programs are more efficient than others. One of the major claims that has been made for "Sesame Street" is that it was less expensive than programs with partially overlapping aims. Headstart, for example, cost $1,056[10] per child in 1970 in comparison to "Sesame Street's" $1–$2. Though financial expenditures represent only one dimension of cost and though the comparison of expenditures does not even refer to benefits, these two figures are strikingly different and illustrate the policy appeal of a popular television program like "Sesame Street" when compared to "face-to-face" programs with low teacher–pupil ratios.

However, it is usually extremely difficult to compare programs from a cost-effectiveness perspective. First of all, programs rarely have similar results, and so it is difficult to develop comparable cost-benefit scales. For

---

[9] The budget only mentions rental at two sites. The offices being used at the other sites may have been ETS field offices or buildings that were already being used by community agencies.

[10] This estimate is given in Grayson, p. 1217.

instance, Headstart has much broader aims than "Sesame Street," including the amelioration of problems of nutrition and health, as well as problems of preschool learning, affective development, and social development. How would one compare Headstart and "Sesame Street" if Headstart failed to cause cognitive gains but facilitated affective development while "Sesame Street" had the opposite effects? The answer to this would have to depend on how cognitive and affective gains are weighted—but by whom and with what weights? It is possible to determine weights with appropriate scaling techniques,[11] but the problem that precedes this is: Who will be called upon to determine the weights by being asked to scale?

In addition, programs with some overlap are often compared after being evaluated by different persons using different designs of differing strength. As a consequence, when one program appears stronger than another, it is difficult to know whether the programs really have different benefits or whether they have been evaluated with different degrees of skill or according to different models of evaluation research (e.g., tailored or medical).

It should also be noted that some programs are standardized in the sense that a central agency determines the information that children should be given the chance to learn. "Sesame Street" is a program of this kind. Other programs are more variable, and the autonomy of their local practitioners entails the development of a heterogeneous collection of programs rather than a single standard program. Headstart is a collection of heterogeneous programs, and it is not clear what the average of all Headstart programs represents (if anything at all) and whether this average, or the very best individual programs,[12] should be compared to a competing program that is implemented in standard fashion.

Finally, a comparison on the basis of dollar costs alone is dangerously simplistic if the less expensive program has social costs that are left out of the dollar cost per child formula. "Sesame Street" is stimulating most of the children it reaches to a small extent; but it may well be widening the achievement gap in doing this. Conversely, because Headstart is available only to economically disadvantaged children, it cannot be widening the gap in any obvious way, although it is not clear at this time just how effective Headstart, when globally conceived, is in teaching simple cognitive material.

---

[11] Ward Edwards' procedure is described and commented upon favorably by M. Guttentag, "Subjectivity and its Use in Evaluation Research," *Evaluation* 1 (1973): 60–65.

[12] A summary of the cognitive effects of the better evaluated Headstart programs is contained in the chapter by E. L. McDill, M. S. McDill, and J. T. Sprehe, "Evaluation in Practice: Compensatory Education," in P. H. Rossi and W. Williams, *Evaluating Social Programs* (New York and London: Seminar Press, 1972).

What we need for the future are experiments in which several programs are evaluated within the same design. All the programs should have similar aims, all should be designed to have maximal impact, and all should be maximally different from each other in their methods. Instead of comparing program X with a no-program control group we might compare programs X, Y, and Z on the outcomes that all are intended to influence and on the side effects that each might cause. In this way, relative cost-effectiveness analyses can be conducted. Of course, each program will have to be evaluated on the basis of its unique goals as well as its shared goals, and this feature will make the comparison of programs somewhat difficult and open to dispute. Nonetheless, comparing programs in a single design will permit some points of valid comparison, and policymakers will be spared the problem of comparing programs that have little overlap in that each was tested in a different fashion. Whether the advocates of a program would be willing to see their product directly compared to other programs is a different matter. We would hope they would; if they did not, however, funding agencies might require them to submit their program to tests of relative cost-effectiveness as a prerequiste for funding. The direct comparison of programs, while not without very considerable problems, is probably the best tool that social scientists have to offer policymakers.

Chapter 10
Placing a Value on "Sesame Street" and on Three National Objectives for Preschool Programs

INTRODUCTION

Defining Values

Values are the central beliefs in our cognitive systems from which attitudes and lower-order beliefs are derived. Terminal values, such as freedom or salvation, are those which do not need justifying in other terms, whereas lower-order beliefs—e.g., belief in the current American electoral system—need to be justified in terms of the extent to which they promote values like freedom (to vote) or equality (of representation). Values can also be instrumental, and once again the crucial attribute is irreducibility. Thus, honesty needs no further justification for most persons, but a belief in Sunday School attendance might have to be justified as a means of promoting salvation or honesty or whatever.[1] The function of values is to guide behavior. Thus, when we contemplate a certain course of action we have to ask ourselves: How can this action be justified in terms of its consequences for specific values like honesty, or my self-esteem, or democracy, or equality, or freedom, or good life, or salvation?

There is a second meaning of the word "value" that has to do with

---

[1] The definition of values is sensibly discussed in M. Rokeach, *Beliefs, Attitudes, and Values* (San Francisco: Jossey Bass, 1968) and in W. A. Scott, "The Natural Structure of Cognitions," *Journal of Personality and Social Psychology* 12 (1969): 261–278.

assigning a value to objects. Such evaluations can be of persons, events, or social programs, and from this perspective evaluation research is a process of establishing the outcomes of some social program by empirical means and then assigning a value to these outcomes. Interestingly enough, values can be assigned to values as we defined them in the first paragraph. For instance, it is patently obvious that some persons value salvation in its religious sense more than others, and the same is true of equality.

The Difficulty of Assigning Value to a Program

How does the evaluation researcher assign value to data? In small part, he can use statistics for this purpose by conducting (rather arbitrary) conventional tests of social significance. We have done this where possible. But for the most part he has to rely on judgments as to the nature and value of the social values that may be promoted or jeopardized by a program's effects. Hence, if an educational program is increasing the reading speed of children by 5 percent without any loss of comprehension, he has to ask: What social values are being realized by an increase of 5 percent? Personal happiness (enjoying school more, enjoying more reading of pleasant material); economic security (getting better grades, spending more years in education, and gaining a better job); an increase in personal freedom (spending less time in onerous academic tasks where performance was slow before the improvement in reading); etc. Then, once this list is established, the researcher has to evaluate how valuable it is to realize each of these particular values.

The overall task is obviously a difficult one for several reasons. First, not all conclusions about outcomes are equally well supported by the data. There are typically outcomes that one can consider well corroborated (as with the effects of encouragement to view in the case of "Sesame Street"), or outcomes that are circumstantially indicated by the data (as with the effects of "Sesame Street" on the achievement gap), or possible outcomes that were not even tested by the data (as with most possible effects of "Sesame Street" in the non-cognitive domain).

Second, there is usually an inferential leap to be made from the outcomes to the values being promoted. Thus, in the example of the speed-reading program, we would have to assume that reading 5 percent faster will permit better grades, more years in education, and a job before we could assume that it promotes economic security. Because some of the postulated causal links between outcomes and the promotion of social values may not be true, the transition from outcomes to values is fraught with danger.

Third, unlike the speed-reading example, most programs have both positive and negative consequences. Hence, one can draw up a list of values being promoted *and* jeopardized, and this increases the researcher's need to know how to weight the importance of achieving each value. Thus, if two values were being promoted by some program and four were being jeopardized, it would appear at first glance as though a global negative value should be assigned to the program. But if the two values being promoted were valued highly by everyone, but the four being jeopardized were of little consequence, then the program would be assigned a positive overall value. Despite the need for a scaling system to assign weights to values, none exists today of which we are aware.[2]

Fourth, the process of assigning weights to values can result in what might be called political problems. Imagine that we were to conclude that "Sesame Street" promotes freedom of choice (almost anyone can watch who wants to) as well as pleasure (the program has a large and regular audience of volunteers) but is jeopardizing equality (because the average disadvantaged preschooler lags even further behind the average advantaged preschooler when he enters school than he did before the series went on the air). For social groups whose members place a high value on freedom and the happiness of the greatest number, their global evaluation of the program will be positive. But for social groups whose members place a lower priority on these two values and more on equality, their evaluation of "Sesame Street" might be negative. Hence, before making their decisions policymakers who are responsible to various constituencies have to consider, as one input into their decision-making process, how their constituencies weight the specific values that a program probably is, or is not, promoting. These value weights determine, or reflect, whose interests are to be promoted by the program, and we should be very clear that assigning value to a program has political overtones relating to whose interests shall and shall not be furthered.

It is in many ways easier to place value relatively than absolutely. In the case of "Sesame Street" this would mean assessing whether a higher value can be assigned to the series than to other preschool educational programs or to the alternative television programming that is available to children today. But the problem with a relative evaluation of "Sesame Street" is that there is little evidence currently available about the outcomes of comparison programs with which one would like to contrast "Sesame

---

[2] There is no technical reason to prevent the development of ways of assigning weights to values by empirical means or—indeed—of eliciting a list of the values that are believed to be relevant to given program outcomes. Our comment refers only to the fact that such procedures have not been used to date in evaluation research as far as we know.

Street's" effects. Hence, we cannot assign relative values in this instance, except on an impressionistic basis.

These difficulties should make it obvious that assigning value to outcomes is a different kind of task from establishing outcomes and that the evaluation researcher speaks more as a person who has reflected on the outcomes—as any citizen might—than as an "expert." To be sure, this fact must not be license for the evaluator to indulge his own values. He should attempt to minimize their intrusion as much as possible by consulting with persons who have radically different perspectives on the program in question. But we find it difficult to believe that his own values will not be present in synthesizing these perspectives. Hence, we especially invite readers to be skeptical of the analyses which follow, and we ask them to remember the warning of Lumsdaine that we cited at the end of Chapter 3. He warned that, if evaluators do decide to try and place a value on programs, they should do this so that the line between data-based findings and interpretation is as clear as possible. We are concerned in this chapter with interpreting data.

ASSIGNING VALUE TO "SESAME STREET'S" SUCCESS AT TEACHING

Our Major Conclusion

We consider our findings from the analyses of the effects of viewing without encouragement as the best available "facts" about the effectiveness of "Sesame Street" in teaching American children who are disadvantaged. If we assume that the best measure of viewing came from the Posttest Parent Questionnaire measure, then these findings are:

1. The show taught statistically significant amounts of learning on two of eight tests in the first year—Letters and Numbers.
2. It taught statistically significant amounts of learning on one of nine tests in the second year—Object Relations.
3. Since the Relations Test was also almost marginally related to viewing among nonencouraged children in the first year and was significantly related among the encouraged, and since the Grand Total was also marginally related to viewing in the second year and is disproportionately weighted in terms of Letters and Numbers, we conclude that viewing "Sesame Street" taught knowledge of Letter, Number, and Relation skills.
4. Viewing the program accounted for 5 percent of the variance in posttest knowledge level for Letters in the first year but for no other tests.
5. The strong design of Minton's "siblings control" study indicated that, when 54 percent of all children reported daily viewing and 97 percent reported some viewing during the season, the knowledge mean of these children increased to a statistically significant degree on the letter recognition subtest of the Metropolitan Readi-

ness Test but not on the other subtests which included a test of number recognition and of matching visual forms.
6. "Sesame Street" is viewed more often in homes where the income and education level of the parents are higher. This was indicated by at least four bodies of independent data.
7. As a group, economically advantaged children are probably making larger gains in letter-related skills than are the disadvantaged. This conclusion was suggested by our analyses of the ETS data, by Minton's analysis of her different SES-level subsamples, and by the obvious implications of the average advantaged child being a heavier viewer of "Sesame Street."

We can confidently assign a relative value to "Sesame Street" in the sense that our findings about the effects of viewing are less optimistic than the ETS findings about the effects of encouragement-and-viewing. In particular, we are less optimistic about the size and generality of learning gains, and we have identified one unexpected and undesirable probable side effect of the show.

It is more difficult to assign an absolute value to our findings. What are the gains in numbers and relations worth if they do not meet conventional statistical criteria of pedagogic significance? What are the larger gains in letter skills worth if they are associated with a widened gap in such skills, especially in light of Cooney's recognition of the national importance of the general gap issue? What would any gains in other and unmeasured skills be worth if, because of the positive correlation of viewing and social advantagement, they too were accompanied by a widening of gaps? Though the decision is a difficult one, we are not inclined to place a high value on the size and generality of the cognitive gains that have been demonstrated to date, particularly in the light of any costs that might result from wider gaps. We therefore find it difficult to go from a listing of "Sesame Street" effects to a discussion of the social values being promoted or jeopardized by these effects. However, it must be stressed that our current knowledge about "Sesame Street's" effects is imperfect in four major ways that are dealt with below.

The Program's Value Depends on More Than Six-Months' Viewing

Most children watch "Sesame Street" for more than one season. This means that we need to know the effects of viewing for a longer period before we can use the size and generality of gains, and the differential social impact of the series, as definitive criteria for assigning value to "Sesame Street." Obviously, viewing for several seasons might increase both the size and generality of gains. At first glance, it would seem that prolonged viewing might also exacerbate the gap problem. This would happen: (1) if the more advantaged continued to be heavier viewers on the average and did not stop learning from the show, or (2) if the average advantaged child tired of the show at an earlier age and went on to learn more advanced skills from other sources. But it is also possible for extended viewing to narrow, or at least not to widen, gaps. This would happen (1) if the more advantaged continued watching the show, because it entertained them, but did not continue learning from it since they had already mastered its curriculum, or (2) if the advantaged stopped viewing at an earlier age and did not use the time and opportunity made available to them for learning new material. The general point to be noted is that, though many means of increasing the size and generality of learning gains will also widen achievement gaps, it does not necessarily follow that all means of increasing gains will inevitably increase gaps.

The Program's Outcomes and Value Depend on Changes in the School System

In considering the need for more knowledgeable and more intelligent citizens, a striking consistency emerges in how the need is defined. In Jerome Kagan's words that Cooney cites, the need is assumed to be for people who know "how to think and not what to think," and the emphasis is more on cognitive style than on information. In the same vein, Bloom and Hunt stressed in their works that we cited earlier that there was more of a need to increase the intelligence of children than there was to increase their knowledge level. While it is difficult to maintain a rigid distinction between the dimensions of information/knowledge and intelligence/cognitive style, there is nonetheless a general difference, and "Sesame Street's" demonstrated impact to date has been in the area of simple knowledge acquisition rather than in the area of enhancing problem-solving skills or increasing intelligence.

The nature of "Sesame Street's" national impact probably depends on how schools respond to the show and on whether they transform any knowledge it imparts either into knowing how to think, or into information gains that are larger and more useful than those that have been demonstrated to date. Unfortunately, we do not yet know how schools are reacting to the program, and this reaction is crucial for determining the value we should assign to the show.

In the paragraphs that follow, we shall examine three ways in which schools might have reacted. Let us first assume that schools have not adjusted their curricula because of "Sesame Street." We would then expect that some heavy viewers, who would otherwise have struggled in school, would find the going easier. It is less clear what would happen to those heavy viewers who would have found school easy even without "Sesame Street." They may relish the edge in performance that the series confers on them or they may be bored with a partial repetition of what they already know. In any event, if schools have not modified their curricula, we would not expect to find many more knowledgeable students at the end of the first grade than at present, for the schools would still be teaching what they had taught before the series appeared. However, there might be less overall variability in knowledge if the schools have not changed. This is because there would be an unknown number of heavy viewers who would have done poorly in school but who would do somewhat better because of the series. Thus, the most probable consequences of schools not changing are: (1) a failure to capitalize upon the skills of those heavy viewers who are good students and (2) a decrease in the variability in achievement relative to the variability before "Sesame Street."

Let us now assume that schools have modified their curricula and that the degree of change has been similar across all the schools in the nation. In this case, the brighter "Sesame Street" graduates would be stimulated and new knowledge may be imparted in schools, thereby creating the potential for gains in areas related to intelligence and cognitive style. But the less bright graduates, the infrequent viewers, and the nonviewers would be at even more of a disadvantage in the classroom because of the curriculum change. An unknown percentage of these children would presumably rise to the new challenge, but others would not and would lag even farther behind the "Sesame Street" graduates. Thus, if schools have changed there might be an increase in the overall variability in achievement, and the children who gained most would be those who watched "Sesame Street" most, and those who suffered most would be those who watched the program least.

Finally, let us imagine that the schools which modified their curricula were those with the highest percentage of "Sesame Street" graduates. In this case, new information would be made available to those groups of children who viewed "Sesame Street" most heavily, and the knowledge level of the graduates might be increased in ways that could be relevant to children later "knowing how to think." But it must be noted that if curricula change were correlated with "Sesame Street" viewing, the program would be exacerbating the academic achievement gap and would be compounding the inequalities that already exist between schools and that make the schools, in John Holt's words, "rigged against the poor" in such a way that "curing 'learning deficits' by Headstart, 'Sesame Street', or any other means, is not going to change that."[3]

The upshot of this discussion is that the value we assign to "Sesame Street" has to depend upon how schools change because of the show. This might seem unfair at first glance because CTW cannot make schools change.

---

[3] J. Holt, "Big Bird Meets Dick and Jane, *Atlantic,* May 1971.

However, the educational system of the United States is an interdependent one and—whether planned or not—"Sesame Street" has become part of that system. Programs whose positive effects are capitalized upon by other educational institutions are those we most need to find and fund, for they bring about desired significant changes without a more generalized educational reform that is difficult to achieve. Programs whose positive effects are not capitalized upon have a potential for future significant changes, but only if other institutions also change. The fundamental issues thus become: Have schools changed because of "Sesame Street"? If so, which schools have changed in which ways?

The Program's Value Partly Depends on Non-cognitive Kinds of Educational Growth

"Sesame Street" is supposed to modify children's knowledge of the social world and their feelings about themselves, but we saw in previous chapters that these goals were assigned a lower priority than knowledge of letters and numbers and that statistically significant effects of viewing have not yet been demonstrated outside of the cognitive domain. We cannot obviously put a value on effects that we do not know about. This would not matter, of course, if the value of demonstrated effects were slight. But in the present instance, viewing might increase children's academic self-concept or desire for knowledge, thereby making the child into a more autonomous learner than he would have been without the show.

However, we think it fair to state that, like so many other preschool programs, "Sesame Street" implicitly assumes that the need for more knowledgeable children is more pressing than the need for children who are happier or more tolerant or more self-aware or more socially adept. This may be true, but it is only a difficult-to-test assumption at this time. Moreover, such an assumption raises achievement and knowledge to the status of terminal values, and it is not clear that they should occupy this status. Instead, many persons see achievement and knowledge merely as means to gaining better jobs and economic security, as means of raising one's social status by virtue of a diploma or a degree, or as means of pleasing parents. Indeed, Young[4] and Herrnstein[5] have raised serious concerns about elevating achievement and IQ to values to be pursued in their own right. Their fear is that such a stress will lead to a new kind of social stratification in which the most intelligent obtain the best jobs, seek out similarly intelligent spouses, beget relatively intelligent children, and thereby

---

[4] M. D. Young, *The Rise of the Meritocracy, 1870–2033* (New York: Random House, 1958).

[5] R. Herrnstein, "IQ," *Atlantic Monthly,* Sept. 1971, pp. 43–64.

create a structure in which the brighter will tend to get brighter and the duller duller.

Chomsky[6] has criticized this general argument, and one of his many points is worth mentioning. The fear of Young and Herrnstein is based on the assumption that achievement and intelligence are so highly valued in our culture that they form the major basis for selecting spouses. In a pluralist society which encourages and rewards the free expression of multiple values, intelligence would be no more dominant a basis for selecting spouses than, say, kindness or leisure preferences or ethnic identification. By stressing the need to raise the academic achievement and intelligence level of American children, "Sesame Street" may be inadvertently contributing to those social forces that assign intellectual competence a predominant role among the values of our society and that may be contributing to the problem outlined by Young and Herrnstein.

It would be incorrect to see "Sesame Street" as *exclusively* concerned with academic achievement or to see it as a *major* social force in placing stress on the development of achievement and intelligence. It is only one of many forces. Parents and schools are probably more potent than "Sesame Street" could ever be, and they may also be more consistently achievement-oriented than "Sesame Street." Nonetheless, the policymaker has to consider whether "Sesame Street's" emphases reduce or preclude an attack on different and significant social problems from those chosen by CTW. He has also to wonder whether "Sesame Street" is affecting non-cognitive growth at all, and how he could test whether it is.

The Value We Assigned to the Program Depended on Our Interpretation of the Findings

As we mentioned previously, there are no cut and dried criteria for assigning value to a program. Some persons may think that it is an achievement to obtain *any* statistically significant effects. They may even think that the analyses conducted by us and by Minton were not powerful enough to detect true effects of viewing which, though possibly small in magnitude, may nonetheless apply to millions of children. These same persons, or others, may additionally believe that the evidence of a widening gap is not convincing, or they may think that the gap problem is not as serious a national problem as the need to increase the knowledge or intelligence level of the vast majority of American children. Persons with some or all of these beliefs may well disagree with us about what the

---

[6] N. Chomsky, "IQ Tests: Building Blocks for the New Class System," *Ramparts,* July 1972, pp. 72–78.

"facts" are and may also disagree with our decision not to move from the listing of the "facts" that we demonstrated to a discussion of the value implications of these "facts."

ASSIGNING VALUE TO "SESAME STREET'S" SUCCESS AT ENTERTAINING

The Implications of the Program's Success in Entertaining Children

"Sesame Street" has demonstrated that a television program can reach a large audience of preschool children and can make faithful adherents of them. Indeed, though the absolute costs of the series run in the $7,000,000 to $8,000,000 range per annum, the large audience size means that "Sesame Street's" per capita cost of entertaining each child is in the $1 to $2 range per annum. We know of no other entertainment program aimed at this audience which is so effectively promoting happiness at such relatively low per capita cost. Moreover, in being available over the national airwaves to whoever wants to tune in, the program promotes the happiness of a greater number than would be possible if its circulation were restricted to children of any particular social group (e.g., the economically disadvantaged).

Its success in the entertainment dimension takes on an even more favorable aspect when we note that encouragement-to-view did not have the effect of increasing total television viewing time (as reported by parents). Rather, it had the effect of switching television programming preferences from other shows to "Sesame Street." If such an effect could be demonstrated for viewing as well as encouragement, it would have one important implication. It would mean that children were being entertained by a program which is frequently acknowledged to be in better taste than most of the television shows which preschoolers would otherwise watch if there were no "Sesame Street." In this sense, "Sesame Street" might be promoting the learning of "better taste" in entertainment, especially if the series were used as a model for developing other television shows.

The fundamental issue to which "Sesame Street's" success in entertaining gives rise is: Can the absolute financial expenditures of the program be justified solely in terms of the pleasure it causes for large numbers of children and the better taste that it might also inspire? Put another way: Can these expenditures be justified without reference to the prereading gains that the children were supposed to make from "Sesame Street"?

We have a great deal of sympathy for the position that "Sesame Street" can be justified without reference to learning gains. On the one hand, the series would be helpful if it decreased the level of violence and commercialism that is currently found in children's programming or if it led to a future generation of adults who will demand more of its television programs than is currently demanded. (Unfortunately, we do not yet know whether such effects will take place). And on the other hand, many individual parents could probably justify their children's viewing of "Sesame Street" solely in terms of the pleasure that the series brings. After all, most parents want their children to be amused.

However, the perspective we have to adopt is that of someone concerned with national needs in the preschool area. From this perspective, we do not see as great a need for more entertainment as there is for more knowledge. And this seems to be reflected in the comments on national needs by Bloom and Hunt, by the mandate to teach that was given to "Sesame Street" (which received half of its funds from the Office of Education), and by the frequent references in CTW publicity material to the position that entertainment is used on the program as a means of gaining attention rather than as an end in itself. CTW is to be congratulated on having successfully completed the first hurdle towards mass instructional television—the hurdle of creating and sustaining viewer interest—and we need to know the techniques whereby this was achieved so that they can be used again. But in the last analysis, gaining and holding the audience is only a necessary prerequisite to the end of learning.

The Implications of the Program's Success in Creating a Constituency of Satisfied Parents and Educational Policymakers

We have no systematic data to support our next contentions. However, our discussions of "Sesame Street" with parents from a wide range of social backgrounds—mostly living in the Midwest—have given us the impression that "Sesame Street" is popular with many parents. They seem to like the program, because it amuses their children, and because they think that it teaches them. Moreover, some parents seem to think that it frees them from having to supervise their children and gives them time to devote to other things. And they may be especially reassured while doing these other things, since their child is spending his or her time with a television program that is more tasteful than the current alternatives on other channels. Thus, it is our impression—and nothing more—that "Sesame Street" promotes the well-being of parents by giving them pleasure at their child's pleasure, pride at his or her learning, leisure because of their liberation from supervision, and reassurance that their child is spending his or her time constructively.

Our discussions with educators and our reading of public statements by officials of the agencies funding "Sesame Street" (particularly the Office of Education) have suggested to us that the series is popular with educational decision-makers at local and national levels. These persons seem to be sensitive both to "Sesame Street's" widespread popularity among parents and children and to the "fact" that it has been demonstrated to be an effective means of mass teaching whereas many other large-scale programs have not. One implication is that "Sesame Street" seems to be seen as a program with few opponents and it can therefore be supported with a minimal fear of adverse public reaction. A second implication is that references to "Sesame Street" can be used either as an example to illustrate that mass educational programs can indeed be successful or—for agencies funding "Sesame Street" (especially the Office of Education)—to help justify the agency budget in that "Sesame Street" is conspicuously cited as one agency-funded program that "worked."

The basic issue that follows from the series' popularity with parents and some policymakers is: Would it be politically feasible to modify a popular program like "Sesame Street" even if (1) its funding could not be defended on entertainment grounds alone, and (2) few educational benefits of value could be attributed to six months' viewing? The first obvious rejoinder, of course, is to state that the six months' criterion is restrictive and that the program might teach more over several seasons. If so, its educational benefits would be more meaningful than the ones that have been demonstrated to date with economically disadvantaged children. This point, however, merely gives rise to an even more thorny value question. Could a popular series like "Sesame Street" be modified even if (1) it could not be justified on entertainment grounds alone; (2) it was teaching children to an educationally significant degree but (3) in so doing, it was also widening the academic achievement gap? We must make no mistake in this. If larger gains do result from several seasons' viewing, it will probably mean that "Sesame Street" is promoting whichever values are associated with knowing more. But, because viewing the program is positively correlated with both income and education, the larger gains will probably also mean that "Sesame Street" is widening the achievement gap.

THE BROADER VALUE ISSUE

Some persons may disagree with our contention that the size and generality of the learning gains attributable to six months' viewing of "Sesame Street" do not justify an analysis of the values that would be promoted or jeopardized by the program. The following sections may help such persons, for the sections detail the different value implications of attempting *(1) to stimulate the development of all American preschoolers without regard to their home background; (2) to especially stimulate the development of economically disadvantaged preschoolers, irrespective of what happens to the more advantaged;* and (*3*) *of attempting to narrow the achievement gap.* Thus, persons who believe that the gains that have been demonstrated to date underestimate true gains or are more socially significant than we believe may want to ask: Which values are being promoted because so many preschoolers of all backgrounds know more than their predecessors and because many disadvantaged preschoolers know absolutely more than their pre-"Sesame Street" brothers and sisters did at the same age?

The section may also help readers who are interested in the broader issue of assigning relative priority to the three general objectives listed above, for one or more of them is a guiding objective of most attempts at educational reform. However, it is difficult to reach one objective without prejudicing the others so that the relationship among the objectives is especially important.

Even if there were a consensus that most resources should be concentrated on the economically disadvantaged—which there is not—this would only raise a further issue that was not relevant to past compensatory programs because they were only made available to the poor. The issue is: Are the economically disadvantaged best helped by knowing more—an absolute criterion that is stressed in the second objective above, or by narrowing achievement gaps—a relative criterion that is stressed in the third objective? More pointedly, are the gains of knowing more worth the costs of falling further behind? A value analysis may stimulate thought on this very important topic which relates to defining the nature of the problem facing disadvantaged children and which may be pertinent to defining priorities for future educational television programs.

Our own position on these issues is somewhat complicated, and we want to elucidate it before going on to discuss the broader value issues. It has been held that attempts to change society by making it more egalitarian (i.e., by reducing the variability in prestige, income, and wealth that is currently associated with different social groups) will reduce the efficiency of society, if efficiency is defined in terms of society's ability to increase its total output of income and wealth. Translated into the "Sesame Street" context, this argument would imply that targeting the show at the disadvantaged (by making it available only to them, or by gearing the content to learning deficiencies found only in them, or by some combination of each strategy) might facilitate an egalitarianism of educational attainment, but it might also limit the total increase in knowledge that would be possible if the series were available to all who wanted to watch it and if its content were geared to the learning needs of the maximum number of preschoolers. It might also mean that the failure to maximize the total output of knowledge would, in its turn, generate less income and wealth than would have been the case if more preschoolers had learned more. It is difficult to assess the validity of this argument about the negative relationship between equality and efficiency, especially since the equality in question relates to educational attainment rather than to income or wealth. Thus, we are unable to specify the relative value of using preschool education to pursue egalitarian or utilitarian social goals.

However, if it were to be acknowledged that an egalitarian goal should be pursued in the preschool domain, or if it were acknowledged that a particular preschool program was primarily aimed at helping the economically disadvantaged, then the weight of the currently available social science evidence suggests to us that most of the problems of the economically disadvantaged result from their social standing *relative* to other social groups rather than from processes relating to the *absolute* needs of the disadvantaged when these needs are considered in isolation from other social groups. This being so, we find it difficult to accept arguments that use the absolute learning gains that might be made by disadvantaged preschoolers to claim that the major problems of the disadvantaged are being alleviated. We find this especially difficult to accept if the absolute gains are accompanied by relative losses, as is probably the case with "Sesame Street."

HOW VALUABLE IS PROMOTING THE INTELLECTUAL AND CULTURAL DEVELOPMENT OF ALL PRESCHOOLERS?

Meeting the Daily Demands of an Increasingly Complex World

One justification that can be advanced for preschool programs aimed at a large and socially heterogeneous voluntary audience is that they may help many individuals better meet the daily demands of living in an increasingly complex world. These demands are especially heavy for the functionally illiterate since a minimal level of literacy is required of everyone who would participate fully in modern life. Everyone needs to be able to read a letter or newspaper and needs to be able to express his wants in writing. Preschool programs which stimulate persons who would otherwise have become functional illiterates are a boon, and the size of the boon obviously depends on the number of persons saved from illiteracy. Unfortunately, the number of potential illiterates reached by voluntary preschool programs like "Sesame Street" is likely to be low since the less gifted are least likely to use such programs. The most obvious way to have a program used by those who most need it is to target the program at the particular kind of child in need. But since most children become literate during their early school years, such a targeting strategy would lose the financial advantage that comes from large audiences.

A point of greater relevance, because it concerns more children, is that preschool programs may help children acquire literacy skills at an *earlier* date. Such premature literacy would presumably help children cope better with school (this point assumes, of course, that schools do not make their curricula more exacting because of "Sesame Street"); it might also decrease the number of young children who fail to understand poison labels or street signs and are endangered because they cannot read; and it might also affect the amount and scheduling of reinforcements that parents give to their children. These are the probable gains of earlier literacy. But Bloom and Hunt advocated universal preschool education on the grounds that large and permanent gains in IQ could be made which would eventually result in many brighter adults—as opposed to many prematurely knowledgeable children or fewer adult illiterates. Moreover, it is a long step from successful preschool programs to adults feeling more comfortable in an advanced technological society, and it is not clear that even the 15-point IQ gains that have been demonstrated for some preschool programs are maintained over the school years and affect adult functioning.[7]

To put the issue more bluntly: Schools have to capitalize on preschool programs if preschools are to help their graduates live more comfortably as adults. If all or some schools do change in response to the challenge from successful preschool programs, then such programs will probably be valuable from the perspective of living one's daily life more easily. But if schools do not change, preschool programs will only be valuable (1) to the extent that they succeed in reaching the potentially illiterate, who are among the most difficult to reach with educational programs anyway; or (2) to the extent that helping young children acquire literacy skills at an earlier date is useful to them during the period when they are literate but would not have been literate without a preschool program.

Meeting Job Needs in an Increasingly Complex Technological Society

One reason why academic achievement has been stressed in preschool research is that it is presumed to have a direct bearing on the nation's job structure, and one of the most important functions of education is to help individuals find better jobs and to prepare manpower for serving the needs of the nation's present and planned economy. To be sure, not

---

[7] Many of the successful compensatory programs with a focussed instructional philosophy are discussed in an unpublished paper by C. Bereiter, "An Academic Preschool for Disadvantaged Children: Conclusions from Evaluation Studies," that is elaborated upon in a paper by E. L. McDill, M. S. McDill, and J. T. Sprehe, "Evaluation in Practice: Compensatory Education." The latter appears in P. H. Rossi and W. Williams, *Evaluating Social Programs* (New York and London: Seminar Press, 1972).

all educators or parents conceive of education as a means of meeting national manpower needs, but we think that policymakers cannot afford to ignore this function and we know that many already assign it a high priority. Let us now examine whether preschool programs aimed at a large, heterogeneous audience might help individuals find better jobs or help the nation meet its manpower needs.

Many of the jobs that our present preschoolers will eventually take may differ from the kinds of jobs that are presently available. Some future jobs cannot yet be imagined; others will involve more knowledge of technology; others may demand a greater diversity of skills than is typical today; others may become quickly obsolescent and a job holder must possess enough flexibility so that he or she can be easily retrained. One important sense in which our increasingly complex society needs more intelligent citizens is so that these jobs can be competently filled. Whether preschool programs will have such effects obviously depends on how the schools react to them and on the exact nature of the future manpower needs.

From the perspective of someone who is concerned about future manpower needs, one important question is: What percentage of the work force will be able to work because there are jobs for them? There seems to be no reason why preschool programs (including "Sesame Street") should create more jobs, except for the marginal effect involved by the creation of organizations like CTW. Moreover, it seems likely that the absolute number of unemployed and underemployed persons will continue to rise. If this happens, there will be more unemployed persons when the graduates of programs like "Sesame Street" enter the labor market, and though the general intellectual level of the graduates might be higher than that of their fathers because of preschool education, there might simply be a greater discrepancy between the number of jobs available and the number of job seekers.

A more important justification for preschool programs has to be that they will help provide a more talented labor pool than is available at present. But three implications of this need to be pointed out for anyone who believes that the more an individual knows, the easier it will be to get a good job. First, preschool programs only help people obtain better jobs to the extent that selection into jobs depends on intellectual skills. Entry into some jobs, however, is determined by whom one knows, social skills, good fortune, or by need achievement. Moreover, even when intellectual skills play a part in job recruitment, it is often a global part in the sense that the skills are necessary but not sufficient for the position. This is especially the case where the intellectual skills required for a job are imprecisely defined and cover a wide range of talents (e.g., a high school diploma is required for the job, or a B.A. degree, or a Ph.D.). In such cases, the decision to hire will depend on non-achievement factors that differentiate between persons who have similar academic backgrounds.

Second, there are constraints of social function that determine social structure. For example, trucks need to be driven, and they will continue to be driven for many years to come. If the general knowledge level of all persons were raised, this would mean that we would have more knowledgeable truckers but it would not necessarily mean that future trucking jobs will be available to persons who have the talents that are currently required for the job. A person applying for a trucking job would only have an advantage if his achievement level were raised and everyone else's was held constant. Competition for jobs typically involves a relative judgment between the talents of different job applicants rather than an absolute judgment of the talent of a single applicant. Hence, increasing knowledge levels may help recruit persons into new jobs on technological frontiers where absolute knowledge counts more, but it may not have any job-related consequences for most other persons whose jobs are determined by relative knowledge levels. However, it might be possible to retrain people more easily if their achievement levels have been increased by preschools and schools.

Third, preschool programs are a very indirect way of influencing the work force. The best way of exercising such influence would probably be to intervene in the work situation directly and to create new jobs or train persons for specific new jobs as they occur. This is probably more useful than providing four-year-olds with letter and number skills for jobs which require more advanced knowledge.

Another reason why a more talented labor pool would be desirable is that the position of the United States in the world economic system depends on developing and marketing technological innovations like computers, photo-reproduction devices, machine tools, new agricultural devices, and new weapon systems. Supplying trained persons to further high technology is sometimes thought to require the early identification of as large a pool of child talent as possible, and it is from this pool that the more talented will be selected for advanced education. Seen from this perspective, programs like "Sesame Street" are important because they are meant to stimulate the talent of a wide range of children at an early age, thereby decreasing the likelihood that many of the truly talented will be missed. Moreover, it is argued that programs which aim at particular groups of children such as the disadvantaged cannot be advancing the high technology to an appreciable degree because they fail to reach so many other children and so do not cause a significant increase in the overall level of talent in the larger pool of all children. To persons concerned about the future technological development of our economy, the social background of children is irrelevant; what counts is that as many of the talented as possible be identified, stimulated intellectually, and helped to gain jobs developing our advanced technology.

If the policymaker decides that a high national manpower priority is the creation of a large pool of persons with more advanced technological skills than are found at present, then he has to ask himself whether this will be best accomplished by expending his resources as evenly as he can across all preschoolers in the nation or whether it will be best accomplished by concentrating greater efforts on the social groups more likely to "have" the talents he wants to see developed. If the latter were his decision, he would want preschool programs to be universally available to all children, and he would especially want schools to modify their curricula if most of their children had used preschool learning opportunities. Such a pattern of curriculum change would build upon the skills acquired from preschool education and would produce more of the talent needed. However, this strategy runs the risk that the talent might be even more disproportionately composed of the economically advantaged than was the case before preschool programs—like "Sesame Street"—became universally available.

Depolarizing Social Group Levels

An important consequence of programs that are aimed at preschoolers of all social groups is that they provide some relief from traditional compensatory programs that are aimed exclusively or predominantly at social groups like the economically disadvantaged, or Spanish-speaking Americans, or some other social category. Compensatory programs probably contribute to the polarization of social differences. Recipients of such programs are reminded that they need help, and in order to receive the help they are forced to see themselves in socially stigmatized categories like "the disadvantaged," "the unemployed," "the crippled," etc., and they may hear themselves described as "culturally deprived." Moreover, their frustration is probably increased by the knowledge that, even if these categories were accurate labels, they point out weaknesses rather than strengths that could be built upon.

Persons who receive no compensatory advantages and who pay for those of others are often resentful because they are providing help and do not see any obvious returns for this. Moreover, they may be threatened by any improvement in the lot of the economically disadvantaged because this can imply a shrinking status or income differential between the advantaged and disadvantaged. Furthermore, the advantaged may also feel that the political activities which brought benefits to the disadvantaged used inappropriate tactics or led to the economically disadvantaged receiving political favors *at the expense of the more advantaged.*

Social forces like the ones mentioned here probably attend the development of compensatory programs, and their impact on society is probably divisive in the short-term. Universally available programs like "Sesame Street" avoid these problems because they are available to all children and because the issue of social class differences in the use of such programs has a low profile nationally. Universal programs are important, therefore, to all persons who cherish a peaceful society in which group differences are played down. Moreover, the "Sesame Street" case adds an interesting twist to this. The series is available to all, yet it has black actors and an inner-city location, and there are some public statements to the effect that the economically disadvantaged are a target group of special interest. This means that the program may depolarize, because it is available to all and may also be successful in gaining the support of economically disadvantaged groups because they perceive that a special effort is being made to reach them.

Universally available preschool programs probably help some disadvantaged children move further into the mainstream of American life, which may be another process that leads to the depolarization of group differences. They would presumably do this by stimulating the potential of the children so that they will do better in school than some of their advantaged contemporaries. It is thus important to ask: Which kinds of disadvantaged children are most likely to benefit from preschool programs? One possibility is that the benefits might accrue to the relatively more advantaged of the disadvantaged. If so, this would provide more models of advanced achievement from among members of the disadvantaged group, but it would also increase the variability in achievement within the group. The question that decisionmakers have to ask themselves, therefore, is whether it is better to pursue policies that aim to create opportunities for an unknown number of the relatively more advantaged of the disadvantaged or whether to pursue policies that are aimed at the totality of the disadvantaged. Said differently, do we want to open some doors or lift the entire floor?

Universally available preschool programs may well depolarize. But if a particular preschool program is not equally used by all groups or does not provide equal benefits when it is equally used, it will increase group differences. If this were to happen, it would widen the present group differences in class, status, or prestige so that many of the gap-related social forces that led to polarization in the first place will persist or even increase. Since the problems associated with the achievement gap will probably not go away—certainly not because of "Sesame Street," at least—some basis will have to be found sooner or later for providing extra resources to the less fortunate in our society. It seems to us that the policymaker interested in depolarization has to look at individual preschool programs and ascertain whether they may be widening the gap. If they are, he may have to decide whether the depolarization of today is worth the possibly exacerbated polarization of tomorrow.

None of the preceding permits us to estimate the degree to which preschool programs aimed exclusively at the economically disadvantaged do in fact polarize social group differences. When compared to busing or to giving jobs to disadvantaged persons in preference to advantaged persons with superior formal qualifications, it would seem that compensatory preschool programs are a minor source of divisiveness, in part because they are often labeled "experimental" and in part because they have a low profile politically. Nonetheless, we do not feel that the possibility of long-term polarization can be ruled out when we come to examine the consequences of universal preschool programs.

Meritocracy Reaffirmed and Exemplified

The ideal principle for the distribution of social rewards in the United States today is a meritocratic one in which rewards come to those whose abilities and effort merit them. The success of a society in reaching the meritocratic ideal can be measured in terms of four fundamental criteria. The first is that all individuals should have an equal opportunity to pursue rewards and that no individual should have a headstart on another by virtue of race, class, religion, or any similar factor. The second criterion is that each individual should be free to avail himself of the opportunities that are available so that, if he does not want to pursue certain rewards or if he wants to devote most of his energies to specific rewards, then he is free to do so within certain legal constraints. The third criterion is that, since men are born with unequal genetic endowments, some will gain more rewards than others even if they all have equal opportunities which they use in equal amounts. The fourth criterion for a merit-ordered society is that the person who puts more effort into the pursuit of rewards (time or energy) should be disproportionately rewarded because he has used his talents better. In short, the ideal meritocracy uses equality of opportunity and freedom in the pursuit of happiness as fundamental rights which permit differences in reward to be justified in terms of differences in both talent and effort.

Universal preschool programs like "Sesame Street" reaffirm meritocratic principles by attempting to provide an educational opportunity on a nonpreferential basis. Actually, if we look to "Sesame Street" as a particular example of such programs, it may do more than merely reaffirm meritocratic principles. It may even exemplify them. Compare the degree to which "Sesame Street" creates equal opportunities which are freely and equally used with the degree to which other social institutions (e.g., the home or school) create equal opportunities or the equal use of opportunities. Impressionistically, it would seem from such a comparison that "Sesame Street" is less biased against the economically disadvantaged than are homes and schools, for the series is available in any home with a working television set—and most homes have one—and its content is identical—within certain constraints of set quality—in rich or poor homes reached by the same transmitter. And, even though it may be used more by the relatively advantaged, the extent of this preference is probably less than many persons expected of a program on educational television. Thus, compared to other educational institutions like the home or school, "Sesame Street" may seem especially able to create the two conditions that are prerequisites for talent and effort to flourish in a democratic fashion. The important value question that follows from this is whether the possibility that "Sesame Street" is *relatively* more meritocratic than other educational institutions in the United States today would be sufficient to justify it if the series were *absolutely* non-meritocratic, either because it significantly widened the academic achievement gap over several years or because schools capitalized upon the series in a way that widened the gap.

HOW VALUABLE IS NARROWING
ACADEMIC ACHIEVEMENT GAPS?

Narrowing the Achievement Gap: Is it Possible?

In a provocative article, Jensen[8] suggested that compensatory education had been tried and failed. By failed he meant that intelligence gains had not been demonstrated in economically disadvantaged children as a result of compensatory educational efforts. Clearly, if the disadvantaged do not learn, then the gap in IQ scores cannot be narrowed.

Jensen's argument has been widely criticized.[9] It is sufficient at this point to note that he mostly discussed the failure to influence intelligence scores rather than scores on tests that were tailored to a particular program's strengths, as the "Sesame Street" tests were, or that involved the learning of simple associations, as many "Sesame Street" test items did. Moreover, he examined global programs like Headstart rather than specific preschool programs like that of Bereiter and Englemann, or the Ypsilanti Perry preschool project, or Susan Gray's Nashville project, all of which

---

[8] A. R. Jensen, "How Much Can We Boost IQ and Scholastic Achievement?" *Harvard Educational Review* 39 (1969): 1–123.

[9] The major criticisms of Jensen's paper were contained in *Environment, Heredity, and Intelligence*, Reprint Series #2, *Harvard Educational Review*, 1969, and in *Science, Heritability and IQ*, Reprint Series #4, *Harvard Educational Review*, 1969.

have caused increases in IQ or aptitude.[10] "Sesame Street" also showed that disadvantaged children can learn from a program aimed at them, and the second ETS evaluation even demonstrated that encouragement to view "Sesame Street" prevented a decline in intelligence, as measured on one vocabulary-based test for preschoolers. It is clear, then, that the economically disadvantaged *can* benefit from some kinds of compensatory education and that intelligence test scores *can* be affected by some preschool programs, although most programs are not demonstrably effective in this.

Increasing the Perceived Legitimacy of the Social Order among Economically Disadvantaged Groups

There is a good deal of evidence to indicate that economically disadvantaged Americans, particularly blacks, feel alienated from much of the mainstream of American life. It might be hypothesized that narrowing the academic achievement gap would help disadvantaged children do better at school, experience greater success in the competition for jobs, and feel that they have a greater vested interest in preserving the basic framework of American society. Hence, they might come to consider the society and its major institutions as legitimate and needing reforms that are less than radical.

It is not at all clear that narrowing the academic achievement gap at age four will result in greater acceptance of American social institutions at age sixteen. For this to happen, we would have to assume that the schools will build upon a preschool program's initial achievements and that non-achievement related factors that cause alienation (e.g., lack of control over one's own life, poor community-police relations) will not increase. If neither of these happened, the achievement gap might be as wide after a preschool program as before it, and many other social pressures would induce alienation as they did before. There is probably no concrete event that cements the perception of societal legitimacy like having a steady, well-paying job and owning significant possessions. But access to well-paying jobs would not necessarily be guaranteed if the achievement gap were narrowed, though the situation might be improved. The guarantee could not be made because, for reasons mentioned earlier, the correlation between academic achievement and the quality of one's job is far from perfect even after all the social background factors have been partialled out that currently inflate the correlation.[11]

---

[10] Details of the appropriate studies are available in the references cited in footnote 1.

[11] See P. M. Blau and O. D. Duncan, *The American Occupational Structure* (New York: John Wiley & Sons, 1967).

In considering the argument that narrowing the gap will promote greater societal integration, the policymaker cannot afford to ignore the effects of the narrowed gap on social groups who expect to have higher status than the economically disadvantaged and who might be threatened by the rise of the disadvantaged. The social group most threatened at this time probably consists of lower middle class whites, and the phrase "white backlash" probably refers to the threat that arises because persons in this group perceive that their share of national resources is diminishing. A complexity is introduced if the legitimate authorities in the society are seen as promoting this threat because they are seen to condone and encourage the preferential treatment to the disadvantaged. This will not increase the degree to which the white (or other advantaged) groups feel committed to their societal institutions, and it implies that any increased societal acceptance by the economically disadvantaged might be achieved at the cost of increased societal rejection by the groups most threatened by the success of the disadvantaged.

The policymaker may thus have to choose between integrating the disadvantaged further into society or risking an increase in the alienation of those social groups just above the disadvantaged in the social prestige hierarchy. In this context, a sentence of Gans' is particularly appropriate:

> In a democracy that is 90 per cent white and about 60 per cent affluent, the elected officials of the executive and legislative branches of government will not be able to institute many programs that require reductions in power and privilege from the majority. . . .[12]

What Gans' sentence indicates is that the political cost of alienating the relatively affluent majority is so high that it would be difficult to support social programs that might reduce their power or privilege. However, these short-term costs have to be weighed against the possible costs of failing to narrow the gap or—more directly—the costs of instituting universal programs that exacerbate it and so polarize further. This means that decisionmakers might have to opt between furthering the interests of the economically advantaged or disadvantaged. If this were to happen, how could we morally justify a choice for the advantaged when they are absolutely deprived of less and when there is an unknown segment of the disadvantaged that is cold, hungry, ill-housed, and sick to a degree that could be interpreted as absolutely deprived of some of life's most basic needs? Moreover, how could we opt for the economically advantaged when their dissatisfaction has to be expressed within a social context where they have

---

[12] H. J. Gans, "The White Problem," in H. J. Gans, ed., *People and Plans* (New York: Basic Books, Inc., 1968), p. 363.

more to lose by their actions than the disadvantaged. To be sure, the disadvantaged have things to lose (the roofs over their heads and—in some cases—their jobs). But they do have less to lose and so they may be prepared to risk more when they express their dissatisfaction in behavior. In other words, the probability and intensity of behavior that disrupts our system may be higher from the economically disadvantaged than from the advantaged.

Let us make no mistake: the issue of gap narrowing makes salient the age-old problem of whose interests shall be promoted at whose expense—a problem that has political and ethical dimensions. Moreover, it is a problem that the goal of reaching and teaching all children seems to side-step neatly. However, if universal programs are selectively used they do promote some groups' interests more than others. This being so, the crucial issue is: Should we allow different groups to pursue their different interests freely if this furthers inequality of performance; or should a deliberate decision be made to pursue one group's interests more than another's in order to further greater equality of performance?

Promoting Some Basic American Values (But Not Others)

One important reason for narrowing the gap is that not all children are presumed to have equal home opportunities for gaining the kind of knowledge that is tested in schools. Hence, in order to give all groups an equal chance in school, it is reasoned that they should be made as equal as possible on entering school even if this means giving the economically disadvantaged more government-supported educational opportunities than the advantaged. Underlying this is the assumption that group equality of performance on entering school is a social value that should be promoted. This is not to say that all individuals should be equal. Rather, there should be no correlation between variables like SES or race and preschool performance.

The problem is that equality can be defined in different ways. Some of these can be seen as conflicting with other basic American values and these apparent conflicts often enter into political debate. For example, attaining the equality of group preschool achievement averages might entail providing unequal educational opportunities for groups that initially score lower. To be sure, we might argue that this government-provided difference in opportunities only makes up for home-provided differences in educational opportunities. However, the former are typically more visible than the latter, and it is often not *perceived,* or it is not accepted, that unequal government-provided opportunities merely compensate for unequal home-provided opportunities. As a consequence, it is sometimes argued that there is a basic contradiction in advocating unequal opportunities to promote either a greater equality of achievement or a greater equality of opportunity.

Equality of preschool performance can also be interpreted as conflicting with freedom which is the most prized of all American abstract values.[13] At one level, freedom is violated because economically advantaged persons cannot elect how their taxes are spent; and at another level, economically advantaged children are often not free to enjoy compensatory educational opportunities because income cutoff points are established and children whose parents earn more than the cutoff cannot take advantage of the educational opportunity even if they want to. Also, the provision of unequal opportunities can be interpreted as conflicting with a "self help" value that is symbolized by the Horatio Alger myth. According to this value, individuals have to improve their lot by virtue of their own endeavors rather than through the intervention of others. It is likely, then, that any accomplishments due to the intervention of others are not respected, and this might cause negative attitudes towards the recipients of compensatory programs.

Since most decisionmakers are responsible to politically minded constituencies they have to ask themselves which of these values their constituencies consider most important, for groups that value freedom (in the abstract) most highly will often want to take different actions from groups that value equality more highly.[14] But even if decisionmakers are not responding to the real or anticipated preferences of their political constituencies, they still should ponder the importance of maximizing equality as an end if this implies either unequal means to reach this end or a restriction to some of the freedoms of others.

Comparison Processes in American Education

There is a growing body of theoretical data which indicates that we develop our estimation of our abilities by comparing ourselves with others

---

[13] M. Rokeach, *Beliefs, Attitudes, and Values* (San Francisco: Jossey-Bass, 1968).

[14] Rokeach found that policemen ranked freedom first of eighteen values while they ranked equality twelfth. Unemployed blacks ranked freedom tenth and equality first. Moreover, persons sympathetic to civil rights demonstrations, ranked freedom first and equality sixth, while among persons unsympathetic to demonstrations freedom was ranked second and equality eleventh. It is not clear, of course, whether each of these groups interprets freedom and equality in the same way. It is possible, for instance, that some of the groups define freedom in terms of freedom from external constraints and others in terms of freedom to pursue opportunities.

in the immediate environment.[15] Social comparison theory has been used in education to explain why the academic self-concept of black children declines when they enter integrated classes.[16] What is hypothesized is that black children, who compared themselves to other black children (and hence indirectly to black achievement norms) when they were in all-black classes, now compare themselves to higher norms when they enter mostly white classes. Since they fare badly in this last comparison, they decrease their estimate of their own ability. Unfortunately, we are not yet sure of the causal relationship between estimates of one's own academic ability and one's school performance, or school-leaving age, or job performance, or self-concept. Hence, it is impossible to estimate the consequences that might result because economically disadvantaged children in the post-"Sesame Street" era will sometimes be comparing themselves to advantaged contemporaries who outperform them by more than was the case before "Sesame Street."

Comparison processes are also used by teachers for determining the relative ability of children, and it is clear that the teachers' expectations of a child's academic performance bias his or her treatment of that child and influence the grades and aptitude scores of the child in question.[17] Thus, if academically disadvantaged children are even further behind advantaged children in the first grade because of some preschool program, it is likely that teachers will expect less of them on the average and will also teach them less.

Finally, it is worth noting that children compare each other's performance, and they attach evaluative labels to individual children or to groups of children as a consequence of these comparisons. In this way, the lowest-scoring might be labeled as "dumb," or "backward," irrespective of their absolute performance level. The consequences of these comparisons and labels will be deleterious in most cases, and we might expect the frequency

---

[15] Social comparison theory dates its systematic elaboration to a paper by L. Festinger, "A Theory of Social Comparison Processes," *Human Relations* 7 (1964): 117–140. More recent empirical work and extensions to the theory are contained in a special 1966 supplementary number of the *Journal of Experimental Social Psychology* which was entirely devoted to social comparison issues.

[16] The use of social comparison theory in this context has been most noteworthy in the chapters by T. F. Pettigrew and by I. Katz that appear in the *Nebraska Symposium on Motivation* (Lincoln, Neb., 1967), and the theory is also used in the paper by D. Armor, "The Evidence on Busing," *Public Interest* 28 (1972): 90–126.

[17] The research on the effects of teacher's expectancies has been recently summarized by J. P. Baker and J. L. Crist in a chapter in J. D. Elashoff and R. E. Snow, *Pygmalion Reconsidered* (Worthington, Ohio: Charles A. Jones Publishing Co., 1971) and, in great detail, by R. Rosenthal, "On the Social Psychology of the Self-Fulfilling Prophecy: Further Evidence for Pygmalion Effects and their Mediating Mechanisms" (unpublished manuscript, Harvard University, 1973).

or intensity of such labeling to increase if achievement gaps are widened over their current levels.

Comparison processes like those we have just outlined imply that part of the achievement problem of the economically disadvantaged depends on group differences in achievement. Narrowing the gap would not prevent these comparison processes from operating between individuals, but it would reduce the probability of such comparison processes operating at the level of social groups—at a level that does not respect the individuality of members of the social groups in question.

Relative Deprivation in American Society

One correlate of dissatisfaction with life in the United States seems to be relative deprivation. Absolute deprivation occurs when a person totally lacks a specific resource. Relative deprivation occurs when one person perceives that he lacks some resource that another has and when he also believes that the second person has no greater right to that resource.[18] Thus, I might feel relatively deprived of justice if I thought that some other person was obtaining better legal service or more favorable verdicts from the courts when there was no explicable basis for such preferential treatment. Relative deprivation is similar to perceived injustice, and three features about it deserve consideration. First, it is not sufficient that I consider only how the courts treat me; it is the difference between my treatment and others' treatment that counts. Second, it has been claimed that relative deprivation can be egoistic or fraternal.[19] Egoistic deprivation refers to me comparing myself to someone else, while fraternal deprivation refers to me comparing a group of persons like myself (e.g., blacks) to a group of other persons (e.g., whites). Third, relative deprivation has been demonstrated in field studies to vary with dissatisfaction with jobs,[20] reported participation

[18] N. G. Runciman, *Relative Deprivation and Social Justice* (Berkeley: University of California Press, 1966).

[19] T. F. Pettigrew, "When a Black Candidate Runs for Mayor: Race and Voting Behavior," in H. Hahn, ed., *Urban Affairs Annual Review* (Beverly Hills, Calif.: Sage Publications, 1972), as well as in R. D. Vanneman and T. F. Pettigrew, "Race and Relative Deprivation," *Race* 13 (1972): 461–486.

[20] Patchen found that workers in an oil refinery seemed to base their satisfaction about wages, not on the difference between what they and others earned, but on what they earned relative to their job responsibility and seniority when this was compared to what others earned relative to their responsibility and seniority. J. S. Adams has formalized this relationship between input-outcome comparisons and dissatisfaction in a chapter, "Equity Theory," that appears in L. Berkowitz, ed., *Recent Advances in Experimental Social Psychology,* vol. 2 (New York: Academic Press, 1963). The original idea in the social sciences goes back to Stouffer's work in *The American Soldier,* vol. 1 (Princeton, N.J.: Princeton University Press, 1949).

in urban riots,[21] and voting for George Wallace,[22] while in laboratory experiments it has been demonstrated to cause low morale.[23] Obviously, if relative deprivation were definitively demonstrated as a cause of alienation from the mainstream of American society, it would imply that any program increasing the difference in academic performance between social groups may also be increasing the potential for groups and individuals to make comparisons that cause dissatisfaction. Alternatively, if individuals or groups did not spontaneously make comparisons that caused dissatisfaction, it is nonetheless possible for other persons, particularly the politically active, to make particular comparison groups salient whose outcomes are more favorable than the outcomes of one's own group.

What is not clear at this time is how much relative deprivation will result because of preschool programs that exacerbate the achievement gap. In the case of "Sesame Street," the limited impact that can be attributed to the series at present indicates that it probably did not increase the gap by a significant amount in one season. Even if it did, it is not clear whether knowledge of an increase in the gap is sufficient by itself to generate much dissatisfaction. Compare, for example, the dissatisfaction that is likely to occur from knowing about a widening gap with the dissatisfaction that might result if such group differences in knowledge or education led to differential access to jobs and hence to an exacerbation of group differences in income.

It is also worth noting that, if social comparison processes determine dissatisfaction it is also likely that they determine satisfaction.[24] Furthermore, in most social situations there are many comparisons that we could make, some of which would cause dissatisfaction and others satisfaction. Hence, an important and unsolved question is: What determines which group is selected as a comparison group? The presence of a comparison group that *could* cause dissatisfaction does not imply either that this comparison will be made or that those comparisons will be overlooked which would cause an overestimation of feelings of satisfaction. It is therefore difficult to predict when a particular "objective" social situation that could cause relative deprivation is translated into feelings of dissatisfaction.

---

[21] The concept of relative deprivation is used in part to explain riot participation by J. M. Paige, "Political Orientation and Riot Participation," that appeared in the *American Sociological Review* 36 (1971): 810–820.

[22] T. F. Pettigrew.

[23] A. J. Spector, "Expectations, Fulfillment, and Morale," *Journal of Abnormal and Social Psychology* 52 (1956): 51–56.

[24] For a discussion of this, see P. Brickman and D. T. Campbell, "Hedonic Relativism and Planning the Good Society," in M. H. Appley, ed., *Adaptation-Level Theory: A Symposium* (New York: Academic Press, 1971).

Thus, while the narrowing of achievement gaps that help reduce income disparities between groups might well reduce the relative deprivation experienced by some groups, it is not clear in the case of preschool programs whether narrowing group differences in prereading skills will make economically disadvantaged children or their parents any more satisfied with the outcomes that the social system provides for them. Of course, the issue would warrant more attention if schools succeeded in capitalizing upon preschool programs and converted a narrowed gap in prereading skills into a narrowed gap in advanced skills that have a direct relationship to obtaining a better education or better job. And the issue would warrant especially grave attention if schools capitalized upon group achievement differences that were widened by particular preschool programs, for then gaps in more advanced skills would be widened and this would more obviously work to the detriment of the disadvantaged.

Race, Caste, and Class

Blacks in the United States today tend to be poorer, to know less, to get worse jobs, to have children who are poorer, know less, and get worse jobs. A major difficulty arises if observers attribute this cycle of poverty to blackness rather than to, say, social class and the education that goes with this. To attribute a necessary causal relationship to blackness and lower scores on achievement or IQ tests can entail taking one trait—blackness—which may be irrelevant to achievement and then using it to justify excluding some persons from social opportunities. This is how caste systems operate, and they are quite out of keeping with basic American individualist values since persons in some social groups are treated in terms of visible global attributes like skin color rather than in terms of their individual characters. So long as there remain elements of such a caste system in the United States, black Americans will be angry and there will be a "racial problem."

There are obvious differences of social class in American society as well as differences in caste. These class differences mean that children with parents who are poorer, less educated, more rural, and more inner-city live in less pleasant surroundings than children with parents who are more affluent, better educated, and suburban. Moreover, children with each of these sets of background characteristics score differently on achievement and IQ tests when they enter school. Unless we assume that there are genetic differences between classes, including genetic differences between classes *within each race,* it does not seem that the resources of the lower class section of the talent pool are being fully exploited. An important practical issue of concern to a nation intent on increasing the size and quality of its technological elite is this: Will one do better to direct one's efforts at all preschoolers, thereby stimulating the more talented among the advantaged and disadvantaged, or should one direct one's efforts especially at disadvantaged preschoolers (whether from disadvantaged racial or class backgrounds)?

The latter would seem desirable if it could be concluded from intensive preschool programs that: (1) advantaged children with high talent and high educational test scores increase their performance less than disadvantaged children with high latent talent and depressed educational test scores; or (2) the pool of latent talent among the disadvantaged is large enough to be worth cultivating, but needs an intensive cultivation that can only be afforded by directing more effective resources at the disadvantaged than the advantaged. To our knowledge, there is no definitive answer to these issues at this time. However, the issue of the potential of the disadvantaged for providing many persons with advanced skills is worth raising. It illustrates that there may be practical as well as moral consequences of narrowing the achievement gap between different castes and different classes.

Beyond Meritocracy: To Increase or Decrease Individual Variability in Academic Achievement?

Even if all opportunities were equal for a whole generation of children, they would not finish their lives on an equal social, economic, or intellectual footing. More importantly, their children would not start life on an equal footing, because parents have an understandable tenacity to pass on to their children whatever advantages they have gained by virtue of their own talents or effort. Since a result of this tenacity is that some children will have fewer opportunities in life than others because of the parents they were born to, it is difficult to argue that underprivileged children have deserved their disadvantagement by virtue of talent or effort. Indeed, even if they had the same opportunities as other children from birth and were just as free to avail themselves of the opportunities *but did not do so,* in what sense would their lower use of opportunities be merited? After all, it cannot be readily assumed that they made less use of opportunities because they had less talent or because they acted in full knowledge of the consequences of their low effort. Even if a social system could miraculously unconfound race and achievement or SES and achievement for one generation, it would still be faced with the fact that parents create inequalities anew each generation and with the problem of justifying such apparently undeserved inequality among small children. A major difficulty facing meritocratic societies is to create a framework of justice that can explain the disadvantagement of persons whose fate was not determined by their own talent or effort.

A second difficulty with meritocracies concerns the degree to which they foster interpersonal competition. Meritocracies stress how talent and effort can bring rewards; they try to create the freedom to pursue rewards; and they also institute selection processes that weed out the more meritorious from the less meritorious. This value system leads to pressures on individuals to work hard, but it can also lead to the development of other, less desirable, talents which help persons appear meritorious. These talents include: cunning, secrecy, sabotage, forming coalitions to crush competitors, and other related attributes that have to do with "getting ahead." In a sense, then, a value system that emphasizes equality of opportunities and liberty to pursue one's own definition of happiness will often conflict with fraternity.

Meritocracies create values which particularly justify rapid economic development, as in nineteenth-century America. However, it is not clear to us, as it is not clear to social philosophers like John Rawls,[25] that these values are as appropriate to the last half of the twentieth century as they were to the nineteenth. The major task facing this country in the early nineteenth century concerned its rapid economic development which was partially accomplished by adopting values which stressed free competition among men so that the most meritorious could rise to positions of wealth and power. Hence, the value system slighted equality and fraternity in favor of freedom in the economic marketplace. The last half of the twentieth century may well need to place greater stress than in the past on social interdependency and on the need to create social justice for those with lesser talents.

One way of beginning to move in this direction is to direct social policy toward decreasing the national variability in achievement instead of increasing it. To do this, a higher proportion of resources would have to be directed towards children in the lower part of the achievement distribution and, instead of selecting the most talented for special advantages, one would choose the least advantaged to a greater degree than is presently the case.

We must be careful at this point to reiterate that attempts to decrease variability and narrow gaps can have serious drawbacks, and the mistakes of some of the compensatory education programs of the 1960s have to be avoided. In particular, strategies may have to be adopted at this time that do not stress the "cultural deficiency" of the economically disadvantaged, that do not stigmatize them, that include the rural poor as well as the urban poor, and that involve concrete programs aimed at very specific and carefully chosen goals. Strategies may also have to be developed that minimize any perceived conflict of interest between economically disadvantaged

---

[25] J. Rawls, *A Theory of Justice* (Cambridge, Mass.: Harvard University Press, 1971).

groups and persons who are working class or middle class.[26] This could be achieved by methods such as introducing new programs with a low national profile exclusively to the disadvantaged, or by introducing nationwide programs with a higher profile among the economically disadvantaged than the advantaged, or by introducing programs that specially cater to the economically disadvantaged and from which disadvantaged children of a certain age stand to gain more than other children.

One strategy to be avoided, in our opinion, is taking opportunities away from the children of more economically advantaged groups, and it should be noted that our previous remarks were directed at the *introduction of new educational programs rather than at the withdrawal of current programs* from these children. It should also be noted that no program has to be exclusively aimed at an undifferentiated audience or at a highly specific one. Programs can reach many but concentrate on few, and in this sense "Sesame Street" is already a universal program but with a selective concentration on the disadvantaged. The key issue is whether the program's total compensatory inputs (principally represented by utilization centers) should be increased to counteract the increase in individual difference variability and the widening of the academic achievement gap that are probably taking place because of the program.

HOW VALUABLE IS IT FOR ECONOMICALLY DISADVANTAGED CHILDREN TO KNOW MORE IF THE MEANS OF ATTAINMENT WIDEN THE ACADEMIC ACHIEVEMENT GAP?

If we teach all children, we teach economically disadvantaged children. Hence, we might assume that some of the benefits of teaching all children are also relevant to teaching the disadvantaged. For instance, the disadvantaged will benefit from any short-term reductions in group polarization and from knowing more in a complex world. But if the means of knowing more also lead to the average disadvantaged child falling further behind his advantaged counterpart, then we might also assume that he will experience any problems associated with a wider gap. These problems include the way he is treated at school by teachers and peers; how he estimates his own academic skills; how difficult he will find the competition for jobs; and

---

[26] We should note, once again, that there may be considerably less perceived conflict of interest when it comes to compensatory preschool programs as opposed to, say, busing or situations where jobs are dispensed according to a quota system that favors applicants from disadvantaged backgrounds whose formal qualifications may be less than those of unsuccessful applicants from more advantaged backgrounds.

how justly he might feel treated when he compares his own life chances with those of the economically advantaged or with those that are promised him as a person who is supposed to have the same opportunity as anyone else to benefit from school.

We now have to ask the crucial question of whether there is anything special about the economically disadvantaged which would make the absolute gains they make outweigh any relative losses. This question has obvious relevance to "Sesame Street," for the show is probably causing some absolute gains but also widening gaps in those domains where learning takes place.

How the Parents of Economically Disadvantaged Children Probably Define Their Children's Educational Problems

If we were to ask the parents of economically disadvantaged children what they want of a preschool program we suspect that they would reply: "We want it to teach our children something" or "We want it to help them do better in school." It is less likely, in our opinion, that they would say they wanted the program to narrow an academic achievement gap. Moreover, if it were pointed out to parents that the most fundamental way of narrowing the gap was to make a preschool program less widely available (i.e., selective in its dissemination), it might arouse the fear that their own child might not receive the program and so might not directly benefit from it all. Hence, from the perspective of parents who are primarily concerned for the welfare of their own child, the major problem is probably to teach their child more—an absolute criterion—rather than to narrow gaps —a relative criterion. It follows from this that respecting the desires of disadvantaged parents might entail defining their children's educational problem as an absolute one.

But the expression of parental wishes for a child will vary with the context in which the wishes are enunciated. In particular, if a list of possible wishes were drawn up, and the consciousness of parents raised by the list, would the choice still be for wanting their child to know more? Imagine answers to the open-ended question "What do you want for your child from his preschool experiences?" *versus* answers to the close-ended question "What do you want for your child from his preschool experiences?" "Please rank order the importance of the following alternatives: (a) that he knows more; (b) that he knows more if this means falling further behind his advantaged contemporaries; (c) that he knows more and draws ahead of his advantaged contemporaries; (d) that he probably will know more but that, even if he does not, it is certain that the achievement gap between advantaged and disadvantaged children will be increased; and (e) that he might know more but that, even if he does not, it is certain that the gap will be narrowed." To put the matter bluntly: We do not always express our wants at a high level of consciousness. Thus, while simply expressed wants should be considered in determining social policy, they should not be paramount. Moreover, even when wants have been determined from a long array of sophisticated alternatives, individual or group wants are not identical with national needs. It is the latter that should be paramount in decisionmaking.

The Minimal Level of Absolute Knowledge for Participation in American Society

There are minimal levels of absolute knowledge which our society requires for even minimal citizen participation, and it can be argued that we should only worry about educational problems like achievement gaps once we have made sure that as many children as possible have elementary literacy skills and can read a telephone directory or a newspaper. Functional illiterates come disproportionately, but by no means exclusively, from economically disadvantaged groups. A popular preschool program like "Sesame Street" presumably attracts potential functional illiterates from all social groups, and it might provide the groundwork on which literacy skills are built. The crucial social importance of such skills suggests that the economically disadvantaged may especially benefit from universal and popular preschool programs, because they are more likely to have children who are potential functional illiterates.

Unfortunately, we do not know how many potential illiterates from among the economically disadvantaged would be stimulated by mass preschool programs. If we are prepared to assume that this target group scores extremely low on tests of cognitive ability, it is a reasonable guess—at least with "Sesame Street" because of the correlation of viewing and knowledge level—that the potentially illiterate are among the least likely to avail themselves of mass educational programs of a voluntary nature. Indeed, if a show like "Sesame Street" were to be justified on the grounds of preventing illiteracy, we would have to ask ourselves whether the same financial outlay might not be better spent on a program to identify and work with the children who are most likely to become illiterate. In other words, should the remedy of functional illiteracy be a beneficial side effect or a target problem? As a beneficial side effect, the absolute gain of reduced illiteracy has to be so great as to outweigh the costs of the economically disadvantaged falling behind the advantaged. But as a target problem, only the potentially illiterate would receive the program and, since these would come disproportionately from disadvantaged groups, the disadvantaged would gain both absolutely and relatively and a national problem of illiteracy would be reduced.

Models of Achievement from Economically Disadvantaged Groups

Programs that reach and teach a heterogeneous group of children will reach and teach some children from disadvantaged social groups, however these are defined, and will permit some talented children from these groups to take advantage of opportunities and to develop their full potential. Such children may later become models of what members of particular disadvantaged groups can achieve. It is not clear how such models influence the less fortunate members of economically disadvantaged groups. One result may be increased pride in one's membership group; a second may be belief in the efficacy of the social system to promote members of one's own group; a third may be the awakening of children's desire to emulate the model; and a fourth may be actual imitation of the model by the child.

It is important to note two reasons why efforts directed at all children might be more effective in promoting achievement models than efforts especially targeted at disadvantaged groups. First, if the strategy behind the special effort to reach the disadvantaged stressed the need to lift the floor of the disadvantaged this would mean that efforts would have to be disproportionately directed towards the least talented among the disadvantaged. This, in its turn, should hinder the development of the most talented from whose ranks later models of achievement would be most likely. And second, if the strategy were to direct resources at all the disadvantaged and if their mean achievement or reward levels were increased without a corresponding increase in variance, then it is not obvious that the most talented among the disadvantaged would stand out in the same way that they would have if their achievement and reward levels had been raised but those of other group members had not.

However, there are some difficulties that arise if one attempts to justify a preschool program on the grounds that it helps models from disadvantaged groups develop their potential even though the average advantaged and disadvantaged child may grow further apart academically. First, we do not know all the effects of such models. It is conceivable, for example, that the standards set by the model are so high that children despair of reaching them. Second—and more importantly—it is not clear how many models of achievement would emerge if the mean achievement level of the economically advantaged were raised more than that of the disadvantaged, for this means that the most talented among the disadvantaged would face even stiffer competition for advancement. And third, a better way to create more models would be to concentrate efforts on the more talented of the economically disadvantaged children rather than on all children.

CONCLUSION

Assigning a Value to "Sesame Street"

It is difficult to assign a value to viewing "Sesame Street," because (1) we know little of the effects of more than six-month's viewing; (2) we know little of the non-cognitive effects of the show; (3) we do not know if schools capitalize upon any gains due to the show; (4) we cannot readily weight the positive consequences of many children knowing a little more and enjoying the program against the negative consequences of widening gaps in those cognitive domains where "Sesame Street" teaches. Our personal judgment is not to assign high value to the gains that have been demonstrated to date, although we wish to stress that so much still remains to be learned and our judgment is a judgment—nothing more.

It would be desirable if nationwide voluntary preschool programs could be developed which teach children from all social groups, including the economically disadvantaged, and which also narrow the achievement gap. But we would be naive to claim that we know how to develop such programs. Two crucial issues thus arise:

1. To what extent should we concentrate our efforts on teaching all children, rather than on primarily teaching the economically disadvantaged?

2. If we decide that the problems of the economically disadvantaged deserve special preschool treatment, is the national problem to narrow the achievement gap or to teach disadvantaged children more irrespective of what happens to the gap?

Teaching All Children versus Narrowing the Achievement Gap

It is difficult to assess whether the need to teach prereading skills to a wide range of children is more pressing than the need to narrow the academic achievement gap, and we have come to no answer to this problem. As we saw previously, reaching and teaching all children by means of a universal program (1) may promote some happiness for a large number of parents and children who like the program; (2) may help children understand their social world better at an earlier age by speeding up the acquisition of elementary literacy skills; (3) may help produce a larger pool of child talent from which more persons will later emerge to advance the high technology on which the United States depends economically; (4) may promote equality of opportunity in the restricted sense that all persons have access to the same opportunities; (5) may promote the freedom to use or not use opportunities as one sees fit; and (6) may temporarily depolarize the situation that emerges when the children from one social group are treated preferentially over the children from some other group.

But the universal program may also increase the academic achievement gap. If it does, the following consequences are possible: (1) equality of opportunity will not be promoted in that disadvantaged children will enter school even further behind their advantaged contemporaries and so will not have an equal opportunity to benefit from school; (2) strict meritocratic principles will be violated because economically disadvantaged children will lag further behind for reasons that are probably not related to their own effort or talent and so cannot have been personally merited; (3) group polarization may increase with time if preschool programs inflate existing achievement differences and if these differences, in their turn, are so affected by the schools that they become differences in skills which are related to adult income; (4) the widening gap should increase social stigmatization on the basis of caste and class, thereby creating social system strains as well as moral problems stemming from a failure to respect individuality.

The advantages of narrowing the achievement gap are in part the obverse of the four points just made. We would be fostering (1) equality of opportunity and (2) adherence to stricter meritocratic principles and these might (3) diminish caste and class distinctions and (4) lead to a long-term group depolarization. In addition, narrowing the gap requires that special resources be devoted to the economically disadvantaged so that (5) a particular section of the national talent pool will be stimulated that has been systematically understimulated in the past. Hence, aiming programs exclusively at the disadvantaged might not be detrimental either for developing the technological elite that the nation requires or for developing models of high achievement that could spur on children from economically disadvantaged groups.

Targeting effective educational resources exclusively or predominantly at particular groups of children has obvious drawbacks. It prejudices equality of access to resources in favor of equality of achievement standing, and this can create severe political problems for policymakers who believe that the social standing of their advantaged constituencies is adversely affected if the disadvantaged gain by more than the advantaged. Moreover, it is not at all clear that targeting resources at the disadvantaged will accomplish much in the sphere of producing more persons with higher technological skills. It might; but it might not.

From a purely practical perspective, assigning a relative value to teaching all children *versus* narrowing the achievement gap depends on the following consideration. If schools were to capitalize upon a preschool program's successes, then we would have to ask ourselves whether the national needs for more persons with advanced technological skills and for a more knowledgeable citizenry are more pressing than the national need to reduce the ingrained caste and class differences that many persons have presumed to lead to many of the country's major social and moral problems? That—in our opinion—is the question which universal educational programs pose for us, and there is no easy answer at this time. Indeed, moral philosophers across the ages have posed the dilemma that the need for "efficiency" seems to be in fundamental conflict with "social justice" and that there is no obvious way of determining which of these ends should be furthered in particular cultures at particular times. We do not know which should be furthered in the United States today.

The dilemma only arises in the context of modern preschool education if the regular schools do in fact capitalize upon any learning caused by preschools. If they do not, the major practical question is: How valuable is it (1) to have many children achieve elementary literacy skills at a younger age than they would otherwise have acquired them? This must be seen, however, in the context that the children's knowledge on leaving school will probably not be any greater than it would have been without the preschool program. And, (2) how valuable is it to have n children saved from functional illiteracy by a mass voluntary preschool program? However, this question must be seen in the light of the possibility that $n + k$ children might be saved by a similar-cost program that was exclusively targeted at the potentially illiterate.

The Preschool Problem of the Economically Disadvantaged

We found it difficult to assign a value priority to narrowing the gap *versus* teaching all children. However, if a decision were made that the preschool problems of the disadvantaged are more important than the problems of all children, it would then be necessary to assign a priority to narrowing the achievement gap *versus* increasing the achievement levels of disadvantaged children even if such increases are accompanied by a widened achievement gap. This particular priority question is easier to decide.

Absolute gains by the disadvantaged (1) would probably save some children from functional illiteracy; (2) would promote the development of some models of achievement from disadvantaged groups; and (3) would probably correspond with the expressed wants of disadvantaged parents. In addition, such gains might (4) be associated with a short-term depolarization of group differences and (5) might promote certain conceptions of freedom and equality.

Against these points, however, are the following considerations: (1)

the persons least likely to use new resources among the economically disadvantaged are likely to be the potentially illiterate so that it is doubtful how many such children will be helped; (2) achievement models emerge because they do better than other persons, and so a relative criterion is used. Yet if the gap widens, the competition for excellence will increase and standing out from the economically advantaged will be all the more difficult for disadvantaged children; (3) the simply expressed wants of parents are not necessarily a good basis for estimating either national needs or the wants that parents would express if they were to choose from a sophisticated list of possible wants which raised the parents' consciousness above its normal level.

We should also not forget that economically disadvantaged children who had absolutely gained and relatively lost from a preschool program would have a more difficult time in school because of (1) their lower standing relative to their classmates, which might make school all the more punishing; (2) the increased expectancy of teachers that disadvantaged children should perform badly; (3) the attribution by advantaged peers that the disadvantaged are "backward"; and (4) even self-attributions by the disadvantaged to the effect that they are not as bright as others or are better only at less academic school activities. Moreover, (5) there are some jobs in our society which are allocated on the basis of achievement, and what counts in this respect is not what one knows but how much more one knows than others; and (6) unless one invokes caste or class-related genetic differences in ability, it is impossible to invoke meritocratic concepts to account for group differences in academic achievement among four-year-olds. Meritocracies justify adult differences in social rewards; but they cannot easily justify preschool differences in abilities that have some probable causal connection with adult rewards. Thus, we would suggest that the educational problem of the economically disadvantaged is relative, relating to their standing below the advantaged, and is not absolute, relating to how much they do or do not know.

Chapter 11
Some Implications of Our Evaluation for Social Policy Relevant to "Sesame Street"

POLICY CONSIDERATIONS RELEVANT TO FUTURE EVALUATIONS OF "SESAME STREET"

In the proposal for funding the third year of the Children's Television Workshop, it was mentioned that "Sesame Street" would not be evaluated in its 1971–1972 season, but that it might be evaluated again in its 1972–1973 season. Although never undertaken, it was proposed that a 1972–1973 evaluation should be similar to the two ETS evaluations that we previously examined. Since there seems little point in another demonstration of the adequacy of encouragement to view "Sesame Street" in the cognitive realm, we propose an outline of evaluation designs that are meant to examine important questions that have not yet been adequately probed. We outline four kinds of studies, dealing with them in what we consider to be the order of their priority. The studies are not described in any detail other than a brief sketch of the major design features.

A Study of the Long-term Effects of "Sesame Street" in Multiple Domains

"Sesame Street" would be more important as an educational innovation if it could be demonstrated that the program caused changes in academic achievement or personal development that are observable during the child's career in school. Fortunately, it is fairly simple to learn of "Sesame Street's" long-term effects in these areas.

363

The encouraged and nonencouraged groups in Durham, Phoenix, and Los Angeles were randomly constituted, and we know that the manipulation affected the amount of reported viewing, especially in Los Angeles. Schools keep records of the academic achievement of their pupils and of the tracks they are in. With the permission of parents and school authorities, these records could be retrieved and used to examine the effects of encouragement on whatever outcome measures are regularly kept in schools' records. Such records would probably include grades and standardized achievement scores and would be available for several years after the children stopped viewing "Sesame Street" on a regular basis. In fact, data could be compiled right through the child's school years, and with them we would be able to draw conclusions about long-term effects, including those that generalize to achievement test scores.

Since the encouraged and nonencouraged groups were randomly formed, it is also possible to collect interpretable data directly from the children as well as from their records. The neglected areas of social knowledge and affective development could be explored in this way, in the full realization that such measures have greater reliability and validity with older children than with four-year-olds. There is no reason why teachers and parents could not also be asked to rate the children in the experiment, and in this way we would be able to collect information from different relevant sources who know something about the child's interest in school, his academic aspirations, his attitudes, and typical behavior.

It may be argued on two grounds that the study of such long-term transfer effects is not a fair test of "Sesame Street." One is technical and has to do with the fact that the difference in viewing between the encouraged and nonencouraged children was not absolute (because some nonencouraged children viewed), thereby biasing the experiment against demonstrating effects of "Sesame Street." This bias occurred least of all in the Durham, Phoenix, and Los Angeles samples that would be part of the experiment proposed here; and, in particular, the bias at Los Angeles was noticeably small. We think that, if attrition were not too high, a strong test could be developed, especially at Los Angeles. A second objection might be that the long-term study would not be a test of "Sesame Street" but would be a test of the ability of schools to capitalize upon the opportunities that the program offers its viewers. This is true up to a point. The proposed experiment would not be a test of "Sesame Street" at its strongest. But it would be a test of the effects that have greatest social utility and that help define "Sesame Street's" importance. Unless we have clear evidence that our nation's schools can capitalize upon the probably slight advantage offered by "Sesame Street," it will be an educational innovation that has some effects by itself but no long-term effect in the larger educational context into which it has to fit.

A Large-Scale Evaluation of Economically Advantaged and Disadvantaged Children Who Are Not Encouraged to View

The ETS evaluations had only one sample of children who were clearly economically advantaged, and this is the major part of the data we had at the time of our study for determining the series' effects on the advantaged and its relative effects on the advantaged and disadvantaged. We think it important to know about possible SES and race differences in the frequency of viewing, about similar possible differences in how parents interact with their children in the context of "Sesame Street," about how much is learned by children from the various social groups, about the extent of transfer in each group, and about the extent to which schools in middle-class and working-class areas use "Sesame Street" or have revised their curricula because of it. We cannot answer such questions unless we can generalize more confidently to economically advantaged children in general, and at the time we could only generalize to children from the Philadelphia suburbs. It is probably unrealistic to expect that we should obtain a truly random sample of economically advantaged and disadvantaged children. But we could at least follow the excellent guidelines of Ball and Bogatz' strategy with economically disadvantaged children, and we can choose several advantaged sites that are different from each other geographically, on an urban-rural dimension, etc. Obviously, a heterogeneous sample of purposively chosen sites is much better than a single site.

The conditions of viewing to which we want to generalize are those where the child views at home without encouragement from outsiders. Any study of economically advantaged and disadvantaged samples should concentrate on these conditions. Moreover, the study should capitalize upon the advanced measurement skills of persons like Ball and Bogatz so that the latter, in whatever capacity, could advise CTW on the selection of measures of personal and social growth. "Sesame Street's" success in this general, hard-to-measure area has been chronically underexplored. Yet, modifications of social behavior and personal attitudes have always been stated as goals of "Sesame Street." The television medium would seem especially appropriate for social learning via modeling and for acquiring knowledge and pride through seeing individuals or social groups of personal relevance who do things that disconfirm popular stereotypes. Schools and preschools may find such teaching more difficult than television with its strong immediacy and its ability to capture the past and present, the near and far. It seems entirely plausible to us that "Sesame Street" may be as effective in teaching a wide range of knowledge *incidentally* as it is in teaching its present range of cognitive skills *directly,* but the issue has not yet been adequately explored.

We call, therefore, for a study of nonencouraged, at-home children from a mixed sample of economically advantaged and disadvantaged sites. The tests for the study should measure personal and social development as well as cognitive development, and care should be taken so that the testers do not know how much the children viewed. Such a study would be very much like the one that CTW originally proposed for "Sesame Street." As we saw in Chapter 3, the workshop called for an evaluation stressing (1) typical conditions of viewing; (2) long-term learning; and (3) the use of well-known tests of cognitive and affective development.

An Audience Survey with Stratified Random Sampling

We already know that "Sesame Street" is regularly viewed by about 40 percent of the total national audience of children from two to five years of age and that it is probably watched more in the relatively more affluent homes of the nation. The big question still unanswered is how black and white children view. We feel that the annual audience survey of the Corporation for Public Broadcasting should be expanded so that its sample of black households is increased. This would not be an expensive addition, and it would permit a more reliable assessment of viewing in black homes. Alternatively, a new survey should be conducted.

The sample for such an audience survey should be so stratified, and the size of subsamples so weighted, that we can examine how race and socioeconomic status *together* are related to viewing. There is a positive correlation between viewing and socioeconomic status in the nation at large, and we know that black Americans tend on the average to be of lower socioeconomic status than whites. However, it seems that blacks and whites may view in equal amounts. An obvious way that these apparently discrepant facts can be reconciled is to assume either that the data for blacks are wrong or that the relationship of socioeconomic status and viewing is different for black Americans than for white Americans. These two possibilities can only be explored with a stratified random sampling design that ensures an adequate number of black households of different SES levels.

There are difficulties involved in assessing the number of child viewers as opposed to the number of viewing households. It should not be difficult to discover the number of households where multiple viewing by target children takes place. The problem is more complicated with multiple viewing in day-care centers. While it would be relatively easy to draw up a universe of licensed day-care centers, proprietary and otherwise, it would be very difficult to draw up a universe of unlicensed ones. This means that extra effort would have to be expended to discover the homes and centers that take in children on a fee-paying basis, and the urgency of the need for such information depends on the number and social composition of the children attending unlicensed homes and centers during the day. An audience survey would be a difficult, but not impossible, task.

Formative Research on Enhancing the Power of the Encouragement Manipulation

It is clear that encouragement facilitated learning. Let us assume for the moment that the effects of encouragement were not due to the tester knowing of the child's encouragement status and treating him differently because of this. If tester artifacts did not operate, encouragement is an important process that enhances learning, and it would be useful to know how encouragement facilitates learning and how it can be modified so that its effectiveness is increased. We do not yet have enough knowledge about valid, controllable determinants of learning that we can afford to ignore any single gift horse such as encouragement-to-view.

However, we think that the conditions increasing the effectiveness of encouragement are best studied at this stage in experiments of a formative kind. In this way, various patterns of encouragement could be experimentally manipulated and their relative effectiveness assessed in different areas. The encouragement manipulation of the ETS researchers was relatively slight by all appearances, for the parents in the second-year evaluation were only visited once a month after the initial interview. It is possible, then, that more frequent or more structured interaction might increase the size of the relationship between encouragement and viewing.

Any powerful determinants of learning that emerge from formative research on the encouragement process should later be tested in a field experiment so that we could be sure of the transfer between the controlled formative research setting and the less structured setting of summative research. If they could be practically implemented, these determinants would be particularly valuable, because they involve the child and his parents in the learning process in their home setting at an early stage in the child's personal development and at an early stage in the development of his relationships with his parents that have to do with more formal schooling.

The reason why we have assigned such relatively low priority to specifying what encouragement stands for is that the factors causing learning may be interpersonal rather than purely technological. Part of the attractiveness of "Sesame Street" as a new addition to our national preschool resources is that it does not seem to require face-to-face interaction to cause small amounts of learning. If increasing the program's effects requires face-to-face interaction then the program becomes less and less a relatively inexpensive way of causing simple cognitive learning and more and more like other expensive preschool programs. The novelty of "Sesame Street" is that it is a new technological system for the delivery of education. It should be made more effective by improving the program's delivery, and especially by improving its content, rather than by making it more like other programs. After all, it is the very absence of face-to-face interaction with paid agency personnel that really capitalizes upon what is unique and inexpensive about "Sesame Street"; and modifications of the show's content provide obvious means of increasing the series' impact. We think that "Sesame Street's" national importance would be reduced if future research indicated that the complex encouragement treatment had the effects it did because of social rather than technological factors. However, if the treatment were inexpensive to implement, this would increase its value. The $100 to $200 range that we computed as the annual costs of encouragement does not seem high when compared to the costs of other face-to-face programs. Hence, while the priority accorded to understanding the encouragement process may not be as high as other priorities—in our eyes—the question should not by any means be ignored. As stated previously, there are so many no difference results in the preschool area that we cannot afford to overlook any demonstrated, large effects.

It would be naive to equate the encouragement process implemented on a one-to-one basis by ETS field staff members in the child's home with the encouragement process that is implemented to groups of mothers and children by CTW officials in utilization centers or with the encouragement that individual parents give their children for watching "Sesame Street." Though they share the same name, these encouragement processes may be different in content and setting, and it would be wrong to conclude from our positive findings about the effects of encouragement-and-viewing that greater emphasis should be placed on utilization centers or that many parents are already implementing an equivalent of the ETS treatment. They may be doing so, but they may not. We simply do not understand encouragement yet.

POLICY CONSIDERATIONS RELEVANT TO EVALUATING EXPANSIONS OF "SESAME STREET"

Apart from making new learning programs for television, there are two major directions in which future expansions of "Sesame Street" could well take place. Since public money may be involved in such expansions, it is important to examine how research can be used to make sure that the public's money is well spent. These two directions (not necessarily independent ones) are toward the increased use of "Sesame Street" on cable television and toward its use in day-care centers that are totally or partially controlled by CTW.

"Sesame Street" and Cable Television

The importance of cable television for "Sesame Street" is twofold: It is a means of expanding the home-viewing audience by eventually penetrating into some of the areas where public television is not available today; and, more importantly, it has the potential to overcome some of the interactional limitations of television. Cable offers the chance to a child, or to selected children, of interacting with adults or other children via cable. This was brought out in a statement that Dr. Edward Zigler read into the minutes of the subcommittee of the Committee on Appropriations of the House of Representatives. (At that time, Dr. Zigler was director of the Office of Child Development.)

> There is now experimental use of cable television in several remote parts of the country. Cable television is most promising as a vehicle for developmental programming, inasmuch as it will provide for two-way conversation, on-the-spot monitoring, and specific educational instructions to take place. This type of television programming would allow children to take part in conversation with people on the screen, to play in an orchestra, to act in a drama, etc.[1]

Cable television offers, then, one way in which some type of interaction and feedback could be built into fun-oriented learning of the kind that "Sesame Street" embodies, and it is one way of correcting part of television's limitation as a learning aid. Indeed, it might even be one way of bringing to children in their homes the kind of encouragement process that caused learning in the two ETS evaluations. However, it must not be forgotten that it may be especially difficult to use cable television with preschoolers, whose skills in interacting with adaptations to the television set might be limited. Moreover, it would be an expensive process. Quite apart from initial capital costs, there are the costs of the labor and/or computers that are needed for providing performance feedback or motivation to view.

"Sesame Street" aside, formal research is urgently needed on how cable television can be optimally integrated into educational curricula. Within the context of "Sesame Street," we think that formative research should be undertaken before any significant amount of public money is spent by CTW on cable television. Such formative research is particularly needed if plans are made to integrate the CTW nonbroadcast materials (books, toys, records, etc.) into the curriculum. If these materials are to be paid for by parents, it would be particularly burdensome to the less affluent who would be forced to spend proportionately more of their total

---

[1] This statement was made on May 19, 1971 in Hearings before a Subcommittee of the Committee on Appropriations of the House of Representatives, 92nd Cong., p. 64.

income. As a result, fewer might buy the learning aids. (We are assuming here, of course, that the aids make a difference, which is not certain.) Alternatively, materials could be distributed to the less affluent, hopefully in a way that minimizes stigma. But this would mean that public tax monies are supporting the distribution of nonbroadcast materials from which CTW stands to benefit financially, and this gives the general public the right to know that its money is being spent wisely. It is for these reasons that the potential of cable television should be explored with formative research before any large-scale program is launched.

"Sesame Street" and Day-Care Centers

From time to time, public demand for day-care centers arises, and we may one day experience a new growth in the number of proprietary and nonproprietary day-care centers. "Sesame Street" could easily be utilized in these centers either as a live program or via video cassettes. The series' potential in day-care centers is enormous, for it could be shown and other programs relating to nutritional, health, and developmental matters could be implemented at the same time. Moreover, CTW could well aspire to use the nonbroadcast materials it has developed as learning aids and might even want to add after-school reading or other programs (e.g., "The Electric Company") for children already in school. In addition, there is no reason why parents could not be involved in the educational process.

To implement "Sesame Street" in day-care centers has three major implications. First, it fits the program into a perspective as one of many resources that are needed to combat a national educational problem that has more facets than just the development of prereading skills. Seen from this broader perspective, "Sesame Street's" major cognitive goal is only part of the definition of the nation's preschool problem.

Secondly, the use of nonbroadcast materials in conjunction with the program would imply that these materials facilitate learning, a proposition that is still to be tested in the atmosphere of a day-care center. It would be premature to assume offhand that the nonbroadcast materials improve the child's performance, for we have heard, in trying to gain information about unsuccessfully implemented evaluations of CTW's utilization centers, that conditions at these centers are not always conducive to uninterrupted viewing and playing with toys or books about "Sesame Street." This is because children want to play together when they get together and mothers want to talk. However, if the conditions of learning in day-care centers were structured "correctly," then we would expect well-constructed learning aids to aid learning. Unfortunately, it is not possible at this stage to identify all of the conditions that are conducive to the "correct" use of such learning aids. Nor is it obvious that these conditions could be created in the relative hurly-burly of day-care centers.

Third, "Sesame Street" becomes a considerably more expensive proposition in the context of day-care centers. Though one of the major attractions of the centers might be a curriculum built around "Sesame Street" and though the televised part of the curriculum might be extremely inexpensive when computed against a base line of all viewers in present and future years, it nonetheless remains the case that the remainder of the day-care center expenses would be considerable. They would include the capital cost of building and equipment, together with the salary costs of the professionals and nonprofessionals who would be employed at the centers.

An expansion of CTW into the day-care business, either alone or in partnership, would require a rigorous analysis of the ways in which CTW's day-care centers would differ from others and of the gains in cost-effectiveness that result from incorporating "Sesame Street" into the curriculum. Moreover, some assurance would be required, before widespread implementation took place, that nonbroadcast materials add to the child's development, and that the day-care centers are set up in such a way that they can be evaluated with better success than the CTW utilization centers have been evaluated.

OUR POLICY RECOMMENDATIONS REGARDING THE USE OF "SESAME STREET"

Universal and Selective Social Services

Titmuss has discussed the distinction between universalist and selective social services. Universalist services are open to anyone, and prime examples of this are the American public school system and the British National Health Service. All American children can attend school irrespective of parental income, and all British citizens can claim health services irrespective of income. Selective social services are targeted towards certain select individuals, be they the crippled, the aged, the culturally disadvantaged, or the oil companies whose resources are being depleted and for which they are compensated via tax laws.

One problem with most selective services is that they stigmatize the recipients; another is that they lead some persons or groups who do not receive the service to feel that they are being deprived relative to those who do receive it. The major problem with universalist social services is that they are not used equally by all the potential recipients. Titmuss has written of the British health services system that:

We have learned from fifteen years' experience of the Health Service that the higher income groups know how to make better use of the Service; they tend to receive more specialist attention; occupy more of the beds in better equipped and staffed hospitals; receive more elective surgery; have better maternity care, and are more likely to get psychiatric help and psychotherapy than low income groups—particularly the unskilled.[2]

Titmuss then goes on to document the same income bias in the area of state-provided housing and schools.

"Sesame Street" offers yet another example of how the economically advantaged take greater advantage of universally available social resources than is the case with the less advantaged. "Sesame Street's" problems have to do with the small amount it probably teaches disadvantaged children, on the one hand, and with its probable failure to stimulate all groups of children to make equal use of the opportunity that the program represents. It does not seem to be a problem of providing equal opportunities or of stimulating similar gains by various social groups if viewing does take place.

It should be stressed that the distinction between selective and universalist social services describes the end points of a continuum rather than a simple dichotomy. "Sesame Street" is universally available over the airwaves, but the utilization centers that CTW installed in inner-city areas were one attempt to provide unequal auxiliary services so as to increase the usage of "Sesame Street" by one particular group—the economically disadvantaged. In this sense, "Sesame Street" is already partially selective, although it is obviously more universalist than selective.

Any policy decisions about "Sesame Street" have to deal with one paramount issue: To what extent should the program be selective and thus compensatory? To say it should not be selective and that it should be equally available to all would increase the preschool knowledge level of millions of children to an as yet unknown extent over their viewing career, but it might also increase the achievement gap since resources that are equally available to all children are not necessarily equally used. To what extent, and in what ways, should "Sesame Street" be a selective social service? We ask this question again because it is the most important single policy issue that this report raises.

If a decision were taken that "Sesame Street" should be universal and that the gap problem can be ignored, then no policy change is called for with respect to "Sesame Street." But if a decision were taken that the gap problem is worth alleviating, then policy changes are called for. The next section deals with three ways of preventing "Sesame Street" from widening gaps and, hopefully, of causing it to narrow them.

---

[2] Richard M. Titmuss, *Commitment to Welfare* (London: Allen & Unwin, 1968), p. 196.

Increasing Viewing by Economically Disadvantaged Children

It is unfortunate that we had no reliable evaluation of the utilization centers. In particular, we would like to know: How many children are regular attenders; whether these are the children who would have watched the show at home had there been no utilization center; and whether viewing in such surroundings causes learning. These questions are important, because one strategy for increasing viewing is to create centers where group viewing and rehearsal can take place. However, it does not seem likely that such centers will alone make a great impression in the national viewing problem, because the centers enroll so few children when compared to the absolute numbers of disadvantaged children who need to become regular viewers across the nation if the gap is to be narrowed.

Another possibility might be to use the resources of Carl Byoir and Associates, the CTW publicity agents, to try and increase the publicity for the program in areas where the disadvantaged live. Such publicity should be aimed, not at improving the program's "image," but rather at getting parents and children to tune in and watch the show. However, we are not very convinced that a massive publicity campaign would, by itself, make enough of a difference to be worthwhile, for it could be assumed that the persons not yet reached by CTW publicity are going to be among the very hardest to reach. Moreover, it is not clear as a general principle whether mass publicity campaigns have much effect on behavior.[3]

Another potential solution might be to make the program available more times a day on public television. It becomes more likely, thereby, that the child will get to see "Sesame Street" when he tunes in on a "random basis" or at times when no attractive alternative is available on other stations. Unfortunately, we suspect that this alone might not be a radical enough strategy, for we know that public television is watched less in more disadvantaged homes and so just switching on the set is not likely to make "Sesame Street" appear. Moreover, it is hard to imagine even more programming time being devoted to "Sesame Street" on public television than is currently the case.

The show would be more likely to appear if it were screened on commercial television channels. We can infer from the Yankelovich New York data that availability on commercial stations increases viewing and that removing it from commercial stations decreases viewing, even though many of the children who originally saw the program on commercial stations transferred their station allegiance and watched on public television when it was only available there. What we do not know is how many of

---

[3] H. H. Hyman and P. B. Sheatsley, "Some Reasons Why Information Campaigns Fail," *Public Opinion Quarterly* 11 (1947): 412–423.

these New York children would never have come to view "Sesame Street" if it had not been on commercial television in the first place.

None of the foregoing methods of increasing viewing involves directly approaching economically disadvantaged children or their parents and urging them to view. Members of the staffs of utilization centers do spend some of their time trying to persuade parents to have their child watch "Sesame Street," and it is possible to imagine two contexts in which this activity could be expanded. First, we know that the encouragement manipulation in the first year (a weekly home visit) increased the amount of reported viewing by disadvantaged children so that it reached the level of the advantaged children. It would be possible to train local residents from economically disadvantaged areas to act as encouragement staff who would visit the homes in their area where there was a child of target age. No such encouragement would be made available to economically advantaged children.

This solution would not be without problems, however. First, it would be difficult to contact the many nonviewing and low-viewing homes that would be required to narrow the viewing gap. Second, the cost of the program escalates as we move from the cost of transmitting a technological innovation to a large audience to the cost of hiring a large field staff whose job it is to see that the transmissions are received by the target audience. Third, we have to ask whether the added expenditure and intrusion into people's lives is worth the learning it achieves when we do not know at present whether this learning advantage persists over time or includes growth in non-achievement areas.

Another alternative would be to seek out settings where large numbers of economically disadvantaged children are available anyway. Day-care centers are obvious settings of this kind, and "Sesame Street" could be made available either on regular airwaves or by video cassettes or even by cable. Moreover, such facilities could be provided free of charge if the center contained a specified proportion of children who can be defined as economically disadvantaged, and they could be made available at a price to other day-care centers that wanted to use them.

The major problems with this approach are that, at present, only about 25 percent of the nation's disadvantaged children attend day-care centers of the Headstart nonproprietary kind. Of course, we do not know what the percentage will be if day-care facilities become more common. Second, it is not clear at this time what proportion of the persons responsible for day-care centers would welcome incorporating "Sesame Street" into their curricula. Third, political problems could arise in giving a service free to some sections of the community and charging others for it. Proprietors of day-care centers in advantaged areas may well ask for free "Sesame Street" cassettes if they know that day-care centers in disadvantaged areas are getting them, and they may be successful in these requests. Fourth, we do not know whether imposing financial penalties on the advantaged for watching "Sesame Street" would deter them from paying for the program. It would not be expensive on a per capita basis for day-care centers to purchase a series of cassettes, particularly when the capital cost is divided by the number of children who are to watch it over several years. Hence, the more affluent sections of society might be prepared to pay for "reasonably" priced cassettes. Finally, the effectiveness of using day-care centers in this fashion is predicated on the fact that the children who attend come from the homes least likely to watch "Sesame Street." However, it is not clear that it is the most disadvantaged among the disadvantaged who attend day-care centers. May not the same status-correlated tenacity for educational opportunities (day-care centers and "Sesame Street") work even within the restricted range of the disadvantaged? Our data certainly show that the more fortunate among the economically disadvantaged are the heavier viewers of "Sesame Street."

Most of the foregoing strategies are aimed at providing the economically disadvantaged with a greater number of resources than the advantaged. They are compensatory strategies within a universalist framework that is provided by the free availability of "Sesame Street" over the airwaves. As we hope to demonstrate, this very universal availability imposes a ceiling on the usefulness of attempting to remedy the deficiencies of "Sessame Street" by focusing the attack *exclusively* on increasing the program's distribution to the disadvantaged.

In their 1971 poll, Louis Harris and Associates asked parents which programs they had viewed on public television in the last three or four months. "Sesame Street" was spontaneously mentioned by the parents of 80 percent of the households with a child under six years of age where one family member had college experience, and it was mentioned by the parents of only 44 percent of the households where no family member had graduated from high school. If we make the assumption that the percentage of regular viewing homes was 65 percent *at each level of education,* then 52 percent of the "college" homes and 29 percent of the "non-high school graduate" homes will be regular viewing households. (The figures may be underestimates because they include all the households where there are children from zero to two years old and no children from three to five years old. Moreover, the 52 percent figure is based on the assumption that regular viewers are as likely to be found among the college-trained as the non-high school graduates, and this assumption may be incorrect. Thus, there are two reasons for believing that 52 percent is an underestimate of regular viewing in households where someone has had college training, but we do not know by how much it is an underestimate.)

The 1971 audience survey by Daniel Yankelovich, Inc., found that the percentage of regular viewers in Bedford-Stuyvesant was 45 percent, while it was 68 percent in East Harlem, 70 percent in Chicago, and 34 percent in Washington, D.C. In all of these areas, there was a utilization campaign, winter testing, and questions that indicated how interviewers wanted respondents to reply. Given that the 52 percent estimate from the 1971 Harris survey is probably an underestimate of regular viewers, how plausible is it to assume that attempts to increase viewing by the disadvantaged will result in their viewing more than their advantaged counterparts?

It would be difficult to achieve this, we think, since the ceiling of economically advantaged regular viewers is so high. There are just too many distractions that take children, whatever their family background, away from the television set once or twice a week during viewing hours, and there are just too many other household members who command the knob that selects a station. Could any campaign to increase viewing be so effective that it raises the level of regular, disadvantaged viewers to above 60 percent? And could it achieve this without increasing the level of viewing by advantaged children? Obviously, we do not know. But we are skeptical that a regular audience of 60 percent plus is possible across all of the economically disadvantaged children in the nation. We suspect, therefore, that attempts to increase viewing by the disadvantaged may narrow or even close the viewing gap, and as such they would be beneficial. But it is unlikely that they would reverse the gap.

Increasing the Learning Gains of the Economically Disadvantaged

A second way of developing a compensatory thrust would be to increase the learning gains that are made by economically disadvantaged viewers while increasing the learning gains of advantaged viewers by a lesser amount.

It might seem that one way of doing this would be to determine the academic, social, and affective areas in which economically disadvantaged children are out-performed by their more advantaged contemporaries and then to design the "Sesame Street" program so that, for a given age group, it teaches what the disadvantaged need to know and what the advantaged already know. However, this strategy may not succeed, for, quite apart from defining these problem areas with children of so young an age, there is the distinct possibility that advantaged children who view the show will be younger than the disadvantaged. As a consequence, we might have four-year-old disadvantaged children and three-year-old advantaged children overrepresented among the audience of children who can potentially learn from the program. If this were the case, the gap might not be narrowed. Any use of television content that is aimed at the particular learning needs of disadvantaged children of a particular age has to be such that advantaged children of a younger age, and with comparable learning needs to the older children, do not want to watch the content.

A second compensatory strategy would be to learn which social and educational processes facilitate learning from "Sesame Street" and then make these processes more available to the disadvantaged than to the advantaged. Imagine that formative research on "encouragement" were to result in techniques for increasing learning. Such techniques could then be widely disseminated and made available, on request, in preschools, day-care centers, or—if suitable—in homes, and they would be most effective in narrowing the gap if they were only made available to the economically disadvantaged.

There is currently a growing interest in educational technology, techniques for both the distribution of learning opportunities and for interaction between the child and technological innovations. In his capacity as acting director of the Office of Technology Development in the Office of Education, Lawrence P. Grayson wrote in the context of formal school learning:

> By the end of this decade, the range of applications and the pervasiveness of technology in education will be greatly increased, primarily for two reasons. First, there is the growing demand for change in the present educational system, because of its high and still increasing costs, its low productivity, and its inability to be fully responsible to identified national needs. The second reason is the recent advances and growth in the number of cable systems, the potential expansion of Instructional Television Fixed Service for both video and nonvideo services, the appearance of new and specialized microwave common carrier systems, the development of domestic satellite communications, advances in film and tape cartridges, the emergence of minicomputers and computer time-sharing, and the growing acceptance of microfilms.[4]

It may well be possible to implement some of these innovations in order to provide performance feedback to economically disadvantaged children. For example, a cable system would permit selected children to rehearse what they have learned or are learning from a program, and it would be possible to work directly on such important features as transfer or knowledge of the social world in a way that would promote long-term retention. It would be entirely possible in this way to link the innovation of cable television (the medium) to computer-assisted instruction (the feedback operator to the child). Alternatively, instructional films or cassettes might provide the medium of instruction, and the computer could be used to test performance relevant to specific films.

The capital costs of such selective attempts to modify the learning of

---

[4] Grayson, p. 1216.

economically disadvantaged children would be high, and the only way to derive a reasonable benefit from them would be to ensure prolonged usage of the technical facilities by as many children as possible. Given this, it is unlikely that such technological innovations will affect the child in his home in the next years. Rather, cable and its auxiliary services are more likely to be utilized in centers where many children come together. This makes the effectiveness of such technological innovations dependent on the growth of day-care centers, for unless substantial numbers of disadvantaged preschoolers receive the opportunity to practice newly acquired skills, there is no way in which the achievement gap is going to be narrowed at age four.

These technological innovations will require time before they can be implemented successfully. We do not yet have a well-tested system that combines either cable and computer-assisted instruction, or video and computer-assisted instruction, or cable and human instruction, or video and human instruction. (It may well be especially difficult to work out such systems that can be used by preschoolers.) While such systems are being worked out, children across the nation will be viewing "Sesame Street," and the achievement gap may be widening, especially if schools do in fact capitalize upon "Sesame Street" and develop new curricula that, by assuming knowledge of letters and numbers, penalize lighter viewers and nonviewers of the program even more than the program directly penalizes them.

Another problem relates both to the preparedness of economically advantaged parents to pay for educational opportunities and to the profits that are anticipated by the businesses that develop technological innovations in education. Developers will want to market their products as widely as possible and there will be a ready market for some of them beyond nonproprietary day-care centers. If advantaged parents whose children attend privately owned day-care centers are prepared to pay for a developmental education, then the developers of technological innovations will be more than willing to supply them. As a consequence, any relative advantage that the economically disadvantaged might enjoy because of federal purchasing of technological learning aids will diminish as these aids become available to advantaged children on the open market.

It is noteworthy that strategies for increasing the learning of economically disadvantaged children involve financial costs which are higher than those associated with the cost of television alone. It is the providing of *individualized instruction* that is relatively so expensive, whether through teachers or through technological innovations that have to be used with great frequency if per capita costs are to decline. Given the constraints that operate on any plans for individualized instruction, it should come as no surprise to note that in considering attempts to increase learning by individuals, "Sesame Street" looks less different from present or planned practices in other areas of preschool education, and that it looks less like the radical alternative it seems to be at first glance—an alternative that involves a mass audience, no face-to-face interaction, and no individualized instruction. It is going to be a difficult and expensive task to reach a significant percentage of economically disadvantaged children with a preschool television package that permits these children to learn more than their advantaged counterparts.

Decreasing the Viewing or Learning Gains of the Economically Advantaged

In the previous paragraphs we have stressed the possibility that advantaged parents may be tenacious in providing educational opportunities for their children and in helping their children use such opportunities. We do not mean to imply by this that the greater tenacity of advantaged over disadvantaged parents may be due to the former's greater concern for their children's education. It may well be due to such mundane structural factors as having more time to spend per child, having more money to spend per child, etc. Whatever the origin, there is a noteworthy consequence of this greater tenacity: It will be difficult to provide non-stigmatized opportunities to the economically disadvantaged that do not sooner or later, through economic market mechanisms, become available to the more advantaged whose advantagement is so widespread anyway. Reflections like these prompted Robert Fisher to conclude that:

> We have been working on the wrong group. We have been trying to help poor kids acquire middle-class values, middle-class motivation, middle-class language patterns, middle-class learning styles, middle-class competitive values; but the poor never will be able to compete on even terms with middle-class mothers and fathers.[5]

He therefore proposes a preschool program for the advantaged that instills values about the importance of play, love, and spontaneity rather than about cognitive learning and delayed gratification. In short, he proposes to instill in advantaged children a motivational system that has affective development rather than academic achievement as its core construct and that should slow down the cognitive development of these children.

The most obvious strategy to reduce the learning of the economically advantaged would be to take "Sesame Street" off the public airwaves so that it could not be viewed by any economically advantaged children at all. Access to the program would be via specific cables that are selectively distributed to homes and day-care centers or via films and cassettes that are only distributed to preschools that have a significant percentage of

---

[5] Robert Fisher, "Project Slow Down: The Middle-class Answer to Head Start," *School and Society,* Oct. 1970.

economically disadvantaged children. This general strategy would be much more selective than any proposed earlier, because it destroys the universalist framework of distribution over the airwaves that permits the advantaged to view more. It would almost certainly be the most effective of all the strategies we have discussed for narrowing the gap and it would almost certainly be the least effective of all the strategies for stimulating the growth of all children.

There are a number of reasons why we would not expect or desire the implementation of any policy based on the withdrawal of "Sesame Street" from the economically advantaged. First, the program is very popular, and there might be a considerable outcry if the program were taken off the air, particularly if this act were associated by some segments of the public with the need to make the distribution of the program more compensatory. Policymakers would have to answer, either directly or indirectly, for such an act, and many will be loath to do what they think will bring about public dissatisfaction.

Second, the withdrawal of funds by the Office of Education—the major supporter of CTW—would probably be resisted at this time by some of its high-ranking members, for "Sesame Street" is one of the projects that the Office of Education has funded and that has clearly been a success in the general public's estimation.

Third, even if funds for "Sesame Street" were withdrawn or made contingent on the series' selective dissemination, it would not necessarily preclude the possibility of "Sesame Street" continuing on the air with other sources of funds. CTW derives an income from nonbroadcast materials and from foreign sales of old programs, and this source of revenue must be expanding. Moreover, funds from private industry are increasing, and CTW should have little difficulty in finding sponsors if the decision were taken to broadcast the program commercially. There would be drawbacks to this last strategy for CTW (particularly, a loss of independence), but it might be a more preferable alternative than the loss of the program's nationwide preschool audience.

Fourth, it should be noted once again that the objectives of "Sesame Street" have never been stated precisely enough that a priority could be established between promoting the growth of all children and narrowing the achievement gap. To take the program off the air at this time would imply the primacy of narrowing the gap, but such may not be the primary objective of "Sesame Street" in the eyes of CTW officials, the general public, or the program's sponsors. It might be sufficient that the economically disadvantaged may be learning something.

Finally, there is a value question that is important in its own right. It is offensive to most persons, we think, to provide a service and then to retract it selectively when the means to deliver that service continue to exist.

By withdrawing the program we would be causing a drop in achievement, and we would be robbing economically advantaged children of a program they liked, and harm might result. Contrast the selective withdrawal of a service to its selective introduction. By not introducing a program to the advantaged we would prevent a gain in achievement (rather than cause a loss), and we would prevent the children from seeing a program toward which they had no opinion (rather than one they liked). Thus, we think it likely that less harm will result from the selective introduction of an effective and popular program than from its selective withdrawal. In "Sesame Street's" case, it is clear that selective withdrawal would be involved, and it is not likely, or even desirable, that this withdrawal should take place. Thus, it does not seem to us to be a viable option with "Sesame Street" to resort to strategies designed to reduce the learning of the advantaged.

MODIFYING CTW'S PRIORITIES AND OUR RECOMMENDATION

The officials at CTW have shown remarkable problem-solving skill in the past, and we call upon them to continue to do the same in the future in specific ways that we outline here. In the past, the creativity of CTW employees has been channeled into the development of new programs. We feel that there is less need for new programs at this time since they may inadvertently do harm if there is a social class bias in who views them. Instead, we call for a frontal attack by CTW on assessing whether there are social biases in who already views their shows, "The Electric Company" included, and in developing ways in which any such biases could be eliminated or even reversed. Some combination of the strategies outlined in the foregoing section may help in this, but we believe that CTW should be free to use whatever means it develops itself.

What we propose is that the foundations and federal agencies that fund "Sesame Street" require of CTW that, within two years, proof be furnished either that regular viewers are equally likely at each of several levels of socioeconomic status or that, if any inequalities exist, these favor the less economically advantaged. Alternatively, if viewing is heavier among the more advantaged, then proof should be furnished that this discrepancy is "reasonably" compensated for by the greater gains of economically disadvantaged children in areas of development that include prereading skills, social learning, and self-worth.[6] If such information is not provided or the

---

[6] By the time such data are available, we might also have reliable information about how the encouraged and nonencouraged children from Durham, Phoenix, and Los Angeles fared in their passage through school, and this will be important input for decisionmakers.

data turn out unfavorably for the program, then the continuation of funds for "Sesame Street" and for similar programs should be made contingent on their selective dissemination to the economically disadvantaged in some ethical way.

We also propose that proof be furnished that the learning gains from viewing without encouragement are of a magnitude that is conventionally considered educationally significant. There is no conclusive evidence for this at present either for one season's viewing—where some data were at least available—or for more than one season's viewing—where no reliable data were available. Unless such information is forthcoming, "Sesame Street" will remain a popular program with children and parents whose effects on learning cannot be demonstrated to be large. Since its effects on learning are not large, its possible effects on the gap cannot be large— at least, not large in any one season.

If future funding is made contingent on specific performance criteria, and if CTW takes seriously the task of meeting these criteria, the result would probably be a redefinition of CTW's priorities. Ensuring that the academic achievement gap is not increased would take higher priority over the more successfully achieved goal of promoting some intellectual growth in economically disadvantaged heavy viewers. Also, ensuring that viewers make larger and more widespread gains would turn CTW's attention away from the development of new programs to the development of a more powerful "Sesame Street." We want to stress that CTW should be free to use its creative talents in any way it wants to achieve the objectives we have outlined. But we think two constraints are worth mentioning.

First, the federal government and foundations should not increase their funding of CTW. Any extra funds for CTW's new task should come from CTW's own sources of additional revenue or from the cutbacks in some areas which would result from reordered priorities. There is no point in increasing the appropriation to CTW if the program may be causing little learning and even some social harm by widening the achievement gap. The only situation where increasing funds could be countenanced, we think, is if CTW decided to test several different strategies for narrowing the gap and wanted to conduct true experiments concerned with the relative efficiency of various strategies. Such information would be useful to CTW. But it would also have a wider applicability, for we shall be confronted for many years with the problem of providing resources universally and desiring them to be used equally by all sections of society or even desiring them to be used more by those social groups that are likely to use them least. This is an important area for social research quite independent of CTW and "Sesame Street."

Second, we would propose that the secretary of the Department of

Health, Education, and Welfare and the presidents of the Ford Foundation and the Carnegie Corporation appoint officials from their agencies to accomplish two tasks. One would be to coordinate among themselves the outline of the directives to be given to CTW, and the second would be to appoint a research advisory council (independent of CTW's Advisory Council) to monitor the steps that CTW would be taking in its efforts to increase learning and to prevent the achievement gap from widening. This council would also be responsible for establishing the performance criteria for determining whether "Sesame Street" is reaching the objectives that are set for it. If no cooperation among these agencies could be worked out, any single one could appoint such a council to monitor whether the particular funds that it allocates are having the desired effects and are having no undesired side effects on society.

POLICY CONSIDERATIONS RELEVANT TO THE USE OF TELEVISION FOR SOLVING EDUCATIONAL PROBLEMS

The contribution of "Sesame Street" does not lie in demonstrating that most groups of preschoolers can learn from television. Rather, the program's contribution lies in demonstrating that a program which is (1) deliberately tailored to the interests of a wide range of preschoolers and which is tested for appeal before being televised can succeed (2) in gaining the attention of millions of children and can help them learn some simple things (3) in the absence of benign coercion from teachers or parents who, in other educational contexts, have enough power over children that they can force them to attend to the educational material. Since it is not novel to find that individual children can learn from television, we shall discuss some other problems that policymakers might consider when confronted with making decisions about televised instruction.

A first consideration has to do with the distribution of the televised information. Some material will be relevant to specific groups of children (e.g., those with learning disabilities, or wanting to learn Spanish, etc.) and will be distributed only to persons in special classes. Alternatively, the material may be distributed over the regular airwaves but may have such a restricted appeal that it will be of minor importance to society at large. In each of these cases, there would be little danger that the televised information would be learned by more members of a non-target group than by members of a target group.

The major problems with program distribution arise when a popular curriculum is made universally available on the assumption that it will be universally used or that it will be used more by a certain social group. Such curricula will frequently be more heavily used by the economically advantaged, which will directly countervail against achieving either universalistic or compensatory outcomes. It might be useful in the future if policymakers considered any proposed instructional television program in the light of distinctions between universal and selective goals, the universal and selective distribution of televised material, and the universal and selective use of such material.

A second consideration has to do with the fact that it is the content of a television program and not television itself which teaches. We do not yet know exactly what it is about the content of "Sesame Street" which gains the interest of preschool children and teaches them. It is entirely possible, for example, that puppets, simple tunes, and advertisement-like presentations, are effective in teaching. If so, could we assume that they are as effective with adolescents or drug addicts or senior citizens as they seem to be with preschoolers? Television is only a medium, and the message has to meet audience needs if it is to hold and teach the audience. But there are numerous audiences in the United States today, so that we cannot generalize from a children's program and imply that we know how to cause learning about health matters in adults. Indeed, adult and adolescent audiences are probably more differentiated than preschool audiences because they represent a wider range of age, interest, and knowledge. It will thus be more difficult to tailor a television program to a large audience of adults or adolescents than it will be to tailor a children's program. This implies that a policymaker is better advised not to ask: "Will television teach this?", but to ask: "What evidence is there that this particular instructional material will hold the target audience's interest and will be effective in teaching?" This last question makes no reference to television at all, although the policymaker also has to know if the intended recipients of the program have television sets and can tune in to the channel involved.

A third consideration for policymakers has to do with the adequacy of learning from television. For programs aimed at a large audience, there is the inevitable problem that the curriculum cannot be fitted to the knowledge level or learning skills of small groups, as it can with classes in schools. Instead, the curriculum must be fitted to some particular global standard (e.g., the average four-year-old child who is economically disadvantaged), thereby entailing that it will be too advanced for some members of the target audience and too elementary for others, and that it might progress too slowly for some target children and too quickly for others. Moreover, unless there are other teaching aids, television cannot detect and correct learning errors. There *may* therefore be a ceiling to the limits of television as a mass instructional tool designed to teach a standard school or preschool curriculum. We obviously do not know this yet, but the policymaker is nonetheless advised to consider whether television *by itself* can affect learning gains that are large enough to be educationally significant, and he is also advised to consider television in the context of an instructional package rather than as the package itself.

A fourth issue concerns the relative dearth of our information about television and its effectiveness in instructing large voluntary audiences. We do not, in general, know the kinds of information and techniques of presentation that will hold interest and cause learning in different audiences, and policymakers should consider the possibility of funding prebroadcast formative research on a particular topic before they fund large-scale and expensive television programs on the same topic. As the "Sesame Street" case so ably demonstrated, formative research can help producers make some of their inevitable mistakes in a context where they are relatively inexpensive, and it can also be useful in permitting producers to use learning techniques that are demonstrably effective. The general success of "Sesame Street" in the public's eyes and in the eyes of some policymakers should not lead to the hasty implementation of other programs without some kind of formative research period. New televised programs should be funded as experiments and not as new programs; as high risk innovations and not as low risk applications of a purportedly well-tested technology. Moreover, it might not be wise to fund new large-scale television programs and cut established programs that are only partially effective or that have not yet been evaluated. One "Sesame Street" is no automatic blueprint for producing programs whose success in reaching and teaching large, voluntary audiences can be predicted. But it should certainly be an impetus to future, responsible experimentation that will help establish a body of knowledge about the conditions under which different techniques of presenting televised information will gain, hold, and teach various large audiences.

Some Thoughts on this Secondary Evaluation

by Samuel Ball and Gerry Ann Bogatz

This chapter is a brief response to Cook et al.'s *report. We argue from the viewpoint of primary evaluators whose data have been reexamined in both appropriate and inappropriate ways. Cook* et al. *seem to be arguing two contradictory points—on the one hand that "Sesame Street" has had minimal educational impact on viewers; and, on the other hand, that it has noticeably widened the educational achievement gap between lower- and middle-class children. If "Sesame Street" is teaching so little, how can it be having such a bad effect on the ubiquitous "gap"?*

The argument that the series has little educationally useful impact on viewers is based, in part, on erroneous notions of what is measured by the instruments we developed. (For example, the authors wrongly assume that most of the test items assess association-level, rote learning.) It is also based on highly conservative statistical comparisons which are often misinterpreted. For example, Cook et al. *compare the learning of "very frequent" with that of "frequent" viewers. Failure to find large achievement differences between these treatment levels can hardly be regarded as an indication that the program is only minimally effective. The authors, however, choose this interpretation.*

Cook et al. *agree with us that both lower- and middle-class children learn about as much as each other when they view. However, they argue that a higher proportion of middle- than lower-class children do view. This argument is the basis for their "gap" criticism. We question the representativeness of the viewing data (e.g., Harris Poll) upon which the authors base this assertion—data that are based, as they point out, on imprecise measures and on a sample of lower-class children with remarkably few black members. Data, ignored by Cook et al., indicate that the vast majority of inner-city preschool children view "Sesame Street," making it impossible for a sizeable proportion of middle-class children to view it more. In any case, we question the usefulness of the "gap" issue at this stage and we ask whether any widely available educational program with an extensive curriculum has ever been able to decrease the gap.*

We have examined this work in great detail, and we reject its major conclusions. In our view, "Sesame Street" did achieve many of the goals it set for itself over a wide range of preschool children. However, we do not question the authors' right to raise the issues they have raised, and we hope that the resulting discussions will lead to a better understanding of the evaluation process and to better ways of responsibly examining important educational programs.

INTRODUCTION

In 1969, Howard Freeman of Russell Sage Foundation asked for the cooperation of Educational Testing Service in a new project that was to improve the capabilities of social scientists in conducting evaluative research on social programs. The project involved the funding of three metaevaluations or, oversimply, evaluations of evaluations.[1] The basic purposes at the time and subsequently reiterated included:

- Providing "case studies" so that students and practitioners of evaluative research could examine the processes of this kind of research in detail
- Providing independent and timely assessment[2] of the evaluations being studied
- Examining problems and strengths across evaluations in different social sciences.

We agreed to cooperate, and Thomas Cook of Northwestern University was selected by Russell Sage Foundation to conduct a metaevaluation of our "Sesame Street" evaluations. We were especially pleased at the prospect that many of the neglected problems associated with large-scale field studies would be given the attention they deserved—such problems as developing instrumentation quickly and at relatively low cost, obtaining

---

[1] One was a study of an evaluation of the negative income tax experiment, another of performance contracting, and the third is presented in this book.

[2] The metaevaluator would have access to the evaluator's data as they were collected. Thus, the metaevaluator would be able to provide the scientific community with an assessment soon after the evaluator's report was published.

community cooperation in low-income sites, training indigenous personnel to collect data, arranging priorities given conflicting demands on the evaluation, and analyzing data and writing reports in short periods of time.

We had misgivings too. All research in the social sciences is open to criticism; and when studying the work of others, it is not difficult to find fault. The difficulty is to maintain a balance in which weaknesses are seen in relation to capabilities given current professional knowledge, the funding level, and time constraints. For example and hypothetically, it would be unsophisticated to criticize an evaluator of a preschool program for constructing measures in the attitudinal domain that had lower reliability coefficients than measures in the cognitive domain. Similarly, it would be simple (but simplistic) to criticize without qualification an evaluation design for failing to allow a question to be answered when the evaluation was not designed or funded to answer that question.

Our prime concern was that someone inexperienced in the craft of metaevaluation (who is experienced?) and without much firsthand experience in conducting evaluations might be insensitive in conducting this case study. We found that Cook shared our concerns and had misgivings about the hazards of auditing someone else's work. This sharing of concerns resulted in a close working relationship during the first year of the project. Communication between Cook and us was frequent, and exchanges of data, information, and results were mutually profitable. The first year's efforts resulted in the analysis of our data and analyses; and Cook *et al.* found that they arrived at the same answers we did when addressing the same questions. As Cook humorously put it in May 1971: "Quite frankly, the combination of the Age Cohorts study and your latest analyses of the inferential study leave little meat on the research carcass for professional vultures like myself—or is it professional nit-pickers."[3]

During the next two and one-half years, however, Cook *et al.* decided to make some major adjustments to the task in which they were engaged. In so doing, they conducted what they have termed a secondary analysis—posing new evaluation questions and using data from our evaluations and from as many other sources as seemed to them to be relevant to answer these new questions. The evaluation of our evaluation thus became secondary; and the major purposes of the Russell Sage Foundation project were considerably neglected. The "case study" aspect of the work comes through only occasionally, and a primary emphasis of this book is on further data analysis and interpretation. The question of design is also examined in this book but mainly in the context of what our design should have been, if it had been developed to answer the different questions posed by Cook *et al.* This

---

[3] Personal communication, May 5, 1971.

leaves important areas of the evaluative research process unattended. The independent assessment purpose of the metaevaluation is left mainly to an indirect approach. Thus, for example, Cook *et al.* point out that since they are asking different questions from ours, it is not unlikely that they will arrive at different answers. A third purpose of the Russell Sage Foundation project—to examine problems and strengths across evaluations in different social sciences—was dropped because there was little coordination across the three metaevaluations which were carried out independently of each other. This book then is a secondary evaluation whose major purpose is to provide an evaluation of "Sesame Street."

Though it was not the original purpose of this Russell Sage Foundation project, there is little doubt that it is a legitimate enterprise for a social scientist to conduct a secondary evaluation of a given program. Specifically, Cook *et al.* chose to evaluate "Sesame Street" using data collected by others in order to answer questions of their own choosing.

THE QUESTIONS

Two major questions posed by Cook *et al.* were:

1. Does "Sesame Street" reduce the gap between the achievement of middle-class and lower-class children?

2. Does viewing "Sesame Street" cause learning?

A Theoretical Issue—the Gap

The first of these involves some background and theoretical issues that ought to be addressed before proceeding further. The second question we shall address as we examine the data and the major analyses conducted by the authors.

We wish to emphasize that the question of the gap posed by Cook *et al.* is of their own choosing. There is a lengthy attempt made to show that reducing the gap was a major purpose of "Sesame Street."[4] However, the "gap" was not important to Children's Television Workshop, and "Sesame Street" was not built on a deficit model of lower-class attainment. As Gerald Lesser, a major educational architect of "Sesame Street," pointed out:

> With middle-class characteristics as a standard, some preschools are designed to bring disadvantaged children up to that standard. Aimed at giving the

---

[4] It is worth noting that despite the authors' argument that they knew the intentions of CTW and the real goals of "Sesame Street" they did not interview CTW officers, staff, or major advisors. This detachment is a stance advocated by some evaluators, but it hardly puts the evaluator in the position of expert with respect to the program's goals or the developer's intentions.

have-nots what the haves already possess—it must be good or why would the haves have bothered to get it?—these compensatory education programs are based on what has been called the "deficit model." We rejected this model.[5]

Later, Lesser added:

To reduce the educational gap between children from poor and well-to-do families, national television would need to meet either or both of two implausible conditions: Either poor children would have to watch more than middle-class children; or if poor children did not watch more, they would have to learn more from the same amount of watching as middle-class children. . . . We hoped that poor children would learn as much and that the gap would not be widened . . . .[6]

In our first-year evaluation report, our evaluation plan stated:

No mention has been made of direct comparisons between lower SES (socioeconomic status) and middle SES subjects, between black subjects and white subjects or between Spanish-speaking and English-speaking subjects. Such comparisons are not of interest to the Children's Television Workshop. The purpose of the show is to benefit all children regardless of language background, SES, and race. Major statistical comparisons will be made within groups rather than between groups. That is, CTW is more concerned with whether lower SES viewers learn more than lower SES non-viewers than with whether lower SES viewers learn more than middle SES viewers.[7]

In the five years since that statement was written, no one except Cook *et al.* has questioned us on the reasonableness of this statement. We think that it is an incredible hope that a universally available educational program which is broad in scope can close the gap. The history of educational innovations attests to this—that programs tend to increase diversity rather than decrease it. We would certainly counsel any group whose aim is to close the gap *not* to use publicly available television as the delivery medium.

Cook *et al.* also make the point that they chose the question of the gap, because we had addressed it in our reports. Actually our first report of 373 pages and numerous appendices contained six lines addressed to this question. The second-year report presented an analysis of first-year data on advantaged and disadvantaged children; but in the second-year study we purposely collected no data on advantaged children because our

---

[5] G. S. Lesser, *Children and Television: Lessons from Sesame Street* (New York: Random House, 1974), p. 51.

[6] Ibid., pp. 80–81.

[7] S. Ball and G. A. Bogatz, *The First Year of Sesame Street: An Evaluation* (Princeton, N.J.: Educational Testing Service, 1969), p. 16.

primary concern was to evaluate "Sesame Street's" effects on the disadvantaged irrespective of its effects on the advantaged.

Of course, the authors have every right to ask any question they wish, and secondary evaluators should not feel obliged to tie their questions to those of the program developer or primary evaluator. However, is the gap a critical social and educational issue to raise at the outset? Is it not more important that every preschool child has the opportunity to acquire sufficient knowledge and skills so that entering school presents no major problem? In other words, is it the relative standards between lower- and middle-class children that should worry us or some absolute acceptable level of children's attainments?

We shall return to this question later as we examine Cook *et al.*'s work in detail; but the main point we wish to make here is that closing the gap was not a goal of "Sesame Street." More important, we consider it to be a peripheral issue in the sense that it does not get to the main problems underlying low-achieving children[8] and that it asks of "Sesame Street" an achievement no other universally available educational program, on or off television, has been able to achieve. If narrowing or closing the gap were a criterion of a universally available educational program's value, what program would get a passing grade?

The Impact of "Sesame Street"

To be able to answer the question whether "Sesame Street" affects the gap between lower-class and middle-class children, it was first necessary to answer the question: Does viewing "Sesame Street" cause learning? Clearly, if it does not, there could be no effect on the gap. To answer the question, Cook *et al.* carried out a number of different analyses, and with each there is a set of conclusions. We became confused as to what the overall conclusion was even with respect to a given analysis. Here are some examples of different kinds of conclusions reached:

> We have demonstrated that learning was caused as a result of ETS staff members distributing promotional material about "Sesame Street" to parents and children and then visiting the children once a week in their homes in

---

[8] At one stage, Cook *et al.* seem to countenance (but reject) the idea of providing "Sesame Street" to disadvantaged children only. By preventing the advantaged from learning, the disadvantaged might catch up. Argument by analogy can be tricky, but since there is also a gap in the dental health of advantaged and disadvantaged children, would they then argue we should deny fluoride to advantaged children to reduce that gap? See S. Swinton, "Faculty Critique," in M. Apple, M. Subkoviak, H. Lufler, Jr., eds., *Educational Evaluation: Analysis and Responsibility* (Berkeley, Calif.: McCutchan, 1974), p. 229.

order to encourage them to watch the program (Chapter 5, p. 152).

. . . [T]he only children in the nation who have ever received this particular encouragement treatment are in the ETS research samples. We can, therefore, be certain that encouragement is not promoting the growth of many children in the United States today . . . (Chapter 1, p. 13).

. . . [W]e demonstrated that heavy viewing was required for gains to appear . . . Chapter 1, p. 15).

. . . [E]ffects of viewing could only be demonstrated on a minority of the ETS tests, albeit the more reliable ones, and only one test (Letters) reached conventional statistical criteria of educational significance[9] (Chapter 1, p. 20).

If these conclusions are true, there is little problem with respect to "Sesame Street" widening the gap. If one were to take the argument to its logical conclusion, it would appear that if the ETS staff members could have been kept from distributing promotional material about "Sesame Street," the gap would not be affected. However, there are other, more optimistic statements about the effects of "Sesame Street."

. . . It seems, then, that learning was related to encouragement only if encouragement was related to viewing "Sesame Street" (Chapter 5, p. 128).

. . . [I]t is warranted to conclude . . . that "Sesame Street" taught some Letter and Number skills and some knowledge of comparative relationships to a statistically significant degree (Chapter 7, p. 238).

Our analysis and Minton's dissertation suggested that one season's viewing of "Sesame Street" taught nonencouraged children (Chapter 7, p. 263).

. . . [E]ncouragement-and-viewing . . . prevented IQ . . . from declining. . . . [V]iewing "Sesame Street" for six months without encouragement caused learning gains in some letter, number, and relationship skills (Chapter 1, p. 20).

. . . [T]he size of the learning differences was such that they met several different criteria of social significance, and there were no observed differences between the program's effects on viewers who were boys or girls, blacks or whites, or on viewers who were at different levels of IQ, age, or socioeconomic status (SES). It [encouragement] seems, therefore, to be a powerful treatment that promoted the growth of all children (Chapter 1, p. 13).

It is instructive to look further into this ambivalence as to the impact of "Sesame Street," for it illustrates problems likely to arise in any secondary evaluation. In the first two quotes and again in the last two quotes, Cook *et al.* suggest that "encouragement" is the major causal agent of

---

[9] In our view, statistical tests do not relate to educational significance, but to the question of whether observed differences are "believable." Whether these differences are "educationally significant" is a different kind of question, and one that cannot be answered merely by referring to a standard error of measurement or a standard deviation.

learning. In every educational experiment, it is necessary for the actual content to be delivered in some way. That is, if a new curriculum is introduced in mathematics, teachers have to be asked, in some fashion, to teach it. If it is a new textbook, someone has to give it to the students. Somehow, the treatment being studied will include some peripherally related elements. Thus, we wanted to study viewing "Sesame Street," and it was important to a true experiment to ensure that the randomly selected experimental subjects viewed more than the control group. In fact, before "Sesame Street" was ever telecast, members of our research advisory committee seriously suggested that we pay children in the experimental group to view. The expectation then was that the "natural" audience would be so small there would be hardly any viewing (experimental) subjects. "Encouragement" was the insurance process we finally settled on.

We recognized that the encouragement to view may have had reactive effects, and we conducted an analysis to break out these effects.[10] We, as did Cook *et al.,* found *viewing* apart from encouragement to be a significant factor. But, in any case, it is strange to interpret the overall results as being due to the peripherally, possibly reactive effects—as in the statement: "Learning was caused as a result of ETS staff distributing promotional material and then visiting the children once a week. . . ." It is rather like a study of the new math curriculum concluding that children were more adept at set theory as a result of teachers being influenced by salespeople to buy the new program.

THE DATA BASE AND RESEARCH DESIGN

It is important for the secondary evaluator not only to employ new statistical analyses, but also to understand the data base and research design upon which those analyses rest. We wish to provide examples of problems that arise when the measures and design are not fully understood.

The conclusion reached about our dependent measures was that ". . . the ETS evaluation [was] primarily an evaluation of 'Sesame Street's' effectiveness in teaching the association between verbal labels and numerical, alphabetic, or physical shapes" (Chapter 4, p. 88). The reader will find references to the Letters Test or as one of the "associative tests" (Chap-

---

[10] In Chapter 7, p. 201, Cook *et al.* indicate that they do not understand the analysis. A letter to Cook (June 21, 1972) from Dr. Albert Beaton, director of the Office of Data Analysis Research at ETS, explained the procedure in a lengthy enclosure and pointed out that we pool the interaction variance into the error term for testing mean effects and test interactions against the within cells residuals. The letter ended with an offer to provide further explanations, if they were desired.

ter 4, p. 87). This is quite misleading, because the Letters Test[11] contained:

Number of Items First Year	Number of Items Second Year
10 matching (visual discrimination)	5 matching (visual discrimination)
2 recognition of uses of letters	12 letter names
36 letter names	10 letter sounds
4 initial sounds	17 decoding and sight vocabulary
6 reading words	4 left-right orientation

In footnote 7, Chapter 4, Cook *et al.* note that of all items in the battery, 46 percent were "associative" in the first year, but they provide no breakdown for the second year. They also state that 72 percent of the items in the Letters Test were "associative" in the first year but only 17 percent in the second year. For the Numbers Test, their own breakdown indicates 49 percent (first year) and 13 percent (second year) were "associative" items.

It is hard to reconcile those figures with the previously quoted statement that the ETS "evaluations were primarily evaluations of 'Sesame Street's' effectiveness in teaching associations."[12] And, more seriously, it raises questions about a secondary evaluation that largely ignores subtests and assumes the Letters and Numbers tests in the first-year evaluation are measuring the same things as similarly named tests in the second-year evaluation. This kind of problem arises when numbers (scores) are regarded as the data base without due regard to the processes that underlie those numbers—the test items. Thus, when Cook *et al.* obtained significant effects from viewing, they denigrated the result by pointing out that it is mainly in the "simple associative" test of letters of the alphabet. The test contained aspects of reading, decoding, letter sounds, transfer of training, and visual discrimination. For a preschool child, these should not be regarded as simply associative in learning style.

It is not only in the area of these dependent variables that problems

---

[11] Renamed in the second year as the Prereading Test, a title we felt more appropriate to the content.

[12] This book, as published, is a revision of an earlier draft. Some of our comments on the earlier draft probably caused changes to occur and footnote 7 in Chapter 4 is likely such a change. However, at least in places, the textual references to "associative" tests remained. The point we wish to make here is that an extensive and detailed knowledge of the measuring instruments is essential to a satisfactory secondary analysis.

arose. Viewing indices and design were misunderstood.[13] For example Cook *et al.* complain that the "most serious problem" with the Viewing Records (one of the viewing indices) was that they "were not collected from the nonencouraged children" (Chapter 4, p. 93). It would have been absurd to collect Viewing Records about "Sesame Street" from nonencouraged children. Imagine the reactive effect of asking the mothers of nonencouraged children how many times their children had watched "Sesame Street." To overcome this problem for nonencouraged children, we collected a disguised viewing record—viewing logs which requested similar information in a different context.

Cook *et al.* also argue that we should have had more affective measures in our test battery in the second-year evaluation. We had three. One came from the preschool children themselves, the second from the parent questionnaire, and the third from the teacher questionnaire. The measurement of affect is difficult, and specific suggestions of other measures we might have used will be warmly welcomed.

Similarly, the authors argue that there should have been more transfer items and less duplication of the first-year's measures in the second-year evaluation battery. Of the thirty-one subtests in the second-year study, fifteen monitored "old" goals from the first year; and fourteen, "new" goals. Over 10 percent (twenty-five items of 214 in the Grand Total) were transfer items. In addition, the Peabody Picture Vocabulary Test,[14] items measuring attitudes and interests, and parent and teacher questionnaires provided much information about transfer of learning effects. We found it difficult (in cases where tests were individually administered, budgets and time were tight, and purposes were diverse) to satisfy all the demands.

In our view, the data base is the single most important aspect of empirical evaluative research. We think it is an area demanding the greatest attention of secondary evaluators.

VALUE ORIENTATION

We believe it is incumbent upon all those involved in evaluative research to indicate the value orientation they bring with them to a given

---

[13] On a number of occasions, Cook indicates that if certain information had been provided or if certain extra facts were known, his analyses would have been different. No request for information was ever refused, and we know of no instance where any was withheld.

[14] The Peabody Picture Vocabulary Test should not be used as "an indicator of growth in knowing how to think." (Chapter 1, p. 11). This use of a receptive vocabulary measure was not so intended by us, and we think its use by others in this way is also unwise.

study. Cook *et al.* in their secondary evaluation have been splendid in their explicit statements of values. It is apparent, for example, that they see narrowing the gap in achievement between lower- and middle-class preschool children as a major social purpose of "Sesame Street." Joan Cooney, president of Children's Television Workshop, sees as a more urgent problem the moving of children across the basic literacy line which she sees as the key to obtaining a good education.

In their design and analyses, Cook *et al.* value a conservative stance. That is, if there is any doubt about the impact of "Sesame Street," they want to resolve that doubt against "Sesame Street." As the authors see it, *"If there has to be bias, then we want to . . . make it conservative in direction"* (Chapter 4, p. 98). According to this argument, it is better to reject a good program (a conservative error) than to accept a bad program (a liberal error).

We find this stance harmful when evaluating new programs in an area where all agree a problem exists and a solution to the problem should be found. The conservative stance will be seen by many as rigorous, perhaps "scientific" and even "hardheaded." And it is a useful stance if current programs are satisfactory, change costly, and the need for change not pressing. Cook *et al.,* however, make a virtue out of being conservative and the reader should be clear on this point. While accepting an ineffective program is an error, and more likely to occur with a liberal stance, rejecting an effective program is just as much an error, and more likely with a conservative stance. The more one strives to eliminate either kind of error, the more one is likely to commit the other kind of error. The apparent "rigor" of the conservative stance is, in fact, only apparent, and the cost to solving social problems when current programs are unsatisfactory is obvious. The need for preschool education and the poor quality of children's television programming, especially in 1969–1970, are not even in question. Thus, not only is the "rigor" of the conservative stance a moot point but the worthiness of the stance in this situation seems at least equally doubtful.

Conservatism, the value, permeates this secondary analysis both in the data analyses and their interpretation. This conservatism appears in two forms. If some impact is found, typically it is explained away; if some potentially damaging evidence is found, it is emphasized. This was already noted in terms of the Letters Test. When an impact was found there, it was pointed out, and we think erroneously, that the test assessed associative skills and the test was even renamed on one occasion "Letters of the Alphabet." It could have been renamed "Symbolic Encoding and Decoding."

DEEMPHASIZE THE POSITIVE

Consider the finding in Chapter 5 that viewing "Sesame Street" "mediated the relationship between encouragement and learning" (Chapter 5, p. 153). (Incidentally, "mediated" is an interesting word in the context of this analysis and we suspect it is partly a conservative euphemism for "caused.") The empirical evidence for this comes from a very conservative analysis in which relatively heavy viewers are compared with slightly less heavy viewers.[15] Nonetheless a relationship was found favorable to "Sesame Street" in that in sites where encouraged children viewed more than nonencouraged children, they also learned more; but in sites where both groups viewed as much, there were no clear differences in amount learned.

In the pages following the presentation of this result (Chapter 5, pp. 151–152), three reasons why the favorable result might be an artifact are provided. The first is that encouraged and nonencouraged children might have learned different amounts only if they were light viewers. The point of this argument and how this means viewing does not mediate (cause) learning are not presented. The second is that parents or testers[16] might have introduced a bias. This supposes parents, in the sites where the encouraged-to-view children learned more, inflated their amount of viewing measures; but parents in the sites where the encouraged-to-view children did not learn more did not inflate the same estimates. That would be incredible! As for testers, it is argued by Cook *et al.*, on the basis of information we supplied, that in some cases testers also carried out encouragement.[17] As we also pointed out to Cook, however, this occurred in very few of the posttest tester assignments; and almost all these were in Boston where results in this analysis were *not* favorable to "Sesame Street." If

---

[15] This is rather like looking for the effects of schooling by comparing those gains of children in one kind of school with the gains of children in a different kind of school. Such studies usually find the effects of schooling to be minimal, but it is a highly conservative finding. A better test of schooling effects needs a group who did not go to school; here we need children who could not watch "Sesame Street."

[16] We must admit to some irritation in another of the author's assertions that the "Sesame Street" test (one index of viewing we used in the first-year evaluation), if it were given first on the posttest, would also have biased the testers. We made it quite explicit in our evaluation report that this test was administered last. We realized the potential danger of early administration of this test; and we showed Cook the way the tests and manuals were bound and color coded to prevent tester error.

[17] Unfortunately, in a few cases in Boston a subject's mother or field testing schedules demanded the posttest not be done "blind." After the great care and almost total success in blind testing, it was with some affect we read: "Future evaluations should take pains to employ testers who are ignorant of the treatment. . . ." (Chapter 5, p. 152).

tester bias created the favorable result, why did it not do so in Boston and Philadelphia, where nonencouraged viewed about as much as encouraged children?

The third reason Cook *et al.* provide to explain away the results showing viewing mediates learning is that "other correlates" are involved. Later (Chapter 5, p. 153), these "other correlates" are called "other unknown factors," and we are told they may have "caused" (not "mediated") the "encouragement-learning relationship." Unfortunately, there is no clue as to what the unknown factors might be. The major point is that *in any research* unknown factors *might* produce a particular positive result. This should not preclude researchers from reaching positive conclusions if they are indicated.

ACCENTUATE THE NEGATIVE

As positive results and conclusions are deemphasized, so too results leading to negative conclusions are emphasized. For example, consider the role of the amount of viewing which is crucial in Cook *et al.*'s thesis. They argue at one point that all who viewed learned, irrespective of group membership. In order to show that the gap is being adversely affected, it is, therefore, necessary to show that disadvantaged children viewed less than advantaged children.[18]

Cook *et al.*, of necessity, use other primary sources when studying national-level viewing trends. The Harris surveys which he calls "the best available data" (Chapter 1, p. 17), indicated that the advantaged viewed more than the disadvantaged. Cook *et al.* also point out that by 1971 the same Harris surveys seemed to show black children viewing more than white children. This result was at variance with the other Harris results, and Cook *et al.* dismiss it with the remark that the estimate of black viewers may not be stable "since the Harris sample of black households with a child under six years of age in public television areas was about sixty in 1971" (Chapter 1, p. 17). This leads the authors to dismiss the idea that black children were viewing more than white children. Of course, by the same token, it could have led him to dismiss these Harris data on disadvantaged children entirely, for if those data were unstable and included such a few black households, how can they have been any better when used to compare with

---

[18] Actually the chances of there being important differences in amount of viewing are quite slim. Intensive Yankelovich surveys of various ghetto areas indicate very high viewing rates by lower-class children (e.g., inner-city Chicago averaged over 90 percent, East Harlem, 86 percent, and Bedford-Stuyvesant from 77 to 91 percent). These data were available to Cook but he did not use them. [See Lesser, pp. 203–206.]

middle-class children's viewing? Blacks make up a sizeable proportion of the lower-class population.

After examining other weaknesses in the various survey data, Cook *et al.* reach no overall conclusion, and the reader is left with the statement that the evidence "suggests" that "Sesame Street" was watched more in homes of higher socioeconomic status—and three demurrers of which the inadequate sample mentioned earlier was but one. Later, indeed, in their in-depth treatment of the topic in Chapter 8, we are told: "It was therefore impossible to examine how regular viewing is related to indicators of SES" (Chapter 8, p. 295). However, in the overall review chapter, Cook concludes that "Sesame Street" ". . . is *in fact* selectively used by children in a way that especially benefited advantaged children who were heavier viewers of it" (Chapter 1, p. 22). (The emphasis is ours.)

We think the reader will find other instances in which a positive finding is deemphasized or a negative one accentuated. It helps to explain the difficulty in discovering what Cook *et al.* really thought the impact of "Sesame Street" was. (See pp. 392–394.) It stems from a conservative value that they adopted, and we think is generally pervasive. Cook *et al.,* the secondary evaluators, have every right to adopt that value; but the reader should remember it when reading their general conclusions.

SOME TECHNICAL ISSUES

Inevitably in reacting to an enterprise as large as this secondary evaluation, there are many areas where we, the suppliers of much of the primary data, have concern. If we were to list these and discuss them even briefly, it would be too tedious for the reader. However, here are some of our concerns:

1. In Chapter 4, Cook *et al.* discuss "the major problems" of confoundings in our design. We purposely included partial confoundings in our design in order to conduct a number of side studies. (See our first-year report, Table 2.) Partial confoundings are not the same as full confoundings. It simply involves using proper analyses if the partial confounding is to be overcome.[19]

2. The estimates of the program's effects that Cook *et al.* refer to frequently as "biased" are not. They are less precise. Bias and precision are different concepts and should not be confused. Thus, in a randomized experiment,

---

[19] The list of confoundings in Table 4.1, pp. 68–69, is an example of where a secondary evaluator objects to the primary evaluation because it may not allow the secondary evaluator to achieve his purposes. In Table 2 of our first-year report, we present our sample plan and explain in the text why supplementary studies such as the effects of "Sesame Street" on three- and five-year-olds were carried out only in two sites.

blocking and covariance adjustments are used to increase precision, not to remove bias.

3. Cook *et al.* indicate that from a particular analysis only 5 percent of the variance in gains is accounted for by viewing. This is not particularly meaningful. The question of what percentage of the variance is accounted for by a particular treatment is highly dependent on the amount of variance available by virtue of the research and sampling designs. Thus, if eight grades and various SES groups had been included in the study, the percent of variance accounted for by the treatment would have been very small because of large between grade and between SES variation, although within any grade level and SES level, the percent of variance might have been quite high.

4. Space precludes a comprehensive critique of the new analyses conducted by Cook *et al.,* but let us consider here one set of analyses given considerable weight by them in arriving at their conclusions.[20] (See Chapter 6: "An Analysis of Obtained Posttest Means.")

Let Y be posttest, X be pretest, and the subscripts e and c represent experimental and control groups. Thus, gain score estimates of the effect of treatment are of the form:

$$(1)\ (\bar{Y}_e - \bar{Y}_c) - (\bar{X}_e - \bar{X}_c)$$

and covariate adjusted estimates are of the form:

$$(2)\ (\bar{Y}_e - \bar{Y}_c) - b_{y.x} (\bar{X}_e - \bar{X}_c)$$

where $b_{y.x}$ is the estimated regression coefficient of Y and X from the pooled-within samples. In a true experiment both (1) and (2) as well as simple posttest differences:

$$(3)\ \bar{Y}_e - \bar{Y}_c$$

are unbiased estimates of the treatment effect. One generally uses (2), because if the sample sizes are not very small, it is almost always more precise than (1) or (3). If age, A, is a better covariate than X (i.e., Y is more correlated with A than X) rather than (2), one should consider the unbiased estimate:

$$(4)\ (\bar{Y}_e - \bar{Y}_c) - b_{y.a} (\bar{A}_e - \bar{A}_c)$$

where $b_{y.a}$ is the estimated regression coefficient of Y on A from the pooled within samples. If Y is more correlated with A than X, (4) will be more precise than (2); if Y is more correlated with X than A, (2) will be more precise than (4). Now Cook's analysis of expected and obtained posttest means yields an estimate of the form:

$$(5)\ (\bar{Y}_e - \bar{Y}_c) - b_{x.a} (\bar{A}_e - \bar{A}_c)$$

---

[20] We are indebted to Dr. Donald Rubin, research statistician, Educational Test-

where $b_{x.a}$ is the estimated regression coefficient of pretest on age from the pooled sample. This estimate is also unbiased, but in all but the most unusual of circumstances (very small samples, $b_{x.a} = b_{y.a}$, variance of A very large compared to the variance of X or Y), (5) will have *larger* variance than (4). Hence, Cook *et al.*'s estimate is not to be preferred to the standard covariance adjusted estimates (2) or (3) or to the covariance adjusted estimate using both X and A. Cook *et al.* have preferred a form of analysis less useful than the one used in the original evaluations.

5. Chapter 9, "The Dollar Costs of 'Sesame Street,' " is a relatively trivial view of the cost function describing the relationship between costs and outputs where costs are budgets and outputs are regular viewers. Constant marginal costs are assumed regardless of audience size or year of the show. And many important residuals of "Sesame Street" are not discussed. These include attitudinal and zeitgeist effects on our society in reference to preschool education and children's television programming.

CONCLUSIONS AND RECOMMENDATIONS

As in most educational exercises, two kinds of lessons can be learned —a specific and a general. A partial view of the specific problems we have found in this secondary evaluation has been presented in the preceding pages of this chapter. As well as these specific problems, there are more general lessons to be learned about the process of secondary evaluation.

We recognize the need for review and open debate, if evaluative research is to progress. It is to be expected that this will lead, at times, to increasing levels of affect as well as increasing levels of understanding. The primary evaluator may well consider that the secondary evaluator did not give proper weight to the problems of data collection—problems not shared by a secondary evaluator—or to the hosts of considerations that impinge on the primary evaluator. The secondary evaluator, coming late to the scene, may well feel in a more privileged, objective position.

As we see it, Cook *et al.* have addressed most of their work to the issue of the gap, carried out highly conservative and at times misguided analyses, and arrived at conclusions that are not very sensitive to the positive impact of "Sesame Street." Our view, however, is doubtlessly based on our value that a television program that helps preschool children in a variety of areas judged to be related to academic or cognitive development is to be encouraged for its successes rather than put down for what it might be failing to do.

Indeed, the sources of potential conflict are many, and we consider it

---

ing Service, for his help in preparing this chapter and especially this section. However, the opinions expressed in this chapter are those of the authors.

a matter of good fortune that our relationship with Cook has been generally cordial. It is clear, of course, that we have many differences of opinion. The reader, we certainly hope, will look not only at this book, but also at the original studies in order to resolve these differences.

More importantly in the long run, all of us should consider whether this model of primary evaluation followed by secondary evaluation is particularly useful. Would it be better, for example, to take the advice of such theorists and practitioners as Robert Stake and Wesley Churchman and attempt to develop within an evaluation a majority and perhaps adversary, minority opinion? Or would it be preferable, though more costly, to ensure that a number of independent primary evaluations are carried out when a potentially important educational program is put into effect?

In our first-year evaluation of "Sesame Street," we pointed out rather pessimistically that educational evaluators have typically been the historians of educational policy and practice and that rarely has their work been used to affect greatly what is happening. It is doubtful whether Cook *et al.*'s or our work on "Sesame Street" will have much impact on the viability of the series. We both seem to agree that "Sesame Street" teaches preschoolers some educationally useful elements, and Cook argues that the show provides "happiness" too. The argument then is mainly about how much is learned and whether this learning has undesirable side effects. But even if the main effect of this book is itself not significant, we hope there will be a significant side effect—turning the readers' attention to the problems of evaluative research. These are problems which, if solved, might enable educational evaluators to have a more potent impact on educational policy and practice.

Index